Pentecostal Manifestos

James K. A. Smith and Amos Yong, *Editors*

PENTECOSTAL MANIFESTOS will provide a forum for exhibiting the next generation of Pentecostal scholarship. Having exploded across the globe in the twentieth century, Pentecostalism now enters its second century. For the past fifty years, Pentecostal and charismatic theologians (and scholars in other disciplines) have been working "internally," as it were, to articulate a distinctly Pentecostal theology and vision. The next generation of Pentecostal scholarship is poised to move beyond a merely internal conversation to an outward-looking agenda, in a twofold sense: first, Pentecostal scholars are increasingly gaining the attention of those outside Pentecostal/charismatic circles *as* Pentecostal voices in mainstream discussions; second, Pentecostal scholars are moving beyond simply reflecting on their own tradition and instead are engaging in theological and cultural analysis of a variety of issues from a Pentecostal perspective. In short, Pentecostal scholars are poised with a new boldness:

- Whereas the first generation of Pentecostal scholars was careful to learn the methods of the academy and then "apply" those to the Pentecostal tradition, the next generation is beginning to interrogate the reigning methodologies and paradigms of inquiry from the perspective of a unique Pentecostal worldview.
- Whereas the first generation of Pentecostal scholars was faithful in applying the tools of their respective trades to the work of illuminating the phenomena of modern Pentecostalism, the charismatic movements, and (now) the global renewal movements, the second generation is expanding its focus to bring a Pentecostal perspective to bear on important questions and issues that are concerns not only for Pentecostals and charismatics but also for the whole church.
- Whereas the first generation of Pentecostal/charismatic scholars was engaged in transforming the anti-intellectualism of the tradition, the second generation is engaged in contributing to and even impacting the conversations of the wider theological academy.

PENTECOSTAL MANIFESTOS will bring together both high-profile scholars and newly emerging scholars to address issues at the intersection of Pentecostalism, the global church, the theological academy, and even broader cultural concerns. Authors in PENTECOSTAL MANIFESTOS will be writing to and addressing not only their own movements but also those outside of Pentecostal/charismatic circles, offering a manifesto for a uniquely Pentecostal perspective on various themes. These will be "manifestos" in the sense that they will be bold statements of a distinctly Pentecostal interjection into contemporary discussions and debates, undergirded by rigorous scholarship.

Under this general rubric of bold, programmatic "manifestos," the series will include both shorter, crisply argued volumes that articulate a bold vision within a field as well as longer scholarly monographs, more fully developed and meticulously documented, with the same goal of engaging wider conversations. Such PENTECOSTAL MANIFESTOS are offered as intrepid contributions with the hope of serving the global church and advancing wider conversations.

PUBLISHED

Frank D. Macchia, *Justified in the Spirit: Creation, Redemption, and the Triune God* (2010)

James K. A. Smith, *Thinking in Tongues: Pentecostal Contributions to Christian Philosophy* (2010)

Wolfgang Vondey, *Beyond Pentecostalism: The Crisis of Global Christianity and the Renewal of the Theological Agenda* (2010)

Justified in the Spirit

Creation, Redemption, and the
Triune God

Frank D. Macchia

WILLIAM B. EERDMANS PUBLISHING COMPANY

GRAND RAPIDS, MICHIGAN / CAMBRIDGE, U.K.

Published 2010 by
Wm. B. Eerdmans Publishing Co.
2140 Oak Industrial Drive N.E., Grand Rapids, Michigan 49505 /
P.O. Box 163, Cambridge CB3 9PU U.K.
www.eerdmans.com

Printed and bound in Great Britain by
Marston Book Services Limited, Didcot

16 15 14 13 12 11 10   7 6 5 4 3 2 1

Library of Congress Cataloging-in-Publication Data

Macchia, Frank D., 1952-
    Justified in the Spirit: creation, redemption, and the triune God /
    Frank D. Macchia.
            p.   cm. — (Pentecostal manifestos)
        ISBN 978-0-8028-3749-3 (pbk.: alk. paper)
        1. Justification (Christian theology) 2. Pentecostal churches —
    Doctrines.   I. Title.

BT764.3.M33   2010
234′.7 — dc22

2010005262

Unless otherwise indicated, all Scripture quotations are from the HOLY BIBLE: NEW IN-
TERNATIONAL VERSION. Copyright © 1973, 1978, 1984 by the International Bible Society.
Used by permission of Zondervan Bible Publishers.

In memory of my father, the Reverend Mike D. Macchia (1927–2010),
who preached and exemplified the gospel of God's grace

Contents

Acknowledgments

There are many who have offered some form of encouragement and support to me in writing this book. Of greatest importance, of course, are my wife, Verena, and my daughters, Desiree and Jasmine, who willingly sacrificed valuable time with me as I sat long hours at the computer. Their gracious support and encouragement were meaningful signs of the grace of which I write in the pages that follow. I also wish to express gratitude to my parents and the Pentecostal church of my upbringing for raising me to cherish a gospel that was substantially about the gift of God's indwelling presence. My father's preaching was the first and enduringly most important exposure to the grace involved in that divine embrace. The dedication is but a small token of my gratitude to him.

No theologian is an island, but he or she works as part of a community of scholars. The Vanguard University School of Religion has responded with understanding and patience to those key moments when I hunkered down to bring this manuscript to completion. In addition, various colleagues have taken substantial time to engage me in conversation on salient points related to justification or parts of this manuscript. Ralph Del Colle, Dale Coulter, D. Lyle Dabney, Thomas Finger, Dale Irvin, Rich Israel, and Edmund Rybarczyk need to be mentioned in particular. Dabney was the first to spark my interest in the topic of justification and the Spirit, and in this role he has done much to launch me in my thinking, especially with regard to the fascinating ways in which he has elaborated on the work of his mentor, Jürgen Moltmann. Moltmann himself has graciously encouraged me when my seminal thoughts on this issue first appeared in print. Numerous others who have worked with me during my years of participation in the Justification and Justice Study Group of the National Council of Churches Faith and Order Commission have also served to inspire my thinking. Jeffrey Gros, Donald Dayton, Despina Prassis, and Ann Riggs deserve special mention here. Last but not least, the dedicated work of my graduate assistants, Walter Alexander and David Peddie, was invaluable as they proofread the chapters, formed indices, and discussed aspects of my thinking with me in insightful ways. It goes without saying, of course, that the contents of — and any errors in — the ensuing chapters are my own.

As I write these acknowledgments, I am deeply aware of the fact that I have brought to completion a project that has been on my mind for nearly a decade. I give God the glory for sustaining me in my work and keeping the fires of interest alive despite the necessary time periods in which I had to place this manuscript on the back burner. The completion of this volume is a blessing for me that I trust will inspire others.

ONE Reaching for the Spirit

Contrasting Models of Justification

1 Introduction

Framing the Issue of Justification and the Spirit

"All the works of God end in the presence of the Spirit."[1] This statement by Jürgen Moltmann represents the assumption from which this book proceeds. And this insight applies as much to justification as to sanctification and glorification. At its essence, "justification" refers fundamentally to the gift of *righteousness* (or "just relation") that is granted to the sinner, what might be called a "rightwising" or "righteousing" of flesh.[2] This gift of righteousness involves God's self-justification as the faithful Creator and covenant partner to creation; but it also involves the participation of the creature, for the kingdom of God is "righteousness, peace, and joy in the Holy Spirit" (Rom. 14:17). Seen from the lens of the Spirit, this right relationship is a *mutual indwelling* that has communion and the "swallowing up" of mortality by life as its substance (2 Cor. 5:4). It is based on the self-giving embrace of the triune God and is manifested in new birth, witness, and, ultimately, resurrection. There is no lens through which to view salvation that is not realized and perfected in the presence of the Spirit and that does not, therefore, also begin there for the sinful creature.

I refer here not merely to the presence of the Spirit as realized now in the context of the Christian life, community, and witness. I refer also and especially to the eschatological fulfillment of the Spirit's indwelling in the

---

1. Jürgen Moltmann, *God in Creation: A New Theology of Creation and the Spirit of God*, trans. Margaret Kohl (New York: Harper and Row, 1985), p. 96.

2. E. P. Sanders proposes the term "righteousing" rather than the old English "rightwising." See Sanders, *Paul, the Law, and the Jewish People* (Philadelphia: Fortress Press, 1983), p. 6.

resurrection of the dead and the communion of saints in the fullness of God's presence. One might be said to rise from the dead in the fullness of the Spirit, for the resurrection is, according to Paul, the ultimate in pneumatic existence (1 Cor. 15:44-46), in which mortality is "swallowed up by life" (2 Cor. 5:4) or baptized in the Spirit.[3] This connection between pneumatic and resurrected existence is why the indwelling of the Spirit in this age is the "down payment" and guarantee of the immortal existence of resurrection in the new age (Eph. 1:14; Rom. 8:11; 2 Cor. 5:5).

My point here is that there can be no justification apart from the fullness of life in the Spirit, for Paul says that we were created for this very purpose of bearing the Spirit:

> For while we are in this tent, we groan and are burdened, because we do not wish to be unclothed but to be clothed with our heavenly dwelling, so that what is mortal may be swallowed up by life. Now it is God who has made us for this very purpose and has given us the Spirit as a deposit, guaranteeing what is to come. (2 Cor. 5:4-5)

Genesis notes that humanity became a living soul through the breath of God's Spirit (Gen. 2:7). We were made to bear the Spirit in the pneumatic existence of the Son and in communion with God. Things cannot be made right for creation unless we are granted the fulfillment of this very life for which we were created. When Paul wrote of the "justification that brings life" (Rom. 5:18), he was referring to the life of the Spirit and of the resurrection as essential to the just relationship for which we were created.

To be justified in the Spirit ultimately means being justified in Spirit possession, resurrection, glorification, and the ultimate communion of love given in the Spirit's presence (Rom. 5:5; 8:30). If we are to have any hope of a Trinitarian understanding of salvation that gathers up and integrates all soteriological categories, we must not exclude the Spirit from the substance of any of them. I refer here to the very substance of justification as a divine act and a creaturely gift in the world. The Spirit must be allowed to leave its impress on the gift of justification, mainly because the Spirit has left this same impress on the risen (justified) Christ (Rom. 1:4; 4:25), for Jesus "appeared in a body, was vindicated by the Spirit" (1 Tim. 3:16). There is no justice for creation in Christ apart from the Spirit's presence.

---

3. I like David Cooke's reference to Jesus' rising "into the full Spirit-life of the resurrection." See Cooke, *The Distancing of God: The Ambiguity of Symbol in History and Theology* (Minneapolis: Fortress Press, 1990), p. 366.

It is interesting to read the history of justification theology in the light of the Spirit, since both Catholic and Protestant traditions have been ambivalent about the role of the Spirit in justification. They both have — in different ways — tended to keep the Spirit at arm's length from the substance of justification; yet they have also assumed at points a more intimate connection, which would later dominate some of the most interesting recent ecumenical efforts at rapprochement.

Many traditional Protestants describing justification, if they mention the Spirit at all, have the Spirit function from the outside, inspiring faith in the gospel but not at work as the very substance of justification itself. In fact, the emphasis has been on *imputed* righteousness, or the act of transferring Christ's righteous status to those who do not deserve it. The prominent image is one of a law court and is often termed "forensic." The metaphor is commonly explained so as to highlight our breaking of the law and the subsequent judgment of condemnation that we deserve. As the heavenly Father, God justly levels precisely this judgment against us; but as our advocate, Christ stands in our place as the mediator necessary to redeem us. Christ makes adequate payment on our behalf by the sacrifice of his life and his perfect fulfillment of the law. God as judge is then happily compelled to acquit those who trust in Christ, canceling their sin and removing its condemnation.

This metaphor contains enough truth to be compelling. It shows that justification is about a divine judgment that is based on the sacrifice of the cross and involves pardon for sin. Furthermore, it shows that justification is fundamentally a right relationship that is based on the merciful act of another. Indeed, "when we were still powerless, Christ died for the ungodly" (Rom. 5:6). Nonetheless, there is much that is missing that can serve — and has served — to distort the total picture. God the Father, in this metaphor, seems to be a relatively passive spectator who happily accepts Christ's advocacy but had nothing fundamentally at stake in its outcome and played no active role in it. Even if the Father's sending Jesus as the advocate is somehow included, the Spirit is entirely absent. The Spirit in this story is, at best, reduced to the instrumental function of communicating the declaration of freedom to the criminal's soul or inspiring trust in the judge (or the advocate). If the sacrifice of Christ as the advocate were a Trinitarian event that had anything to do with the resurrection or with Pentecost, one would not know it from the telling of this story. One would also not know from this story that our sin is not the mere breaking of a commandment but our deeper alienation from life. There are such serious theological gaps in this metaphor that it obscures as much as it clarifies.

Even if one highlights the *legal* overtones of justification, the Spirit cannot be excluded as a major player in the drama. After all, the Spirit is an advocate, too (John 14:16, 26; 15:26; 16:7), and a witness to what God has done through Christ (John 15:26). The court scene is incomplete without its transformation through the Spirit into a circle of divine advocacy and witness, life and communion that mercifully draw in the condemned sinner, who is alienated from life. Since the gift of justice through God's offer of life and communion faces opposition in the world, justification through Christ and the Spirit involves witness and vindication. The judgment enacted pardons by engulfing the condemned in the ultimate victory of life, vindicating God and the repentant sinner over against the opposing forces of alienation and death.

This development of the court scene would cause it to look very unlike any legal setting familiar to us. If developed further, it bursts the entire metaphor to pieces. Perhaps this is the point. No metaphor of legal exchange or process can ultimately capture justification in the Spirit: the Spirit is an abundant and overflowing gift that ultimately defies legal explanations. The very fact that God plays the role of judge, advocate, *and* witness in this "trial" should tell us that this is not the kind of trial that we can identify with anything familiar to human experience. The fact that justification brings life in the midst of death (Rom. 5:18) tells us that here we are dealing with something that transcends a mere legal acquittal. Justification in Scripture has legal overtones but cannot adequately be grasped by any legal metaphor. Righteousness is not *imputed;* it is *accessed* or *participated in* through faith and by the life of the Spirit.

The traditional Protestant defender of forensic justification might protest at this point that the Spirit is only properly substantial to salvation under the rubric of new birth and *sanctification.* This is because the inclusion of the Spirit as essential to justification bases our favor with God in significant part on the quality of the creature's spiritual or ethical life. We could respond to this protest in a number of ways. First, one cannot collapse the Spirit into the quality of the believer's spiritual or ethical life. This *subjective* understanding of pneumatology, which identifies the Spirit with the enlightened religious consciousness or with moral progress, is precisely what is wrong with the Protestant soteriology that dominated the modern era prior to Barth and left an influence even beyond him. The gift of the indwelling Spirit is also quite *objective* to the believer in the sense that the Spirit proceeds from the heavenly Father to win God's favor for us in the Christ event and to communicate this favor to us in a divine embrace that is integral to — but also distinct from — our transformed responses. The indwelling Spirit bears witness *to* our spirits within a divine embrace that then allows the Spirit to also witness *through* us or through the new life imparted to us (Rom. 8:15-16). There are thus both objective and subjective elements to the Spirit's justification of life.

Our transformed witness participates in the Spirit's witness to righteousness and may be said to "incarnate" justification in history; but our witness to divine justice cannot be simply identified with the Spirit's in an unqualified sense. Only in the resurrection can we speak of perfection and fullness of life and witness in the Spirit. Therefore, the Spirit's transformation of the creature through resurrection/glorification cannot be reduced to any penultimate schema of moral or spiritual progress. We are speaking here about the divine victory over alienation and death in the resurrection from the dead. This liberty and transformation granted by the justifying Spirit in the immortal existence of the risen body is outside the reach of flesh, even its most noble intentions and accomplishments this side of eternity, for "flesh and blood cannot inherit the kingdom of God, nor does the perishable inherit the imperishable" (1 Cor. 15:50). Paul's intentions concerning the law were good, but he was still "unspiritual, sold as a slave to sin" (Rom. 7:14) and in need of liberation "from this body of death" (Rom. 7:24). Only the first fruits of the Spirit gave Paul the foretaste of the liberty involved in the immortal existence yet to come (Rom. 8:23). Paul did not work his way to the new birth (a nonsensical thought), and even the good works inspired by the Spirit could not produce the resurrection from the dead. Basing justification in part on the Spirit's embrace, even its immediate effect in the new birth and in its ultimate fulfillment in the resurrection, does not base it on our accomplishments — spiritual or otherwise. We can no more win justification by works than we can raise ourselves from the dead.

Second, not only can we not collapse the Spirit into the subjective life of the believer; we cannot separate the cross from its goal in the impartation of life. Though the cross is indeed an event of reconciliation in its own right, it also mediates reconciliation through the resurrection and Pentecost by mediating the Spirit. As the Pentecostal pioneer Frank Ewart wrote, "Calvary unlocked the flow of God's love, which is God's very nature, into the hearts of his creatures."[4] The Spirit blasphemed at the cross is the hid-

---

4. Frank Ewart, "The Revelation of Jesus Christ," in *Seven Jesus Only Tracts,* ed. Donald W. Dayton (New York: Garland, 1985), p. 5.

den advocate of creation present within the experience of abandonment
and death suffered by the Son in his self-giving for creation. This is the
Spirit that empowered Christ's self-sacrifice on the cross (Heb. 9:14), raised
Jesus from the dead (Rom. 1:4), and was poured by Christ onto creation to
impart God's favor and to continue to advocate for — and witness to —
divine justice in the world. One cannot, therefore, separate the cross from
the resurrection and Pentecost along the lines of justification and sanctification. These events represent a seamless mediation of the Spirit, the mediation of life and justice in communion with God. Grace is not a divine
disposition but an abundantly poured-out gift of divine self-giving to the
sinner. The right relationship is not a distant agreement but an intimate
communion of love involving a *mutual indwelling.*

The "rightwising" of sinful flesh occurs for the one-sidedly forensic
metaphor described above only as the distant Judge's declaration to be
believed. To be sure, this declaration is thought to have many rich consequences, but none of these has anything essentially to do with justification itself. Without justification in the Spirit we could end up neglecting
the insight into the cross as the mediation of the Spirit or into the Christ
of the cross as the single seed that produces "many seeds" by dying (John
12:24) or who draws people in by being lifted up to a shameful death
(John 12:30). Neglected is the resurrection of the second Adam as the
"life-giving spirit" (1 Cor. 15:45), who is elected to be the "firstborn among
many brothers" (Rom. 8:29). Unclear would be the seamless flow from the
cross to Pentecost as the means by which the Spirit is mediated to sinful
flesh, and the powerless are both embraced and pardoned by the divine
presence, the divine embrace (Rom. 5:5-6). In short, the prominent New
Testament description of Jesus as the baptizer in the Spirit is missing from
a one-sided forensic justification theology based only on the cross. Therefore, absent from the essence of justification is the eschatological reach of
the Spirit-empowered witness to God's justice in the world or its fulfillment in the resurrection and glorification of flesh in Christ's image. Neglected is the communal dimension of justification among the radically
"other" and the many.

Third, rather than justification and sanctification representing two
thoroughly distinct stages or dimensions in one's salvation, they are to be
viewed as two overlapping and mutually complementary lenses through
which to view the entire rightwising of creation. How indeed can one eliminate from justification the advocacy and witness of the Spirit to and
through the community of the faithful throughout history and in eschato-

logical fulfillment? Neither can we view the gift of the Spirit as a mere addendum to justification nor a collateral gift only logically connected to justification by Christ. All soteriological categories occur in Christ *and* in the Spirit, or "in the name of Jesus Christ and by the Spirit of God" (1 Cor. 6:11). In fact, throughout the pages that follow I will propose that divine *koinonia*, or the mutual indwelling of God as Father, Son, and Spirit, is the most fruitful context for qualifying the rigid distinction that has existed more broadly in the West between creation, justification, and sanctification.[5]

ALLOW ME TO SHIFT GEARS at this point and speak of the typically Catholic metaphor of justification. Inspired early on especially by Augustine in the fifth century, the traditional Catholic metaphor has been more oriented to the infirmary than the courtroom when it comes to justification. The infirmary is not an image entirely foreign to Luther, to be sure, but it dominates the Latin West prior to the Reformation. The focus here is not on condemned criminals who are acquitted; rather, it is on persons critically wounded in sin against the Lord of creation, but who are mercifully taken up by the Lord and gradually brought back to health. Under Aquinas in the thirteenth century (and under the influence of Aristotelian anthropology as well as a church prominently concerned with penance), this image took on a strongly moral direction, so that the process of healing was understood predominantly in the context of moral formation. The ethically misguided soul is healed by grace in order to bring forth the fruit of justice. This is the prominent image of justification in the Catholic West.

This metaphor has much to commend it. There is more potential here than in the forensic model for involving the Spirit in the justification of creation. The Augustinian image of justice through the restoration of life will provide a valuable point of departure for my own constructive proposals. Problematically, however, Augustine's quarrel with Pelagius directed the entire discussion about justification toward a preoccupation with questions of "grace" with respect to human nature, especially in the light of freedom, law, and moral rectitude. Theology was eventually eclipsed by anthropology via a preoccupation with such concerns. Dominant was a phenomenology of conversion or an explanation of how the individual cooperates with grace. In order to preserve the integrity of the creature's free response to the

---

5. I agree here with Kelly M. Kapic, "The Trajectory of Trinitarian Eschatologies," in *Trinitarian Soundings in Systematic Theology,* ed. Paul Louis Metzger (Edinburgh: T. & T. Clark, 2006), p. 190.

Spirit, the idea of habitual grace was developed in the thirteenth century: it understood the Spirit to be mediated to the soul by a supernatural but created enabling. The Spirit was kept at arm's length from the creature under renewal in a concentrated effort to work out an understanding of human cooperation that grants grace the initiative while avoiding an overwhelming of the soul by the divine presence.

As well intentioned as this development may have been, the anthropological concentration gave the impression that justification is a cooperative partnership between the enabling of grace as a supernatural force and an autonomously free moral agent. Rather than developing first the foundation of divine favor by the Spirit in the Christ event, and then in the embrace of the indwelling Spirit that raises us from death to new life, the scholastic maneuver, when speaking of justification, was to move immediately to the issue of human preparation for justice and to the process by which one cooperates with grace toward renewal. The cross tended to be reduced to the funding of merits necessary to grant the sinner the enabling of grace. The granting of meritorious value to this human cooperation only added to the Pelagian implications, despite consistent efforts to avoid these by granting grace the priority.

Though one cannot separate God's turning to the sinner through the cross and the outpoured Spirit from human freedom and cooperation, the latter must be seen as locating the basis of life and justice in the self-giving and embrace of another. Our cooperation comes only through the Spirit's embrace and indwelling. Cooperation is properly caught up in something deeper and higher, namely, *participation* in God. Participation is thus the basis and qualification of cooperation. Infused virtues live from God's constant offer of Godself to us in the Spirit. Our moral witness participates in the divine favor bestowed in the cross and the embrace of the Spirit and is empowered by it. But the cross and Pentecost alone — as divine acts of self-giving, embrace, communion, and transformation — form the basis of justification, and not the results of the transformation in the outward witness of the church in history. Thus, the relative lack of attention to the cross and the embrace of the indwelling Spirit in the medieval concept of justification by grace only served to feed the distorted stereotype of autonomous cooperation that I have described above.

I will attempt to show that historic Catholic and Protestant understandings of justification were never confined to the legal and moral understandings of the just relationship stereotypically described above. Both have drifted in significant ways toward basing everything in participation in God by the Spirit. Augustine, Aquinas, Luther, and Calvin shared some affinity with the typically Eastern notion of a partaking of the divine nature through participation in God. This seminal beginning toward a pneumatological theology of justification needs to be developed.

The reader may indeed be aware of the fact that more recent ecumenical discussion has moved even more significantly beyond the stereotypical Protestant and Catholic approaches to justification described above. The recent Lutheran-Catholic and Lutheran-Orthodox ecumenical exchanges are prominent parts of this newer trend. Article 15 of the 1999 *Joint Declaration on the Doctrine of Justification* agreed to by the Vatican and the Lutheran World Federation defined justification as coming about via the triune God, in whom we partake of Christ by the Spirit: "Christ himself is our righteousness, in which we share through the Holy Spirit in accord with the will of the Father." Notable Catholic theologians are now emphasizing participation through the indwelling Spirit over cooperation and habitual grace. Similarly, in dialogue with the Russian Orthodox, the Finnish Lutherans have emphasized faith as participation in Christ through the indwelling Spirit rather than as a mere assent to the proclaimed Word or a reception of an imputed status. This participatory understanding of faith has allowed these Lutherans to discern an essential connection between justification and *theosis,* a connection that has been meaningful for others, such as the Methodists in the context of their dialogue with Catholics. Add to this the attention that has been paid to the ecclesial and eschatological dimensions of justification in the so-called "new perspective on Paul," and one has a new atmosphere for reflection that explores the third article of the creed to move significantly beyond the oppositions of the past.

What is not always entirely clear in this new ferment of theological reflection on justification is the role of pneumatology in its possible mediating between the classic Protestant concern for extrinsic or legal righteousness granted to us through faith and the Catholic concern for the impartation of righteousness through moral formation and the attainment of virtues. The Spirit as the link between the legal and the transformative is significant, since the Spirit functions as both advocate and vivifier. Arguably, a theology of justification that integrates various biblical accents is only possible through a Trinitarian framework that grants the Spirit proper emphasis. The idea that we partake of Christ through the indwelling Spirit is a valuable point of departure for discovering the relatively neglected pneumatological link.

However, even the role of the Spirit in faith and/or baptism in facilitating one's participation in Christ as the righteousness of God needs to be developed. The role of the Spirit in the Christ event — as well as the witness and advocacy of the Spirit among the "other" and the "many" — are eschatologically of equal importance. In developing the pneumatological and Trinitarian theology of justification, I will eventually make the case that the substance of divine justification is based in the communion of divine love, which is opened to creation through the Christ event and the embrace of the Spirit's indwelling that leads to the eschatological fullness of life in resurrection and glorification. Life in the Spirit is at the core of justification and is thus communal as well as individual, while it involves a faith that is expressed in love and is nourished by hope. Current ecumenical conversations may be said to intensify the historic Catholic and Protestant "reaching for the Spirit" at the core and substance of justification. There is a growing recognition that the time is ripe to grant concentrated attention to this subject.

I approach these issues from a Pentecostal background. The Pentecostal metaphor of salvation would accent the battlefield in which humanity is held captive to the forces of darkness and made to serve its purposes. Christ and the Spirit invade alien territory in overthrowing the enemy and setting the captives free. The condemned are offered liberation and healing by Christ and the power of the Spirit. Those who accept are saved and mightily filled with the Spirit in order to join the Spirit in witnessing of God's mercy to the world. The goal is the outpouring of the Spirit on all flesh so that all may be won back to Christ. This metaphor is similar to the Protestant one in the sense that the liberty of the proclaimed Word of God is at the base of justification. But it is even more similar to the Catholic one in the sense that this justification is connected to the undeserved healing of the condemned. In justification, the condemned are not only pardoned but restored to abundant life with God. The condemned struck down on the battlefield are justified by being restored to life.

This Pentecostal background might not seem significant given that Pentecostalism has not been known for cultivating a theology of justification. Significantly, however, justification is often described in early Pentecostal literature as an initial stage in one's *possession* of the Spirit. Spirit baptism, or the fullness of life in the Spirit, is commonly viewed as the crowning moment of one's possession of the Spirit; but this moment influences everything else, since what precedes it is thought to prepare for it and what follows flows from it.[6] However, significant Pentecostal voices

6. As we will see, there is a debate within Pentecostalism over whether Spirit baptism is

are now proposing that one can draw from Pentecostal theology to move beyond the thorny issue of "stages" to view Spirit baptism as an *eschatological* gift that is rooted in regeneration, involves experiences or breakthroughs in life, and culminates in the resurrection. If one were to view justification as a lens from which to view this Spirit baptism as an expansive journey involving divine justice as a gift to the sinner, it becomes possible to see both metaphors as complementary to one another. In fact, it is possible biblically to see Spirit baptism as a root metaphor of the history of salvation within which justification and sanctification can be integrated as overlapping metaphors of the eschatological rightwising of creation.

Developing a Trinitarian theology of justification with an accent on the indwelling or baptism in the Spirit is my goal in the chapters that follow. The right relation that constitutes justification will thus be viewed as pneumatological in substance, consisting of pardon, the victory of life over death, divine witness and vindication, and participation in the divine *koinonia*. The first part (chapters 2, 3, and 4) will attempt to reflect on three models of justification in relation to the indwelling of the Spirit: Catholic, Protestant, and Pentecostal. I do not mean these to be histories of justification but rather indications of how stereotypical approaches to justification emerged historically and were qualified, especially by an implicit reach for the Spirit as the realm of divine favor and justice. I will show that the Catholic emphasis on habitual grace and the Protestant accent on declared or imputed righteousness implicitly reach for the life of the Spirit as essential to justification, and they can be blessed by turning to the distinctively Pentecostal emphasis on Spirit baptism.

The second part (chapters 5, 6, and 7) represents a biblical and constructive treatment of justification as a divine act, first in the Old Testament, especially in the promise of the outpoured Spirit as that which will fulfill righteousness, and then worked out in the context of the Christ event, especially the atonement as seen in the light of the baptism in the Spirit. The third part (chapters 8, 9, and 10) furthers the biblical and constructive treatment of justification, but this time as it is worked out eschatologically in the life of faith, the communion of saints, and the life of the triune God.

To be justified is to participate in the fullness of pneumatic existence,

---

the crowning moment of Christian initiation (including justification) or distinct from this as the doorway to Christian witness and mission. All agree, however, that Spirit baptism makes the creature the dwelling place of the Spirit, which is the chief point of emphasis.

which means the risen and glorified Christ as well as the communion of love enjoyed among Father, Son, and Spirit. The legal overtones of justification in Christ's and the Spirit's advocacy and witness point to this deeper justice as its core and essence. This is why the court scene seems to be appropriate on the surface, but it ultimately bursts apart as inadequate to describe it. Similarly, the moral virtues that emerge from our cooperation with the Spirit bear outward witness to the divine favor granted to us in the Christ event and the indwelling of the Spirit, but justification is not based on the virtues. At the base of the virtues is the divine self-giving and gift of life. Justification in the Spirit involves the virtues and our weak and ambiguous witness to justice, but it is based on the Spirit's embrace, or the Spirit's life overcoming and reaching beyond ambiguous human life, reaching beyond to the resurrection of the dead.

Without the Spirit's embrace and inner witness, which points to an eschatological fulfillment that exceeds both legal exchange and moral achievement, both the divine legal declaration and the infused virtues continue to be placed in opposition to each other without their proper link or point of integration. Without the Spirit's embrace, which is the embrace of the triune God, both traditions have tended to put forth ultimately inadequate metaphors of the justification of the sinful creature. In the following chapters I will attempt to develop a pneumatological theology of justification inspired by a Pentecostal metaphor, the baptism in the Spirit. I refer here to a justification "in the Spirit" toward a Trinitarian soteriology.

2 Imparted Righteousness

The Catholic View of Justification

Justification "was anything but a commonplace in patristic thought, Eastern or Western,"[1] and it was not considered a topic of major concern by medieval exegetes.[2] When the subject does come to significance in Augustine, he calls on it to combat Pelagianism — what he perceived to be a personal effort to win salvation by works of the law.[3] This concern with personal salvation tended to tie justification in medieval Catholic theology to questions of free will and conversion. The larger biblical issues of pneumatology in the contexts of Christology, ecclesiology, and eschatology are not entirely forgotten (especially in Augustine); but the emphasis definitely shifts over time to the moral formation of the individual penitent. A properly theological concentration on justification through the divine gifts of Christ and the Spirit shifts to an anthropological concentration on a phenomenology of human conversion and moral formation.

I do not mean to imply that we can separate the theological from the anthropological in a pneumatological theology of justification. Rather, I refer to the restrictive concentration on the anthropological in the historical development of justification prior to the Reformation. In discussing this anthropological preoccupation with justification in the West, I

1. Jaroslav Pelikan, *The Christian Tradition: A History of the Development of Dogma,* vol. 4: *Reformation of Church and Dogma* (Chicago: University of Chicago Press, 1982), p. 157.

2. Charles P. Carlson, *Justification in Earlier Medieval Theology* (The Hague: Martinus Nijhoff, 1975), p. 65.

3. I realize that there may indeed have been a difference between what was perceived in the West as Pelagianism and Pelagius's actual soteriology.

will draw on the Eastern tradition (both positively and negatively) to illustrate the importance of rooting justification through cooperation with grace more fundamentally within *participation* in Christ through the Spirit's *indwelling* of the creature. Ultimately, I wish to explore the metaphor of *Spirit baptism* brought to the fore of theological discussion by the Pentecostal movement in an effort to arrive at a larger narrative framework for interpreting justification than the individual's moral conversion and formation. In the journey toward this larger narrative, I will begin with Augustine.

Augustine and Justification as the Renewal of Life

In response to Pelagius, Augustine connected justification to the Spirit's renewal of the creature but concentrated its formal definition on the fruit of righteousness *in us*. Theologically, his struggle was indeed anthropological from the start: he faced the challenge of creating a balance between a Pelagian confidence in the human ability to gain salvation and the Manichean detachment of humanity from grace entirely. Between these poles, Augustine believed in an element of free will in the choice to turn away from God and even in a natural human yearning for God. One may simply recall his invocation in Book One of his *Confessions:* "[O]ur hearts are restless until they find rest in thee." But Augustine also felt that the Spirit was necessary to assist the will in turning to God. He wrote of "this Spirit of God by whose gift we are justified" in response to Paul's statement that, where the Spirit of the Lord is, there is liberty (2 Cor. 3:17).[4] Augustine expresses his carefully forged balance this way: "Not that the result is without our will, but that our will does not accomplish the result, unless it receive the divine assistance."[5]

Augustine even linked justification by the Spirit to partaking of the divine nature or becoming like God, for people "are to be like unto God, — even the love which is 'shed abroad in our hearts,' not by any ability of nature or the free will within us, but 'by the Holy Ghost which is given unto us.'"[6]

---

4. Augustine, *De Spiritu et Littera*, in *St. Augustine's Anti-Pelagian Works*, trans. Peter Holmes and Robert Ernest Wallace, Nicene and Post-Nicene Fathers (hereafter NPNF), 1st ser., ed. Philip Schaff (reprint; Peabody, MA: Hendrickson, 1994), p. 28.

5. Augustine, *De Perfectione Justicia Hominis*, in Schaff, *St. Augustine's Anti-Pelagian Works*, NPNF, 1st ser., 5:19.40.

6. Augustine, *De Natura et Gratia*, in Schaff, *St. Augustine's Anti-Pelagian Works*, NPNF, 1st ser., 5:77.

He also said that by the Spirit we "burn to enter upon the participation in that true light" that is God.[7] Indeed, Augustine wrote: "He who justifies is the same as he who deifies in that by justifying He makes us sons of God."[8] This "deification" (becoming like God) is not via our being generated from God's substance (so that we are essentially divine) but rather from being adopted by God's indwelling Spirit. Quoting John 1:12, Augustine says further that the "power" granted to believers to become the children of God is the "love which is only communicated to us by the Holy Ghost bestowed upon us."[9] Insightfully, he understands justification and regeneration as overlapping concepts that span the new creation from the resurrection of Jesus to the resurrection of the dead, since Jesus "heals the sick or raises the dead, that is, justifies the ungodly."[10] Justification is a broad concept for Augustine: it "establish[es] the rectitude of the created order."[11] These insights will prove to be vital to an expansively pneumatological and Trinitarian view of justification.

This expansive pneumatological and Trinitarian framework could very well have led Augustine to view justification as essentially a *divine* judgment to indwell the creature that triumphs over sin and death in Christ and in the gift of the Spirit, a judgment in which we participate by the Spirit through faith, and which vindicates faith in God. Here I am referring to justification as a theological truth concerning the triumph of God's righteousness or justice in the world over all that threatens or resists it. Unfortunately, however, Augustine's preoccupation with the question of both the potential and the limits of the human will in the attainment of human righteousness caused him, instead, to take a distinctly anthropological turn in his understanding of justification.

Most telling is Augustine's conclusion that the righteousness by which we are justified "is not that whereby He is Himself righteous but that with which He endows man."[12] This statement is justifiable in the sense that justification does impart something new in transforming the creation. In an-

---

7. Augustine, *De Spiritu et Littera*, p. 5.

8. Augustine, *Enarratio in Psalmos*, in *St. Augustine's Exposition on the Psalms*, trans. A. Cleveland Coxe, ed. Philip Schaff, NPNF (reprint, modified; Peabody, MA: Hendrickson, 1994), 8:49. l. 2.

9. Augustine, *De Natura et Gratia*, p. 77.

10. Augustine, *De Natura et Gratia*, p. 29.

11. Alister McGrath, *Iustitia Dei: A History of the Christian Doctrine of Justification*, vol. 1: *The Beginnings to the Reformation* (Cambridge: Cambridge University Press, 1982), p. 34.

12. Augustine, *De Spiritu et Littera*, p. 15.

other sense, however, this statement is misleading, since justification is first and foremost a revelation and vindication of divine righteousness, or the divine self-giving that fulfills justice for creation. As a corrective to Augustine, we should note that is given primarily in justification is not a material capacity or a moral virtue, but God's very presence and embrace. This self-giving is precisely the very substance of divine righteousness. God is righteous in that God mercifully gives of Godself in embracing the other. In this sense, justifying righteousness *is* divine righteousness, which draws in the condemned sinner to participate. Moreover, there can be no separation between the mercy shown creation in the rightwising of sinners and the righteousness of God, since in justifying sinners God is indeed being true to Godself as righteous.[13] By insisting that justification is not divine righteousness but rather the righteousness "in us" (or emergent in us as the fruit of justice), justification as a theological truth becomes essentially an anthropological one. It would be helpful for us to note here Aquinas's contribution to this anthropological turn in the medieval understanding of justification.

Aquinas and Habitual Grace

The anthropological turn intensifies after Augustine. By the time one reaches the thirteenth century, grace becomes distinguished from the indwelling Spirit, and justification takes a more radically anthropological turn through the doctrine of habitual (created) grace or the elevated human capacities necessary to cooperate with God in the moral formation of the believer. Aquinas became even more preoccupied with issues of human will and conversion. This increased emphasis developed in an ecclesiastical atmosphere in which penance had gained prominence. Moreover, Aristotle's virtue ethics challenged one to believe that right action leads to human virtue. This position was decisively rejected through the medieval doctrine of *infused* virtues. Virtues did not arise from right action but rather through cooperation with enabling grace. Aristotle's influence, however, was still vital in the moral theology of justification that developed in the high Middle Ages. Aquinas sought to understand how the soul can be turned toward God through the infusion of virtues in a way that still preserved free will. To avoid both Pelagianism and an overwhelming

---

13. See Eberhard Jüngel, *Justification: The Heart of the Christian Faith*, trans. Jeffrey F. Cayzer (Edinburgh: T. & T. Clark, 2001), pp. 74-75.

of the soul by a forceful God, one must conceive of a human's turning toward God that is not forced by God but is still enabled by God. Habitual or created grace (elevated human capacities) provided such an aid to the human will — in its graced but also its willful cooperation with God.[14]

Aquinas thus rejected Peter Lombard's idea that the love infused in the soul at the base of the virtues was the indwelling Spirit; the former's fear was that this idea would undermine a willful turning of the soul to God. However, it is interesting that Lombard made his case quoting Augustine in his favor:

> Moreover, there are some, who say, that the Holy Spirit, God Himself, is not given, but His gifts, which are not the Spirit Himself. And as they say, the Holy Spirit is said to be given, when His grace, which, however, is not Himself, is given to men. And this they say Bede thought in the words above, with which he says, that the Holy Spirit proceeds, when His grace is given to men, not as if His very Self is given, but His grace. But that the Holy Spirit Himself, who is God and the Third Person in the Trinity, is given, (St.) Augustine openly shows in the fifteenth book *On the Trinity,* saying thus: "That the same Holy Spirit (has been) given, when Jesus breathed upon [them], concerning whom He then said: *Go, baptize all the nations in the Name of the Father and of the Son and of the Holy Spirit,* we ought not doubt. He Himself is, therefore, the One who has been given from Heaven on Pentecost Day. In what manner, therefore, is God not the one who gives the Holy Spirit? Nay how much is God the one who gives God?" Behold with these words he openly says that the Holy Spirit, that is God Himself, is given to men by the Father and the Son.[15]

Lombard rightly appeals to the Augustinian (and Athanasian) principle that salvation is God's self-impartation and indwelling. God is both the giver and the gift of salvation. All human cooperation with God would then be couched within the human *incorporation and participation in God.*

14. Aquinas, *Treatise on Grace,* Q. 113, art. 3, in *Basic Writings of St. Thomas Aquinas,* ed. and trans. Anton C. Pegis (New York: Random House, 1945). See Wolfhart Pannenberg, *Systematic Theology,* vol. 3, trans. Geoffrey Bromiley (Grand Rapids: Eerdmans, 1998), pp. 197-98; see also John Hardon, *History and Theology of Grace* (Ypsilanti, MI: Veritas Press, 2003), pp. 138-39.

15. Peter Lombard, *The First Book of the Sentences,* Distinction 14, chap. 2, *The Four Books of Sentences,* http://www.franciscan-archive.org/lombardus/I-Sent.html (italics in original).

Aquinas was indeed aware of the problem of detaching God's indwelling gifts from their source in the Spirit, even noting in response to John 4 that the Spirit "is correctly called the living water, because the grace of the Holy Spirit is given to man in such a way that the source itself of the grace is also given, that is, the Holy Spirit."[16] Bruce D. Marshall has thus argued that habitual grace for Aquinas does not function as an intermediate reality that precludes the possibility of the soul's direct contact with the Spirit. He quotes Aquinas that "the rational creature . . . touches God himself" and that "by grace we are joined to God himself, with nothing created intervening."[17] The assumption here is that habitual grace elevates the soul so as to facilitate the indwelling of the Spirit. In a sense, grace as a created *forma* prepares the soul to touch the Spirit.

Yet, if what is elevated to touch the very Spirit of God is an accident of the soul (which it was for Aquinas), does it not function to mediate between the soul and the indwelling Spirit? As a result of Aquinas's rejection of Lombard's granting the priority to the indwelling Spirit, the Spirit was said to indwell the soul in high medieval scholasticism, "always on the supposition that in some mysterious way the Third person was united to the soul through some created *forma* of unique character."[18] This mediation of habitual grace in between the human soul and the Spirit only meant that justification was driven further in the direction of an anthropological emphasis.[19] Catholic theologian Karl Lehmann thus candidly remarks, "Frankly, one can refer here to the fact that the doctrine of grace, especially of 'created grace,' has replaced pneumatology in the Western tradition."[20] Though justification was solely by grace understood as the power or efficacy of the Spirit, it was concentrated on the fruit of justice that arises in

16. *In. Io.* 4:10-26 [577], quoted in Daniel A. Keating, *Deification and Grace* (Naples, FL: Sapientia Press, 2007), p. 58.

17. Aquinas, *Summa Theologiae*, I, 43, 3, c, quoted in Bruce D. Marshall, "Ex Occidente Lux? Aquinas and Eastern Orthodox Theology," *Modern Theology* 20, no. 1 (Jan. 2004): 29. Marshall provides his own translation of the Latin text found in the Blackfriars edition, 60 vols. (London: Eyre and Spottiswoode, 1964-1973).

18. See Hardon, *History and Theology of Grace*, p. 138.

19. Johann Auer, "Grace (II. Theological, A. History of the Doctrine)," in *Sacramentum Mundi: An Encyclopedia of Theology*, ed. Karl Rahner et al. (New York: Herder and Herder, 1968), 2:414; Aquinas, *Commentary on the Sentences*, 2:24-28; Aquinas, *Summa Theologiae*, I. Q. 110-14, quoted in Auer, "Grace," p. 414.

20. Lehmann, "Heiliger Geist, Befreiung zum Menschsein — Teilhabe am göttlichen Leben," in Walter Kasper, hrsg., *Gegenwart des Geistes: Aspekte der Pneumatologie* (Basel: Herder, 1979), p. 202.

the believer's moral formation. Justification was thus "treated as a subsidiary and theoretical element in the general theology of grace," to explain "how and why the sinner is translated into a state of righteousness."[21]

Therefore, the "justification of the ungodly is brought about by God moving man to justice," says the angelic doctor.[22] Concretely for Aquinas, grace is the "habitual gift bestowed on us" so that we could grow in our tendency to respond favorably to God.[23] This is because God bestows on people "certain forms and powers . . . in order that they may of themselves be inclined to these movements."[24] As operative, habitual grace heals human nature and initiates justification; as cooperative, it grants the believer the capacity to participate in meriting eternal life and furthers justification. As Aquinas says, habitual grace is the grace "whereby corrupted human nature is healed, and after being healed is lifted up so as to work deeds meritorious of eternal life, which exceed the capability of nature."[25] The emphasis on the nature of human cooperation with God's grace calls forth numerous distinctions, such as between grace that is "actual" (what we might call "prevenient") and grace that is "habitual" (what we might call "sanctifying") — and, within both, as "operating" and "cooperating." As Aquinas explains, operating grace is God's grace acting on the soul, while cooperating grace involves the human will. Such is the mature development of Aquinas's theology of grace, which he arrived at through a complex and changing development.[26]

That one can "merit" eternal life is thus itself a gift of grace, for "a man can merit nothing from God except by His gift."[27] As the Council of Trent would later say in agreement, the "bounty toward all men is so great that he wishes the things that are His gifts to be their merits."[28] Aquinas did note that human moral progress was entirely by the power of God's Spirit, and he was even sensitive to themes of participation and *theosis*.[29] Yet he

---

21. Carlson, *Justification*, p. 77; cf. p. 108.

22. Aquinas, *Treatise on Grace*, Q. 113, art. 3.

23. Aquinas, *Treatise on Grace*, Q. 111, art. 2, 1005.

24. Aquinas, *Treatise on Grace*, Q. 110, art. 2, 998-99.

25. Aquinas, *Treatise on Grace*, Q. 109, art. 9, 993.

26. See Bernard Lonergan, "St. Thomas' Thought on Gratia Operans," *Theological Studies* 2, no. 3 (Sept. 1941): 289-324; see also McGrath, *Iustitia Dei*, 1:103-9.

27. Aquinas, *Treatise on Grace*, Q. 114, art. 3, 1041.

28. *Canons*, Sixth Session, chap. 16.

29. See Otto Hermann Pesch, *Die Theologie der Rechtfertigung bei Martin Luther und Thomas von Aquin* (Mainz: Grünwald, 1967), esp. pp. 634ff.

shifted the locus of justification further from a revelation of divine righteousness in God's embrace, or the indwelling of flesh, to the achievement
of human righteousness by grace. From the late fifteenth century onward,
the *habitus* of habitual grace tended to be described as a detached quality
that overlaid the soul.[30] Though there was late medieval resistance to this
trend (for example, among the fourteenth-century Augustinians), the emphasis on habitual grace threatened to undermine Augustine's earlier effort to continuously grant priority to the Spirit of God in the person's
moral progress. The danger here, as Vladimir Lossky has shown, was in
making salvation a "creaturification" rather than a deification process "in
which we really participate in the nature of the Holy Trinity."[31]

   This overall distinguishing of grace from the Spirit also resulted in a lack
of attention to the *Christological* locus of justification as well as the communal, cosmic, and eschatological dimensions of justifying righteousness.[32]
Fortunately, the modern Catholic theology of justification has turned at
least implicitly in the direction of the Spirit. I will explore this point next.

The Modern Catholic Reach for the Spirit

While not necessarily denying the significance of habitual grace, modern
Catholic theology has moved decisively in the direction of granting the divine indwelling and participation in God the fundamental and enduring
role in the justification of the believer. Important in this development is
the nineteenth-century theologian M. J. Scheeben. The more Scheeben
studied the role of the Spirit in the Trinitarian life of God, the more he became convinced "that the Spirit exercised more than merely exemplary ef-
ficient causality in our sanctification."[33] He began to see in the justified

---

   30. Henri de Lubac, *The Mystery of the Supernatural,* trans. Rosemary Sheed (New
York: Herder and Herder, 1965), esp. pp. 7-11, 143-50.
   31. V. Lossky, *The Mystical Theology of the Eastern Church* (Crestwood, NY: St. Vladimir's Seminary Press, 1997), pp. 213-14, quoted in Marshall, "Ex Occidente Lux?" p. 28. The
Eastern tradition protects the transcendence of the hypostasis of the Spirit by noting that
the Spirit indwells through the divine energy, which is still the presence of the Spirit and not
a created reality.
   32. See Lehmann, "Heiliger Geist," and Kenan B. Osbourne, *Reconciliation and Justification: The Sacrament and Its Theology* (Eugene, OR: Wipf and Stock, 1990), p. 124.
   33. Malachi J. Donnelly, "The Indwelling of the Holy Spirit according to M. J.
Scheeben," *Theological Studies* 7, no. 2 (June 1946): 269.

soul a formal relationship that looks to the Holy Spirit as the *causa formaliter efficiens* of our holiness. As Ralph Del Colle observes of Scheeben: "[T]he Holy Spirit is not just the channel of divine love or present through gifts but that the Spirit is present in the creature as a hypostatic identity. Scheeben therefore proposes that the Spirit is present not just as donation but as person."[34] Scheeben wanted to follow the Greek fathers in emphasizing the objective communicability *ad extra* of God's very substance in the life of the believer, looking upon the Spirit as "entering formally into our sanctification."[35] Scheeben's soteriology was helpful in beginning to move beyond the medieval emphasis on habitual grace. However, it is problematic that he viewed the union with God in largely moral terms.[36]

In more recent Catholic theology, there has been a renewed appreciation for a pneumatological understanding of grace. A priority has been placed on the indwelling of the Spirit and on participation in God as the contexts in which to understand created grace and human cooperation with God. The Catholic statement in the *Joint Declaration on the Doctrine of Justification* (1999) maintains that "justifying grace never becomes a human possession to which one could appeal over against God" (no. 27). In a similar vein, Hans Küng concedes that Catholic theology since Trent — and in opposition to Peter Lombard — has placed too much emphasis on grace as a kind of "third reality" between God and humanity that humanity can use to cooperate with God as autonomous partners.[37] Küng does not deny that grace as *charismata* and as fruit refers to gifts that enable us toward genuinely renewed human capacities. After all, the divine indwelling has a profound effect on the vessel in which it dwells! But a notion of "grace" as renewed human capacities for God is derivative, a specialized usage that is not to be emphasized at the expense of the indwelling of the Spirit as the locus of God's fulfillment of justice in the creation.

Küng notes further that the greater emphasis is to be placed on grace

34. Ralph Del Colle, *Christ and the Spirit: Spirit Christology in Trinitarian Perspective* (Oxford and New York: Oxford University Press, 1994), p. 44.

35. See M. Jos. Scheeben, *Handbuch der katholischen Dogmatik* (Freiburg im Breisgau: Herder'sche Verlagshandlung, 1873), 1:857. Donnelly, "The Indwelling of the Holy Spirit," p. 269.

36. Donnelly, "Indwelling of the Holy Spirit," pp. 279-80.

37. Hans Küng, *Justification: The Doctrine of Karl Barth and a Catholic Reflection*, trans. Edward Quinn (Philadelphia: Westminster, 1981), pp. 201-3. Hereafter, page references to this work will appear in parentheses in the text.

as a divine indwelling and "thus not primarily a physical entity in the human subject but rather something entirely *personal* — the character and behavior of the living God Himself" (pp. 197-98). Bestowing grace on humanity means that "God Himself bestows Himself" (p. 201). "Created grace" is hence simply the ongoing result and effect in human nature of the divine self-giving and indwelling (p. 201). As Karl Rahner has also pointed out, grace is only habitual "inasmuch as God's personal self-communication is permanently offered to man."[38] Thus, "created grace" is simply the ongoing result and effect in human nature of the divine self-giving and indwelling (p. 201). Avery Dulles follows Rahner in viewing union with God as effected by the indwelling Spirit rather than created grace, so that the categories used to describe grace are personal rather than physical.[39] In this light, the Catholic theologian Piet Franzen developed a theology of justifying grace as primarily an indwelling and also as an ongoing encounter with God's personal presence.[40] Charles Moeller and Gérard Philips conclude: "At the present moment, theology is moving in the direction of a synthesis between the doctrine of indwelling and that of created grace."[41]

This recent Catholic turn toward the Holy Spirit in justification raises the issue of the subordinate place of cooperation to incorporation and participation in a properly pneumatological (and thus Trinitarian) understanding of justification. The benefit of the Catholic emphasis on the integral relationship between justification and renewal cannot be fully appreciated without a proper focus on the indwelling Spirit as the means by which believers are incorporated into and come to participate in *God*. Cooperation is thus defined by the divine embrace. This issue deserves separate treatment, especially in terms of its ancient and Eastern roots. In particular, I want to clarify the proper place of cooperation with grace in regard to the more formative concepts of indwelling, incorporation, and participation.

---

38. Karl Rahner, "Grace (II. Theological, B. Systematic)," in *Sacramentum Mundi*, p. 419.

39. Avery Dulles, "Justification in Contemporary Catholic Theology," in H. George Anderson, T. Austin Murphy, and Joseph A. Burgess, eds., *Justification by Faith: Lutherans and Catholics in Dialogue*, No. 7 (Minneapolis: Augsburg, 1985), p. 259.

40. Franzen, *The New Life of Grace* (New York: Herder and Herder, 1972), p. 91; see also Dulles, "Justification in Contemporary Catholic Theology," p. 259.

41. Moeller and Philips, *The Theology of Grace and the Ecumenical Movement* (London: Mowbray, 1961), p. 23; see also Dulles, "Justification in Contemporary Catholic Theology," p. 370 n. 8.

The Indwelling Spirit: Cooperation through Participation

What I am referring to here is the priority of the Spirit's indwelling to co-operation and concrete changes in the justified life, so that the latter two are viewed as caught up in one's participation in the triune life. Justification brings life (Rom. 5:18), but it has its substance in the indwelling Spirit. This is not to deny the importance of cooperation with God, even within an understanding of justification. After all, the creature is not destined to act without any element of choice involved, and God does not commit violence on creation.

Cooperation — or graced synergy — with respect to God is an ancient and well-established aspect of soteriology. Thomas Torrance has shown that the apostolic fathers identified grace with the work of the Spirit, but their concern was to explain how the sinner gains the capacity to cooperate favorably with God in the process of moral formation.[42] Similarly, in the second century, Origen resisted various fatalistic doctrines proposed by the Gnostics or the Stoics by emphasizing the capacity of humans to respond favorably to the Spirit or grace of God. For example, Origen notes that Valentinus's doctrine of unchangeable, predestined natures (good or evil) cannot account for the change that one makes from an evil to a virtuous life in cooperation with the grace of God, or from righteous to unrighteous living in the case of one who turns away from God.[43] The reality of change in life implies a significant element of choice in human behavior, including one's response to the grace of God.

Origen, however, also implies that this cooperation is taken up into a larger *participation* in the divine life leading toward deification. He says that the "*nous* which is purified is lifted above all material realities so as to have a clear vision of God, and it is deified by its vision."[44] Though participation and *theosis* were minor themes in the West (as we saw in Augustine), they became a distinguishing characteristic of soteriology in the

42. Thomas F. Torrance, *The Doctrine of Grace in the Apostolic Fathers* (Grand Rapids: Eerdmans, 1959), pp. 138-41, esp. p. 140.

43. See Thomas P. Scheck, *Origen and the History of Justification: The Legacy of Origen's Commentary on Romans* (Notre Dame, IN: University of Notre Dame Press, 2008), pp. 20-30.

44. Origen, *Commentary on John*, 32.27, quoted in J. A. McGuckin, "The Strategic Adaptation of Deification," in Michael J. Christensen and Jeffrey A. Wittung, eds., *Partakers of the Divine Nature: The History and Development of Deification in the Christian Traditions* (Grand Rapids: Baker Academic, 2006), p. 101.

Eastern churches. The Alexandrian theologians Clement, Origen, and Athanasius "elevated the soteriological theory of *theosis* to new heights."[45] The Cappadocians were also taken with *theosis,* partly due to Gregory Nazianzus's reading of Origen and his commitment to base his soteriology on Athanasius. Many know Athanasius's famous statement, "God became man so that man might become God."[46] Significantly, Gregory altered this statement in the following way: "And since, then, God is made man, so man is perfected as God, and that is my glory."[47] This is our vocation, our glory, our righteousness, our *justification* as creatures of God. Indeed, those whom God justified God also glorified (Rom. 8:30).

The issue to be faced in these early centuries of the church was whether or not graced cooperation with God was part of a deeper incorporation into God and participation in God through the divine indwelling. This cooperative view of grace thus brought up the question of whether or not this cooperation is rooted in something deeper and truly participatory. In other words, this cooperation must in reality come by way of a participation in God if synergy is to avoid the impression of an autonomous self acting toward God or making claims on God. Participation implies that divine indwelling must be the assumption of cooperation.

Most importantly, the prior emphasis on incorporation and participation must be used to prevent human cooperation with grace from shifting the attention from theology to anthropology, especially since the focus of participatory terms remains on the divine life and action. Incorporation and participation can be used to keep the emphasis on something beyond (though not apart from) oneself, since the question remains about what exactly we have been incorporated into or in what are we now made to participate. The terms "cooperation" or "synergy," by themselves, cannot adequately direct us outside of ourselves toward a theocentric view of justification. But "incorporation" and "participation" are terms that we can use to focus on the wide expanses of the pneumatological and Trinitarian dimensions of justifying righteousness. The door is thrown wide open from this participatory perspective to develop a *Trinitarian* structure for justification, so that we may see justification as both a divine judgment and a life-transforming action that in-

---

45. J. A. McGuckin, "The Strategic Adaptation of Deification," p. 97.

46. Athanasius, *De Incarnatione,* quoted in McGuckin, "The Strategic Adaptation of Deification," p. 101.

47. Gregory Nazianzus, *Carmina Dogmatica,* 10.5-9, quoted in McGuckin, "The Strategic Adaptation of Deification," p. 101.

volves human participation, even cooperation, but also encompasses the entire cosmos.

The anchor for this Trinitarian perspective will be the indwelling of the Holy Spirit, which is the principal means by which God enacted justice in Christ and possesses the human vessel in order to bring this vessel into participation in Christ and, through Christ, in God or the divine *koinonia*. Only from this foundation can cooperation with grace play a properly secondary, though still significant, role. The goal of resurrection shows the limits of cooperation as a soteriological category. One does not cooperate in one's own resurrection! We can gauge the pneumatological and broader Trinitarian deficit in our justification doctrine in part by noting the degree to which we have developed this doctrine apart from the indwelling Spirit.

When we speak of the Eastern church, the struggle between Antioch and Alexandria over the doctrine of salvation is relevant to our discussion. The tragic consequences of a cooperative view of grace cut loose from a prior emphasis on divine indwelling and participation in God or in Christ is illustrated for us in the soteriological struggle surrounding the Council of Chalcedon in the fifth century. Douglas Fairbairn has convincingly made the case that the conflict leading up to Chalcedon can be described as waged between an understanding of grace as something *merely* passed on to us to aid in our cooperation with God (typical of Nestorius and the Antiochene tradition) and grace *primarily* as God's personal presence to redeem by indwelling believers and incorporating them into God (typical of Cyril and the Alexandrian tradition, which triumphed at Chalcedon). Fairbairn says that "there was a question of whether grace consisted of Christ giving the Christian power, aid, and assistance in reaching that perfect human condition or whether God gave the believer participation in his own immortality and incorruption."[48]

Fairbairn noted that this soteriological struggle had profound implications for the debate that was resolved at Chalcedon. The Nestorian attempt to keep the divine and human natures separate in Christ located the center of Christ's personhood in the union of natures rather than in the divine person of the Logos. The result was that the emphasis of redemption was on the relatively autonomous work of the *human* Christ as a graced man, the archetype of cooperative grace engaged in by humanity. Con-

---

48. Donald Fairbairn, *Grace and Christology in the Early Church*, Oxford Early Christian Studies (Oxford: Oxford University Press, 2003), p. 14. Hereafter, page references to this work will appear in parentheses in the text.

cerning Jesus, the Nestorians held that "God the Logos gives that man the power and cooperation he needs to be our pioneer in the march to the perfect age" (p. 28). The focus for them was on God's partnership with Jesus as the graced man rather than on the divine indwelling in Jesus or the assumption of Jesus into the divine life (p. 52). Grace became something that Christ possessed and then handed down to us in order that our lives might be graced for cooperation as well.

Cyril advocated an understanding of grace very different from that of the Nestorians: "Rather than viewing grace as God's giving power, assistance, and cooperation to help people progress . . . Cyril understands it primarily as God's giving *himself* to humanity" (p. 63, emphasis added). The breathing of the Spirit on Adam and Eve became the initial stage of God's self-giving to humanity, which is then in need of fulfillment through the indwelling of the sanctifying Spirit (pp. 64-65). The Christology that arose from this emphasis on grace as God's self-giving implied a foundational emphasis on the person of the divine Logos as the seat of personhood in Christ, as well as the person of the Spirit as the divine presence from which Jesus and then we are taken up into the Son's communion with the Father: "The idea that God gives us himself through Christ and the Holy Spirit virtually demands a strongly unitive Christology, in which the personal subject of Christ is the Logos himself" (p. 69).

A soteriology that focuses on the divine self-giving also demands a strong sense of the Spirit's indwelling as that which fulfills the vocation of the creature before God. The Spirit gives the Word a Spirit-indwelt body so that, through the Word, all bodies could be indwelt. The incarnational Christology of Chalcedon granted Jesus the wherewithal to impart the Spirit from his Spirit-indwelt humanity, for, as Augustine observes, "How much must he who gives God be God!"[49] God is both the giver and the gift of salvation (Athanasius). A unitive and a pneumatological Christology are complementary realities in describing salvation as the divine self-giving and indwelling of the creature as well as the creature's dwelling and participation in God. God does not give us grace as something detached from Godself; rather, God constitutes that grace through the divine indwelling or the mutual indwelling between the creature and God: "Salvation is receiving God and not simply something from God" (p. 70). Christ's redemptive work on the cross and in the resurrection flowed from

---

49. Augustine, *De Trinitate*, 15.46, in *On the Holy Trinity*, trans. Arthur West Hadden, 1st ser., ed. Philip Schaff, NPNF (reprint; Peabody, MA: Hendrickson, 1994), 15:26.46.

the divine self-giving in the incarnation and leads to the divine self-giving at Pentecost. Of course, Cyril also wrote of grace as a divine enabling that is granted to us in our cooperation with God; but this is a secondary and derivative understanding of grace in his thought. Basic to the notion of grace that supported the unitive Christology of Chalcedon was God's very self directly present to us in Christ and his impartation of the Spirit and active in us granting immortality and communion to dying and alienated beings.

In short, to overcome the stereotype of an autonomous agent cooperating with God from the basis of elevated human capacities, a Catholic understanding of justification will continue to highlight the indwelling Spirit at the base of human transformation, the very fulfillment of the creation of humanity as the bearer of the Spirit (Gen. 2:7). There is no question but that a pneumatological understanding of grace will continue to represent the way forward for a Catholic theology of justification. I agree with Pannenberg's view on this:

> The link between the Spirit's works in the souls of believers and the indwelling of the Holy Spirit himself has . . . received stronger emphasis in modern Roman Catholic theology than in the trend of its doctrine of grace that has been dominant since the High Middle Ages. It has not abandoned the idea of a created grace (for gifts of grace) but has closely related it to the uncreated grace of the Holy Spirit and his indwelling in the soul.[50]

The newer Catholic emphasis on the indwelling Spirit for its understanding of grace can refocus on participation in the triune God for salvation, as has already been highlighted in theologians such as Hans Urs von Balthasar.[51] The way forward will consist of a stronger recognition of justification as a divine self-giving to flesh, even involving divine self-vindication as the just God who justifies the ungodly by granting them a share in the very Spirit of life that vindicates the Son (Rom. 1:4; 3:26). This is the action that makes justification a revelation of *divine* righteousness

---

50. Pannenberg, *Systematic Theology,* 3:201. See also I. Willig, *Geschaffene und Ungeschaffene Gnade: Bibeltheologische Fundierung und systematische Erörterung* (Münster: Aschendorff Verlag, 1964), pp. 283ff.

51. See Anne Hunt, *The Trinity and the Paschal Mystery: A Development of Recent Roman Catholic Theology,* New Theology Series 5 (Collegeville, MN: Liturgical Press, 1997); see also Hans Urs von Balthasar, *Mysterium Paschale: The Mystery of Easter,* trans. Aidan Nichols (Grand Rapids: Eerdmans, 1990).

and not primarily human righteousness, contrary to the tragic detour of Augustine and those who followed in his anthropological emphasis. This is the action in which we are allowed by the Spirit to participate, a participation that is Trinitarian in framework, Christologically focused, communally and eschatologically oriented, and taken up into a hope for the liberation from bondage of the entire creation in the resurrection and the new creation, the ultimate outpouring of the Spirit on all flesh. Only in this outpouring can creation take on the image of Christ and participate in the revelation of divine justice. Augustine stated rightly that God not only restores us to moral virtues but also transforms us, for "through 'the one mediator between God and men, the man Christ Jesus,'" God "spiritually heals the sick or raises the dead, that is, justifies the ungodly."[52]

It is for all of these reasons that justification can best be understood within the context of the baptism in the Holy Spirit. Before we leave the Catholic reach for the Spirit in its developing justification doctrine, we need to address one more issue: the recent Catholic turn to the Spirit as descriptive of grace that is inherent in all of creation.

Bearing the Spirit as the Chief Vocation of Creation

Expanding justification to involve the Spirit and the wide spaces of the triune life takes us back to creation. Pneumatology implies that we need to expand the narrative of justification beyond the Christian's conversion and development, even beyond the explicit details of the Christ event, to involve creation and its calling. Significantly, the modern reach in Catholic soteriology for the Spirit involves mining the ancient tradition of viewing human existence itself as determined by the reality of the Spirit. Irenaeus's broadly salvation-historical framework for understanding the mutual work of Christ and the Spirit for salvation implies that all of life is in some sense "graced" by the Spirit. There can be no "autonomous" moral agent using grace toward some form of moral self-determination if the Spirit is fundamental to human existence to begin with. Grace, not just as extrinsic empowerment but now intrinsically, constitutes what it means to be human by the Spirit of God.

Küng, for example, refuses to see the creature only through the lens of

---

52. *St. Augustine's Anti-Pelagian Works*, trans. Peter Holmes and Robert Ernest Wallace, NPNF, 1st ser., ed. Philip Schaff (reprint; Peabody, MA: Hendrickson, 1994), vol. 29, p. 131.

its opposition to God, but more deeply in the context of the creature's being held up by the grace of Christ, since all things were made by and for Christ (John 1:1-4; Col. 1:15-16). Using Barth's (as well as the legitimately Catholic) notion of creation as itself a salvific act in Christ and in the triune God, Küng regards creation as graced from the beginning and not autonomous. Küng quotes L. Bouyer approvingly in the following:

> The *habitus* of sanctifying grace, far from establishing us in some sort of autonomy in regard to God, involves precisely a permanent hold of God, not only on our actions but on the source of our being, in so far as this could have been alienated from God by sin, and has to become his again, in the strictest possible sense, in Christ. In consequence, sanctifying grace, so far from conferring any power of our own to perform any independently supernatural acts, is simply a disposition maintained in us by God to act no more but under the impulse of actual grace.[53]

An autonomously graced self is an illusion in the light of the fact that human existence is in Christ and exists from (even if also alienated from and in opposition to) the Spirit of Christ. The graced self lives from the Spirit by virtue of being human even before participating in Christ's sonship by the redemptive indwelling of this same Spirit.

Küng thus participates in the modern Catholic effort, forged especially by Karl Rahner and Henri de Lubac, to understand actual human historical existence as graced so as to see the grace of Christ as already implicit within human life. The wrongful separation of the orders of the natural and the supernatural is associated with the twelfth century. The recent effort of Küng, de Lubac, and Rahner is to revise this scholastic bifurcation of nature and grace as two separate categories, as though grace is "an appendage to an already constituted nature."[54] Sensitive to Pope Pius XII's desire to maintain the gratuity of grace, Rahner understands grace as determinative for human historical existence but nevertheless as distinct from nature as a supernatural reality.[55] Henri de Lubac takes particular aim at the notion of "pure nature" (nature constituted independently of grace or the divine vocation for

---

53. L. Bouyer, *The Spirit and Forms of Protestantism*, trans. A. V. Littledale (Westminster, MD: Harvill Press, 1956), pp. 207-8, quoted in Küng, *Justification*, p. 206.

54. David L. Schindler, introduction to Henri de Lubac, *The Mystery of the Supernatural* (Warren, RI: Crossroad, 1998), p. xxiii, n. 41.

55. See Rahner's response to Henri de Lubac in "Eine Antwort," *Orientierung* 14 (Zürich, 1950): 141-45. I am grateful to David L. Schindler for this reference in his introduction to Henri de Lubac, *The Mystery of the Supernatural*, p. xxiii, n. 41.

humanity). The medieval concept of salvific grace as perfecting nature assumed that nature was in some sense graced but not in the sense that the supernatural characteristic of sanctifying grace is denied as a result.[56] Grace was thus viewed in the Middle Ages as an accident of the soul rather than as that which determines human existence.

Denying this view of grace as an accident but also uneasy with the formal distinction that Rahner assumes between the supernatural orientation toward God within human existence and human existence in itself, de Lubac suggests that the desire for God implicitly characteristic of human existence is constitutive of humanity as called of God. He explains:

> God's call is constitutive. My finality, which is expressed by this desire, is inscribed upon my very being as it has been put into this universe by God. And, by God's will, I now have no other genuine end, no end really assigned to my nature or presented for my free acceptance under any guise, except that of "seeing God." (pp. 54-55)

Finality is not extrinsic to humanity but rather "a destiny inscribed in a man's very nature, directing him from within, and which he could not ontologically escape" (pp. 68-69). There is no other human reality that is relevant to our understanding of grace than this one that actually exists in history as called of God for God and thus as graced (pp. 60-62).

Of significance to our pneumatological interest, de Lubac notes that God's gift to the creature, "that gift which is himself," is like no other (p. 75). This gift is unlike any gift given from one human to another, for in the divine self-giving, humanity is given its very being. This divine self-giving keeps the gift of salvation functioning as true gift, inexplicable by human systems of justice and in excess of any response that we could make. In this being of which the creature participates, "God imprinted a supernatural finality; he has made to be heard within my nature a call to see him" (p. 76). This being is not added to human nature but constitutes it. "For it is a gift totally interior to me; nothing is left out of it, and nothing of myself is without it" (p. 77). In creation, God gives us — and continues to give us — to ourselves as gift, in the sense that we have no existence apart from this gift (p. 77). The result is that refusing God constitutes a radical denial of oneself that threatens one's own reason for being at its very core.

---

56. Henri de Lubac, *The Mystery of the Supernatural*, p. 23. Hereafter, page references to this work will appear in parentheses in the text.

There are both Protestants and Catholics who resist the implication that grace is merely the development of an aptitude or orientation already essential to human nature.[57] Yet, for de Lubac, one is not to posit a *natural* link between graced human existence and supernatural or sanctifying grace. Human existence as graced by God is not a divine seed that must grow into supernatural grace (p. 84). The modalities of creaturely and sanctifying grace are still distinct. To pass from the promise of the call graciously constitutive of human existence to the fulfillment in salvation requires a divine action that is inaccessible to human ability. Notice carefully what de Lubac says in this regard:

> Between nature as it exists and the supernatural for which God destines it, the distance is as great, the difference as radical, as that between non-being and being: for to pass from one to the other is not merely to pass into "more being," but to pass to a different type of being. It is a crossing by grace into an impassible barrier. One does not merely need extra strength, such as an actual grace would give: one needs a new principle, that principle of divine life which we call "sanctifying grace." (p. 83)

I would like to emphasize that this "new principle" is to be regarded as the redemptive indwelling of the Spirit. The difference between graced existence, the divine call constitutive of human nature, and sanctified existence in fulfillment of this call is the difference between the creature created to become a living soul by the breath of God (Gen. 1:2; 2:7) — for in God's very presence we "live and move and have our being" (Acts 17:28) — and the divine indwelling of the Spirit and its fulfillment in the resurrection to new life as deliverance from sin and death (Ezek. 37:13-14; Rom. 8:11). Grace fundamentally determines and fulfills human existence as it is called of God to bear the divine Spirit.

This call to bear the Spirit is not fulfilled in creation, though creation by the Spirit constitutes human existence according to this call. The creation thus groans for the liberty of pneumatic existence (Rom. 8:22). The divine indwelling and the future resurrection are gifts of God that alone

---

57. For example, the Catholic theologian John Hardon sees this as an erroneous Protestant view of grace. Hardon, *History and Theology of Grace,* pp. 13-15. Lutheran theologian Robert Jenson agrees with a naturally human *openness* to grace but not an *aptitude* for grace, since grace is an ongoing conversation initiated continuously by God with humanity. Jenson, *Systematic Theology,* vol. 2: *The Works of God* (Oxford: Oxford University Press, 1999), p. 68.

fulfill the call. Through these, humans are justified in their fundamental existence as creatures of God. Without these, we have no reason for being. No justification as creatures of God is possible apart from the indwelling of the Spirit. No righteousness is possible apart from the communion of love opened up to us in the Spirit's embrace. No justification is possible apart from the fullness of the Spirit in the immortal or pneumatic existence of the resurrection.

If I may invoke a Protestant voice to help here, human existence and salvation as pneumatological has been beneficially developed, as Hans Küng has pointed out, in the Reformed perspective of Karl Barth. The latter also understood creation as an implicitly salvific act in Christ and viewed natural existence as fundamentally determined by the *Spirit* of God: "The whole man is of the Spirit, since the Spirit is the principle and power of the life of the whole man." For Barth, humanity is not divine by nature, nor is grace in its essence a human quality. Rather, creatures as creatures live from the Spirit of God, meaning that "the whole man lives by the fact that God is there for him." Barth notes of the human being: "Every moment that he may breathe and live he has in this very fact a witness that God turns to him in His free grace as Creator."[58] Barth says concerning the sinner that, even in the far country of human alienation, God "surrounds and maintains him with His own life!"[59] Thus, for Barth, the "relationship between the Spirit and man even in its anthropological sense is to be represented on the analogy of expressions used in the soteriological context." Creatures are graced by the Spirit in their creaturely existence. But this work of the Spirit in the sustenance of creaturely existence is also, for Barth, transitory and ambiguous. Creatures still perish. Therefore, he emphasizes the fallenness of natural existence and its opposition to its own true calling and orientation as a creature of God destined for the Spirit. Sinfulness is not just something inside the human person, "qualities or achievements or defects, but his very being." The human for Barth stands "in contradiction to God his Creator, but also to himself and the end for which he was created."[60] Sin is utter alienation from life: from the life of God but also life as God intended it for the creature.

The fundamentally pneumatological core to creaturely existence ex-

58. Barth, *Church Dogmatics*, vol. 3, *The Doctrine of Creation*, pt. 2, trans. Harold Knight et al. (Edinburgh: T. & T. Clark, 1960), pp. 362-63.

59. Barth, *Church Dogmatics*, vol. 4, *The Doctrine of Reconciliation*, pt. 1, trans. G. W. Bromiley (Edinburgh: T. & T. Clark, 1956), p. 542.

60. Barth, *Church Dogmatics*, vol. 3, pt. 2, p. 363.

plains the very need for our "justification" before God. This need is not first and foremost due to our status as sinners, for even sinning within a condition of bondage to alienation and death requires a relationship with the Creator of which we are hardly worthy apart from creation as a graced reality. When one considers the vastness of the cosmos, the billions of galaxies and the billions of stars within each one, why should homo sapiens, who occupies the tiny dust particle called earth require any "justification" at all? How do we rate to even appear on God's radar screen? "When I consider the heavens," wrote the psalmist, "what is man that you are mindful of him, the son of man that you care for him?" (Ps. 8:3-4) Not only humanity's minuteness, but also its temporality, makes humans insignificant apart from their Creator: "O LORD, what is man that you care for him, the son of man that you think of him? Man is like a breath; his days are like a fleeting shadow" (Ps. 144:3-5). How do we rate even to require "justification" at all? The answer is in Genesis 2:7: in creating us, God awakened us through the divine breath as living souls responsive to God and fundamentally dependent on God for our very being (cf. Acts 17:28). Paul thus notes that we were created for the very purpose of attaining the immortal life of the Spirit (2 Cor. 5:4-5). Creation involves the calling to bear the very breath of the Creator and Redeemer and to be the first fruits of the renewal (and justification) of the entire cosmos as the dwelling place of God. We may thus refer to the "evocative, ecstatic soul which is more itself the more God is in it and it is in God."[60] The very need for justification implies that we were from the time of creation "graced," or earmarked, for the indwelling Spirit.

Of course, we cannot neglect the Fall in our understanding of graced human existence. But it is possible to see in the self-contradiction of human existence elements of both grace and the opposition to it, so that we view existence in Christ as coming through a genuine shift in loyalty at the core of one's existence. But this shift is not one that obliterates the self as a creature created by God in Christ and sustained by the Spirit to still implicitly yearn to be possessed by God and to possess God. As Augustine wrote, "Thou hast formed us for Thyself, and our hearts are restless until they find rest in Thee."[61] It is interesting to note, with respect to our inter-

---

60. Michael Hanby, *Augustine and Modernity,* Radical Orthodoxy Series (New York: Routledge, 2003), p. 3.

61. Augustine, *Confessions,* in *The Confessions and Letters of Augustine with a Sketch of His Life and Work,* trans. J. G. Pilkington, NPNF, 1st ser., ed. Philip Schaff (Peabody, MA: Hendrickson, 1994), 1.I.1.

est in the indwelling of the Spirit, that the Old Testament makes an implicit distinction between humanity as living from the breath of God (Gen. 2:7) and yet, because of sin and death, humanity's need to have the Spirit placed within in order to be brought to new life and obedience (Ezek. 36:26; 37:14). In the New Testament, therefore, the indwelling Spirit became the description of the creature's awakening to new life and subsequent intimate communion with God and participation in the mission of God in witness to Christ (e.g., Eph. 3:16-19; Acts 1:8). A qualitative distinction is assumed between the creature's transitory and ambiguous relationship to the Spirit as a fallen creature and the redemptive indwelling of the Spirit that brings new life, justification, sanctification, and glorification in conformity to Christ's image (Rom. 8:29-30).

Conclusion

Though the historic Catholic doctrine of justification was connected to human renewal, it moved decisively in the direction of a moral view of the justified relationship and an anthropological emphasis on acquired virtues. Having its roots in large measure in Augustine's battle with Pelagius, justification became preoccupied with questions of grace and free will and subsequently became entangled in a phenomenology of conversion from which it was difficult to emerge, despite the eschatological breadth of Augustine's original vision. When dealing with justification, the scholastics tended to rush to the issue of human preparation, and then to cooperation with habitual grace, rather than concentrating first and foremost on God's self-giving to flesh in Christ and on the Spirit's indwelling of sinners.

The modern Catholic reach for the Spirit in its developing doctrine of justification, however, has the potential of expanding the doctrine to involve the indwelling Spirit at its very essence. This pneumatological focus can lead to a basing of justification on the full breadth of the biblical story of redemption, from creation to eschatological consummation, with a special focus on the Christ event as a Trinitarian act involving the Spirit. Cooperation with grace toward moral development can be construed so as to be rooted in *participation* by the Spirit in Christ and through him in the *communion* of the Spirit as the very substance of the righteousness of God. One does not leap from moral formation to the eschatological existence of the resurrection, but rather from the Spirit's indwelling and the new birth to the fullness of the Spirit in the immortal existence of the resurrection.

There is potential here for viewing justification within the wide-open spaces of the Trinitarian *koinonia* and self-vindication as the Creator, who makes the creation the divine dwelling place. I believe that the root metaphor of Spirit baptism can help us greatly in achieving this expanded view of justification. Before we turn to an exploration of this metaphor, we need to examine Protestantism's revival of the emphasis on justification and how this tradition both neglected and implicitly reached for the Spirit as well.

3 Imputed Righteousness

The Protestant View of Justification

I am convinced that mainstream Protestant theology has served the body of Christ well by elevating the doctrine of justification to prominence, though this has not always been recognized ecumenically.[1] In the Reformation's revival of Paul's emphasis on justification, God's own judgment and self-vindication as Creator and Savior took precedence in theologically discerning the nature of divine justice. God was recognized as righteous or just precisely in justifying the sinner, especially through the death of Jesus on the cross (Rom. 3:26). In my view, the great insight behind the elevation of justification in Protestant theology was thus the attempt to return to a theocentric, or God-centered, understanding of the divine-human relationship that held at least the potential of viewing salvation principally as a possession of and participation in the divine life. Though not the only path to theocentrism, this increased attention to justification in the history of theology in the West placed divine judgment and self-vindication both at the base and the horizon of God's redemptive activity in the world. By liberating justification from its medieval anthropological preoccupation with the dynamics of penance and conversion, Protestants

---

1. I was surprised, for example, when I chaired the study group on "Justification and Justice" for the Faith and Order Commission of the National Council of Churches (USA), by how many participants from a variety of traditions outside of the Lutheran and Reformed traditions found a focus on justification alienating to them and unfruitful as a focus of ecumenical dialogue on the relationship between salvation and justice. In addition, it is well known that there is a growing tendency to downplay the significance of this doctrine among St. Paul's own theological priorities, a tendency that I have never found entirely convincing.

allowed justification to once again function as revelatory of *God's* trium-phant and reigning righteousness in the world.

This theocentrism, however, raised new problems, which were due mainly to the historical attempt to secure it through an *extrinsic* notion of justifying righteousness construed as a legal or quasi-legal transaction. By basing justification on declared or imputed righteousness, justification tended to be equated with pardon or acquittal, which was then distin-guished sharply from the more participatory and transformative aspects of salvation. What this neglected was at the very heart and soul of justifica-tion: the gift of the Spirit in embracing the sinners and taking them up into the life and *koinonia* enjoyed by the Spirit with the Father and the Son. Arguably, granting priority to declared or imputed righteousness, though more potentially theocentric, also led to a failure to get entirely beyond the medieval preoccupation with personal salvation. Essential to these prob-lems was a lack of an adequate pneumatology in defining how one is brought into a right relationship with Christ and what the substance of this relationship might be. As such, the justified relationship lacked pneumatological substance and an adequately Trinitarian structure. In the absence of the Spirit at the essence of justification, the role of faith grew large as the means of embracing extrinsic righteousness. The elevated role of faith threatened to usher in a cryptic anthropological emphasis under the guise of a theocentric emphasis.

As a result of the one-sided Protestant polemics of justification, a soteriology with a strong emphasis on justification is still widely assumed to tilt the divine-human relationship in the direction of a legal covenant that tends to confine the life-giving Spirit to the cognitive function of faith or to an addendum that ushers in "additional" riches of salvation beyond God's fundamental "acceptance" of sinners. In response many wish to see the divine acceptance of sinners as a divine *embrace* of sinners through the indwelling Spirit. All notions of divine pardon are to be found in this em-brace, not in a word of acquittal from a distant judge. The Trinitarian God of the Christian faith is known as the God who *self-imparts, indwells,* and *incorporates,* not a distant judge who hands down verdicts from a heavenly court.

But as with more recent Catholic soteriology, so also with Protestant theology, there has been a struggle to overcome its shortcomings by grant-ing the Spirit of life priority in the justified relationship. They have done this largely through a more robustly participatory notion of faith in the context of salvation as *union with Christ.* Though helpful as a step in the right direction, the pneumatological basis for both faith and union needs to receive proper emphasis if one is not to slip into another version of an anthropocentric soteriology. Let us explore these issues more carefully, starting with Luther.

Luther and Forensic Justification

Luther's understanding of justification was complex and contained elements useful for a pneumatological and Trinitarian theology of justification, especially in his statements about the triumph of righteousness in Christ or the significance of union with Christ for salvation. But there is no question about the fact that he was also responsible for the narrowly Christological, forensic, and one-sidedly extrinsic understanding of justification that historically has hampered an adequately Trinitarian understanding of the doctrine. Provoking Luther's turn to extrinsic and imputed righteousness was the medieval anthropological emphasis on penance and moral formation. Given the tendency in the West to locate the Spirit within the arena of the creature's subjective cooperation with God, the shift to Christology and extrinsic righteousness in the Reformers' understanding of justification tended to leave the Spirit behind. *Imputed* righteousness became the alternative to *imparted* righteousness, with the Spirit relegated to the latter.

The Protestant reasoning was as follows: if justification is based, even in part, on the cooperating creature, the danger of Pelagianism is always present. Of course, within the anthropological emphasis on cooperation with God, a dominant effort can be traced in the Middle Ages from Augustine to Aquinas to grant grace the priority. Yet one could also say that there was a "bewildering variety" of approaches to grace and justification in the medieval effort to determine the exact basis of justification in the subjective human response to God. The result was that "[e]veryone professed to be Augustinian and anti-Pelagian, but there was little agreement on what these terms meant."[2] As a result, the Protestants would combat the Pelagian danger by removing justification from the inner renewal. The better strategy would have been to have based justifi-

2. "Justification by Faith (Common Statement)," in *Justification by Faith: Lutherans and Catholics in Dialogue VII*, ed. George H. Anderson, Austin T. Murphy, Joseph A. Burgess (Minneapolis: Augsburg, 1985), §18.

cation in the divine embrace as realized in the story of Jesus and then through Spirit baptism in us; however, this would not turn out to be their dominant strategy.

This is not to deny that the Protestants had reason to be concerned. That there were "Pelagian" tendencies in the Catholic preoccupation with human cooperation with grace in medieval theology seems apparent. One is particularly struck by Gabriel Biel's assumption (taken from William of Ockham and traceable to the much earlier John Cassian) that *facientibus quod in se est, Deus non denegat gratiam* ("God does not deny his grace to the one who does what is in him").[3] This statement became part of the received tradition concerning justification following the twelfth century.[4] The idea that God is obliged to confer grace on those who show an effort (in order to grant this effort meritorious status) was meant as a corrective to Pelagianism; but it ended up as a cause for the terror of conscience among the Reformers.[5] Though Bartholomaeus Arnoldi von Usingen, Biel's student and Luther's teacher, would write that "righteousness and salvation are from God and are due to his grace alone and not to merit,"[6] one finds, on closer examination, his concomitant notion that "the sinner first has to take the initiative to open the door of his heart for God's gracious assistance by an act of penitence."[7] A recent Lutheran-Catholic common statement on justification (which predated the well-known *Joint Declaration*) noted that in popular medieval Catholicism, salvation was widely regarded as somehow earned not only by "the moral law and monastic counsels of perfection but also observances of a vast panoply of penitential disciplines and ecclesiastical rules and regulations."[8]

The "sacrament of penance, often called simply, 'confession,' had in-

---

3. Heiko A. Oberman, *The Harvest of Medieval Theology: Gabriel Biel and Later Medieval Nominalism* (Grand Rapids: Baker Academic, 1963), pp. 175-81. John Cassian (360-435) also advocated the idea of an *initim salutis,* which was a "natural prelude" of human effort to which grace was expected to be offered by way of response. See John Hardon, *History and Theology of Grace: The Catholic Teaching on Divine Grace* (Ypsilanti, MI: Veritas Press, 2003), p. 23.

4. McGrath, *Iustitia Dei,* vol. 1 (Cambridge: Cambridge University Press, 1986), p. 83.

5. See "Justification by Faith (Common Statement)," §§11-12.

6. *Libellius . . . contra Lutheranos, Erphurdie,* 1524, D.1.5, quoted in Oberman, *Harvest of Medieval Theology,* p. 179.

7. *Libellius . . . contra Lutheranos, Erphurdie,* C.4.5, quoted in Oberman, *Harvest of Medieval Theology,* p. 180.

8. "Justification by Faith (Common Statement)," no. 22.

deed come to concentrate in the middle ages on the preparation and the attitude of the penitent as he or she stood before the tribunal of divine justice."[9] Rather than dealing first with the basis of justification in the Christ event as the event of the Spirit par excellence, the tendency was to go immediately to the issue of human preparation for the fruit of justice at work within the penitent. The Christ event was typically reduced to a "funding" of this conversion process with merits. Scotus sought to resist this anthropological preoccupation by arguing that the absolution by the priest, and not the penitential act of the penitent, makes penance a sacrament.[10] Despite this insistence, "the subjective state of the penitent was, on the basis of the ordered will of God, decisive for each of the three components of the sacrament: contrition, confession, and satisfaction."[11] Attention to this subjective state led Johann Fischer, a later opponent of Luther, to write that one may participate in penance from fear and self-love but that eventually this would grow into love for God and righteousness.[12] Aquinas made a similar distinction in motives between attrition (self-love) and contrition (love for God).[13] Such distinctions seemed to beg the question: How does one know which one of these two is descriptive of one's own penance? This penance struggle served in part to form the situation of insecurity that gave rise to Luther's revolution.

The great Protestant insight into justification is in viewing it as a *theological* reality before all else, or as a divine judgment and action that reveals the righteousness of God in a world that has called it into question. Luther arrived at this conclusion when faced with the demands of penance and the uncertainty of the human ability to meet them. The question Luther faced was, "Who could judge the sincerity or adequacy of one's own penance?" As Luther says, "No one is sure of the integrity of his own contrition."[14] Luther elaborates by way of a testimony:

9. Jaroslav Pelikan, *The Christian Tradition: A History of the Development of Dogma*, vol. 4: *Reformation of Church and Dogma* (Chicago: University of Chicago Press, 1982), p. 130.

10. *Oxford Commentary on the Sentences*, 4.16.1.7, quoted in Pelikan, *Reformation of Church and Dogma*, 4: 130.

11. Pelikan, *Reformation of Church and Dogma*, p. 131.

12. *Fruytfull sayinges of Davyd the kynge and prophete in the seven penytencyall psalms* (London, 1508), p. 4, quoted in Pelikan, *Reformation of Church and Dogma*, p. 131.

13. *Commentary on the Sentences*, 4.17.2.2.ad 3, quoted in Pelikan, *Reformation of Church and Dogma*, p. 131.

14. Martin Luther, "Disputation of Doctor Martin Luther on the Power and Efficacy of Indulgences (95 Theses) (1517)," no. 30, *Works of Martin Luther*, trans. and ed. Adolph Spaeth, L. D. Reed, Henry Eyster Jacobs (Philadelphia: A. J. Holman Company, 1915), 1:32.

> When I was a monk, I made a great effort to live according to the requirements of the monastic rule. I made a practice of confessing and reciting all my sins, but always with prior contrition; I went to confession frequently, and I performed the assigned penances faithfully. Nevertheless, my conscience could never achieve certainty but was always in doubt. . . .[15]

As he tried to do penance faithfully, he "transgressed them even more" making his conscience "the more uncertain, weak, and troubled."[16]

In fact, Luther came to hate the justice of God before he discovered the sufficiency of Christ for salvation. No matter how vigorously he made satisfaction through penance, he was never assured of the results. The harder he tried, the more frustrated he became. Then, in the legendary prayer tower, Luther fell upon Romans 1:17, which says that "the just by faith shall live." He remarked concerning this discovery: "Here I felt that I was altogether born again and had entered paradise itself through open gates. There a totally other face of the entire Scripture showed itself to me."[17] Justification by faith alone attained the heights of a hermeneutical principle that unlocked the whole of Scripture in a new light for Luther, revealing the grace of God behind all of God's dealings with humanity. Luther writes: "For if we lose the doctrine of justification, we lose simply everything. Hence the most necessary and important thing is that we teach and repeat this doctrine daily, as Moses says about his Law (Deut. 6:7)."[18]

For Luther, no assurance of salvation is possible ultimately based on the quality or quantity of one's contrition or works. Even the early scholastic phenomenology of conversion, especially the version supported by Gabriel Biel, was not sufficient to grant Luther's troubled conscience its needed peace. God was too absolute in demands and too transcendent in holiness to be adequately satisfied by the subjective state of the penitent or by subsequent acts of charity. Such thoughts ended up creating a situation of terror for the young monk who sought a gracious God so fervently but found this God out of reach by even the noblest of acts of penance or

15. Martin Luther, "Lectures on Galatians 1535," *Luther's Works*, ed. Jaroslav Pelikan (St. Louis: Concordia, 1963), 27:13.

16. Luther, "Lectures on Galatians 1535," *Luther's Works*, 27:13.

17. Luther, "Preface to the Latin Writings," *Luther's Works*, ed. Lewis Spitz (Philadelphia: Muhlenburg Press, 1955), 34:337.

18. Luther, "Lectures on Galatians 1535," *Luther's Works*, 26:26.

works of charity. Luther had to flee to the place where satisfaction was made for him, namely, the cross of Jesus Christ.

Despite the limitations of Luther's struggle within the medieval system of penance, he fortunately directed attention to the righteousness of the cross. In some tension with the satisfaction theory of the atonement, Luther also tended to involve a notion of divine righteousness of the cross that was triumphant and liberating, essentially involving the resurrection.[19] Concerning the righteousness of God that justifies in Romans, Luther says:

> By this righteousness alone we are justified, and by it we shall also be raised from death to eternal life on the Last Day. But those who are trying to undermine the righteousness of Christ are resisting the Father as well as the Son and the work of both of them. Thus at the very outset Paul explodes with the entire issue he intends to set forth in this epistle. He refers to the resurrection of Christ, who rose again for our justification (Rom. 4:25).[20]

It is important to add to what Luther says above that, in resisting divine righteousness, one resists the Spirit as well, and not just the Spirit's witness to this righteousness but the Spirit's role in its inauguration in Christ and its impartation to the creation. Luther implies as much when he says that the righteousness of Christ that justifies the sinner "flows and gushes forth from Christ, as he says in John 4:14: 'The water that I shall give will become in him a spring of living water welling up to eternal life.'"[21] Such quotes beg for pneumatological development so that one understands more about the very substance of this righteousness. In Romans the apostle Paul writes: "For the kingdom of God is not a matter of eating and drinking, but of righteousness, peace and joy in the Holy Spirit" (Rom 14:17). Though the faithfulness of Christ as the man of the Spirit grants specific substance to this righteousness, so does the Spirit of life revealed in that righteousness and involved in the communion into which Jesus was taken up through his anointing, incarnation, and faithfulness.

Also true to his Godward direction, Luther was convinced that an in-

---

19. This understanding of atonement in Luther is highlighted in the one-sided treatment of it in Gustaf Aulen's classic work *Christus Victor: An Historical Study of the Three Main Types of the Idea of the Atonement* (Eugene, OR: Wipf and Stock, 2003).

20. Luther, "Lectures on Galatians 1535," *Luther's Works*, 26:21.

21. "Lectures on Galatians 1519," *Luther's Works*, 27:222.

ordinate emphasis on penance diverted attention from the all-sufficiency of the cross for the creature's experience of grace. Such was certainly Luther's criticism of the medieval preoccupation with indulgences. These were "the temporal punishment for actual sins that was owed in accordance with divine justice" (Pope Leo).[22] Applied to the penitent was the superabundance of merits of Christ and the saints. Luther responded that the "true treasure of the church is the most holy gospel of the glory and grace of God."[23] For Luther, indulgences took the focus off the gospel and resulted in the trivialization of divine justice.

By placing the focus of attention on the sufficiency of God's redemptive work in Christ for our justification, Luther redefined justice in his reading of Romans 1:17 ("the just by faith shall live") as a passive justice, a gift given from Christ to faith.[24] Rather than serving as one virtue among others, faith became the all-encompassing posture of a believer wholly dependent throughout life on God's mercy revealed in Christ. Luther arrived at a notion of grace as the divine righteousness revealed in Christ and alien to us as sinful creatures, thus setting in motion a notion of justification that removed all human transformation and the consequent cooperation with divine grace — all human moral progress and works — from the realm of justification.

All of the elements of human transformation belonged for Luther under the rubric of regeneration and sanctification, which he formally distinguished from justification: "For Scripture does not give man his name in a metaphysical sense, according to his essence . . . but Scripture speaks theologically and names him as he is in the eyes of God."[25] Scotus had already shifted the weight of divine acceptance from metaphysical realities to the divine will, since what basically matters is the divine judgment and not something external to God compelling the divine choice.[26] This shift in defining righteousness from a moral quality to the divine will or judgment

22. Pelikan, *Reformation of Church and Dogma*, p. 134.

23. Luther, "Disputation," no. 62.

24. Luther, "Preface to the Latin Writings," *Luther's Works*, ed. Jaroslav Pelikan (St. Louis: Concordia, 1963), 34:337.

25. Luther, "Lectures on Galatians 1519," *Luther's Works*, 27:181.

26. Alister McGrath notes that Scotus has been viewed as Pelagian due to his assumption that humans are involved in justification but that this view of Scotus is flawed because it neglects the latter's doctrines of predestination and the priority of divine acceptance, "which emphasize the priority of the divine will in justification." McGrath, *Iustitia Dei*, 1: 144-45.

opened the way for Luther's notion of justifying righteousness as an alien righteousness rooted only in the divine judgment. Following Scotus, Luther would write:

> The Scripture interprets "righteousness" and "unrighteousness" quite differently from the way the philosophers and jurists do. This is shown by the fact that they consider them as qualities of the soul. But in the Scripture, righteousness depends more on the reckoning of God than on the essence of the thing itself.[27]

By placing the weight of justification on the divine judgment, God could reckon persons righteous or just in Christ despite their status as sinners, and justification becomes a legal transaction distinct from their renewal. Thus, for Luther, God's righteousness is outside of us and in Christ, and the righteous are paradoxically sinners as well *(simul justus et peccator)*. This was also true for Calvin: "The gift of justification is not separated from regeneration, though the two things are distinct."[28] Such a distinction implies that justification is not substantially *pneumatological*: it would have been impossible to speak of justifying righteousness only as extrinsic to us and in Christ alone had the Reformers understood it as substantially pneumatological.

They intended to counter imparted righteousness with imputed righteousness, or to shift the substance of our relationship with God from human virtues and progress to the merciful judgment of God revealed and enacted in Christ. Luther makes this motive clear:

> This is the reason why our theology is certain, it snatches us away from ourselves and places us outside ourselves, so that we do not depend on our own strength, conscience, experience, person, or works but depend on that which is outside ourselves, that is on the promise and truth of God, which cannot deceive.[29]

Though there is value to Luther's theocentrism, is it not also too one-sidedly extrinsic and legal, with its notion of justifying righteousness still

27. Luther, "Lectures on Romans," in *Luther's Works*, ed. Helmut T. Lehman (St. Louis: Concordia, 1972), 25:141.

28. John Calvin, *Institutes of the Christian Religion*, trans. Henry Beveridge (Grand Rapids: Eerdmans, 1979), 2.3.11.

29. "Luther's Preface of 1535," quoted in Pelikan, *Reformation of Church and Dogma*, pp. 149-50.

too anchored within a divine disposition rather than abundantly poured out as a divine gift? Lacking the Spirit, the Protestant theocentrism, inspired by its justification theology, lacked Trinitarian fullness. There can be no question but that Luther's revolution shifted the attention from human qualities or virtues to the divine mercy and righteousness enacted in Christ, liberating many from the anthropological preoccupation of medieval theology and spirituality. But in shifting the attention away from anthropology to the Christ event, did not Luther neglect the substance of righteousness in the Spirit? Without developing the role of the Spirit's indwelling in and through the Christ event (and its larger Trinitarian framework), as well as its goal in the creature's participation in divine *koinonia*, the necessary link between justification as a divine judgment and as a creaturely reality remained unclear, explainable only by the questionably biblical notion of "imputation."[30]

This distinction between justification and the Spirit of renewal was indeed unique to the Reformation. As Albrecht Ritschl notes, the separation of justification from human renewal was unknown in the Catholic West prior to Luther, and it was one of the most unusual contributions of the Reformation to soteriology.[31] The modern Reformed theologian G. C. Berkouwer still found this distinction to be essential to Protestant soteriology: he says that if justification becomes "involved in the relativity of our human existence and development . . . our hearts will be cast into doubt even as the doctrine of justification itself will be poisoned at its very root."[32]

But God has become involved in the relativity of our human existence in Jesus of Nazareth, and through him in us, and in a way that justifies creation as the bearer of the Spirit and as participant in divine communion. By way of response, we can say further that our participation in the righteousness of God cannot be severed from justification if justification is truly to be a *relational* reality in the richest sense of that term's depiction by the work of the Spirit. Justification is based on the Christ event and the embrace of the Spirit through him and not on the quality of our participa-

30. Even the evangelical New Testament scholar George Eldon Ladd says: "Paul never expressly states that the righteousness of Christ is imputed to believers." Ladd, *Theology of the New Testament* (Grand Rapids: Eerdmans, 1993), p. 491.

31. Albrecht Ritschl, *The Christian Doctrine of Justification and Reconciliation* (Edinburgh, 1872), pp. 90-91, referred to in McGrath, *Iustitia Dei*, 1:184.

32. G. C. Berkouwer, *Faith and Justification*, trans. Lewis B. Smedes (Grand Rapids: Eerdmans, 1954), p. 100.

tion in response. Yet justification does involve such participation, granting it by grace the dignity of a Spirit-empowered witness to the justice of God in the world. Of course, the separation of justifying righteousness and our inherent righteousness has historically served the critical function of slashing at the roots of all human idolatry and presumption involved in simply *identifying* one's notions of virtue or progress with justifying righteousness. One need only read Barth's classic 1922 commentary on the book of Romans, with its emphasis on God as the "wholly Other God" *(der ganz andere Gott)*, to understand how this Reformation heritage has had an impact on twentieth-century theology. But more needs to be said; this separation cannot be the final word.

Though Barth's theology spoke powerfully and meaningfully to multitudes between World War I and World War II, one cannot rest secure with his message in an emerging postmodern church that is well aware of human idolatry and is currently confronting other challenges, such as cultural and religious pluralism and the destruction of life in all of its beautiful diversity.[33] In this light, one must wonder whether the Reformation heritage's severing of justification from renewal cannot be used as a means of shutting the door on the importance of the creature's diverse participation in the wide expanse of Trinitarian righteousness. One could end up lacking appreciation for the "incarnation" of justification throughout the eschatological expanse of genuine and diverse elements of grace that are present within the Spirit-inspired witness of the churches among various cultural contexts, as well as implicit in the cries for justice throughout the oppressed creation. Simply consider the lengthy essay on the history of justification by the contemporary German theologian Gerhard Sauter to discover how thoroughly justification has been removed from human renewal and virtue in the Reformation tradition. Here justification stands "alone" as a divine judgment that is completely hidden in Christ and impenetrable by human virtue or moral reasoning. When I read Sauter's essay, I had the impression that I had just read something akin in spirit to Barth's 1922 commentary on Romans.[34]

The Protestant protest thus gives the impression that one is viewing only one side of an incomplete dialectic that has come forth with a re-

---

33. See D. Lyle Dabney, "Starting with the Spirit: Why the Last Should Now Be First," in *Starting with the Spirit,* ed. Stephen Pickard and Gordon Preece (Hindmarsh, Australia: Australian Theological Forum, 2001), pp. 22-25.

34. Gerhard Sauter, "God Creating Faith: The Doctrine of Justification from the Reformation to the Present," *Lutheran Quarterly* 11, no. 1 (Spring 1997): 17-102.

sounding "No!" toward identifying justifying righteousness with human righteousness without moving toward the needed "Yes!" to the Spirit-inspired witness to the same. Neglecting the Spirit — and dominated by Christology — Protestant theology lacked the pneumatological resources necessary to speak of justification as both a divine judgment and a renewal of life. Participation and witness are pneumatological categories that neither identify nor separate justifying righteousness and human renewal. Both can exist within the creative and dynamic dialectic involved in the justification of life. I do not refer here to a "dialectic" as a formal principle or a static reality without room for growth, progress, or participatory communion; rather, I refer to the dialectic of the *Holy Spirit* as the one who realized perfect justice in Christ and is approximating us to this righteousness as a community and as persons through our participation in communion.[35]

In transforming us, the Spirit thus conveys both a resounding "No!" and an affirming "Yes!" to our own witness to divine righteousness. Rather than discouraging growth, the dialectic is its engine, keeping us humble and striving ever onward and upward in our witness in living hope to its eventual perfection in the *eschaton*. As Galatians 5:5 points out, "by faith we eagerly await through the Spirit the righteousness for which we hope." Such righteousness will not come until the resurrection of the dead, the living communion of saints with God, and the new heavens and new earth. As Paul Tillich observes, "transcendent justice fulfills ambiguous human justice."[36] Until this fulfillment, justification is something in which we participate through the Spirit, who, as the great "Dialectician," both affirms our witness to justice and grants us as a community of faith a critical eschatological reservation toward our inner transformation and movement toward justice.[37]

Interestingly, the classic Protestant concern begun by Luther with justification *by faith* could not rest secure merely with a justification doctrine that only involved extrinsic and imputed righteousness. The hefty role granted to faith, though occasioned by an emphasis on extrinsic and im-

35. I appreciate Amos Yong's discussion of how the Spirit drives the dialectic of church and kingdom, in *Spirit-Word-Community: Theological Hermeneutics in Trinitarian Perspective*, Ashgate New Critical Thinking in Religion, Theology, and Biblical Studies (Hampshire, UK: Ashgate, 2002).

36. Tillich, *Systematic Theology* (Chicago: University of Chicago Press, 1976), 3:226.

37. See Jan Milič Lochman, *Dogmatik im Dialog: Die Kirche und die Letzen Dinge*, Bd. 1 (Gütersloh: Gütersloher Verlagshaus, 1973), p. 35.

puted righteousness, actually implied something truly *participatory*. Justification by faith implied that justifying righteousness is an eschatological reality in which one currently participates in hope. Viewed from the angle of participatory faith, declared or imputed righteousness tends to be inadequate to capture the full depth and breadth of justification. There is potential here for granting the indwelling Spirit proper emphasis in justification as an incorporation and participation in the Trinitarian justice and self-vindication in history. Without an adequate emphasis on the indwelling Spirit, however, faith as the principle of participation can thrust us into a new form of anthropocentric soteriology. To probe this matter further, I will explore Luther's tendency to base justification on union with Christ and how this is developed among the Finnish Lutherans. Then I will look at Calvin's wrestling with Andreas Osiander over the same issue.

Union with Christ: The New Protestant Frontier

There is a growing Protestant effort to overcome the overly legal and extrinsic notions of justification by basing justification in part on union with Christ or participation in Christ by faith. In fact, union with Christ by faith is arguably the basis of soteriology in both Luther and Calvin. This discovery has sometimes, in more recent theological work, involved a conscious return to the ancient, especially Eastern, emphases on divine indwelling and participation in God (even *theosis*). The outstanding example of this trend is found in the Finnish Lutheran response to the Russian Orthodox notion of *theosis*. We should also note that a turn from forensic to participationist understandings of faith and justification has also been important for Anabaptist, Reformed, Methodist, and various evangelical groups, forging connections with both Catholic and Orthodox traditions.[38] For example, Article 13 of the Methodist/Catholic Honolulu Report of 1981 declares that justification is "not an isolated forensic episode, but is part of a process which finds its consummation in regeneration and sanctification, the participation of human life in the divine." Similarly, Article 15 of the Lutheran/

---

38. See Veli-Matti Kärkkäinen, *One with God: Salvation as Justification and Deification* (Collegeville, MN: Liturgical Press, 2005), pp. 67-86. For insight into the evangelical debates surrounding recent participationist and incorporation language for justification, see Michael F. Bird, "Incorporated Righteousness: A Response to Recent Evangelical Discussion Concerning the Imputation of Christ's Righteousness in Justification," *Journal of the Evangelical Theological Society* 47 (2004): 253-75.

Catholic *Joint Declaration on the Doctrine of Justification* (1999) also implies
a participatory notion of justification by noting that justification "thus
means that Christ himself is our righteousness, in which we share through
the Holy Spirit in accord with the will of the Father."

This development was supported by Pannenberg's criticism of the
classical Protestant notion of forensic justification for so emphasizing the
extrinsic and alien righteousness of Christ *imputed* to us that it neglected
the role of faith (and baptism) as *participation* in the righteousness demonstrated in Christ (Rom. 3:21-26).[39] This development was also encouraged by renewed appreciation for the fundamental role of union with
Christ in Luther's and Calvin's understandings of salvation. This discovery
is important, since it implies that union with Christ by the Spirit is at the
very essence of justification as an eschatological reality.

Indeed, in places in Luther's writings, justification arises from union
with Christ, by which the believer participates in Christ and is identified
with him in his crucifixion and resurrection. For Luther, faith is not the
body and love as a virtue the form, as in medieval scholasticism; faith is
the body and *Christ* is the form. Luther says that faith "takes hold of
Christ in such a way that Christ is the object of faith, or rather not the object, so to speak, but the One who is present in faith itself."[40] Luther also
notes that faith is the temple and Christ sits in the midst of it.[41] In these
statements by Luther, faith facilitates a mutual indwelling between Christ
and the believer.

As noted above, this emphasis on union with Christ by faith is most
powerfully present in the Finnish Lutheran understanding of justification.
The rapprochement between Finnish Lutheran and Russian Orthodox
churches, or between justification and *theosis,* is not artificial, in Tuomo
Mannermaa's view, but rather facilitated historically by Luther's implicit
sharing in the ancient patristic understandings of Christ as the real presence of God in the world and of salvation as a partaking of Christ in mystical union. Such themes can be found in Augustine and Aquinas as well.[42]
As Christ the divine Logos is one person, so also are Christ and the believer
in dynamic union.[43] According to Mannermaa, Luther also shared the

---

39. Pannenberg, *Systematic Theology,* trans. Geoffrey Bromiley (Grand Rapids: Eerdmans, 1997), 3:229-30.

40. Martin Luther, "Lectures on Galatians 1535," *Luther's Works,* 26:129.

41. Luther, "Lectures on Galatians 1535," *Luther's Works,* 26:130.

42. See Otto Hermann Pesch, *Die Theologie der Rechtfertigung bei Martin Luther und
Thomas von Aquin* (Mainz: Matthias-Grünewald, 1967).

classic epistemology that assumed actual participation in the being of the one known rather than merely being affected by the other from the outside. The knower and the object known can become one. The result is a transformational view of justification that implies a deeper reality than the mere rise of moral behavior due to habitual grace or the neo-Protestant union of wills.[44] However, the believer who shares mystical union with Christ is indeed transformed so as to be Christ to the neighbor. The devotion to Christ in faith's union with Christ is turned outward toward the other.[45] Mannermaa concludes: "When seen in the light of the doctrine of *theosis,* the Lutheran tradition is born anew and becomes once again interesting."[46]

There is no question but that Luther has become quite interesting when viewed through the lenses of the Finnish Lutheran theologians, even if elements of Luther's thought that are not consistent with Finnish systematic reconstructions become marginalized in the process. I have found their rediscovery of Luther enormously helpful, but I think we need to exercise some caution so that the emphasis on the participation of faith in Christ does not shove justification toward a new anthropological emphasis. For example, though there is precious little detail in Mannermaa's *Christ Present in Faith* that describes the work of the Spirit in justification, one finds a rich variety of phrases describing "faith" in terms only comparable to Christ in significance. Mannermaa says that "only faith, that is, Christ alone, can give birth to a new human being."[47] He says that faith "denote[s] the full and complete divinization of the human being." Therefore, "[f]aith is 'heaven.'" Faith means "the real presence of the person and work of Christ." Faith "creates a new 'tree,' that is, a new 'person,' which bears good fruit." Faith is even "the 'divinity' that becomes incarnate in works"![48] Mannermaa thus makes *faith* the basis of justification, because faith makes Christ and God present: "Faith is the basis for justification

43. Tuomo Mannermaa, *Christ Present in Faith: Luther's View of Justification,* trans. Kirsi Irmeli Stjerna (Minneapolis: Augsburg/Fortress, 2005), pp. 39-42.

44. Mannermaa, "Why Is Luther So Fascinating? Modern Finnish Luther Research," in *Union with Christ: The New Finnish Interpretation of Luther,* ed. Carl E. Braaten and Robert W. Jenson (Grand Rapids: Eerdmans, 1998), pp. 4-12.

45. Mannermaa, "Why Is Luther So Fascinating?" pp. 5-19.

46. Mannermaa, "Justification and Theosis in Lutheran-Orthodox Perspective," in Braaten and Jenson, *Union with Christ,* p. 25.

47. Mannermaa, *Christ Present,* p. 31.

48. Mannermaa, *Christ Present,* pp. 45-54.

precisely because faith means the real presence of the person of Christ, that is, the real presence of God's favor and gift."[49]

For the New Testament, however, the Spirit, not faith, is the referent when it comes to the presence of Christ or of God in us and the substance and realization of God's righteousness in the world. For Paul, righteousness is first "in the Spirit" before it is ever "by faith" (e.g., Rom. 14:17), and the latter is dependent on the former (Gal. 3:1-14). Justification is by faith merely because it is a *pneumatological* reality affirmed in Christ in the absence of sight and in anticipation of the new heaven and new earth in which righteousness dwells. Thus Paul writes that we "eagerly await through the Spirit the righteousness for which we hope" (Gal. 5:5). As John Henry Newman says, "Faith is the correlative, the natural instrument of the things of the Spirit."[50] Participation in Christ is first and primarily a pneumatological reality as believers are caught up in the communion of the Spirit with Christ and, through Christ, with the heavenly Father. A greater emphasis on the immediate work of the Spirit of communion as the point of convergence with Eastern Orthodoxy might have led Mannermaa further away from the anthropocentrism of medieval piety, from which Luther attempted (not entirely successfully) to disentangle himself. We cannot replace a preoccupation with penance with an equally strong preoccupation with the dynamics of faith!

In the context of this danger, Paul Tillich rightly warns that, ideally, justification in the Reformation tradition is primarily by grace as a divine act and presence — and only secondarily through faith. His words are worth quoting in full:

> Not faith but grace is the cause of justification, because God alone is the cause. Faith is the receiving act, and this act is itself a gift of grace. Therefore, one should dispense completely with the phrase "justification by faith" and replace it by the formula "justification by grace through faith."[51]

The principle of participation is primarily theological (in the Spirit) and only secondarily anthropological (by faith).

Therefore, I agree with Albert Schweitzer that Paul's point of emphasis in his teachings about justification is on the contrast between the law and

---

49. Mannermaa, *Christ Present*, p. 57 (italics in original).
50. Newman, *Lectures on Justification* (London: J. G. and F. Rivington, 1838), p. 247.
51. Tillich, *Systematic Theology*, 3:224.

the eschatological life of the Spirit in Christ (Gal. 4–5). Paul's "by faith" slogan was a "linguistic and dialectic convenience" that allowed him to easily contrast his position with that of his opponents, who emphasized the *works* of the law.[52] Though I find the Finnish Lutheran interpretation of Luther insightful in some ways, I want to shift the focus more explicitly and predominantly to the ancient emphasis on the Spirit as the nerve center of the Christian life in all of its aspects. If an emphasis on the Spirit over faith means putting Luther at some distance, so be it. We are obligated first to the biblical witness and not to Luther. Luther, I am sure, would have agreed, at least if he was consistent with his fundamental loyalties.

I realize that Mannermaa intends his concentration on faith to facilitate a higher focus on participation in Christ as the righteousness of God. The indwelling Spirit, the habitation of God in us, is not absent in Mannermaa's thought; he even starts his discussion of the significance of union with Christ with the *inhabitatio Dei*.[53] But an emphasis on Christ present in faith (rather than in the Spirit as grasped by faith) tends to shift the focus from Christ to the believer. The nature of faith tends to eclipse the distinct work of the Spirit as the "go-between God" who works with the Son to realize the righteousness of the Father on earth and then to bring us into this righteousness as participants and in fulfillment of our calling as creatures. An emphasis on Christ as present in the Spirit will cause faith as the means by which we embrace the Spirit to take a back seat — a vital back seat, but a back seat nonetheless.

The otherness of Christ (crucified, risen and exalted), even in relationship to faith, can be maintained as well by an emphasis on the indwelling Spirit, since Christ's presence in us is mediated by the Spirit. There is no way in this Trinitarian construal of "Christ in us" to collapse Christ into Christian faith, which, if not subordinated in significance to the Spirit, can stand in danger of replacing the medieval version of the church as the *Christus prolongatus* (extension of Christ). It is not faith that is the real presence of Christ, provides the basis of justification, gives birth to a new person, bears fruit, or represents the "divinity" incarnated in works. The Spirit does all of these things *by means* of faith in Christ, and even without or beyond it. By means of the Spirit within, God is able to do exceedingly above and beyond all that we ask or think (Eph. 3:16-21). The Spirit — and

52. Schweitzer, *The Mysticism of Paul the Apostle* (reprint; New York: Seabury, 1968), pp. 206-7.

53. Mannermaa, *Christ Present*, pp. 3-4.

not faith — is the abundant and excessive gift; faith is a weak vessel empowered by God. Faith is the instrument by which Christ is accessed in the Spirit rather than the Spirit being the instrument by which Christ is accessed in faith.

It would be interesting at this point to look at the role of union with Christ in Calvin's understanding of justification. Unlike Luther, who viewed justification as the overall hermeneutical principle for interpreting the gospel, the very linchpin of the total life of grace, Calvin saw justification as one branch of the grace or benefit available through union with Christ, equal in significance to sanctification. But both branches of justification and sanctification are rooted in union with Christ for Calvin. He writes: "The whole may thus be summed up: Christ given to us by the kindness of God is apprehended and possessed by faith, by means of which we obtain a two-fold benefit: first being reconciled by the righteousness of Christ . . . and, secondly, being sanctified by his Spirit."[54] Does this mean that justification takes place in the Spirit because it is received and participated in through union with Christ? Calvin will reveal his ambivalence concerning that question. To explore this ambivalence, we need to look at Calvin's critique of Andreas Osiander. I will first discuss Osiander's controversial view of justification through union with Christ.

In a series of terse and provocative statements, Osiander proceeds, in his *Disputation on Justification* (1550), to give us the broad outline of his approach to justification in the Spirit.[55] His basic argument is that justification is accomplished through the victory of life over death, a point usually neglected in summaries of his theology of justification. He notes that the "justification" of the ungodly refers literally to bringing the dead to life (§4). This new life can be experienced now, not as an event of the flesh, "but rather a movement of the spirit, which God awakens in our hearts by his Spirit through the preaching of the Word" (§10). He notes in this light that Paul's rejection of the law as the path to justification was due primarily to the fact that the law could not give life [Gal. 3:21] (§§1-2). Osiander concludes that theologians err, no matter how great in name they may be, "if they think that we are dealing here with anything other than the living God: the Father, the Son, who has become flesh, and the Holy Spirit, who

54. Calvin, *Institutes*, 2.3.11.

55. Andreas Osiander, "Eine Disputation von der Rechtfertigung," *Schriften und Briefe 1549 bis August 1551*, hrsg. Gerhard Müller und Gottfried Seebass, *Gesamtausgabe*, Bd. 9 (Gütersloh: Gütersloher Verlagshaus, 1994), pp. 428-47. Hereafter, all references to this work will appear in parentheses in the text. All quotations in English are my own translations.

justifies, vivifies, and glorifies" (§69). Salvation is by grace, because new life only comes from God: "Our works, as good as they may be, cannot justify, vivify, or glorify, for that belongs to God alone" (§78).

Osiander's assumption that justification regenerates (vivifies, glorifies) led him to emphasize the reality of "Christ in us" as the object of justifying faith. Christ is the fullness of the Godhead bodily and now dwells fully in us (§39). All blessings come to us through Christ's presence within (Rom. 8:32), including justification (§52). We are justified by faith only in the sense that Christ "in us" is present to faith and is accessible to us in faith (§§16-17). In an implicit reference to 1 Corinthians 1:30, Osiander notes that through union Christ is "our righteousness, holiness and redemption" (§18). It is not faith as a virtue or quality essential to us that justifies us, but only "that faith that grasps and is united to Christ, which is its object" (§19).

Osiander does have a notion of the "reckoning" of righteousness, but this righteousness resides within through the mystical union with Christ (§76). To this righteousness we are indebted with our members to live for Christ as he heals us from within (§77). There is little question but that Osiander bases justification on Christ's deity when defining the righteousness that comes from the "Christ in us." It is not Christ's human righteousness that faith grasps but rather the divine righteousness of the Christ present to us in faith (§21). We are thus justified by his essential righteousness (§53). This is the righteousness of all three persons of the Trinity that came into the world when the Son became flesh (§54). This righteousness is shared by the Father and the Son as well as by the Spirit, who makes the godless righteous, which is also now the righteousness of faith (§28). Osiander's concentration on the righteousness of Christ as resident within did not preclude for him the role of Jesus of Nazareth in our access to justifying righteousness. Indeed, the object of the faith awakened in us by God is "Jesus Christ, the Son of God and Mary, who had been born and given to us and is grasped by us in faith" (§14).

Osiander does write that "only the Lord Jesus Christ who has fulfilled the law and all righteousness is righteous" (§26), but then he is careful to add that Christ was not righteous because he fulfilled the law. He was righteous "because he was born from the righteous Father from all eternity as the righteous Son" (§27). Yet the righteousness that comes to us through the Christ within still involved, for Osiander, Christ's death and resurrection, which bring pardon for sin, without which no one can receive righteousness and life from Christ (§29). Justification thus consists of pardon for sin and reconciliation. But this reconciliation with Christ through the Spirit within is not comparable to human reconciliation but is to be understood theologically as a union with deity through spiritual rebirth. After all, "Christ in us" is the object of reconciliation and not another human being (§31).

Osiander had a strong sacramental spirituality within the context of mystical union with Christ in the Spirit. He had an incarnational Christology in which Jesus fulfills human destiny by being the incarnation of the divine Son, an incarnation that is analogously furthered in the presence of the divine Christ in the sacraments and, finally, within believers through the divine indwelling.[56] Christ's death, into which we are baptized, is powerful enough to destroy the old nature as we walk in newness of life through his Spirit (§66). Whoever drinks Christ's blood and eats his flesh in communion with him has the privilege of dwelling in Christ and having Christ dwell within (§41). This is the mystery of Christ and his body (§34). Though Osiander places the emphasis on the incarnation and then the presence of the divine Christ, the fleshly mediation of Jesus (incarnation, death, resurrection) and the material mediation of the sacraments are still vital to the reception of the divine Christ within. Here I agree with David Steinmetz concerning Osiander's Christology:

> It is not the human nature which saves us and with which we are united, but only the divine nature. Nevertheless, the divine nature is not accessible apart from the human. The human nature is the essential means by which the divine nature is communicated to man.[57]

It is problematic that Osiander granted Christ's humanity not much more than an instrumentalist function in our possession of a divine righteousness immediately present within. In fairness to Osiander, for him the life, death, and resurrection of Jesus are needed to mediate the divine presence of Christ to us and do serve to define justifying righteousness as the victory of the living God over sin and death. But the Christ event does not define justifying righteousness any further than this. Therefore, the righteousness present through the indwelling Christ lacks not only christological but also Trinitarian specificity and definition.

Despite this problem, one might expect Calvin to have given Osiander's view of justification a sympathetic hearing. After all, Calvin, even more

---

56. David C. Steinmetz, *Reformers in the Wings* (Grand Rapids: Baker, 1981), p. 96.
57. Steinmetz, *Reformers in the Wings*, pp. 96-97.

prominently than Luther, gave priority to union with Christ by the Spirit in his soteriology. Concerning mystical union with Christ in us, Calvin says: "Therefore, to that union of the head and members, the residence of Christ in our hearts, in fine, the mystical union, we assign the highest rank."[58] Calvin makes the Spirit essential to union with Christ, saying that "Christ breathes into His people, that they may be one with Him" (*Inst.*, 1.3.1). Calvin even made union with Christ through the indwelling of the Spirit theologically prior to justification, declaring that Christ's redemptive work "remains useless and of no value to us" unless Christ dwells within (*Inst.*, 3.1.1).[59] Elsewhere, he declares in a similar vein: "Christ is not external to us, but dwells in us; and not only unifies us to himself by an undivided bond of fellowship, but by a wondrous communion brings us daily into closer connection until he becomes altogether one with us" (*Inst.*, 1.3.2). Indeed, Calvin notes that the twofold grace of justification and sanctification comes only from "embracing" Christ through the bond of the Spirit (*Inst.*, 3.2.8).

So why did Calvin so strongly reject Osiander's understanding of justification? Calvin wanted the righteousness that justifies us to be viewed more clearly and prominently as located *extrinsically,* that is, in the historical accomplishment of righteousness in the human life of Jesus. This emphasis allows faith to function as the means by which we access this righteousness through union with Christ without claiming to yet fully possess it within. Osiander's emphasis on justification through the presence of the righteous Christ within implied for Calvin that justifying righteousness is something we already possess rather than accessing it in faith as something still essentially "apart from us." Thus, Calvin identified Osiander's position as advocating a grasping of justifying righteousness directly without the medium of faith in Christ. He calls Osiander's position a "delirious dream," "a kind of monstrosity called *essential righteousness*" (*Inst.*, 3.11.5). Calvin elaborates: "You see that our righteousness is not in ourselves, but in Christ; that the only way in which we become possessed of it is by being made partakers with Christ since with Him we possess all riches" (*Inst.*, 3.11.22).

Yet, as we have seen, Osiander would also say that we are justified by becoming partakers in Christ by faith. The difference is that, for Osiander,

---

58. Calvin, *Institutes*, 2.3.11. Hereafter, references to this work will appear in parentheses in the text.

59. This quotation from the *Institutes* and the next one are quoted in Bruce McCormack's provocative essay "What's at Stake in Current Debates over Justification? The Crisis of Protestantism in the West," in *Justification: What's at Stake in the Current Debates?* ed. Mark Husbands and Daniel J. Treier (Downers Grove, IL: InterVarsity, 2004), p. 101.

this Christ and his righteousness is prominently "in us." The earthly Jesus was only significant in conveying this to us. Calvin saw this as a collapsing of the historical Jesus into a subjective possession of Christ by the believer. He further perceived such a direct possession of Christ in his divine essence as a blurring of the ontological distinction between the creature and God, and as a rejection of union by faith through the agency of the Spirit. Calvin thus protests: "Osiander, spurning this spiritual union, insists on a gross mixture of Christ with believers" (*Inst.*, 3.11.10). Calvin complains further about Osiander: "Our being made one with Christ by the agency of the Spirit, he being the head and we the members, he regards as almost nothing unless his essence is mingled with us" (*Inst.*, 3.11.5). This alleged blurring of the ontological distinction between Christ's righteousness and our own implied, for Calvin, a kind of realized eschatology, a divinization or a partaking of the divine nature (2 Pet. 1:4), "as if we now were what the gospel promises we shall be at the final advent of Christ" (*Inst.*, 3.11.10).

I consider this charge to be in part a misrepresentation of Osiander's position, since, for Osiander, Christ's essential love is poured out into our hearts through the Holy Spirit given to us (Osiander, §63). Osiander draws from the distinctly Johannine notion of Christ in us and we in Christ, a mutual indwelling by the Spirit (Osiander, §32). The righteousness in us through the divine presence of Christ within is grasped for Osiander by faith and is not to be confused with the righteousness already realized in our ethical behavior. Yet Osiander's largely instrumentalist view of the Christ event and his overwhelming emphasis on the Christ as the deity possessed by believers provoked Calvin's overreaction.

The real difference between the two in my view is that Calvin still wants justification to be based more specifically on the Christ event in a way that essentially involves Jesus' human faithfulness to the Father, especially in Jesus' faithful life and death, rather than primarily and essentially on a divine essence possessed by us. There is more potential here for seeing Jesus' faithfulness as revelatory of God's, indeed, of the divine-human relationship. Justifying righteousness is thus mediated by Christ, for Calvin, "manifested to us in his flesh" (*Inst.*, 3.11.9), being "procured for us by the obedience and sacrificial death of Christ" (*Inst.*, 3.11.5). This objective basis for justification in history allows Calvin to remain faithful to Luther's principle of justification through imputed righteousness: the believer is righteous "not in reality but by imputation" (*Inst.*, 3.11.11). Imputation removes any possibility of justification involving the renewal of the believer. As Calvin says, imputation "vanishes the absurd dogma, that man is justified by faith, inasmuch as it brings him under the influence of the Spirit of God by whom he is rendered righteous" (*Inst.*, 3.11.23).

Calvin was not alone in accusing Osiander of justification through "infused" righteousness. The charge was also leveled by the *Formula of Concord*, which declares that, for Osiander, Christ "dwells in the elect through faith and impels them to do what is right and is therefore their righteousness."[60] Again, Osiander's position was said to maintain "that our real righteousness before God is the love or renewal that the Holy Spirit effects in us and that dwells in us."[61] This caricature is not entirely accurate, since for Osiander it is our participation *by faith* in the indwelling righteousness of the divine Christ that justifies and not primarily the fruit of justice that emerges in us.

The important question here concerns how Calvin connected forensic justification through imputed righteousness to union with Christ. He would attempt to do so through the difficult idea of two distinct but inseparable branches within union with Christ: one based on imputed righteousness (justification/reconciliation) and one on the work of the Spirit (regeneration/sanctification). Calvin says: "The whole may thus be summed up: Christ given to us by the kindness of God is apprehended and possessed by faith, by means of which we obtain a two-fold benefit: first being reconciled by the righteousness of Christ . . . and, secondly, being sanctified by His Spirit" (*Inst.*, 1.3.11). According to Calvin, this twofold grace *(duplex gratia)* of union with Christ — justification and sanctification — is as inseparable as the light is from the heat of the sun, because Christ cannot be divided in two. Yet, as with the light and heat of the sun, so also with justification and sanctification, we cannot transfer "the peculiar properties of the one to the other"; the result is that "to be justified is something else than to be made new creatures" (*Inst.*, 1.3.11).

The difficulty here is that, for Calvin, union with Christ is in a real sense formed by the Spirit of God in its entirety: "Christ breathes into His people, that they may be one with Him" (*Inst.*, 1.3.1). Indeed, Calvin even notes that the twofold grace of justification and sanctification comes only by "partaking" of Christ through the bond of the Spirit (*Inst.*, 1.3.2). If both justification and regeneration come through the possession of the Spirit, it

---

60. Philip Melanchthon, *Formula of Concord*, in *The Book of Concord: The Confessions of the Evangelical Lutheran Church*, trans. Charles Arand et al., ed. Robert Kolb and Timothy J. Wengert (Minneapolis: Fortress, 2000), *Solid Declaration* III, §2.

61. Melanchthon, *Solid Declaration* III, §47.

becomes extremely difficult to thoroughly separate reconciliation from regeneration, especially since neither is the result of good works. Certainly,
there is no union with Christ, not even in its "forensic" implications, without the life-giving Spirit involved directly at its very root and substance.
Even the Christ event is an event of the Spirit (Rom. 1:4; Heb. 9:14). Justification certainly cannot remain distinct from the life of the Spirit if justification occurs through incorporation and union of which the Spirit of
communion is the substance.[62]

Justification participates in the Trinitarian *koinonia* and self-
vindication of God as Creator and Lord, which is inconceivable apart from
the transforming presence of the Spirit. As Calvin himself noted, the "divine favor to which faith is said to have respect, we understand to include
in it the possession of salvation and eternal life" (*Inst.,* 1.3.2). Calvin could
very well have moved in the direction of viewing incorporation and participation language as being more fruitful for his soteriology than "imputation," especially in light of the shaky biblical arguments made for the legitimacy of this latter term.[63] I agree with E. P. Sanders's conclusion: "In Paul's
own letters, righteousness by faith, the Spirit by faith or sonship by faith
mix indiscriminately with participationist language in such a way as to exclude the possibility of a systematic working out of righteousness as the forensic preliminary to life in Christ Jesus."[64] In more recent Reformed the-

---

62. McCormack, "What's at Stake in Current Debates over Justification?" pp. 81-117.
McCormack has made a similar point about Calvin's forensic doctrine of justification as being fundamentally inconsistent with his soteriological point of departure in union with
Christ. McCormack notes: "At several points in Calvin's *Institutes,* Calvin appears to make
'union with Christ' to be logically, if not chronologically, prior to both justification and regeneration" (p. 101). McCormack rightly sees that regeneration cannot be conceptually distinguished from justification entirely if both are based in union with Christ (p. 102). The result is that regeneration takes precedence over justification in Calvin's soteriology, contrary
to the intentions behind his forensic doctrine of justification. Interestingly, McCormack
traces the problem back to Luther's tendency to make faith in Christ prior to justification
(p. 94). However, McCormack views this inconsistency in Calvin (as well as Luther) as more
of a threat than a promise and seeks to change Calvin's point of departure to a revised election doctrine to bring about consistency.

63. As I have noted earlier, George Eldon Ladd wrote: "Paul never expressly states that
the righteousness of Christ is imputed to believers." Ladd, *Theology of the New Testament,*
p. 491. Michael F. Bird notes that the language of incorporation and participation are more
appropriate to Calvin's soteriological vision than imputation ("Incorporated Righteousness,"
p. 274). As Bird shows, this issue has been debated recently among evangelical theologians.

64. E. P. Sanders, *Paul and Palestinian Judaism: A Comparison of Patterns of Religion*
(Minneapolis: Fortress Press, 1977), pp. 506-7.

ology there is a renewed attention to faith as participation in Christ as our righteousness, using Calvin as a resource.[65]

If union with Christ by the Spirit and through faith is basic to Calvin's justification doctrine, there is potential within that doctrine to press the question as to what precisely connects the inauguration of justifying righteousness in Christ with the believer's participation via union with Christ through faith. The theocentric emphasis of the Reformers can best be preserved if the link is the role of Jesus as the one who baptized in the Spirit and the Spirit as the indwelling presence imparted from Jesus to us. Only this link can spare us the unacceptable choice between a christological doctrine of justification and an anthropological one; this link can also spare us the unfortunate bifurcation of justification and regeneration. Though faith is a gift of the Spirit, it is also a human activity. It cannot bear the theological weight of explaining why the Reformation focus on Christ necessarily involves the participation of the creature. After all, the creature was created to become the dwelling place of God, not just to have faith.

There is potential in the category of union with Christ for a Trinitarian understanding of justification so long as the indwelling and incorporating Spirit is the focus of attention. There is potential in the history of Protestant theologies of justification for just such an accent, our final point of concern in this chapter.

The Protestant Turn to the Spirit

Interestingly, as Pannenberg has noted, the Reformers and their spiritual children could not totally avoid the essential connection between justification and renewal through the Spirit of life inherited in the West from the Augustinian legacy.[66] Though Luther clearly distinguished justification as a divine judgment enacted in Christ from inherent change within the believer, he also showed signs of accepting an essential connection between them: this positive relationship is most clearly present in Luther's early commentary on Galatians (1519), where he says that the believer has begun to be justified and healed, like the man who was half dead (Luke 10:30).

---

65. See Julie Canlis, "Calvin, Osiander and Participation in God," *International Journal of Systematic Theology* 6, no. 2 (Apr. 2004): 169-84.

66. Pannenberg, *Systematic Theology*, 3:215.

Meanwhile, however, while he is being justified and healed, the sin that is left in his flesh is not imputed to him.[67]

Tied to the reality of faith as participation in Christ, there is a sense in which justification is in process for Luther: "[W]e are partly sinners and partly righteous, i.e., nothing but penitents."[68] Luther's *simul justus et peccator* ("simultaneously just and sinner") seems qualified here to involve a *partem justis partem peccator* ("partly just and partly sinner") understanding of justification within one's growth in the life of the Spirit. The implication here is that justification is regenerative and healing. I agree with Tuomo Mannermaa that Luther's *simul* statements focus on the believer's relationship with Christ, while the *partem* statements have in mind the believer's subsequent struggle between the old and the new.[69]

At the base of this expressed connection between justification and healing in Luther is the gift of the Spirit. In the same Galatians commentary, Luther notes that the righteousness "imputed" to the believer in faith represents the *same thing as the gift of the Spirit*, so that he sees grace not merely as a divine disposition but also as a divine gift. Luther says the following of Paul's message in Galatians 3:1-5:

> Now is not the fact that faith is reckoned as righteousness a receiving of the Spirit? So either]Paul] proves nothing or the reception of the Spirit and the fact that faith is reckoned as righteousness will be the same thing. And this is true; it is introduced in order that the divine imputation may not be regarded as amounting to nothing outside of God, as some think that the Apostle's word "grace" means a favorable disposition rather than a gift. For when God is favorable and when He imputes, the Spirit is really received, both the gift and the grace.[70]

This quote is significant in that Luther here describes divine reckoning as a pneumatological reality, a divine self-giving. The reckoning of faith as righteous *is* the impartation of the Spirit. The down payment of the Spirit functions here to vindicate faith in Christ as the means of righteousness. Thus the divine reckoning of Christ's righteousness and the granting of the Spirit become the same reality. God does not reckon merits to the believer, but rather life that can be experienced in faith and hope right in the

---

67. Luther, "Lectures on Galatians 1519," *Luther's Works*, 27:227.
68. Luther, "Lectures on Romans," *Luther's Works*, 25:322-23.
69. Mannermaa, *Christ Present in Faith*, p. 58.
70. Luther, "Lectures on Galatians 1519," *Luther's Works*, 27:252.

midst of death, for Abraham believed "the God who gives life to the dead and calls things that are not as though they were" (Rom. 4:17; see also Rom. 4:16-25). Consistent with this implicit link between justification and the Spirit, Luther writes in his Commentary on Psalm 51 that "grace" was "the continuous and perpetual operation or action through which we are grasped and moved by the Spirit of God."[71]

Something of the Augustinian heritage lives on in such statements. What does this understanding of grace say to a doctrine of justification by grace? Does it not imply that we are justified in the Spirit of new life who regenerates us? I think it was with such texts in mind that Steinmetz could say that "Luther had . . . stressed justification as the transforming work of the Spirit."[72] The positive involvement of the Spirit in Luther's doctrine of justification by faith has been a subject of recent research.[73] What is needed further by way of reflection on the early Luther is to view the Spirit as at the very substance of the righteousness enacted historically by the Father in anointing Christ with the Spirit and in raising him from the dead, "according to the Spirit of holiness" (Rom. 1:4). In being drawn into the Son, we are drawn into the Trinitarian *koinonia* as well as the divine self-vindication of God as Lord and covenant partner of creation. Our own participation in this justification involves us as witnesses of the divine justice and fulfills our vocation as creatures to become the dwelling place of God.

Viewing justified existence as pneumatic existence allows justification and regeneration to represent overlapping metaphors of the Spirit's work rather than as conceptually distinct categories only logically connected. Perhaps this soteriological implication lay at the base of Philip Melanchthon's statement in his *Apology of the Augsburg Confession:* "[B]y faith alone we obtain the forgiveness of sins on account of Christ and by faith alone we are justified, that is, out of unrighteous people we are made righteous or are regenerated." Melanchthon declares further: "And because 'to be justified' means that out of unrighteous people, righteous people are made or regenerated it also means that they are pronounced or regarded as

---

71. *Commentary on Psalm 51,* §10, quoted in Pelikan, *Reformation of Church and Dogma,* p. 153.

72. Steinmetz, *Reformers in the Wings,* p. 127.

73. See Kärkkäinen, *One with God,* pp. 61-66. He provides us with a helpful discussion of Miikka Ruokanen's unpublished dissertation on Luther's doctrine of justification in relation to the Spirit, entitled *Spiritus vel gratia est ipsa fide: A Pneumatological Concept of Grace in Luther's De servo arbitrio* (Helsinki: University of Helsinki, 1991).

righteous. For Scripture speaks both ways."[74] The person who made such statements was known for his defense of a forensic doctrine of justification! In such classic Lutheran texts, John Reumann notes a distinction between justification in the narrow sense based on the righteousness of Christ, and in the broad sense involving the indwelling of and renewal of the Spirit.[75] I would say that the narrow sense and the broader sense is in essence the same sense, since Jesus fulfills and inaugurates divine righteousness as the baptizer in the Spirit.

One might also refer to John Calvin's remark in his commentary on Romans 4:25 (". . . he was raised for our justification") that justification is a "renovation" unto new life.[76] Calvin most profoundly intuited the essential role of the Spirit in justification by writing that God is the "fountain of righteousness" in which we participate by faith, for Christ justifies us "by the power of his death and resurrection" (*Inst.*, 3.11.8). What are this "fountain" and this "power" other than the abundant outpouring of God's Spirit? As I have noted, Calvin saw the justified life as possible through the union with Christ forged by the indwelling of the Spirit (*Inst.*, 3.11.1).

Interestingly, Martin Bucer distinguished between justification as an extrinsic righteousness found in Christ and as an intrinsic righteousness that grows within humans toward Christ.[77] A similar position can also be found in Aquinas.[78] This option actually became the ecumenical consensus of the sixteenth-century *Regensburg Agreement*, which was heavily influenced by the Protestant Bucer and the Catholic John Gropper.[79] Both

74. Philip Melanchthon, *The Apology of the Augsburg Confession*, in Kolb and Wengert, *The Book of Concord: The Confessions of the Evangelical Lutheran Church*, 4: §§117-18, §72.

75. John Reumann, *Righteousness in the New Testament: Justification in Lutheran-Catholic Dialogue* (Minneapolis: Augsburg Fortress, 1982), pp. 7-8.

76. John Calvin, *The Epistle of Paul the Apostle to the Romans*, trans. John Owen (Grand Rapids: Baker, 1999), p. 186.

77. See esp. Brian Lugioyo, "Martin Bucer's Doctrine of Justification and the Colloquy of Regensburg, 1541" (PhD diss., University of Aberdeen, 2007; forthcoming from Oxford University Press). See also Steinmetz, *Reformers in the Wings*, pp. 127-29.

78. Aquinas had a notion of our being received by God solely on the basis of God's mercy, but then also this receiving transforms us: Rom. 2:13, Lect. 3; *De Ver.*, q. 27, a.1, quoted in Hans Küng, *Justification*, p. 218.

79. At one time, on the Catholic side were Eck, Cochleus, Gropper, and Pflug and, on the Protestant side, Bucer, Capito, Melanchthon, and Calvin (as observer). See Anthony Lane, *Justification by Faith in Catholic-Protestant Dialogue: An Evangelical Assessment* (New York: Continuum imprint, T. & T. Clark, 2002), pp. 50-57. See also Lugioyo, "Martin Bucer's Doctrine of Justification."

Bucer and Gropper sought to wed imputed righteousness with imparted righteousness, and this ended up as the substance of the Regensburg statement. Article 5 views justification as *based* on the righteousness of Christ but also as *involving* imparted righteousness. Concerning imparted righteousness, the statement notes that "the faithful soul depends not on this, but on the righteousness of Christ given to us as a gift, without which there is and can be no righteousness at all."[80] It is fascinating that Calvin praised the statement as a victory for Protestant soteriology: "For the Protestant delegates have retained the essentials of our true doctrine, so that nothing there is held to that does not exist also in our writings."[81]

The agreement is brilliant but in need of clarification as to how the two righteousnesses (extrinsic and imparted) are actually one. Gropper, the major Catholic influence on the agreement, saw imparted righteousness as primary (with imputed completing imparted), while the Protestant Bucer viewed the extrinsic righteousness of Christ as primary and as the inspiration for participation in actual justice.[82] Bucer maintains that the revelation of God's righteousness embraced by faith is followed by the impartation of the Spirit and the zeal for justice: "Because by faith we embrace this righteousness and benevolence of God, it shines in us, and thus he imparts himself, so that also we, too, are driven by some zeal for righteousness."[83] Bucer ends up as the architect of "double justification" in Protestant theology, although, as Brian Lugioyo notes, the term is problematic because it implies two causes of justification (imputed and imparted). In reality, Bucer advocated one formal cause for justification, namely, God's gracious or beneficent will.[84] However, still problematic, in my view, is the separation implicit in Bucer of a christological (imputed) and a pneumatological (imparted) justification, even if the two are then wedded within justification by the redemptive will of God. I would desire rather to find both imputed and imparted righteousness as abstractions that function in reality as elements embraced in the realm of the Spirit's presence. Bucer implies as much, offering us a fruitful avenue for further reflection.

---

80. See Lane, *Justification by Faith*, p. 235.

81. Letter to Farel (11 May 1541), quoted in Lugioyo, "Bucer's Doctrine of Justification," p. 191.

82. See Lugioyo, "Bucer's Doctrine of Justification," p. 120.

83. Bucer, Metaphrasis et Enarrationes Perpetuae . . . in Epistolam ad Romanos . . . (Bibliographie 76) (Strasburg: Wendelin Rihel, 1536), p. 80, quoted in Lugioyo, "Bucer's Doctrine of Justification," p. 40.

84. Lugioyo, "Bucer's Doctrine of Justification," pp. 38-39, 89.

This evidence that key Reformers made justification a regenerative and (at least implicitly) pneumatological doctrine is due to the fact that these positions arose from the basic structure of a soteriology that was Trinitarian in implication, in which salvation as a whole was rooted within union with Christ through the indwelling of the Spirit. This relational structure implied that justification involves more than remission of sins but also overlaps with regeneration, sonship, communion with God, and other benefits, enriching the notion of justifying righteousness and allowing for both forensic and transformative statements to be made about justification without necessary contradiction. In other words, the forensic quality of justification is not distinct from the Spirit but is rather to be understood as qualities of the Spirit's work as counselor, advocate, intercessor, and the Spirit of adoption (all "legal" metaphors). There is no "imputation" that is not essentially an indwelling. And there is no indwelling that is not essentially a transformative communion of persons.

For pietism, regeneration — and not forensic acquittal — represented the dominant soteriological category.[85] Indeed, in the words of Claude Welch, "conversion overcomes depravity" for the pietists.[86] Within this overarching concept of salvation as new life in the Spirit, justification in pietistic writings is sometimes defined narrowly as pardon for sin, but it is also often described positively and broadly as new birth by the indwelling Spirit of God.[87] One could even say that the regenerative understanding of justification in pietism caused the forensic concept of the doctrine to "fall out of use" for many.[88] Christoph Blumhardt could even quip that the one-sided doctrine of forensic justification is "meaningless" to the one whose mighty hand leads us to give of ourselves entirely in a way that responds to the blood of Christ shed for us.[89] Without new birth, justification is a fiction, concluded Christian Hoberg.[90] Johann Tobias Beck wrote

85. Dale Brown, *Understanding Pietism* (Grand Rapids: Eerdmans, 1978), p. 66.

86. Claude Welch, *Protestant Thought in the Nineteenth Century, 1799-1870* (New Haven: Yale University Press, 1972), 1:29.

87. M. Schmidt, "Spener's Wiedergeburtslehre," *Zur neueren Pietismusforschung*, hrsg. M. Greschat (Darmstadt: Wissenschaftliche Buchgesellschaft, 1977), pp. 9ff.; see also S. Haussammann, "Leben aus Glauben in Reformation, Reformorthodoxie und Pietismus," *Theologische Zeitschrift* 27 (1971): 273-74.

88. J. Ohlemacher, *Das Reich Gottes in Deutschland Bauen* (Göttingen: Vandenhoeck & Ruprecht, 1986), p. 123.

89. Christoph Blumhardt, *Ansprachen, Predigten, Reden, Briefe: 1865-1917*, Bd. 2 (Neukirchen-Nuyn: Neukirchener Verlag, 1978), p. 5.

90. Referred to by Carl Lindberg, "Do Lutherans Shout Justification but Whisper Sanc-

more positively that justification equals "growth in the process of being made more righteous."[91] Albrecht Ritschl thus notes that pietism is in a sense "an approach to the Catholic view" of justification.[92] The difference is that the pietists emphasized the new birth as involving the instantaneous work of the Spirit and the importance of faith as the means by which this work is received.

There is no question but that John Wesley at points sought, in concert with the mainstream Reformation, to clearly distinguish justification as pardon for sin from sanctification.[93] Yet Wesley's uniquely pietistic soteriological emphasis was on justification as itself regenerative. He says: "I believe that justification is the same thing as to be born of God."[94] Wesley notes that "the general ground of the whole doctrine of justification" involves God's remitting the punishment due to our sins, reinstating us in the divine favor, and "restoring dead souls to spiritual life as the earnest of life eternal."[95] Wesley also identifies justification with conversion, saying that "conversion, meaning thereby 'justification,' is an instantaneous work; and that the moment a man has living faith in Christ, he is converted or justified." But Wesley also points out that the regeneration integral to justification is "imperfect" (since there are "degrees" of regeneration) and that the justified believer "has the power over all the stirrings and motions of sin, but not a total freedom from them." The new birth that comes through justification imparts the divine pardon, but the person does not yet have a clean heart or sanctification (a higher degree of regeneration) in a "full and proper sense." Sanctification allows the believer to achieve perfection

---

tification? Justification and Sanctification in the Lutheran Tradition," in *Justification and Sanctification in the Traditions of the Reformation,* ed. Milan Opočenský and Páraic Réamonn, Studies from the World Alliance of Reformed Churches, 42 (Geneva: World Alliance of Reformed Churches, 1999), p. 100.

91. Johann Tobias Beck, *Erklärung des Briefes Pauli an die Römer,* Bd. 1 (Gütersloh: Bertelsman, 1884), p. 85.

92. Albrecht Ritschl, *The Christian Doctrine of Justification and Reconciliation: The Positive Development of the Doctrine,* trans. H. R. Mackintosh and A. B. Macaulay (Eugene, OR: Wipf and Stock, 2004), p. 108.

93. John Wesley, "Sermon 5: Justification by Faith," *The Works of John Wesley,* 3rd ed. (Grand Rapids: Baker Book House, 1979), 5:56; "Sermon 107: On God's Vineyard," *The Works of John Wesley,* 7:204. See also Kenneth Collins's one-sided defense of Wesley's forensic view of justification, *The Theology of John Wesley: Holy Love and the Shape of Grace* (Nashville: Abingdon, 2007), pp. 155-93.

94. Wesley, "The Principles of a Methodist," *The Works of John Wesley,* 8:369; cf. p. 367.

95. Wesley, "Sermon 5: Justification by Faith," p. 55.

in its "last and highest state."[96] Though the regeneration that belongs to justification is not, properly speaking, sanctification for Wesley, it does involve a "change in the soul" from "unholy to holy tempers." It is thus the "threshold" to sanctification.[97] I agree with Moltmann that Wesley thus interpreted "the justification of the sinner with the concepts of regeneration or rebirth rather than with those of judgment."[98]

Also worthy of note are the lectures on justification offered by John Henry Newman in the nineteenth century, before he became a Catholic. Newman began by maintaining that a divinely declared righteousness brings about that which is announced. "A *declaration* on the part of God," he says, "may in itself presuppose, or involve, or attend, or cause, or in any other way imply the actual communication of the thing declared; still it does not thereby cease to be a declaration."[99] Since human renewal through justification is imperfect, justification as a declaration of righteousness in Christ is "at first what renewal could be at last" (p. 79). This implies brilliantly that justification is based in Christ and the impartation of God's favor from him and in the Spirit, while also involving the transformation of the believer in Christ's image.

Christ was also justified both by the Father's declaration and his ultimate vindication in resurrection and exaltation: "He was, by the Spirit, raised again, proved innocent, made to triumph over His enemies, declared the Son of God, and exalted on the Holy Hill of Zion" (p. 238). Eschatologically, our justification will parallel Christ's. The declaration of God's acceptance in Christ will sustain those who accept this word in faith and hope, but justification also involves their regeneration, resurrection, and exaltation. As Newman explains, "Just as Christ was justified by the Spirit but also declared righteous according to the Spirit, so are we. Our declaration, like his, involved inherent righteousness" (p. 83).

The divine declaration for Newman thus functions sacramentally, as "an external word effecting an inward grace" (p. 94). Justification is both a word to be embraced in faith and a process of renewal by the Spirit. For Newman, the Spirit "works out his justification towards us, in us, with us, through us, and from us, till he receives back in produce what he gave us in

---

96. Wesley, "The Principles of a Methodist," pp. 369, 373.

97. Wesley, "Sermon 107: On God's Vineyard," p. 206.

98. Moltmann, *The Spirit of Life: A Universal Affirmation*, trans. Margaret Kohl (Minneapolis: Fortress, 1992), p. 164.

99. Newman, *Lectures on Justification*, p. 74. Hereafter, page references to this work will appear in parentheses in the text.

seed" (p. 102). Essential is the indwelling of the Spirit: "Justifying righteousness, then, consists in the coming and presence of the Holy Ghost within us" (p. 153). Newman continues: "He justifies us, not only in word, but also in power, bringing the ark with its mercy seat into the temple of our hearts, manifesting, setting up there His new Kingdom, and the power and glory of His cross" (p. 113). The Holy Spirit anchors both faith and renewal, linking them both in the overall reality of justification (p. 151). Newman thus saw his position as mediating between the Protestant view that renewal is a "collateral result" of justification and the Catholic tendency to see justification as based on renewal. For Newman, justification is based on a divine declaration that essentially involves renewal (p. 170).

Modern Protestant theology has tended to favor this kind of mediating position. Emil Brunner, for example, tellingly entitled the chapter of his *Dogmatics* on justification "Regeneration as a Special Aspect of Justification."[100] He then used the relational nature of justification to explain how justification and regeneration overlap. Reconciliation is healing for Brunner, a "reintegration of the disintegrated," a healing of the rift between God's being and ours, God's very life and ours (p. 272). Justification as a relational dynamic is thus essentially transformative. He resisted emphasizing the extrinsic nature of the justified self in Christ, which can lead, contrary to Luther's best intentions, to a denial that the new reality in Christ is genuinely the reality of the empirical self (p. 273). Although he found that Wesleyan perfectionism claimed too much for the empirical self, Brunner was quick to add that "rebirth or justification is a creative act of God." This creative act involves Christ as formed in us so that "something new, even if relatively new, comes into visible existence also" (p. 274).

Quite illuminating is Paul Tillich's view of justified existence as pneumatic existence. He starts by accepting the Protestant refusal to base justification on the quality of our renewed lives. God's love for us in Christ is not based on that. Yet this justification essentially involves pneumatic existence, being vital to a larger pneumatological reality: "God himself as Spiritual Presence." In the Spirit and through faith we surrender our own goodness to God in all of its ambiguity. In this courageous self-surrender, the New Being is experienced and the ambiguous good and evil are transcended. In justification, "unambiguous life has taken hold of man

100. Emil Brunner, *Dogmatics*, vol. 3: *The Christian Doctrine of the Church, Faith, and the Consummation*, Dogmatics, vol. 3, trans. David Cairns (Philadelphia: Westminster, 1962), pp. 269-75. Hereafter, page references to this work will appear in parentheses in the text.

through the impact of the Spiritual Presence."[101] Through God as "Spiritual Presence," justification dynamically involves the courageous acceptance of our lives as a witness to the justice of God. It may be said that, for Tillich, God's unmerited grace is experienced in the Spirit as both an affirmation of our ambiguous witness to justice as well as a transcending of that witness in the righteousness of God revealed in Christ. Ultimately, we can add that our ambiguous lives are overcome through the embrace of the Spirit in the communion of Father, Son, and Spirit.

Finding the overcoming of ambiguous life in the embrace of the Spirit's presence shows that one cannot systematically separate an "imputed" righteousness that is christological from an "imparted" righteousness that is pneumatological, meaning that the entire Protestant and Catholic argument as to which is prior theologically is based on a faulty separation to begin with. Tillich taught me more than anyone else that justification is the embrace of ambiguous life by God's indwelling presence. This is a stunning insight that has shone for me like a beacon amidst the confusion that plagues soteriology in the West.

Jürgen Moltmann is also worth mentioning as an example of recent Protestant understandings of justification as occurring in the Spirit or as essentially a transformative reality. Like Brunner before him, Moltmann points out that God's justifying righteousness is a *creative* righteousness that creates a new reality in the Spirit. Moltmann adds: "The Holy Spirit is the righteousness and justice of God which creates justice, justifies and rectifies. . . . That is why we can in this sense also call the Holy Spirit *the justification of life*."[102] Justification cannot be reduced to forgiveness of sins or an abstract standing as a legal reality. Moltmann thus believes that the Reformation doctrine of justification must be expanded to involve the regeneration in the Spirit that leads to new creation in Christ's image. Moltmann concludes: "There is no justification without the Spirit. Justifying faith is itself the experience that the love of God has been poured out into our hearts 'through the Holy Spirit' (Rom. 5:5)" (p. 148).

Moltmann's student, Methodist theologian D. Lyle Dabney, has also written of justification as "by the Spirit," focusing on the Spirit as the very substance of the reconciled and renewed life that justification facilitates through the resurrection of Jesus.[103] Other Protestants could be men-

---

101. Paul Tillich, *Systematic Theology*, 3:222, 226.
102. Moltmann, *The Spirit of Life*, pp. 129, 143, 148 (italics in original).
103. D. Lyle Dabney, "Justification by the Spirit: Soteriological Reflections on the Resur-

tioned as well. For example, Eberhard Jüngel defined justification this way: "To put it briefly: We are talking about the raising of Jesus Christ from the dead and about our participation in his life and resurrection." Jüngel criticizes any notion of grace as a power that we possess and use or that enables the will to act toward justice, calling the historic Catholic doctrine of cooperative grace a "christianized principle of performance." Though favoring participatory language, Jüngel resists viewing justifying grace as cooperative. Grace is rather the freedom that we can never possess, use, or interact with, because it precedes all will and action.[104]

Jüngel is rightly attuned to the need to make participation prior theologically to cooperation, but there is no need to exclude cooperation from justification altogether, since it plays a secondary role in the "incarnation" of justification in life. The same can be said of the faithful life in general. Mennonite theologian Thomas Finger defines justifying righteousness as God's covenant faithfulness revealed in Christ's faithful life, surrender to death, and resurrection from the dead. Justification "by faith" is justification by way of the faithful life that is liberated by participation in Christ's risen life: "Given the dynamism of the righteousness involved in justification, faith that appropriates it cannot be passive."[105]

One is reminded of Dietrich Bonhoeffer's stunning remark that "the only man who has the right to say that he is justified by grace alone is the man who has left all to follow Christ."[106] Grace is not the common property of Christianity as an element of bourgeois culture, as though one can rest content with the idea that "all the world is justified in principle by grace. I can therefore cling to my bourgeois secular existence, and remain as I was before, but with the added assurance that the grace of God will cover me" (p. 54). Such is "cheap grace" for Bonhoeffer, "which is the deadly enemy of our Church" (p. 45). It is grace as a doctrine or a system,

---

rection," *International Journal of Systematic Theology* 3, no. 1 (March 2001): 46-68. I am grateful to Dabney for first bringing this issue to my attention. My initial effort at developing it is found in my essay entitled "Justification through New Creation: The Holy Spirit and the Doctrine by which the Church Stands or Falls," *Theology Today* 58, no. 2 (July 2001): 202-17.

104. Eberhard Jüngel, *Justification: The Heart of the Christian Faith*, trans. Jeffrey F. Cayzer (Edinburgh: T. & T. Clark, 2001), pp. 4, 195-97.

105. Thomas Finger, *A Contemporary Anabaptist Theology: Biblical, Historical, Constructive* (Downers Grove, IL: InterVarsity, 2004), p. 241.

106. Dietrich Bonhoeffer, *The Cost of Discipleship*, trans. R. H. Fuller (New York: Macmillan, 1963), p. 55. Hereafter, page references to this work will appear in parentheses in the text.

an intellectual assent. It is grace without repentance or church discipline. It is, most devastatingly, "grace without discipleship, grace without the cross, grace without Jesus Christ, living and incarnate" (p. 47).

Though a number of modern Protestant theologians provide outstanding efforts at beginning to define justification as a pneumatological reality, or as the justification that brings life (Rom. 5:18), the recent Protestant turn to the Spirit has sometimes been implicit or nonspecific, emphasizing the participatory nature of faith in the context of union with Christ or the Spirit as serving the same instrumentalist function of facilitating an encounter with Christ. As Dabney and others have noted, what is still needed is an effort at defining the indwelling Spirit as the very substance of justifying righteousness.

I will maintain in the following chapters that the role of the Spirit in defining and granting sinners access to divine *koinonia* will best serve to lead us toward a Trinitarian theology of justification. The New Testament metaphor of Spirit baptism can provide a helpful narrative context for this view of justification, thus preserving both the theocentric and participatory aspects characteristic of justification in the New Testament. Within the context of Christ as the Spirit-indwelt Son of the Father who imparts the Spirit of divine righteousness to the creature (see Acts 2:33), justification can be conceived as properly theocentric and participatory, delivering the doctrine from both a Spiritless declared righteousness and an anthropological preoccupation with the dynamics of human cooperation with grace.

Conclusion

The dominant Protestant effort to define the justifying relationship as a legal relationship involving extrinsic righteousness could not be maintained over time, at least not without significant qualification. At some tension with this legal soteriology, the importance of union with Christ by faith implied for both Luther and Calvin a participatory understanding of the creature's involvement in justifying righteousness, which in turn implied a more expansive role for the Spirit in the justification of the creature. Union and participation are implicitly tied to the pneumatological notions of mutual indwelling and *koinonia*, while the more legal categories of reconciliation and imputation are not, at least not without significant qualification. As I will observe, the biblical understanding of forensic rightwising involves divine judgments that are redemptive, liberating, and in service to the triumph of God's will to take up dwelling within the creation, a narrative of rightwising that is actually more at home in concepts like union and participation than in imputation of a status or a mere reconciliation of wills.

It is vital, however, that the Spirit and not faith receive the emphasis as the very substance of justifying righteousness in order to preserve and expand on the theocentric soteriology of the Reformation. Especially within a Trinitarian context, it would be possible to envision the accomplishment of justification in the Christ event so as to involve Christ as the dwelling place of the Spirit and his life as an offering of devotion to the heavenly Father. Death by crucifixion thrusts Christ as the temple of the Spirit into God-forsakenness in fulfillment of all righteousness, and the resurrection vindicates his life with the Father as indestructible. He did this so that we as temples of the Spirit can be rescued from alienation from the justice of the divine communion of persons. The Spirit-indwelt Christ baptizes us in the Spirit so that we can be taken up in him into the embrace of the divine communion.

Creation is in fact destined from its beginning to be "baptized in the Spirit" (Gen 1:2; 2:7) so that mortality might be taken up into life (2 Cor. 5:4-5) and can only be judged as righteous in the fulfillment of this God-ordained purpose of bearing the divine Spirit in the image of the eternal Son. With Spirit baptism as the narrative context of justification, the creature's eschatological participation in justification is inconceivable without the indwelling and regeneration of the Spirit, leading to resurrection, glorification, and final indwelling and communion. As Brunner and Moltmann have noted, the righteousness that justifies is a *creative* righteousness that conquers sin and death and involves new life and communion rather than a static or unidimensionally conceived legal status.

The classic Protestant notion of justification has always reached for the life of the Spirit. Thus has it implicitly reached for a full-orbed Trinitarian notion of justification that involves God as a communion of persons, who seeks through mutual indwelling to bring creation into the divine *koinonia* and the fullness of life. The great insight into justification as a divine judgment or act, however, requires a strong pneumatology so as to clarify its full Trinitarian structure. Spiritual presence overcomes ambiguous human life in the divine embrace and reaches beyond this life to the pneumatic existence of the new creation. A root metaphor involving the Spirit, such as the metaphor of *Spirit baptism* favored among Pentecostals, can help accomplish that. This is our next topic of discussion.

4 Justification and Spirit Baptism

The Exploration of a Pentecostal Metaphor

What can both anchor and unite the Protestant emphasis on imputed righteousness received by faith with the historic Catholic emphasis on justification through the fruit of righteousness in us as we cooperate with grace? Both traditions have at least implicitly reached for the gift of the Spirit as the essential link. The indwelling of the Spirit first in Christ and through Christ in us can provide the link. Only this link can prevent a bifurcation of a christological doctrine of imputed righteousness and a doctrine of imparted righteousness focused on inner renewal. The Spirit-indwelt Christ who inaugurates the triumph of divine righteousness in the world and imparts the Spirit to the creature provides both the objective basis for the justification declared in the gospel and the essential link to the creature's participation in it.

I believe that the emphasis of the Pentecostal movement on *baptism in the Spirit* can thus give the ecumenical discussion about justification the broad narrative framework it needs to develop this link further. The dialogue will also help Pentecostal theologians rethink some of the ambiguities and difficulties of their own diverse tradition. I will now explore the ecumenical promise of Spirit baptism as a context for understanding justification, beginning with the distinctive Pentecostal emphasis on the indwelling Spirit. Within this larger concentration on the indwelling presence of the Spirit, Pentecostals have emphasized both intimate communion and empowered witness; such accents will prove to be fruitful in the context of a Trinitarian theology of justification. Since the Spirit's embrace of creation in pardon and communion faces opposition from the forces of darkness, this embrace requires powerful witness and divine vindication of this witness. Justification within the loving communion with God made possible by the Spirit thus has legal overtones. This is the context in which the "legal" dimension of justification makes sense, but it is forensic in the *Hebraic* sense of God's righteous decisions triumphing over the opposition. In Yahweh's world court, righteousness flows like a mighty river that sweeps up the opposition and engulfs it with the Spirit's redemptive presence. This is what Pentecostals will call the eschatological latter-day rain of the Spirit. However, the rain of the Spirit must be pushed beyond the pale of historical fulfillment to the new creation in which righteousness dwells.

We will begin by exploring the Pentecostal emphasis on the Spirit's indwelling, including its related accents, and then work toward a broadly pneumatological understanding of justification within the larger framework of the Pentecostal emphasis on Spirit baptism, especially in eschatological perspective.

Spirit Indwelling: The Pentecostal Distinctive

There is no question but that the crown jewel of the Pentecostal message is the baptism in the Holy Spirit.[1] Though Spirit baptism was typically described early on as the crowning moment of one's initiation into the life of the Spirit, it definitely cast its shadow backward so as to make the entire initiation process a process of receiving God's eternal life. For example, in 1906, the founder of Pentecostalism as a global movement, William J. Seymour, described the sinner's justification and entry into the Christian life this way:

> The Lord has mercy on him for Christ's sake and puts eternal life in his soul, pardoning him of his sins, washing away his guilty pollution, and he stands before God justified as though he had never sinned. . . . Then there remains that old original sin. . . . Jesus takes that soul that has eternal life in it and presents it to God for thorough cleansing and purging from all Adamic sin. . . . Now he is on the altar for the fire of God to fall, which is the baptism with the Holy Ghost. It is the free gift upon the sanctified, cleansed heart.[2]

1. See my defense of this point with respect to the development of Pentecostal theology over the last three decades in *Baptized in the Spirit: A Global Pentecostal Theology* (Grand Rapids: Zondervan, 2006), pp. 19-60.

2. William J. Seymour, "The Way into the Holiest," *The Apostolic Faith* 1, no. 2 (Oct. 1906): 4.

With his typical Pentecostal holiness soteriology, Seymour saw justification, sanctification, and Spirit baptism (filling and empowerment) as distinct moments in a person's gradual entry into the life of the Spirit. But notice how justification and sanctification for Seymour both have their origin and fulfillment in the indwelling Spirit. The Christian life for Seymour is all about possessing the Spirit. Eternal life enters the soul, bringing about the pardon and cleansing indicative of justification. This presence of the Spirit works to root out the domination of the Adamic nature, an experience known as "entire sanctification." Then comes the climax of the process of possessing the Spirit: the fire from heaven falls, and the creaturely vessel is "filled" with the Spirit, or powerfully experiences the divine indwelling as a force for intense communion and triumphant witness in the world. Seymour's logic is ancient and profound: "The life has to be put into us before we can present any life unto the Lord."[3]

Dare we speak of the finite as having the capacity to bear the Spirit and to participate in the Spirit's witness? As an elaboration on my previous book on Spirit baptism, I wrote an editorial on the divine indwelling, highlighting the *finitum capax infiniti* (the "finite gaining the capacity to bear the infinite"), suggesting that we find in this emphasis on the divine indwelling another way of looking at the Pentecostal emphasis on the baptism in the Holy Spirit.[4] Terry Cross then responded favorably to this editorial in his presidential address at the 2008 meeting of the Society for Pentecostal Studies.[5] He carefully traced the concept of the *finitum capax infiniti* from its roots in the Lutheran notion of the ubiquitous presence of Christ in the Eucharist. Reformed theology responded with suspicion to the suggestion that the finite Eucharist has the capacity to bear the infinite, because it seemed to undermine a proper grasp of the freedom of the Spirit. Cross correctly notes that this Reformed emphasis on the freedom of the Holy Spirit resurfaced in Barth's separation of revelation from the human experience of God. Cross finds in my essay a way beyond this separation so that the full impact of the divine indwelling and the related *finitum capax infiniti* can be appreciated theologically.

After all, the finite capacity to bear the Spirit was focused, for Pente-

---

3. Seymour, "The Way into the Holiest," p. 4.

4. Macchia, "Finitum Capax Infiniti: A Pentecostal Distinctive?" *Pneuma: The Journal of the Society for Pentecostal Studies* 29, no. 2 (2007): 185-87; see also Macchia, *Baptized in the Spirit*.

5. Terry Cross, "Finitum Capax Infiniti," address to the Society for Pentecostal Studies, Duke University Divinity School, March 15, 2008.

costals, on Christ and the community of the faithful — and not on the elements of the Lord's Supper. Richard Whiteman Fox once wrote tellingly that the congregation at a Catholic mass says to Christ, just before taking the sacred meal, "Speak but the word and my soul shall be healed," but that "the genius of Azusa Pentecostalism was to have the Spirit pass through worshipers' bodies while they did the speaking and healing themselves."[6] This should not be read as a denigration of Catholic worship or the central place it gives to the Eucharist. Fox's insight is nevertheless valid. For Pentecostals, the *finitum capax infiniti* is located centrally in the human heart and the communal interaction of gifted lives that have become channels of the Spirit's presence to one another. The Spirit's indwelling and witness in and through us is vital to all theological categories for Pentecostals, including not only worship but also Christology, soteriology, ecclesiology, and eschatology (involving the final outpouring of the Spirit upon all flesh or the "latter rain of the Spirit"). The goal is to turn all of creation into a temple of the divine presence in the image of Christ and to the glory of the Father.

Recently, the Pentecostal historical theologian Dale Coulter has also focused on the indwelling of the Spirit as the chief Pentecostal distinctive.[7] Noteworthy among the several Pentecostal pioneers that he quotes to make his point is the healing evangelist Smith Wigglesworth, who says, "If you are definite with [Jesus], you will never go away disappointed. The divine life will flow into you and instantaneously you will be delivered. This Jesus is just the same today, and he says to you, 'I will; be thou clean.' He has an overflowing cup for you, a fullness of life."[8] Notice that, just as with Seymour, Wigglesworth defines one's becoming a Christian as a reception of the divine life within. Wigglesworth is clear that the divine indwelling represents an actual partaking of the divine nature, "an impartation of His very life and nature within," for "we are made partakers of His very essence and life."[9] Indeed, Wigglesworth's logic, like Seymour's, was simple but

---

6. Richard Whiteman Fox, *Jesus in America: A History* (San Francisco: Harper San Francisco, 2004), p. 342.

7. Dale Coulter, "'Delivered by the Power of God': Toward a Pentecostal Understanding of Salvation," *International Journal of Systematic Theology* 10, no. 4 (Oct. 2008): 447-67.

8. Smith Wigglesworth, "Himself Took Our Infirmities," in *Ever Increasing Faith*, ed. Wayne E. Warner, rev. ed. (Springfield, MO: Gospel Publishing House, 1971), p. 62, quoted in Coulter, "'Delivered by the Power of God,'" p. 450.

9. Wigglesworth, "Have Faith in God," in Warner, *Ever Increasing Faith*, p. 13, quoted in Coulter, "'Delivered by the Power of God,'" p. 450.

profound: "[T]here must be an inflow of the divine life within" before the believer has a transformed witness to offer God.[10] John G. Lake also made the divine indwelling — God's impartation of Godself — the means by which God blesses the world with salvation:

> The medium by which God undertakes to bless the world is through the transmission of Himself. The Spirit of God is His own substance, the substance of His being, the very nature and quality of the presence and nature of God. Consequently, when we speak of the Spirit of God being transmitted to man . . . we are talking about the transmission of the living substance and being of God into your being and into mine. . . . That is the secret of the abundant life of which Jesus spoke. He said, "I have come that they might have life, and that they might have it more abundantly" (John 10:10). The reason we have more abundant life is that, receiving God into our being, all the springs of our being are quickened by his living presence.[11]

The indwelling Spirit for the Pentecostals was not just a means toward some greater end but was itself the living reality to which they bore witness. By bearing witness to both Christ and the reality of the Spirit's presence imparted through him, Pentecostals were able to emphasize pneumatology as much as Christology. Pentecostals spoke of the indwelling of the Spirit in terms of both intimate communion with God and of powerful witness that is vindicated through signs and wonders. In fact, intimate communion, the doxological dimension of Pentecostal experience, tended to take priority over everything else. The blessing of Christian experience for the Pentecostals, as great and powerful as it was, was concentrated on the enjoyment of the divine presence within an intimate communion with God. "Never in my life did I realize so much of the presence of my dear loving Savior," says George E. Berg.[12] T. Hezmalhalch noted favorably that the early Pentecostals among the Native Americans would not call Spirit baptism a "thing," such as a "blessing," but rather a "he," namely,

10. Wigglesworth, "Our Risen Christ," in Warner, *Ever Increasing Faith*, p. 69, quoted in Coulter, "'Delivered by the Power of God,'" p. 451.

11. John G. Lake, "The Ultimate Test of True Christianity," in *Spiritual Hunger, the God-Men, and Other Sermons by John G. Lake*, ed. Gordon Lindsey (Dallas: Christ for the Nations, 1976), p. 65, quoted in Coulter, "'Delivered by the Power of God,'" p. 451.

12. George E. Berg, "Pentecostal Testimonies," *The Apostolic Faith* 1, no. 6 (Feb.-March 1907): 8.

the presence of God dwelling within.[13] Indeed, the "Lord wants us to seek the Giver and the Blesser instead of . . . the blessing."[14] The Oneness Pentecostals (who were known for rejecting the Trinitarian relationship within God) also made the riches of the divine indwelling the key to both their Christology and soteriology. Christ, as the one indwelt by the Spirit, is the "fullness of the godhead bodily" (Col. 2:9), which then accounts for the reception of his Spirit through Spirit baptism. As a Oneness pioneer writes, "Calvary unlocked the flow of God's love, which is God's very nature, into the hearts of his creatures."[15]

This infilling with divine love is a divine embrace of flesh for the Pentecostals, and thus Romans 5:5 became a favored text among many early Pentecostals for its description of Spirit baptism as the flow of divine love into human hearts, a "baptism of love."[16] Their worship encouraged people to bask in the love of God and to find therein reassurance of God's favor. In the Spirit and through faith in Christ, one finds pardon for sin and reassurance that God will be a strong presence in life's most difficult moments. The awareness of the divine presence brings joy, praise, and reassurance. Though this presence is certainly healing, life transforming, and challenging in terms of faithful responses, it is in itself implicitly viewed as an undeserved embrace made possible through faith in Jesus. The declared word of justification or pardon is not merely spoken; it is felt in the divine presence or embrace.

The transformation of life and the empowerment for witness are derivative, as the means by which the rectified life is manifested and vindicated by the Spirit of God. This vindication of life and witness, however, is itself due only to the excessive grace of God, since this witness can never wholly account for the excessive abundance of grace poured forth from Christ at Pentecost. Therefore, a more elaborate Pentecostal theology will base justification on Christ's triumphant act of conquering sin and death as the man of the Spirit and the reality of the Spirit's indwelling or embrace by faith in him. Our healing, witness, and vindication are derivative

---

13. T. Hezmalhalch, "Among the Indians at Needles, California," *The Apostolic Faith* 1, no. 5 (Jan. 1907): 3.

14. Author unknown, "The True Pentecost," *The Apostolic Faith* 1, no. 4 (Dec. 1906): 2.

15. Frank Ewart, "The Revelation of Jesus Christ," in *Seven Jesus Only Tracts,* ed. Donald W. Dayton (New York: Garland, 1985), p. 5.

16. Author unknown, "The Old Time Pentecost," *The Apostolic Faith* 1, no. 1 (Sept. 1906): 1; see also E. N. Bell, "Believers in Sanctification," *Christian Evangel,* September 19, 1914, p. 3; Will Trotter, "A Revival of Love Needed," *The Weekly Evangel,* April 3, 1915, p. 1.

realities that characterize our eschatological participation in justification, but justification cannot be based on this.

Yet, though it is not based on our transformation, healing, and empowered witness, justification still involves these. Righteousness in the Spirit is opposed by the forces of sin and darkness and must be received and lived out in empowered witness. Even a "legal" understanding of justification requires a powerful witness vindicated by God. Seymour says: "O, beloved, we ought to thank God that he has made us the tabernacles of the Holy Ghost. When you have the Holy Ghost, you have an empire of power within yourself."[17] This life-transforming power is characteristic of the Spirit's indwelling from the experience of deliverance from sin to the resurrection of the dead: "[N]ot only is there power to save from sin, power to heal our bodies, and power to baptize us with the Holy Ghost, but it has power to raise us from the dead."[18] There was no gap between purity and power for the early Pentecostals, since the power of the Spirit is victory over sin as well. But neither was the Pentecostal message moralistic, as though redemption is merely equivalent to moral formation. The gospel through Christ and the imparted Spirit overthrows the dark powers and opens up possibilities for new life and hope.

The witness to this new life is to reach the whole world by the overwhelming power of the Spirit, for "God wants us to go on to get filled with the Holy Ghost that we may be witnesses unto Him to the uttermost parts of the earth. . . . He wants a people who have faith in His word and in the Holy Spirit."[19] The key Pentecostal text is thus Acts 1:8: "But you will receive power when the Holy Spirit comes on you; and you will be my witnesses in Jerusalem, and in all Judea and Samaria, and to the ends of the earth." Nothing can stand in the way of God's desire to fill the fleshly vessel with the Spirit: "When all the powers of hell seem settled down upon your soul; there is something in your innermost being that moves away the powers of hell."[20] As E. Kingsley Larbi says of African Pentecostalism, there is no "demilitarized zone" in the Pentecostal worldview.[21]

17. William J. Seymour, "The Holy Ghost Is Power," *The Apostolic Faith* 2, no. 13 (May 1908): 3.

18. Author unknown, "Healing," *The Apostolic Faith* 1, no. 6 (Feb.-March 1907): 6.

19. Author unknown, "Buried with Him in Baptism," *The Apostolic Faith* 1, no. 2 (Oct. 1906): 4.

20. Author unknown, *The Apostolic Faith* 1, no. 10 (Sept. 1907): 3.

21. E. Kingsley Larbi, *Pentecostalism: The Eddies of Ghanaian Christianity* (Dansoman, Accra, Ghana: Centre for Pentecostal and Charismatic Studies, 2001), p. 423.

The Pentecostal emphasis on the power and vindication of life in the Spirit occasioned a transformative, even "material," understanding of salvation that emphasized the healing of the whole person.[22] This soteriology tended to locate justification not only within the divine embrace of the Spirit's presence but also derivatively within the new birth and healing by the indwelling Spirit of God. Although one can find in early Pentecostal literature statements in support of a forensic understanding of justification, more often one finds understandings that identify justification as regenerative and healing in nature. There is indeed in the history of Pentecostal theology a doctrine of healing by grace through faith. Pentecostal literature is filled with titles supporting healing through the atonement and an acceptance of Christ's healing work by faith. One is much more likely to hear a sermon preached to sinners from Pentecostal pulpits today about accepting healing by faith in Christ than about justification in the traditionally forensic sense of the word. Pentecostals are most likely to speak of the pardon of sins in the context of the gift of the Spirit and healing. For example, in Walter Hollenweger's classic work *The Pentecostals,* the chapter on justification does not even mention the traditional Lutheran doctrine of forensic justification, focusing rather on regeneration and healing.[23] A couple of favored texts are: "[God] forgives all your sins and heals all your diseases" (Ps. 103:3). "And the prayer offered in faith will make the sick person well; the Lord will raise him up. If he has sinned, he will be forgiven" (James 5:15). As Miroslav Volf has observed, "for*giveness*" is part of God's "self-*giving*" in the Spirit.[24] Pardon is based on God's self-giving. Healing campaigns draw massive crowds around the world today and are widely regarded among Pentecostals as the chief means of evangelism. Healing and proclamation bear witness to the triumphant faithfulness of God as Lord and Creator, who embraces and pardons sinners by giving them the life-transforming Spirit.

As regenerative and involving new life in the Spirit, justification was spoken of among early Pentecostals as involving not only cleansing but an experience of new life in the Spirit. As Seymour writes, "The Lord has mercy on him for Christ's sake and puts eternal life in his soul, pardoning

22. See Miroslav Volf, "Materiality of Salvation: An Investigation in the Soteriologies of Liberation and Pentecostal Theologies," *Journal of Ecumenical Studies* 26, no. 3 (Summer 1989): 446-67.

23. Walter Hollenweger, *The Pentecostals* (Peabody, MA: Hendrickson, 1991), esp. p. 317.

24. Miroslav Volf, "Being as God Is: Trinity and Generosity," in *God's Life in Trinity,* ed. Miroslav Volf and Michael Welker (Minneapolis: Augsburg Fortress, 2006), p. 7 (italics in original).

him of his sins, washing away his guilty pollution, and he stands before God justified as though he had never sinned."[25] One unknown author in Seymour's *Apostolic Faith* publication put the matter concerning justification rather succinctly: "Man is born with his back toward God, and the only way to get right is to be born of the Spirit through the blood of Calvary."[26]

One early twentieth-century Pentecostal author drew a distinction between the "brazen altar" (justification), the "golden altar" (sanctification), and the "Holy of Holies" (Spirit baptism). This writer explains that justification involves one's initiation into the new life of the Spirit:

> Here we find the brazen altar, which stands for justification. We receive pardon and regeneration right at the brazen altar. On the altar is the sin offering, on the horns of the altar, blood. Here is pardon and regeneration combined.[27]

In this quote, justification is the place where we are cleansed and born anew by the blood of Christ and the Spirit of God. Justification is the new birth by the Spirit for "[i]n the Holy of Holies one finds Aaron's rod that budded, which represents justification."[28] That justification would be likened to a budding rod is indicative of this author's conviction that justification essentially involves a new birth and new life. Another author notes: "In justification we overcome all the power of the enemy. We have no right to live in sin at any time. Whom the Son makes free is 'free indeed.'"[29] Yet another author concurs, saying of justification:

> God washes all the guilt and pollution out of our hearts and we stand justified like a new babe that never committed sin. We have no condemnation. We can walk with Jesus and live a holy life before the Lord, if we walk in the Spirit.[30]

Also emphasizing justification as liberation to new life, another writes: "[I]n a prayer meeting the Lord set me at liberty, and established in me the

25. Seymour, "The Way into the Holiest," p. 4.

26. Author unknown, *The Apostolic Faith* 1, no. 6 (Feb.-Mar. 1907): 6.

27. Author unknown, "Salvation according to the True Tabernacle," *The Apostolic Faith* 1, no. 10 (Sept. 1907): 3.

28. "Salvation according to the True Tabernacle," p. 3.

29. Author unknown, "No Excuse for Sin," *The Apostolic Faith* 1, no. 6 (Feb.-Mar. 1907): 2.

30. Author unknown, "Two Works of Grace and the Gift of the Holy Ghost," *The Apostolic Faith* 1, no. 1 (Sept. 1906): 3.

justified relation."[31] As though there are degrees of justification, one former Catholic even writes, "I praise God for sanctifying me and *justifying me wholly,* and baptizing me with the Holy Ghost."[32]

It is significant that E. S. Williams, a more recent Pentecostal theologian, sees justification/regeneration (the Spirit's initial indwelling) as a preparation for Spirit filling and witness: "In the new birth the temple is fitted for the infilling of the Holy Spirit."[33] Williams then explicitly sides with Osiander against Calvin concerning their debate over justification! He says: "Whatever may be the full teaching of Calvin concerning the matter, the Bible favors the teaching that in salvation man does partake of the 'divine essence' (2 Peter 1:4)."[34] It is interesting to note that Williams would not agree with Osiander if he had actually meant to say that there is a confusion of essence between us and God (which, as I have noted previously, was not the case). However, concerning Osiander's view of justification, Williams hastens to add: "If, on the other hand, he believed it to be possessed through the life of the Holy Spirit's indwelling, he was correct."[35] He feared that justification as a legal acquittal for the believer's entire life can discourage a proper emphasis on "character, or willingness to walk with God" in the Spirit.[36]

Recently, Pentecostal theologian Veli-Matti Kärkkäinen has explored the relationship of justification and *theosis* (divinization) in response to the Finnish Lutheran doctrine of justification as participation by faith in Christ as the righteousness of God. He supports the Finns' emphasis on faith as participation in Christ as a way of building bridges with the Eastern Orthodox emphasis on divinization. For support, he refers to the work of Edmund Rybarczyk on the connections between Pentecostal and Eastern Orthodox soteriologies. Both Pentecostals and Eastern Orthodox theologians emphasize the work of the Spirit in all dimensions of salvation.[37] Moreover, several recent Pentecostal theologians responding to dis-

---

31. H. L. Blake, "A Minnesota Preacher's Testimony," *The Apostolic Faith* 1, no. 6 (Feb.-March 1907): 5.

32. Author unknown, "A Catholic that received Pentecost," *The Apostolic Faith* 1, no. 3 (Nov. 1906): 4 (italics added).

33. E. S. Williams, *Systematic Theology* (Springfield, MO: Gospel Publishing House, 1953), 3:44; see also 2:246.

34. Williams, *Systematic Theology,* p. 249.

35. Williams, *Systematic Theology,* p. 249.

36. Williams, *Systematic Theology,* p. 245.

37. Veli-Matti Kärkkäinen, *One with God: Salvation as Justification and Deification* (Collegeville, MN: Liturgical Press, 2004), pp. 108-15.

cussions between Catholics and Protestants on justification have accented the role of the Spirit in justification as a transformative process. Justification has become a new frontier of research for Pentecostal theologians such as Amos Yong, Steven Studebaker, David Bernard, and myself.[38]

The entire direction of this soteriology does not consist simply of adding a charismatic experience onto a mainstream Protestant understanding of forensic justification. Justification in the above quotations is rather the pardon and liberation experienced in the embrace of the Spirit, which leads to empowered witness, healing, and divine vindication through signs and wonders and, ultimately, resurrection. Combining both communion and vindicated witness, Pentecostals view justification as implicitly "legal" in the Hebraic sense of God's cause triumphing in the world over opposing forces that challenge its legitimacy. There is implicit potential here for a theology of justification that involves both the justice of divine communion (mutual indwelling) and the witness of the Spirit to the victory of God's faithfulness in the world to embrace all flesh. Justification can by regenerative without being anthropocentric.

In exploring the significance of Spirit baptism for a pneumatological theology of justification, we should start with the issue of the cross and the Spirit's embrace in Pentecostal theology, especially as it relates to the difficult issue of receiving the Spirit in "phases" and in narrowly confining Spirit baptism to the crowning moment of the initiation process.

38. Under Moltmann's influence, Methodist theologian D. Lyle Dabney, who writes from a Pentecostal background, broke ground in this area with his essay entitled "The Justification by the Spirit: Soteriological Reflections on the Resurrection," *International Journal of Systematic Theology* 3, no. 1 (March 2001): 46-68. See also Jürgen Moltmann, *The Spirit of Life: A Universal Affirmation* (Minneapolis: Augsburg Fortress, 1992), pp. 143-64. Moltmann's and Dabney's reflections inspired me to develop this theme further in my own direction: Macchia, "Justification through New Creation: The Holy Spirit and the Doctrine by which the Church Stands or Falls," *Theology Today* 58, no. 2 (July 2001): 202-17. Pentecostal theologian Veli-Matti Kärkkäinen has been working in this area of justification and the Spirit with regard to his previous work at Helsinki on the Finnish Lutheran understanding of justification in Luther; see Kärkkäinen, *One with God*. Note also developments of this theme among Pentecostal theologians Steven Studebaker, "Pentecostal Soteriology and Pneumatology," *Journal of Pentecostal Theology* 11, no. 2 (2003): 248-70; Amos Yong, *The Spirit Poured Out on All Flesh: Pentecostalism and the Possibility of Global Theology* (Grand Rapids: Baker Academic, 2005), pp. 81-120; and David K. Bernard, *Justification and the Holy Spirit: A Scholarly Investigation of a Classical Christian Doctrine from a Pentecostal Perspective* (Hazelwood, MO: WAP Academic, 2007).

Phases of the Spirit

The focus of Pentecostalism on the divine indwelling can be helpful for an ecumenical theology of justification that is open to both the forensic and the transformative dimensions of a right relationship with God. However, mining the full potential of the Pentecostal message for help in this area will not be easy given the penchant of the movement to view the categories of justification, sanctification, and Spirit baptism as *moments,* or even phases, in one's initiation into the life of the Spirit. There are impulses within the early development of Pentecostalism that suggest a more integrated and broadly eschatological understanding of these terms. Reflection on justification in the context of the Pentecostal distinctive can not only end up bringing to the table the helpful Pentecostal emphasis on the divine presence and indwelling; it may also help Pentecostal theologians think through some of the difficulties of their own tradition concerning the life of the Spirit. Let us look first at the diversity of options concerning how Pentecostals have understood the believer's initiation into the life of the Spirit.

As we have seen with Seymour, many of the earliest Pentecostals viewed entry into the life of the Spirit as actually involving three phases: regeneration/justification, sanctification, and Spirit baptism (as an experience of the Spirit in power). This schema is typical of those Pentecostals who came most directly under the influence of the Wesleyan Holiness movement. Under the early influence of William H. Durham, however, this threefold pattern was reduced to two, namely, regeneration and Spirit baptism. Pentecostals who joined the movement from outside the Holiness movement found this option attractive, since they were not accustomed to viewing sanctification as an experience distinct from regeneration. The only distinction that remained was between regeneration and Spirit baptism; they understood justification and sanctification as occurring with regeneration. Durham's wing of the Pentecostal movement was called the "finished-work" movement because it emphasized the sufficiency of Christ's completed work of redemption on our behalf for a person's access to the spiritual life, an emphasis that was not foreign to the Pentecostals who preceded Durham (as I will note shortly). Interestingly, Durham himself actually believed that regeneration brought with it *entire* sanctification. Thomas Farkas thus referred to Durham's soteriology as "single-work perfectionism."[39] But the Pentecostals following in the

39. Thomas Farkas, "William H. Durham and the Sanctification Controversy in Early

finished-work wing, now the largest wing of the global Pentecostal movement, did not maintain Durham's understanding of regeneration as consisting of entire sanctification. They merely adopted his belief that sanctification was not a distinct experience following regeneration, but rather that it occurs with regeneration.

Also under Durham's influence, however, the Oneness Pentecostals (known for their rejection of the doctrine of the Trinity) collapsed all of the phases of initiation to the life of the Spirit into one, namely, regeneration. These Pentecostals, who now comprise more than one-fifth of the world's Pentecostal movement (and are growing), view Spirit baptism as the crowning moment of a conversion-initiation complex involving repentance, faith, and water baptism (in Jesus' name). D. William Faupel, a historian of Pentecostalism, has suggested that this Oneness understanding of initiation in the Spirit's indwelling is the quintessential Pentecostal soteriology, since it pulls together the early Pentecostal concentration on the sufficiency of the work of Christ for the spiritual life and the intense awareness of the Spirit's indwelling in all of life.[40] We will return to Faupel's thesis shortly.

First, allow me to mention that there were many variations within the major streams described above for understanding one's initiation into the life of the Spirit. Pentecostals ran the gamut in their efforts to describe the effects and phases of Spirit possession. Some appropriated justification and sanctification to Christ and Spirit baptism to the Spirit, radically separating them from each other. Others blurred the distinctions between regeneration, sanctification, and Spirit baptism: "There is no difference in quality between the baptism with the Holy Ghost and sanctification. They are both holiness. . . . If we follow Jesus, we will never have any other Spirit but the Spirit of holiness."[41] The gift of the Spirit granted at Pentecost for Spirit baptism was sometimes referred to as rivers of *salvation:* "[W]hen we get the baptism with the Holy Ghost, we have overflowing love, we have rivers of salvation."[42] That Seymour penned that statement is implied by

---

American Pentecostalism, 1906-1916" (PhD diss., Southern Baptist Theological Seminary, Louisville, KY, 1993), p. 21.

40. Faupel, *The Everlasting Gospel: The Significance of Eschatology in the Development of Pentecostal Thought* (Journal of Pentecostal Theology) (reprint; Dorset, UK: Deo Publishing, 2008).

41. Author unknown, "The Baptism with the Holy Ghost," *The Apostolic Faith* 1, no. 11 (Oct. 1907-Jan. 1908): 4.

42. "The Feast of Pentecost," *The Apostolic Faith* 1, no. 9 (June-Sept. 1907): 2.

another he wrote concerning the gift of the Spirit at Pentecost with similar language: "The rivers of salvation had come and had filled the whole place, and they were all immersed or baptized in the Holy Spirit."[43] Indeed, the cleansing of salvation is "by the blood of Jesus and the power of the Holy Ghost."[44] Having Christ means having everything that he owns and has purchased for us on the cross: "justification, sanctification, the baptism with the Holy Ghost and healing of our bodies."[45]

Many early Pentecostals followed a middle path between a radical separation of regeneration from Spirit baptism and a blurring of the distinction between them. They saw the initial indwelling of the Spirit as occurring with regeneration/justification and the "fullness" of the indwelling as taking place with the experience of Spirit baptism. As I have noted above, Seymour wrote of the "eternal life" of God's entering the soul at justification/regeneration but climaxing in spiritual fullness when the fire falls from heaven to fill the vessel.[46] Note also how one early Pentecostal author explained the order of salvation: "When you are converted, you are born of the Spirit." But, in Spirit baptism, the Spirit is "perfected in you."[47] Such language implies that Spirit baptism serves to "perfect" the Spirit's indwelling that occurs with regeneration. One author notes that she must be sanctified before the Spirit "takes full possession of my body" in Spirit baptism, implying that the Spirit is already possessing her in some sense in regeneration and sanctification.[48] In Spirit baptism, the Spirit "comes to dwell in his fullness."[49] Especially interesting is Mrs. A. A. Body's belief that, while waiting for Spirit baptism, she gained "more power in speaking for Christ and *more realization of his indwelling*" (as though the difference between regeneration and Spirit baptism is one of the *awareness* of the Spirit within). For Mrs. Body, at Spirit baptism/filling, what was once accepted largely in the absence of sight is now obvious to experience.[50] Such statements point to a process of the Spirit's indwelling and its effect on the

43. Seymour, *Apostolic Faith* 1, no. 6 (Feb.-Mar. 1907): 7.

44. Author unknown, no title, *The Apostolic Faith* 1, no. 8 (May 1907): 2.

45. Author unknown, no title, *The Apostolic Faith* 1, no. 12 (Jan. 1908): 3.

46. Seymour, "The Way into the Holiest," p. 4.

47. Author unknown, no title, *The Apostolic Faith* 2, no. 13 (May 1908): 2.

48. Antoinette Moomau, "China Missionary Receives Pentecost," *The Apostolic Faith* 1, no. 11 (Jan. 1908): 3.

49. Author unknown, no title, *The Apostolic Faith* 1, no. 3 (Nov. 1906): 2.

50. Body, "Testimony of a Vicar's Wife," *The Apostolic Faith* 1, no. 11 (Jan. 1908): 1 (italics in original).

believer beginning in regeneration and coming to penultimate "fullness" in the experience of Spirit baptism. That soon became the "orthodox" position among most Trinitarian Pentecostal denominations in the United States, or among those that distinguished the reception of the Spirit into phases. For example, the position paper on Spirit baptism for the Assemblies of God affirms that "Scripture makes it clear that all believers have the Holy Spirit (Rom. 8:9, 16). However, the constant hunger for 'more of God' is the heartbeat of Pentecostalism."[51]

There has also been a wide spectrum of opinion throughout global Pentecostalism on the relationship between the experience of Spirit baptism and speaking in tongues.[52] Those who regard Pentecostalism as a "tongues movement" may be surprised to discover that the doctrine of tongues as the "initial evidence" of the experience of Spirit baptism is largely confined to Pentecostal denominations in the United States. But opinions vary even in the United States. For example, there is evidence that key pioneers of the Assemblies of God refused to insist on tongues as the necessary evidence of the experience of Spirit baptism.[53] Jack Hayford, the president of the Foursquare Church denomination, has recently written that the experience of Spirit baptism grants one the capacity to pray in tongues but that there is no guarantee that someone would use that gift.[54] There is strong evidence in early Pentecostal literature that, for the Pentecostals, the highest expression of the Spirit's indwelling is the love of God. A number of authors have defined Spirit baptism as a baptism in divine love.[55] "The Pentecostal power,

51. http://www.ag.org/top/Beliefs/Position_Papers/pp_4185_spirit-filled_life.cfm.

52. Henry Lederle has written of a "sliding scale" among Pentecostals and charismatics concerning how intimately tongues are connected to the experience of Spirit baptism. See Henry Lederle, "Initial Evidence and the Charismatic Movement," in *Initial Evidence: Historical and Biblical Perspectives on the Pentecostal Doctrine of Spirit Baptism,* ed. Gary B. McGee (Peabody, MA: Hendrickson, 1991), p. 132.

53. See Glen Menzies, "Tongues as the Initial Physical Sign of Spirit Baptism in the Thought of D. W. Kerr," *Pneuma: The Journal of the Society for Pentecostal Studies* 20 (Fall 1998): 175-89. See also Joseph Roswell Flower, "How I Received the Baptism in the Holy Spirit," *Pentecostal Evangel* 14 (Jan. 21, 1933): 1-12. Flower, a pillar in the history of the Assemblies of God, clearly resisted any necessary connection between tongues and the experience of Spirit baptism.

54. Jack Hayford, *The Beauty of Spiritual Language: My Journey Toward the Heart of God* (Dallas: Word, 1992), pp. 95-98.

55. E.g., Spirit baptism is a "baptism of love" [author unknown], "The Old Time Pentecost," *The Apostolic Faith* 1, no. 1 (Sept. 1906): 2; see also "Tongues as a Sign," *The Apostolic Faith,* 1, no. 1 (Sept. 1906): 2.

when you sum it all up, is just more of God's love. If it does not bring more love, it is simply a counterfeit."[56] The language of the love of God shed abroad in our hearts given in Romans 5:5 became a favored way of describing Spirit baptism among early Pentecostals.[57] Seymour himself led the charge in the direction by making love rather than tongues the supreme evidence of Spirit baptism.[58]

This diversity of options concerning how the possession of the Spirit is experienced reveals that the Pentecostal distinctive is not so much in the *ordo salutis* as in the emphasis on the very presence and indwelling of the Spirit. The fact that Pentecostals also emphasized the experience and outward vindication of the Spirit's indwelling presence tended to encourage many of them to distinguish phases in the possession of the Spirit. This is true because, in their view, many in the churches had the Spirit within but had not yet placed very much emphasis on this. In the typical Pentecostal perspective, many had not yet experienced the Spirit's presence in power or witnessed the vindicating signs of the Spirit among them, especially in various extraordinary gifts of the Spirit that once characterized early Christianity (such as in the book of Acts and 1 Cor. 12–14) but are now not as visible in the churches. As Kilian McDonnell has reasoned, this Pentecostal penchant for phases to the experience of the indwelling Spirit is valuable because it can help the churches be receptive to an ever-deeper awareness of the transformative presence and working of the indwelling Spirit.[59] Steven J. Land indicated earlier that the experiences of the Spirit connected in Holiness Pentecostalism with regeneration, sanctification, and Spirit baptism can be viewed as an igniting of internal affections for the kingdom of God that are in reality "more fused together than even split apart or prioritized."[60]

Under the influence of Wesleyan perfectionism, the early Pentecostals tended to reach for "entire" sanctification, or the "fullness" of the Spirit. People should not take these terms too literally if they are to avoid exagger-

56. Author unknown, no title, *The Apostolic Faith* 2, no. 13 (May 1908): 3.

57. E.g., E. N. Bell, "Believers in Sanctification," p. 3.

58. See Cecil M. Robeck, Jr., "William J. Seymour and the 'Bible Evidence,'" in McGee, *Initial Evidence*, pp. 72-95.

59. Kilian McDonnell and George Montague, *Christian Initiation and Baptism in the Holy Spirit: Evidence from the First Eight Centuries* (Collegeville, MN: Liturgical Press, 1991), pp. 376ff.

60. Steven J. Land, *Pentecostal Spirituality: A Passion for the Kingdom* (Sheffield, UK: Sheffield University Press, 1988), p. 63.

ated claims of spiritual accomplishment that lack an awareness of the eschatological nature of our experience of the Spirit's strength in the midst of weakness. But as rhetorical devices, the quest for fullness can encourage believers to strive for genuine foretastes of the fullness of the Spirit yet to come. Justification involving the inner and outer witness of the Spirit should be a powerful experience in the churches and not just a confession to be recited.

Working counter to the penchant to favor phases in one's reception of the Spirit was the deep conviction ubiquitous in early Pentecostalism that Christ's work was sufficient for one's entry into the life of the Spirit. Durham emphasized this conviction, but it was by no means unique to his "finished work" soteriology. Seymour was a strong supporter of the sufficiency of Christ's death and resurrection for granting the believer access to all the blessings of life in the Spirit. Even Spirit baptism is won on the cross:

> In Jesus Christ we get forgiveness of sin, and we get sanctification of our spirit, soul, and body, and upon that we get the gift of the Holy Ghost that Jesus promised to His disciples, the promise of the Father, *all this we get through the atonement.*[61]

Seymour adds: "Let us lift up Christ to the world in all his fullness, not only in healing and salvation from all sin but in His power to speak in all the languages of the world."[62] In a text that may also be attributable to Seymour, we find that all elements of possessing the Spirit, including Spirit baptism, are won by the cross: "Justification and sanctification come from God through His death on the cross, and He also purchased on the cross the baptism in the Holy Ghost for every believer."[63] Indeed, "through the blood we receive the baptism of the Holy Ghost."[64] As Oneness Pentecostal Frank Ewart says, "Calvary unlocked the flow of God's love, which is God's very nature, into the hearts of his creatures."[65]

---

61. Seymour, "River of Living Water," *The Apostolic Faith* 1, no. 3 (Nov. 1906): 2 (italics added).

62. Seymour, "River of Living Water," p. 2.

63. Author unknown, "The Holy of Holies: The Holy Ghost," *The Apostolic Faith* 1, no. 10 (Sept. 1907): 3.

64. Author unknown, no title, *The Apostolic Faith* 1, no. 11 (Oct. 1907–Jan. 1908): 2. This statement came as part of a question-and-answer section of the paper, hence possibly written by Seymour or one of his associates.

65. Frank Ewart, "The Revelation of Jesus Christ," in Dayton, *Seven Jesus Only Tracts,* p. 5.

This aspect of the Pentecostal message implied that access to Christ by faith involves the indwelling of the Spirit in all of its dimensions. Of course, these dimensions still can be described as needing to be realized experientially in the life of the believer as distinct blessings of the Spirit. One could even refer to vistas of life in the Spirit opened up by the Christ event that allow the Spirit to define the reach of the Christ event as much as that has defined the directions of the Spirit's leading. But from the vantage point of the Pentecostal emphasis on the Christ event as the all-sufficient mediator of the Spirit, there is no possibility of viewing Christ as merely a launching pad for spiritual heights that go way beyond the cross or the resurrection. After all, the ultimate fullness of the Spirit is experienced in the resurrection of the dead and direct communion with God.

There are recent signs, in fact, of an ecumenical rapprochement among Pentecostals over Spirit baptism that recognizes the soteriological significance of the metaphor. Significant is the conclusion reached at a recent round of talks between Oneness and Trinitarian Pentecostals that Spirit baptism is indeed soteriological if one has the entire span and eschatological reach of the life of the Spirit in mind.[66] Of course, justification, sanctification, and Spirit baptism cannot be reduced to a specific experience or a momentary phase. These terms can also function as lenses through which to view the entire eschatological span of the Christian life in the Spirit. They overlap and mutually illuminate each other. The concentration on consciously becoming the dwelling place of God and on Spirit baptism as the most telling metaphor of this experience is the distinct blessing that the Pentecostal movement has given to the larger body of Christ.

The constructive challenge will be for Pentecostals to recognize and to develop the eschatological expansiveness of Spirit baptism, so that the Spirit's indwelling from regeneration to resurrection can provide a framework for understanding justification. Spirit baptism is rooted in the Spirit's indwelling of the creature at regeneration, but it climaxes in the final habitation of God within the creature at the point of glorification, so that Christ may "fill the whole universe" (Eph. 4:10), and God may be "all and in all" (1 Cor. 15:28). There are significant Pentecostal voices already seeking to de-

---

66. "Both teams recognized that 'Spirit baptism' is essential to the Christian life broadly conceived, involving the entire span of one's conformity to Christ." *Oneness-Trinitarian Pentecostal Final Report, 2002-2007*, §51, *Pneuma: The Journal of the Society for Pentecostal Studies* 30 (2008): 203-24.

velop Spirit baptism as an eschatological gift. I will conclude this chapter with an exploration of this development in Pentecostal theology.

Spirit Baptism and Justification in Eschatological Perspective

I have noted in an earlier book that recent Pentecostals and charismatics have begun to expand the boundaries of Spirit baptism to involve broad eschatological and cosmic dimensions.[67] Pentecostals have always implied as much by highlighting the fulfillment of Spirit baptism on a large scale through a "latter rain" of the Spirit poured out on all flesh as a preparation for the fullness of the kingdom of God at Christ's Second Coming.[68] D. William Faupel has convincingly argued that this eschatological vision is distinctive of the Pentecostal "apostolic faith" or "full gospel."[69] Though Donald Dayton is correct in noting that this gospel contains the elements of salvation — Spirit baptism, healing, and the imminent coming of Christ — Faupel showed that the last element is crucial to the others. Following Faupel, Land, in his *Pentecostal Spirituality: A Passion for the Kingdom*, emphasizes the eschatological breadth of the Spirit's work as distinctive of Pentecostalism, especially by contrast to the lack of an eschatological emphasis in Wesley and the Holiness movement. Agreeing with Ernst Käsemann that apocalypticism is the mother of Christianity,

---

67. See Macchia, *Baptized in the Spirit,* pp. 46-49. See also Amos Yong, *The Spirit Poured Out on All Flesh,* pp. 81-120; Peter Hocken, "Baptism in the Spirit as a Prophetic Statement: A Reflection on the New Testament and on Pentecostal Origins," paper delivered at the Society for Pentecostal Studies, Springfield, MO (Nov. 12-14, 1992); Tak-Ming Chung, "Understandings of Spirit Baptism," *Journal of Pentecostal Theology* 8 (1996): 115-28; Narciso C. Dionson, "The Doctrine of the Baptism in the Holy Spirit: From a Pentecostal Pastor's Uneasy Chair," *Asian Journal of Pentecostal Studies* 2 (1999): 238-47; Larry Hart, "Spirit Baptism: A Dimensional Charismatic Perspective," in Chad Brand, ed., *Spirit Baptism: Five Views* (Nashville: Broadman and Holman, 2004), pp. 105-80; Donald Gelpi, "Breath Baptism in the Synoptics," paper delivered at the Society for Pentecostal Studies, Pasadena, CA (Nov. 20, 1982); D. Lyle Dabney, "'He Will Baptize You in the Holy Spirit': Recovering a Metaphor for a Pneumatological Soteriology," paper delivered at the Society for Pentecostal Studies, Tulsa, OK (March 8-10, 2001).

68. Cf., Author unknown, "Signs of His Coming," *The Apostolic Faith* 1, no. 6 (Feb.-March 1906): 6.

69. Faupel, *Everlasting Gospel,* esp. pp. 42-44. Interestingly, Dayton also notes that eschatology is that feature of Pentecostal soteriology that most widely connects very different Pentecostal groups globally. See Dayton, *Theological Roots of Pentecostalism* (Grand Rapids: Zondervan, 1988), p. 143.

Land says: "Pentecostals were adopted by and adopted this 'mother' and became sons and daughters, prophets and prophetesses of the new order of the Latter Rain of the Spirit." In Land's view, the heart of Pentecostalism is the sanctification of the affections so that they become passions for the coming kingdom of God. Within the integrative context of eschatology, justification, sanctification, and Spirit baptism are connected to passions for the coming kingdom that are "more fused together than split apart or even prioritized."[70]

It is important to note, however, that Faupel and Land viewed eschatology and not Spirit baptism as the overarching and dominant distinctive. There has recently been a marked trend, which my own work has sought to develop, that seeks instead to remain true to the overarching historical concern of Pentecostals with Spirit baptism and the divine indwelling. In other words, eschatology is an aspect of Spirit baptism — and not the other way around. The additional emphasis on eschatology for this richer understanding of the dominant Pentecostal accent on Spirit baptism serves to broaden the boundaries of Spirit baptism rather than to transcend them. The divine habitation of the Spirit in all things depicted in the biblical metaphor of Spirit baptism has *eschatological and cosmic* implications and cannot be confined to the powerful and charismatically varied experiences of the indwelling Spirit cherished by Pentecostals.[71]

The Spirit's indwelling is not exhausted as a metaphor in Pentecostal experiences of the presence of the Spirit within. The very fact that the Messiah finally receives the Spirit in order to impart the same Spirit in his glorification and exaltation (Acts 2:33) implies that there is more to come with regard to Spirit baptism than the powerful and immediate experiences of the Spirit's indwelling in the present age. The fact that Christ poured out the Spirit in Acts 2:33 at Christ's final vindication at the throne of the Father indicates that justification has broad eschatological breadth as well. The Pentecostal emphasis on the immediate experience of the Spirit's indwelling served to highlight the divine indwelling in the Pentecostal conception of salvation. But these experiences are not the ultimate fulfillment of Spirit baptism — nor of justification. One must look to the latter rain of the Spirit to even begin to discover how expansive is the long-awaited fulfillment of these terms.

Such an expansive understanding of Spirit baptism is implied by the

---

70. Land, *Pentecostal Spirituality,* pp. 62-63.
71. See Macchia, *Baptized in the Spirit,* pp. 46-49.

biblical witness itself. Matthew opens John the Baptist's announcement of the coming Messiah as the Spirit baptizer by noting that he preached and taught about the kingdom of God (Matt. 3:1-2). John knew that he did not have the power to impart the Spirit and to start the new age. He was not the one who would clear the threshing floor, restore the wheat into barns, and burn up the chaff that blows away in the wind (3:12). The one who comes to impart the Spirit will bring final restoration and judgment, for apocalyptic transcendence belongs to him alone. When John said that he baptized in water but the Messiah baptized in the Spirit, he was saying something akin to the Old Testament prophets' admission that Israel can circumcise the foreskin but only God can circumcise the heart (e.g., Jer. 4:4). John can perform a rite as an occasion for repentance and hope, but only the Messiah can bring the Spirit and open the door to participation in the new life promised by the prophets.

The opening of heaven at Jesus' baptism thus symbolized an apocalyptic revelation.[72] The Spirit's descending on Jesus in the figure of the dove was reminiscent of the brooding of the Spirit on the waters of creation in Genesis 1:2 and of the dove in the Noah story as the sign of a new creation. The Messiah will first become the locus of the indwelling Spirit through crucifixion, resurrection, and glorification before he imparts the Spirit for the inclusion of others within this same realm of the Spirit and of glorification (Acts 2:33). The texts dealing with Jesus' baptism thus anticipate his resurrection and glorification as events of Spirit indwelling preparatory to his end-time impartation of the Spirit; these texts reveal complex eschatological undertones that await fulfillment at the end of history.[73]

The justification of Jesus "in the Spirit" (1 Tim. 3:16) as the end-time redeemer may indeed be tied in part to this baptismal event, for the declaration of his sonship in the resurrection (Rom. 1:4) begins here at Jesus' baptism. Jesus is being commissioned to inaugurate the kingdom by becoming the new dwelling place of the Spirit, the place from which the Spirit sets the captives free: "If I drive out demons by the Spirit of God, then the Kingdom of God has come upon you" (Matt. 12:28). But more than this, there are larger apocalyptic and cosmic implications in Matthew 3, which led to an

---

72. John Nolland, *Luke 1–9:20,* Word Biblical Commentary 33A (Dallas: Word, 1989), p. 162.

73. Donald A. Hagner, *Matthew 1–13,* Word Biblical Commentary 35A (Dallas: Word, 1993), pp. 58-60.

ancient tradition that Jesus' baptism contained a hint of his later role as the one who would fill all things with the Spirit.[74]

Spirit baptism eschatologically facilitates the transformation of creation into the dwelling place of God. This is the kingdom of God and the righteousness of the kingdom (Rom. 14:17); and this is the ideal context for discussing justification by grace. Much like Matthew 3:1-2, Acts thus opens up its Spirit baptism narrative under the topic of the kingdom of God (Acts 1:3-8). The fact that the Spirit will be poured out in Jerusalem, the traditional place connected to the establishment of the kingdom of God, is also significant. The question of the kingdom's fulfillment is clearly posed in Acts 1:3-8, and Jesus answers it with reference to the baptism in the Spirit. Jesus receives the Spirit once more from the Father in his glorification and exaltation as the vindicated Messiah who has ascended to God in a cloud in the fashion of the vindicated Son of man in Daniel 7:13 (Acts 1:9; 2:33). Not only will the gift of the Spirit poured out from him empower the church's witness; it will be poured out upon all flesh with apocalyptic consequences:

> I will show wonders in the heaven above
> And signs on the earth below,
> blood and fire and billows of smoke.
> The sun will be turned to darkness and the moon to blood
> before the coming of the great and glorious day of the Lord.
> And everyone who calls on the name of the Lord will be saved.
>
> (Acts 2:19-21)

In the meantime, the gift of the Spirit allows the saints to share in Jesus' vindication in the Spirit, for "through him everyone is justified" (Acts 13:39).

So also with Paul, the indwelling Spirit is the gift of the kingdom of God: "For the kingdom of God is not a matter of eating and drinking, but of righteousness, peace and joy in the Holy Spirit" (Rom. 14:17). The life of the Spirit, not ceremonial food laws, is what drives us forward in hope toward the fulfillment of righteousness of which the prophets foretold: "But by faith we eagerly await through the Spirit the righteousness for which we hope" (Gal. 5:5). For Paul, the themes of the divine indwelling of creation

74. Kilian McDonnell, *The Baptism of Jesus in the Jordan: The Trinitarian and Cosmic Order of Salvation* (Collegeville, MN: Liturgical Press, 1996), p. 7. Note esp. McDonnell's chapter on "Cosmic Baptism," pp. 50-68.

for its glorification and the triumph of the kingdom of God over death (so that life reigns in its place) converge in the following text:

> For as in Adam all die, so in Christ all will be made alive. But each in his own turn: Christ, the firstfruits; then, when he comes, those who belong to him. Then the end will come, when he hands over the kingdom to God the Father after he has destroyed all dominion, authority and power. For he must reign until he has put all his enemies under his feet. The last enemy to be destroyed is death. (1 Cor. 15:22-25; see also Rom. 8:14-25).

The passage ends with the fulfillment of the kingdom of God — "that God may be all and in all" (1 Cor. 15:28). The kingdom and its righteousness are fulfilled when God inhabits all things.

In the light of creation's eschatological goal of becoming the habitation of God, notice Paul's description of Pentecost:

> But to each one of us grace has been given as Christ apportioned it. This is why it says:
>
> > "When he ascended on high,
> > he led captives in his train
> > and gave gifts to men."
>
> (What does "he ascended" mean except that he also descended to the lower, earthly regions? He who descended is the very one who ascended higher than all the heavens, in order to fill the whole universe.) (Eph. 4:7-10)

Notice that the ascension of Christ and his bestowal of the Spirit have as their goal that Christ "fill the whole universe." The goal of Pentecost is the divine habitation of creation. Indeed, when God fulfills the kingdom and life reigns over death, God will tabernacle with creation and make it the glorified household of the divine presence. This is when the righteousness and vindication of the kingdom are fulfilled. "Now the dwelling of God is with men" (Rev. 21:3), and God will proclaim, "Behold, I make all things new" (Rev. 21:5).

In the meantime, humans experience Spirit baptism as the Spirit is manifested to their experience in moments of ecstasy and of self-giving. Ecstasy is not only an emotion but is also a sense that one can transcend oneself in embracing God and the neighbor. Spirit baptism in the New

Testament thus gives rise to a profoundly personal — but not an individualistic — experience. The original Jewish disciples spoke in tongues as a consequence of being Spirit baptized to symbolize their reconciliation with Gentiles (Acts 2:4ff.), which made the Gentile participation in the same expression all the more meaningful as a fulfillment (Acts 10:44-46). Samaritans experienced Spirit baptism at the laying on of hands by leaders of the Jerusalem church across deeply held biases (Acts 8:14-17), while Paul received it by the laying on of hands by a prophet at a time when the Jerusalem church was not yet ready to trust him (Acts 9:17). Spirit baptism occurred as moments of *koinonia* and a fresh commitment to the righteousness of God dawning in the world across gulfs of prejudice, fear, and hurt. Paul then summarizes the matter by saying, "In one Spirit we were all baptized into one body, whether Jews or Greeks, bond or free" (1 Cor. 12:13). A. T. Robertson and Alfred Plummer note tellingly that in this text "the Spirit is the element in *[en]* which the baptism takes place, and the one body is the end to *[eis]* which the act is directed."[75] Spirit baptism as *koinonia* — mutual indwelling between the creature and God and among creatures — is the eschatological goal. The church is the visible sign of this eschatological goal in history. Spirit baptism constitutes the church and drives it toward its eschatological fulfillment. Such is Spirit baptism, the pouring out of the Spirit on all flesh. Such can function as the narrative context for justification, as I will suggest in the pages that follow.

Conclusion

There is no question that there is ambiguity in the Pentecostal efforts theologically to explain the passion for Spirit baptism or indwelling. The point is that the Pentecostals are unique in their historic emphasis on the outpouring, baptism, and infilling of the Spirit as well as the overall need to see the life of the Spirit principally as both an intimate communion of love and a living witness to the victorious faithfulness of God to creation vindicated by the Spirit. The Pentecostals emphasized both the victory of

---

75. Samuel Rolles Driver, Alfred Plummer, and Charles Augustus Briggs, *A Critical and Exegetical Commentary on the First Epistle of St. Paul to the Corinthians*, 2nd ed., International Critical Commentary (Edinburgh: T. & T. Clark, 1963), p. 272. Thayer also agrees, in *A Greek-English Lexicon of the New Testament* (New York: American Book Co., 1989), p. 94. I am grateful to Howard M. Ervin for these references in *These Are not Drunken as Ye Suppose* (Plainfield, NJ: Logos, 1968), p. 45.

Christ and the renewing presence of the Spirit within that leads to powerful, vindicated witness. These are their "Protestant" and "Catholic" accents, and both are relevant to an ecumenical and pneumatological theology of justification.

Pentecostals have arguably not always understood the full breadth or ecumenical significance of their distinctive. But there is potential from within early expressions of the Pentecostal message for viewing the gospel of justification as an event not only of Christ but of the Spirit and involving not only pardon for sin but a living witness to the victory of God's covenant faithfulness over both sin and death. The incarnation of Christ is not only the Word made flesh but the gift to the Word of a Spirit-indwelt body given by the Spirit. Christ's life ministry, atoning death and resurrection, and the Spirit outpouring are not merely the means to pardon but the victory over the dark powers and the means by which other bodies are indwelt and rectified in him. This is the narrative framework of Spirit baptism that is potentially available to discussions concerning justification, one that offers a vision of justification that is both declarative and transformative because it is pneumatological in substance.

This emphasis, for all of its ambiguity as it is developed among Pentecostal writers historically and globally, implies that the justified relationship is not primarily legal or moral but rather involves mutual indwelling and embrace, which is its ecumenical significance. The key is to draw on Pentecostal theology to expand the boundaries of Spirit baptism and justification so as to discover the vastness of their eschatological scope. There is no greater expanse than communion within the life of the triune God. Rather than representing mere "phases" in one's personal experience of the Spirit, justification and sanctification can be viewed under the basic thrust of the Pentecostal message as mutually informing metaphors of the triumph of God's love and righteousness in the world through the divine indwelling of all things to the glory of God. In the next chapters I will attempt to give a clearer indication of how justification can be developed within the Pentecostal — and typically Lukan — metaphor of Spirit baptism, as well as within other pneumatologies suggested in the New Testament, especially Paul's pneumatology.

TWO

Justification for Us

The Basis of Justification

5 The Promise of the Spirit

Justifying Righteousness in the Old Testament

What is the substance of justification as an Old Testament concept? This is obviously the crucial question in our attempt to investigate a theology of justification as it was developed in the New Testament and, more constructively, within the context of Spirit baptism. The English word "justification" is unfortunate because for many it has the sense of an attempt to rationalize one's actions or even to "cover up" one's guilt.[1] The older term, "rightwise," would represent a more biblical alternative, since it at least hints at the linguistic and theological connections with the biblical terms for righteousness or justice. E. P. Sanders's term for justification, "righteousing," also comes closer to the biblical terms for justification.[2]

J. A. Ziesler could thus say succinctly that "righteousness from God and justification are the same thing."[3] Of course, justification is not the only metaphorical or theological lens through which to view the righteousness of God. But this fact does not mean that justification is only one element or phase of the gift of divine righteousness.[4] It is rather more accurate to say that justification is one lens — though not the only lens —

1. See Eberhard Jüngel, *Justification: The Heart of the Christian Faith,* trans. Jeffrey F. Cayzer (Edinburgh: T. & T. Clark, 2001), p. 5.

2. E. P. Sanders, *Paul, the Law, and the Jewish People* (Minneapolis: Fortress, 1983), p. 6.

3. J. A. Ziesler, *The Meaning of Righteousness in Paul: A Linguistic and Theological Inquiry* (Cambridge: Cambridge University Press, 1972), p. 8.

4. Here I am in disagreement with Michael Bird, *The Saving Righteousness of God: Studies on Paul, Justification, and the New Perspective,* Paternoster Biblical Monographs (Eugene, OR: Wipf and Stock, 2007), p. 17.

through which the *entirety* of God's active "rightwising" of creation can be viewed. A discussion of the doctrine of justification should explore the unique features of the view that this lens provides and give some indication of how it also overlaps with and illuminates other terms, such as "sanctification."

In general, it has been assumed that justification reveals divine righteousness and grants sinful persons access to this righteousness or justice in life. Justification vindicates divine faithfulness to the promises and to the witness of the law precisely by saving sinners. This paradox of fulfilling justice by saving the unjust is the rub in this entire issue of justification. How can we speak of the fulfillment of divine justice or righteousness by showing mercy to creatures who are judged to be fundamentally unfaithful? This unique problem sharpens the focus of justification as the vindication of God's own unique version of justice in history both in terms of God's self-vindication and the participation of the faithful in that vindication by the Spirit in Christ.

The larger context of creation and redemption as substantially pneumatological, in particular, could help us deal with the original problem of whether or not the gift of righteousness bestowed in justification is a forensic/legal "right standing" with God due to the alien righteousness of Christ or the actual results of one's cooperation with grace in bearing the fruit of justice in life. In other words, is "justifying righteousness" forensic or ethical, is it a verb (a divine judging) or a noun (a quality of the soul or of ethical behavior)? It is my contention that, though a diversity of ideas is attached to the biblical promise of righteousness as a gift in the Old Testament, the heart of this promise is essentially neither a legal standing nor the fruit of justice in us; rather, it is God's favor granted in the gift of the Spirit.

This gift creates the conditions for both pardon and renewal, thus fulfilling righteousness for all of creation. I argue that God fulfills the promises as the faithful God by giving the Spirit, for creation was made to bear the divine Spirit (Gen. 1:2; 2:7; 2 Cor. 5:4-5). Creation was made with this promise of life built in. The declaration of legal right standing and the change in our lives and in our communities are both involved in justification only when they are anchored in this gift of God's indwelling. A declaration of favor and the process of moral formation each falls short of anchoring justifying righteousness. Only the gift of the Spirit, as promised in the Old Testament as the fulfillment of righteousness, can serve this role.

How do we understand justifying righteousness at its essence according to the Old Testament? The prominent alternative today in Old Testament scholarship is that justifying righteousness is God's *covenant faithfulness* toward God's people and even toward the larger creation. Righteousness as the faithful response of people toward God is a derivative consequence through which the divine faithfulness or justice is "incarnated" in history. The justice essential to justification is thus not defined according to abstract norms but rather by what is appropriate to God's faithful relationship with humanity. In my view, the notion of covenant faithfulness as a description of justifying righteousness needs to be expanded by such concepts as righteousness as a redemptive reality, justification as vindication of the messianic ruler, and, ultimately, the gift of righteousness through "God with us" or the outpouring of the Spirit. Allow me to explain.

Righteousness as Covenant Faithfulness

The first point to be made regarding the use of the Hebrew *sed* words for "righteousness" in the Old Testament has to do with the situational or contextual nature of these terms and the variety of meanings that accompany them within the context of God's covenant faithfulness. Specifically, *mercy, deliverance, judgment,* and *justice* serve as appropriate adjectives for the use of *tsedeq* in the Old Testament, depending on the situations involving the divine-human relationship. J. A. Ziesler notes: "The activity is seen as being righteous only as it is seen in relation to him."[5] Righteousness is "neither a virtue nor the sum of virtues, it is activity that befits the covenant." Consequently, the forensic and the ethical are inseparable in the Old Testament, and the ethical is geared toward maintaining covenant faithfulness rather than adherence to abstract ethical norms. Primarily, righteousness in the Old Testament referred to the accomplishment of God's faithfulness toward humanity and of appropriately faithful responses from within the community of the covenant (pp. 40-42). Though the term "covenant" may not be mentioned explicitly very often in Old Testament passages that speak of the promise of righteousness as a divine gift, the concept is often implied as the theological context.

Only a minority of uses of the term for "righteousness" in the Old Testament are legal or forensic in ways distinct from issues of covenant faithfulness (about 18 percent), meaning that righteousness has mainly to do

5. Ziesler, *The Meaning of Righteousness in Paul*, p. 34; see also pp. 40-41. Hereafter, page references to this work will appear in parentheses in the text.

with "loyalty rather than legality" (p. 42). Even in clearly legal contexts, righteousness as a creative or redemptive concept is not excluded, leaving Ziesler, after his extensive analysis of the Old Testament *sed* words, to conclude: "Clearly . . . there is no difference between 'make' and 'declare' righteous, for it is simply a matter of bringing sinners into a new relationship" (p. 8). He notes further that "it is not correct to say that *ts-d-q* in its noun and adjective forms is particularly forensic or even legal" (p. 32).[6] Ziesler qualifies this statement by saying that *ts-d-q* is "legal" in implication but in a way that is uniquely Hebraic, involving the triumph of God's righteous will and faithfulness, so that "the Hebrew understanding of justice was such that to use the word 'forensic' is liable to be more misleading than illuminating" (p. 37).

This theocentric and relational view of righteousness has replaced a moral definition involving abstract attributes or norms of righteousness. Hermann Cremer was the first to show that applying the "Hellenistic" quest for the absolute norm to the understanding of righteousness in the Hebrew Scriptures proved misdirected and unsuccessful.[7] More recent research has shown that even Greek notions of ethics were geared primarily to communal loyalty and faithfulness, so that Ziesler could conclude, concerning the *dik* words for righteousness in the New Testament, that if "Paul did use the words primarily for one's standing before God, we must seriously question whether any of his readers, and especially his Gentile readers, would understand him at all" (p. 51). There is no such abstract norm to which God must submit. God could not be confined to abstract systems of law or justice, for God reigns and only the divine presence brings favor and fulfills righteousness.

Righteousness in the Old Testament is a relational and functional concept, stemming from a covenant relationship with Yahweh that is chiefly maintained in the cult. There are claims that this relationship lays on the faithful, but these claims are specifically related to the covenant faithfulness of God as manifested in redemptive deeds.[8] The commandments

---

6. Ziesler notes further of *sed* words: "[I]n the Old Testament as we have it, only a minority of occurrences are forensic, and even if the noun's origins were juridical, it does not follow that they remain 'basically forensic' for all time" (p. 37).

7. Hermann Cremer, *Die Paulinische Rechtfertigungslehre in Zusammenhange Ihrer geschichtlichen Voraussetzungen* (Gütersloh: Bertelsman, 1900).

8. See Gerhard von Rad, *Old Testament Theology*, vol. 1: *The Theology of Israel's Historical Traditions,* trans. D. M. G. Stalker (New York: Harper and Row, 1962), pp. 372-73. See also Cremer, *Die Paulinische Rechtfertigungslehre,* esp. pp. 34-38.

given by God through Moses in Exodus 20 are thus prefaced with election and God's covenant-establishing act of deliverance from Egypt: "I am the LORD your God, who brought you out of Egypt, out of the land of slavery" (Exod. 20:2). With regard to this relational view of righteousness in the Old Testament, Ziesler notes that a "whole galaxy of German scholars held this position" — including both Catholics and Protestants (p. 11).

As an illustration of this trend, Karl Barth describes God's gracious decision and action to save sinful humanity "as a verdict against which there can be no appeal, as a decision the rightness of which cannot be tested on the standards of other decisions because, on account of the One who made it, it is inherently right."[9] This focus on covenant faithfulness and redemptive deeds has gained a significant hearing over the decades of recent discussion on the nature of divine righteousness in the Old Testament.[10] The same is true, incidentally, of the Dead Sea Scrolls: "Your justice has brought me into the service of your alliance; I rely on your truth."[11]

The covenant that cradles justifying righteousness is not quite like any other covenant imaginable, since without it "neither individuals nor the people as a whole can *live*."[12] Rightwising in the Old Testament thus fulfills justice in accordance with the redemptive relationship that the Creator wills and strives to have with the creation. Gerhard von Rad speaks for a generation of Old Testament scholars:

> But in spite of all the variability in what is said about Jahweh's righteousness, expression is given to an idea which was constitutive for Israel — Jahweh's righteousness was not a norm, but acts, and it was these acts which bestow salvation.[13]

9. Karl Barth, *Church Dogmatics,* vol. 2, *The Doctrine of God,* pt. 2, trans. G. W. Bromiley et al. (Edinburgh: T. & T. Clark, 1957), p. 30.

10. See, e.g., Alan Richardson, *An Introduction to the Theology of the New Testament* (New York: Harper and Row, 1958), pp. 79-83; see also E. R. Achtemeier, "Righteousness in the Old Testament," and P. J. Achtemeier, "Righteousness in the New Testament," *Interpreter's Dictionary of the Bible,* ed. George Arthur Buttrick (Nashville: Abingdon, 1962), 4:81-94.

11. 1QH 7:19f., quoted in Walter Grundmann, "The Teacher of Righteousness of Qumran and the Question of Justification by Faith in the Theology of the Apostle Paul," in *Paul and Qumran: Studies in New Testament Exegesis,* ed. Jerome Murphy-O'Connor (Chicago: The Priory Press, 1968), p. 89.

12. Jüngel, *Justification,* p. 62 (italics in original).

13. Von Rad, *Old Testament Theology,* 1:372-73.

The Psalms contain a number of indications that God's righteousness "delivers" (Ps. 31:1; 71:2; 143:1), "vindicates" (Ps. 35:24), and "preserves" (Ps. 119:40), being in one place synonymous with divine faithfulness (Ps. 36:5-7). In the light of such texts, Brevard Childs agrees with von Rad that "Yahweh's righteousness consists, above all, in acts of the saving deeds of redemption . . . by which he maintains and protects his promise to fulfill his covenant obligations with Israel (Ps. 36:7)."[14] In short, "Yahweh's righteous judgments are saving judgments."[15] Though righteousness has a special application to Israel, Childs argues that it had a broader context, including "a redemptive, harmonious order of the world which Yahweh proposed for his creation." It spans the order of law, wisdom, nature, war, cult, and, above all, the king.[16]

Since righteousness is rooted in God's covenant faithfulness to Israel and all of creation and is fulfilled in redemptive deeds, there can be no contradiction between God's righteousness and God's mercy. Those who fall by the wayside into darkness and destruction do so by mocking the righteous mercy of God. This is not to deny, as Walter Brueggemann explains, that in the Old Testament God's righteousness is sometimes made to serve God's own honor or self-regard (e.g., Exod. 14:4, 7; Ezek. 36:23; 39:25). In a number of other places, however, God's righteousness is exercised out of regard for Israel and the larger creation, even to the point of incurring insult to the divine honor. Note the book of Hosea, which describes God's covenant relationship with Israel — in less than strictly legal terms — as a marriage or within a familial context (such as a child reared from infancy, Hosea 11:1-3). God suffers the indignity of a spouse betrayed by an unfaithful partner or a parent defied by an ungrateful or disrespectful child (Hosea 2 and 11). Indeed, God clothes us in righteousness as a bride adorned graciously and out of abundant love from a groom (Isa. 61:10). "Yahweh moves back and forth between self-regard and regard for Israel, sovereignty and pathos."[17] The tension is resolved when the divine righteousness is defined in service to God's mercy, which becomes the standard of orthodoxy for Old Testament faith (Isa. 45:8, 23-24; 51:6-8; Ps. 71:19; 89:17; 96:13; 98:9; 111:3; Dan. 9:16-18). God is ultimately honored and

14. Brevard Childs, *Biblical Theology of the Old and New Testaments: Theological Reflection on the Christian Bible* (Minneapolis: Fortress, 1992), p. 488.

15. E. R. Achtemeier, "Righteousness in the OT," p. 83.

16. Childs, *Biblical Theology,* p. 490.

17. Walter Brueggemann, *Theology of the Old Testament* (Minneapolis: Fortress, 2005), p. 309.

glorified in redemptive deeds that are merciful and gracious. As Hosea shows us, God wishes to be known so intimately that God's suffering love for the unfaithful can be felt as well. Consequently, there can be no contradiction between God's righteous honor or self-regard and God's merciful self-giving to those who do not in any way deserve it. Barth writes eloquently about God's righteousness with respect to the creation:

> [I]n seeking its highest good, He magnifies His own glory. We cannot distinguish God's kingly righteousness from His mercy. We need not deny it for the sake of His mercy. It is in that righteousness that He says yes to the creature in the mystery of His freedom.[18]

The integration of righteousness and mercy or compassion in the Old Testament stands contrary to the notion of justice prevalent throughout Western Christian atonement theories. The penal-satisfaction theory of the atonement, for example, assumes that God holds to a strictly legal notion of justice as retribution for sin or as pardon only in response to an adequate offering or payment. The Old Testament, however, assumes a notion of justice in the fulfillment of mercy and love. This is not to deny that those who mock God's merciful justice can over time fall under its shadow and experience the dreadful loss of such mercy. But the Old Testament does not assume the need for some form of payment in order for justice to be turned to mercy. There is, for example, no evidence from the Old Testament that the sacrificial system functioned in this way, or in any way other than as a symbolic act of worship and devotion.[19] The use of a mediating offering involves a recognition that redemption is out of human hands and in the hands of God. God will use this offering to carry away our sins.[20] Justice in the Old Testament involves mercy already as part of its very definition.

Divine justice thus seemed at times in Israel's history as *injustice*. Jonah is compelled to offer grace to the oppressive Assyrians, which he clearly resisted as an offensive act. Moreover, God reminds the Israelites

---

18. Barth, *Church Dogmatics*, vol. 2, *The Doctrine of God*, pt. 2, trans. G. W. Bromiley et al. (Edinburgh: T. & T. Clark, 1957), p. 34.

19. I have found David A. Brandos's discussion of this issue illuminating, in *Paul on the Cross: Reconstructing the Apostle's Story of Redemption* (Minneapolis: Fortress, 2006), pp. 20-26.

20. See Jüngel, *Justification*, pp. 162-63, where he notes that sacrifices implied the need for a divinely appointed mediation into the holy.

that even the despised Philistines had an "exodus" from oppression (Amos 9:7). God's partiality for justice, mercy, and redemption for the oppressed obviously also involved the possibility of forgiveness and liberation for the repentant oppressor. Jonah did not want God to bestow righteous and re-demptive favor on the Assyrians, and Israel certainly did not want to imag-ine anything among the Philistines comparable to the exodus from Egypt! Such thoughts certainly seemed unimaginable, the very height of injustice. "There is a profound 'injustice' about the God of the biblical tradition," says Jüngel. "It is called *grace*."[21] It is also called justifying justice from the Spirit who seeks to justify sinners by embracing them. There is the possi-bility here of a just community of the repentant faithful dependent on the mercy of God and sharing the same with one another.

Justice in the Old Testament is ultimately redemptive, leading to a jus-tice through a new creation in which the knowledge of God will flood the earth as the waters cover the sea. Such is the only possible definition for ul-timate justice in our ever-changing and complexly relational society. Reinhold Niebuhr declares: "No scheme of justice can do full justice to all of the variable factors which the freedom of man introduced into human history." It is impossible "to define absolutely what I owe my fellow man, since nothing that he now is exhausts what he might be."[22] A justice that calculates in fixed and exact proportions can never be met in any given his-torical moment, especially since the variables of justice are constantly in flux. What is needed, suggests Miroslav Volf, is "nothing less than the un-doing of the world, past and present, and the creation of a new world."[23] Hebrew Scripture wholeheartedly agrees.

Righteousness in the Old Testament is forensic only in the sense that it is rooted in God's gracious judgment, which is self-vindicating and impos-sible to challenge in any higher court of appeal. There is no higher court. Those who are just are those *judged* by God to be in the right (Exod. 23:7; Deut. 25:1). The judgment is not abstract but rather restorative and given or enacted in the redemptive deeds of God as covenant partner (Exod. 23:7-8; Deut. 1:16; 16:18, 20; Ps. 82:3; Prov. 17:15, 26; 18:5; 24:24). Righteous-ness is thus not a mere declaration of acquittal but rather an ongoing di-

21. Jüngel, *Justification*, p. 163.
22. Reinhold Niebuhr, "Christian Faith and Natural Law," in *Love and Justice: Selections from the Shorter Writings of Reinhold Niebuhr*, ed. D. B. Robertson (Cleveland: World Pub-lishing Co., 1957), pp. 49-50, quoted in Miroslav Volf, *Exclusion and Embrace: A Theological Exploration of Identity, Otherness, and Reconciliation* (Nashville: Abingdon, 1996), p. 220.
23. Volf, *Exclusion and Embrace*, p. 221.

vine activity of divine self-giving and liberation. The term "forensic" here is metaphorical, referring to divine judgments that overcome the powers of darkness and forces of oppression and inaugurate the life of the kingdom of God in its place.[24] It is for this reason that the term "forensic," when applied to God's righteousness as the ancient Hebrews understood it, "is liable to be more misleading than illuminating" unless explained and qualified as mentioned earlier.[25] The "legal" component of the covenant is part of an abundant outpouring of mercy and love, since the covenant is not at all between equals. If the Creator created humanity from the divine Word and Spirit, how can the gift of righteousness through Word and Spirit that restores to persons their very fulfillment as creatures of God be construed adequately as a legal transaction between partners? The gift of righteousness delivers and restores by grace what could never be rationally understood within a metaphor of legal exchange or reciprocity.

This emphasis on redemption and covenant faithfulness in the Old Testament notions of rightwising implies that God's righteous favor can be grasped by faith and hope even in the presence of weakness and unworthiness. "It is not because of your righteousness or your integrity that you are going in to take possession of their land; but on account of the wickedness of these nations" (Deut. 9:5). Though adherence to the law is vital to Israel's faithfulness, Israel is ultimately righteous because the nation takes refuge in God and places its trust and hope in the Lord (Ps. 5:12; 14:5; 31:18; 33:1; 36:10; 52:6; 94:15, 21; 118:15, 20). Abraham trusted in God and was reckoned righteous (Gen. 15:6). The message of Deutero-Isaiah is that Israel is not forsaken by Yahweh, even though the nation has forsaken the covenant and is not worthy of restoration, as Elizabeth Achtemeier writes:

> His covenant stands, despite Israel's unrighteousness. God intervenes for the cause of his afflicted folk before all the peoples of the earth (51:22). He will deliver her from exile (43:14); he will forgive her sin (43:25; 44:22; cf. 54:9); he will care for her as a shepherd cares for his flock (40:11).[26]

24. See Thomas Finger, "An Anabaptist Perspective on Justification," in *Justification and Sanctification in the Traditions of the Reformation,* Studies from the World Alliance of Reformed Churches 42, ed. Milan Opočenský and Páraic Réamonn (Geneva: World Alliance of Reformed Churches, 1999), p. 53.

25. Ziesler, *The Meaning of Righteousness in Paul,* p. 37.

26. E. R. Achtemeier, "Righteousness in the Old Testament," p. 85.

In fact, the optimistic hope that people are able to fulfill righteousness is gone in this part of the Hebrew canon. "If righteousness is to be fulfilled, only God's deeds can accomplish it."[27] As I have noted above, God's righteous and redemptive favor is even directed outside of Israel to the nations as well.

The term "righteousness of God" is uniquely coined at Qumran. It captures the Old Testament emphasis on righteousness as primarily God's covenant faithfulness bestowed freely in acts of mercy. It highlights God as both the source and the major player in the fulfillment of righteousness in the world. There is a particularly strong emphasis at Qumran on righteousness as a divine judgment and gift and on our unworthiness to receive it. Note the following quote:

> For mankind has no way,
>   and man is unable to establish his steps
>   since justification is with God
>   and perfection of way is out of his hand. . . .
>
> As for me,
>   if I stumble, the mercies of God
>   shall be my eternal salvation.
> If I stagger because of the sin of the flesh,
>   my justification shall be
>   by the righteousness of God which endures for ever.
> When my distress is unleashed,
>   He will deliver my soul from the pit
>   and will direct my steps to the way.
> He will draw me near by His grace,
>   and by His mercy will He bring my justification. . . .
> Through His righteousness He will cleanse me
>   of the uncleanness of man
>   and of the sins of the children of men,
> that I may confess to His righteousness,
>   and His majesty to the most High.[28]

---

27. Hans Heinrich Schmidt, "Gerechtigkeit und Glaube: Genesis 15,1-6 und sein biblisch-theologischer Kontext," *Evangelische Theologie* 40 (Jan.-Feb. 1980): 407.

28. 1QS 11:10-15, quoted in Peter Stuhlmacher, *A Challenge to the New Perspective: Revisiting Paul's Doctrine of Justification* (Downers Grove, IL: InterVarsity Press, 2000), p. 15.

There is a deep sense in this quotation of human sinfulness and of divine rightwising as an eschatological hope rooted in God's judgment of mercy and act of redemption in drawing us near to the divine life. Note also the following text:

> I have recognized that all hope is in the proofs of your favor, and all expectation in the fullness of your strength, for no man can be just at your tribunal nor [appeal against] your judgment.[29]

Qumran also connects divine rightwising with the restoration of the faithful in the Spirit of truth.[30] Nils Alstrup Dahl could rightly say that at Qumran the "similarity with Paul's doctrine of justification is truly remarkable."[31]

Righteousness in intertestamental Judaism is certainly measured by one's faithful adherence to the law. But there is evidence to suggest that this faithfulness is also rooted at this time in God's faithfulness and is connected to gratitude for righteousness as an undeserved gift. Although — as with the Old Testament — righteousness could imply a divine judgment against those who spurn God's grace, righteousness in intertestamental Judaism is also fundamentally in the extended arm of divine mercy and redemption: "[R]ighteousness and goodness will be declared, when you are merciful to those who have no store of works."[32] Peter Stuhlmacher concludes:

> "God's righteousness" in the Old Testament and early Judaism means, above all, the activity of the one God to create welfare and salvation in the creation, in the history of Israel, and in the situation of the (end-time) judgment.[33]

The hope for end-time righteousness in the Old Testament was also merged with the hope of the coming *Spirit*, who will reestablish God's presence and favor in the world and vindicate the living witness of both the Messiah and his people. This insight will set up the eschatological and

29. 1QH 9:13-17, quoted in Walter Grundmann, "The Teacher of Righteousness of Qumran," p. 96.

30. Of Qumran, Grundmann notes: "God's goodness makes the fallen and sinful men of Israel just through the renewal of the spirit of truth in them" (p. 96).

31. Nils Alstrup Dahl, "Promise and Fulfillment," in *Studies in Paul: Theology for the Early Christian Mission* (Minneapolis: Augsburg, 1977), p. 100.

32. 4 Ezra 8:35-36, quoted in Stuhlmacher, *A Challenge to the New Perspective*, p. 16.

33. Stuhlmacher, *A Challenge*, p. 19.

pneumatological nature of divine righteousness implied in the Old Testament and prominent in the New Testament. Worthy of exploration first in setting up the pneumatological dimension of righteousness as a gift is the important role of the law in divine rightwising in the Old Testament.

The Law's Witness to Life

The law by which one is judged righteous in parts of the Old Testament consequently has its meaning within the context of Yahweh's faithful deliverance of Israel from bondage (Exod. 20:1-2), even of Yahweh's love for Israel as God's bride (Hosea 2:14-16). The greatest law is absolute love for God and the other (Deut. 6:4), but not even this could ever adequately repay Yahweh for the grace inherent in divine love. Living by these statutes simply allowed the covenant community to respond faithfully to God's faithfulness by never forgetting the Lord as the source of all grace and bounty. In Deuteronomy 6:1-12, the Israelites were to remember and adhere to the commandments so as not to forget the Lord once they enter into the land of promise. They were not to forget that the land and its bounty are gifts of God or that God had delivered them from bondage in Egypt. Deuteronomy 6:20-21 summarizes this matter well:

> "In the future, when your son asks you, 'What is the meaning of the stipulations, decrees and laws the LORD our God has commanded you?' tell him: 'We were slaves of Pharaoh in Egypt, but the LORD brought us out of Egypt with a mighty hand.'"

Deuteronomy 8:11-14 makes the same point:

> "Be careful that you do not forget the LORD your God, failing to observe his commands, his laws and his decrees that I am giving you this day. Otherwise, when you eat and are satisfied, when you build fine houses and settle down, and when your herds and flocks grow large and your silver and gold increase and all you have is multiplied, then your heart will become proud and you will forget the LORD your God, who brought you out of Egypt, out of the land of slavery."

The law is thus spiritual or dependent on a heart transformed out of gratitude for the undeserved faithfulness of God. Observing the law is a means of remembrance and acknowledgment concerning the gracious deeds of the Lord. The freedom of the exodus is dependent on Israel's not forgetting the God of the Exodus. The preface to the law brings to their attention that the one behind the giving of the law is their God, who set them free from bondage (Exod. 20:1-2). Grace and freedom precede law, and obedience to the law is a form of acknowledgment and gratitude. Adherence to the law corresponds to the righteousness of God revealed in the Exodus and to the freedom that was essential to that event.

The faithful response also reflected God's preference for the victims of evil over those who seek to exploit it for privilege or gain; but it also had the breadth of mercy to all who genuinely repent. God gave the right to Israel over their oppressors while they were afflicted under slavery (Ps. 103:6); thus the afflicted also have the right over the oppressors within the covenant community (Ps. 14:5; 69:28; 140:13). The hope of the afflicted is in the Lord (Ps. 116:6; 146:8), but mercy is wide and open, even to the repentant among the oppressors.

Righteousness is ultimately a judgment and gift of God. Yet one should not underestimate the importance of the law as a witness to this gift and as a means of grasping it as a source of life. Life is promised to those who live by the law: "Follow it so that you may live" (Deut. 4:1; cf. 30:16). And again: "He follows my decrees and faithfully keeps my laws. That man is righteous; he will surely live, declares the Sovereign LORD" (Ezek. 18:9). The law is thus vital to the fulfillment of righteousness in the world: living by the law "will be our righteousness" (Deut. 6:25). Again, the law is not only a series of commandments but is also a spiritual matter. The righteous "delight" in the law and meditate on it (Ps. 1:2). The law is perfect, "reviving the soul" (Ps. 19:7). The witness and inspiration of the law is a gift of God and even a vehicle for the divine righteousness, for the psalmist asks God to "be gracious to me through your law" (Ps. 119:29). As I have noted, the preface to the law is the gracious deliverance of Israel from Egypt (Exod. 20:1-3). "I will redeem you with an outstretched arm and with mighty acts of judgment" (Exod. 6:6). In the Old Testament the "realization of righteousness is based . . . alone on the powerful actions of God."[34] The law is a vital condition to the ongoing vitality of life in the covenant that was granted by grace. Those who break the law can break the covenant (Isa. 24:5); but God's justice will go out to the nations through the revelation of the law (Isa. 51:4). There is no question but that the law plays a vital role in the Old Testament in the fulfillment of righteousness.

---

34. Schmidt, "Gerechtigkeit und Glaube," p. 407.

As I have noted above, obedience to the law brings blessings, but these blessings have not by any means been earned. Deuteronomy 6:3 promises blessings for those who obey the law: "Hear, O Israel, and be careful to obey so that it may go well with you and that you may increase greatly in a land flowing with milk and honey, just as the LORD, the God of your fathers, promised you." But notice the important qualification just a few verses later (Deut. 6:10-12):

> When the LORD your God brings you into the land he swore to your fathers, to Abraham, Isaac and Jacob, to give you — a land with large, flourishing cities you did not build, houses filled with all kinds of good things you did not provide, wells you did not dig, and vineyards and olive groves you did not plant — then when you eat and are satisfied, be careful that you do not forget the LORD, who brought you out of Egypt, out of the land of slavery.

In other words, obedience to the law was viewed as a condition of blessing, but there is no simple cause-and-effect relationship between them. In fact, it is the disobedience to the law that makes the heart proud, convinced that it has earned the blessings by means of works. Obedience to the law assures the opposite, namely, that one does not forget the Lord as the source of all deliverance and bounty. Ultimately, the Lord as the source of all blessing graciously delivered Israel from Egypt and freely gave them land, vineyards, and houses that the nation did not earn or deserve. Only in the sense of acknowledging the Lord as the source of all grace does faithfulness to the law remain an important condition for the promise and blessing of life.

Obedience to the law will not only occasion the nation's internal blessing but the fulfillment of the nation's destiny to be a channel of blessing to the nations in fulfillment of the covenant given to Abraham:

> Listen to me, my people;
> hear me, my nation:
> The law will go out from me;
> my justice will become a light to the nations. (Isa. 51:4)

The law, however, also condemns Israel in its weakness and rebellion: "All Israel has transgressed your law and turned away, refusing to obey you" (Dan. 9:11). Deuteronomy 27–30 sets out a series of curses for those who transgress the law and blessings for those who obey it. The curse is especially focused on the nation being besieged, taken into exile, and oppressed (Deut. 28:25-57). The law that was intended as a witness to life can thus witness instead to death and despair.

Yet God never cuts off hope entirely with respect to Israel, even in the midst of curse. As I have noted earlier, though the challenge to obey is never softened in the Old Testament, one is ultimately made to depend on the mercy of God for the gift of righteousness: "He does not treat us as our sins deserve or repay us according to our iniquities. . . . As a father has compassion on his children, so the LORD has compassion on those who fear him; for he knows how we are formed, he remembers that we are dust" (Ps. 103:10, 13-14). The hope of righteousness is thus the hope for the gift of divine love: "But from everlasting to everlasting, the LORD's love is with those who fear him, and his righteousness with their children's children" (Ps. 103:17). God gives strength to the weak in the midst of despair (Isa. 40:29) so that "those who hope in the LORD will renew their strength. They will soar on wings like eagles; they will run and not grow weary, they will walk and not be faint" (Isa. 40:31).

The covenant involving the law is not based on the law but rather on God's gracious and liberating presence (Exod. 20:1-2). In particular, God's presence is promised in the *Shekinah,* which that guaranteed Israel's liberation from her oppressors and from the hopelessness of sin and death. In a word, the law cries out for the Spirit. It is ultimately through the promise of the Spirit that the law becomes a living reality that witnesses to the enhancement of righteousness and life. In the midst of the blessings and the curses of the law laid out in Deuteronomy 27–30, there is the implication that the blessing of the law in occasioning life will ultimately depend on the inward work of the Spirit: "The LORD your God will circumcise your hearts and the hearts of your descendants, so that you may love him with all your heart and with all your soul, that you may live" (Deut. 30:6). The prophets bore witness to the same priority of new creation through the Spirit to law: "I will give them singleness of heart and action, so that they will always fear me for their own good and the good of their children after them" (Jer. 32:39). Note also Jeremiah 31:33: "I will put my law in their minds and write it on their hearts." God will indeed refashion their hearts in favor of the law by putting the divine Spirit in them: "I will put my Spirit in you and move you to follow my decrees" (Ezek. 36:27). And again, note Ezekiel 11:19-20:

> I will give them an undivided heart and put a new spirit in them; I will remove from them their heart of stone and give them a heart of flesh.

Then they will follow my decrees and be careful to keep my laws. They will be my people, and I will be their God.

And also Ezekiel 36:26-27: "I will give you a new heart and put a new spirit in you; I will remove from you your heart of stone and give you a heart of flesh. And I will put my Spirit in you and move you to follow my decrees and be careful to keep my laws." The law and its witness to righteousness will only find fulfillment through the indwelling of the Spirit. The law cannot create singleness of heart in devotion to God, new hope in the midst of despair, give new life, or raise up the dead. The law as a letter or a norm cannot fulfill righteousness. The law and its powerful witness to God live from the Spirit and depend on the gift of the Spirit in the Old Testament. The promise of righteousness in the context of living by the law essentially involves even more fundamentally the promise of new life in the Spirit.

How is it that the Spirit will come upon the people and the blessing of the law will find realization? How is it that the witness of the law to life will reach the nations and the promise given to Abraham will be fulfilled? The Old Testament implicitly links the answer to these questions to the anointed Son of man, the one who will be vindicated by the Spirit as the righteous ruler in the world.

Messianic Righteousness as Vindication in the Spirit

The Messiah will have God's favor and will rule in justice as the man of the Spirit (Isa. 42:1). He will proclaim the year of the Lord's favor as empowered by the Spirit (Isa. 61:1). He will judge righteously and bring justice to creation as the one anointed by the Spirit. Consider Isaiah 11:

1 A shoot will come up from the stump of Jesse;
   from his roots a Branch will bear fruit.

2 The Spirit of the LORD will rest on him —
   the Spirit of wisdom and of understanding,
   the Spirit of counsel and of power,
   the Spirit of knowledge and of the fear of the LORD —

3 and he will delight in the fear of the LORD.
   He will not judge by what he sees with his eyes,
   or decide by what he hears with his ears;

4 but with righteousness he will judge the needy,
    with justice he will give decisions for the poor of the earth.
    He will strike the earth with the rod of his mouth;
    with the breath of his lips he will slay the wicked.

5 Righteousness will be his belt
    and faithfulness the sash around his waist.

Notice that the "breath of his lips" brings judgment of a negative nature to those who resist, while his Spirit-inspired rule brings salvation to others. One might say that he will baptize with the Spirit by the divine breath, bringing both judgment and restoration. Jesus as the indwelling of God is named Immanuel, which means "God with us" (Matt. 1:11), the very climax of God's presence and favor returning to the earth. He is the one who will baptize in the Spirit (e.g., Matt. 3:11), and this Spirit baptizer is vindicated as the Son of the Father (Matt. 3:16-17), a vindication that climaxes in resurrection (Rom. 1:4) and exaltation (Acts 2:33; Phil. 2:9-11) and in the Spirit's witness in history, especially through the people of God.

In Daniel 7:13, the "Son of man" approaches the Ancient of Days on a cloud to be vindicated and to receive the divine right to rule, an indication that he ascends to the throne from the earth.[35] In receiving all rule and authority, he is vindicated as God's chosen.[36] The scene is the heavenly court of Daniel 7:9-10.[37] Just as Moses, who spoke to God "face to face" (Deut. 34:10), passed through a cloud in his encounter with God (Exod. 24:10), so too the Son of man, who represents oppressed Israel (Dan. 7:21-22), comes on a cloud to approach the Ancient of Days.[38] Indeed, Yahweh's saving presence is connected to clouds (Exod. 13:21; 19:9; 24:16; 40:34; Num. 11:25). "There is no one like the God of Jeshurun, who

35. I agree with Alexander Di Lella that "the 'one in human likeness' did not *descend* or *come from* God as if he had been an angel in the divine presence, but rather he *ascended* or *came to* God and *was brought* into his presence." Di Lella, "One in Human Likeness and the Holy Ones of the Most High in Daniel 7," *Catholic Biblical Quarterly*, 39, no. 1 (Jan. 1977): 19 (italics in original). N. T. Wright agrees that the figure here "comes *from* earth *to* heaven." Wright, *Jesus and the Victory of God*: vol. 2, *Christian Origins and the Question of God* (Minneapolis: Fortress, 1996), p. 361 (italics in original).

36. "The Danielic story always was one of vindication and exaltation, and was retold as such in the first century." N. T. Wright, *Jesus and the Victory of God*, p. 361.

37. George Raymond Beasley-Murray, "Interpretation of Daniel 7," *Catholic Biblical Quarterly* 45, no. 1 (Jan. 1983): 48.

38. Di Lella, "One in Human Likeness," p. 19.

rides on the heavens to help you and on the clouds in his majesty" (Deut. 33:26; cf. 2 Sam. 22:10; Ps. 104:3).

For Daniel, the term "Son of man" might have been a title with messianic implications, as it did become in late Jewish documents (*Similitudes of Enoch:* 1 Enoch 46:1-4; 48:2; 62:9, 14; 63:11; 69:26-27; 70:1) and in Jesus (Mark 10:45).[39] It may have referred to a personage who was "like a human figure," perhaps even a divine being who ascends to the throne to reign on behalf of the Ancient of Days.[40] The vindication of the Son of man is thus divine self-vindication. Though representative of the saints, the Son of man does seem to be an agent of God in his own right.[41] In the midst of violent oppression below, the Son of man approaches the throne of the heavenly court to receive vindication and the right to rule in the indestructible kingdom of God, along with all of the divine rights that go along with it, including being the recipient of the worship that belongs to God alone (Dan. 7:14).[42]

There are obvious connections between the Son of man tradition in Daniel 7 and the New Testament depiction of Jesus. C. H. Dodd observes, justifiably, that Daniel 7 "is embedded in the foundations of New Testament thought."[43] Jesus noted that his path to vindication and lordship as the Son of man was the self-sacrifice of the cross, which would "ransom" those in bondage to the enemy (Mark 10:45). The vindication of the crucified Jesus comes by way of his resurrection and ascension to the throne to receive the right to rule God's kingdom, as found in Acts 1–2 (as well as Rev. 5 and 12). Acts 1:9 specifically mentions Jesus' ascending in a cloud, and Acts 2:33 has him receiving the Spirit from the Father in vindication as the man of the Spirit to be the judge of the world (cf. Acts 10:38-42), the one who saves others by imparting the Spirit on all flesh (Acts 2:33).

We, too, are "caught up in the clouds" after our resurrection or transformation by the Spirit to ascend with the Messiah and to share in the vin-

---

39. Arnold B. Rhodes, "Kingdoms of Men and the Kingdom of God: A Study of Daniel 7:1-14," *Interpretation*, 15, no. 4 (Oct. 1961): 423-24.

40. Julian Morgenstern, "'Son of Man' of Daniel 7:13f: A New Interpretation," *Journal of Biblical Literature* 80, no. 1 (Mar. 1, 1961): 65-77.

41. I find the idea largely conjectural that the Son of man here is merely a personification of Israel.

42. Rhodes, "Kingdoms of Men," p. 423.

43. C. H. Dodd, *According to the Scriptures* (London: Nisbet, 1952), p. 69, quoted in Michael B. Shepherd, "Daniel 7:13 and the New Testament Son of Man," *Westminster Theological Journal* 68, no. 1 (Spring 2006): 107.

dication of the Son of man (Acts 1:9-11; 2:33; 1 Thess. 4:17).[44] From the lens of the Christian story, Jesus fulfilled Daniel 7 by rising again "according to the Spirit of holiness" (Rom. 1:4) and ascending on high to the right hand of the Father in order to be "justified in the Spirit" (1 Tim. 3:16) and to bestow the Spirit on all flesh (Acts 2:33), the very down payment and eventual cause of our own resurrection and vindication (Rom. 8:11). Our indwelling by the Spirit ushers us into the righteousness and vindication of the Son of man. This point brings us to the Old Testament witness to the significance of the indwelling Spirit as the ultimate fulfillment of the divine rightwising of creation.

Righteousness by the Spirit's Indwelling

Divine rightwising is indeed covenantal and relational but in ways that are not strictly legal. In fact, in rightwising us, God draws us in so intimately that the divine breath becomes once more our inner grace and freedom. Justifying righteousness is ultimately fulfilled in a grace that is near to the soul and to the very heart of creation, namely, God's own presence through the bestowal of the Spirit. God's covenant faithfulness and vindication as covenant partner and Lord through the exalted Son of man in the Old Testament is thus not exhausted in the covenant made with Israel, nor even with the nations. It extends to all of creation and is focused on God's desire to inhabit and be glorified in all things. Righteousness in the Old Testament as covenant faithfulness and vindication also has at its core a pneumatological substance and at its horizon an eschatological hope.

Creation was made by the very breath of God (Gen. 1:2). The human was formed from the dust and became a living soul from the breath of God (Gen. 2:7). As the New Testament would confirm, it is in the divine presence that humanity lives, moves, and has its very being (Acts 17:28). "When you send your Spirit, they are created, and you renew the face of the earth" (Ps. 104:30). It is the divine breath, along with the word of prophecy, that will raise us up and give us hope again, and it is by this divine indwelling that God will vindicate Godself as Lord of creation: "I will put breath in you, and you will come to life. Then you will know that I am the LORD" (Ezek. 37:6). And again Ezekiel is told: "Then you, my people, will know

44. N. T. Wright, *The Resurrection of the Son of God* (Minneapolis: Fortress, 2003), p. 215.

that I am the LORD, when I open your graves and bring you up from them. I will put my Spirit in you and you will live" (Ezek. 37:13-14). On the other side, we can entrust ourselves entirely to God to be vindicated as faithful by rescuing us even in the face of death: "Into your hands I commit my spirit; redeem me, O LORD, the God of truth" (Ps. 31:5).

God is thus the one who will prove to be the Lord, prove to be faithful and true, by ushering in "everlasting righteousness" (Dan. 9:24) — understood as salvation. This is the hope of the Hebrew prophets. "My righteousness draws near speedily, my salvation is on the way," declares Isaiah 51:5, as though the coming righteousness and the approaching salvation are to be equated. Indeed, righteousness is likened to an abundant rain that causes salvation to spring forth in expressions of new life: "You heavens above, rain down righteousness; let the clouds shower it down. Let the earth open wide, let salvation spring up, let righteousness grow with it; I, the LORD, have created it" (Isa. 45:8). Amos also calls for righteousness to rush down as a mighty stream that can enrich life with fruits of justice (Amos 5:24). Though the prophets understood righteousness as something that the faithful show forth in faithfulness to God and God's statutes, righteousness is fundamentally dependent on divine favor, on the divine presence as the source of new life. It is not only something that we "sow" but more fundamentally something that the Lord "showers" upon us:

> Sow for yourselves righteousness,
> reap the fruit of unfailing love,
> and break up your unplowed ground;
> for it is time to seek the LORD,
> until he comes and showers righteousness on you. (Hosea 10:12)

What is commonly neglected in discussions of righteousness as God's covenant faithfulness is that showers of righteousness are not detached from God's personal presence. God's presence is God's favor, the favor that saves, preserves, and vindicates. In this light it becomes clear that the very person of God "became my salvation" (Ps. 118:21). Indeed, "the Lord is my righteousness," says Jeremiah (Jer. 23:6). To trust in one's own righteousness for salvation is to cease trusting in the Lord (Ezek. 33:13). To be rightwised is to receive God's personal self-giving. God reigns and is vindicated as Lord in the personal presence and indwelling of God's Spirit, as the ancient Jewish tradition of the *Shekinah* illustrates. I agree with Walter Kasper: "In the tradition of the Old Testament and of Judaism the coming of the kingdom of God means the coming of God."[45] And as Hosea 6:3 notes, Israel's only hope is in God's coming presence:

> Let us acknowledge the LORD;
> let us press on to acknowledge him.
> As surely as the sun rises,
> he will appear;
> he will come to us like the winter rains,
> like the spring rains that water the earth.

More to the point, the prophets specifically connected the approaching righteousness of God with the coming outpouring of the Holy Spirit. Consider Isaiah 32:14-16:

> The fortress will be abandoned,
> the noisy city deserted;
> citadel and watchtower will become a wasteland forever,
> the delight of donkeys, a pasture for flocks,
> till the Spirit is poured upon us from on high,
> and the desert becomes a fertile field,
> and the fertile field seems like a forest.
> Justice will dwell in the desert
> and righteousness live in the fertile field.

Indeed, the Old Testament indicates that God's covenant is renewed and righteousness fulfilled in this bestowal of the Spirit upon the covenant people and in their living witness that springs forth as a result:

> "As for me, this is my covenant with them," says the LORD. "My Spirit, who is on you, and my words that I have put in your mouth will not depart from your mouth, or from the mouths of your children, or from the mouths of their descendants from this time on and forever," says the LORD. (Isa. 59:21)

Notice that the faithful covenant relationship is essentially defined as the gracious giving of the Spirit to us and to our descendants. One is reminded of Peter's words concerning the outpouring of the Spirit at Pentecost: "The promise is for you and your children and for all who are far off — for all whom the Lord our God will call" (Acts 2:39).

---

45. Walter Kasper, *Jesus the Christ* (Mahwah, NJ: Paulist, 1976), p. 78.

Righteousness, therefore, is described in the Old Testament in ways that appear cryptically pneumatological, or as a sphere of power and new life that causes justice to spring forth among God's people. Note what Gerhard von Rad says in this regard:

> Examination of the numerous references in which צְדָקָה appears in connection with the preposition בְּ suggests that צְדָקָה seems also to have been understood in an oddly spatial way, as something like a sphere, or power-charged area, into which men are incorporated and thereby empowered to do special deeds.[46]

The righteousness of the kingdom of God floods in as a sphere of deliverance, justice, witness, and vindication. This is the righteousness by which we are justified by the Spirit of life.

Though the gift of the Spirit was a future promise, the Spirit was also viewed as present already in advance of future fulfillment. In the Old Testament, God tabernacled with God's people as they journeyed through the wilderness toward the promised land. In the Old Testament, this presence is connected to the *Shekinah*, the presence of God meeting Israel and bestowing divine favor in the context of the cult, in the tent but also on the ark.[47] Israel also had the memory of God's journeying before them in the cloud or the pillar of fire on the way toward liberation from bondage and toward freedom of worship (Exod. 7:16). The God of Israel was on the move and could not be confined to any one place. As the psalmist asked, "Where can I go from your Spirit? Where can I flee from your presence?" (Ps. 139:7).

But Israel still regarded certain times and places as specially chosen of God for God to meet with Israel in the context of devotion, worship, and sacrifices. The Temple was particularly seen as existing at the "cosmic center of the universe, at the place where heaven and earth converge and thus where God's control over the universe is effected."[48] The Temple was the divine dwelling place par excellence, "where the living god designed to dwell."[49] Israelites enjoyed favor and the vindication of their witness from this visitation of God in their midst.

---

46. Von Rad, *Old Testament Theology,* 1:376-77.

47. Von Rad, *Old Testament Theology,* 1:234-41.

48. Carol Meyers, "Temple, Jerusalem," *Anchor Bible Dictionary,* ed. David Noel Freedman (New York: Doubleday, 1992), 6:351, 539, quoted in Wright, *Jesus and the Victory of God,* 2:407.

49. Wright, *Jesus and the Victory of God,* 2:407.

The flip side of this vindication, however, involved a stern warning that rampant injustice in Israel would cause God's departure from the Temple. Jeremiah 7 points out that the Temple was to be the place where God dwells with his people so long as the people do not forget God's ways of justice (Jer. 7:5-7) and do not consequently turn God's Temple into a "den of robbers" (Jer. 7:11). The Temple had become a focal point of hope and national liberation — as well as security — against the pagans, but it also represented an ongoing challenge of covenant faithfulness.[50] The Temple was at the center of Israel's justification by grace, but this grace was considered costly and connected to appropriate covenant faithfulness from Israel by way of response. I particularly like Ezekiel's image of a river flowing out from the Temple so that many water creatures and plants could live and flourish from its nourishment (Ezek. 47:3-12). Such would ultimately be fulfilled not by a building but by Christ, who would come as the ultimate dwelling place of God's Spirit.

The destruction of the Temple led to a theology of the *Shekinah* as the presence of God to bear Israel's suffering in exile and to lead them back to the land of promise. The *Shekinah* becomes God's indwelling presence.[51] As N. T. Wright has pointed out, the final end of exile will not come until the indwelling Spirit brings about the new creation. It is only then, I would add, that the Spirit makes the entire creation the place of God's dwelling.

The presence of the Spirit in the life of Israel was also noticeable in the ministry of Moses and the prophets (e.g., Num. 11), as well as judges. God would sometimes speak through a prophet like Amos outside the mainstream of Israel's religious life and in sharp criticism against it. The Spirit can be found in unexpected places. Even artisans working on the tabernacle are said to have been filled with the Spirit (Exod. 35:35). All of this merely whets the appetite for a future outpouring of the Spirit that will turn Israel into a reservoir of blessing to the nations. God's faithfulness to the promises and Israel's vindication as the elect people are centered ultimately on the gift of life upon the nation as a whole and through it to the world.

That righteousness as a spiritual reality brings about life runs throughout older wisdom and the cultic demands of righteousness. The whole of creation is made for righteousness in the sense that all things were made for

---

50. Wright, *Jesus and the Victory of God*, 2:333-428, esp. pp. 418-20. The NRSV rightly translates Jer. 7:7: "Then I will dwell with you in this place."

51. See Moltmann's development of this theology in *The Spirit of Life: A Universal Affirmation* (Minneapolis: Fortress, 1992), pp. 47-51.

the Spirit. Righteousness in the Spirit opens up possibilities for life, granting transcendent righteousness and eschatological significance.[52] The historic weakness and inability to realize the fulfillment of this hope for life caused the nation to hope for a day when the Spirit will be poured out abundantly on all flesh in renewal of covenant promises. The destiny of Israel to be a channel of blessing to the nations will occur only through an abundant outpouring of the Spirit on them so that they could become witnesses to the gift of righteousness to the world:

> And afterward,
> I will pour out my Spirit on all people.
> Your sons and daughters will prophesy,
> your old men will dream dreams,
> your young men will see visions.
> Even on my servants, both men and women,
> I will pour out my Spirit in those days.
> I will show wonders in the heavens
> and on the earth,
> blood and fire and billows of smoke.
> The sun will be turned to darkness
> and the moon to blood
> before the coming of the great and dreadful day of the LORD.
> And everyone who calls
> on the name of the LORD will be saved;
> for on Mount Zion and in Jerusalem
> there will be deliverance,
> as the LORD has said,
> among the survivors
> whom the LORD calls. (Joel 2:28-32)

Ultimate hope points to the latter day and to the resurrection of the dead as the final vindication of a people rightwised by the Spirit of God: "Then you, my people, will know that I am the LORD, when I open your graves and bring you up from them. I will put my Spirit in you and you will live" (Ezek. 37:13-14).

The opening of the graves functions here as more than a metaphor. Israel is to know in rising from hopelessness and despair that there is no limit to the covenant faithfulness expressed in the gift of the Spirit of life.

---

52. Schmidt, "Gerechtigkeit und Glaube," pp. 404-5.

When the grave itself is conquered, God will be vindicated as Lord, and the hope placed in God will not suffer shame but will be vindicated as well. "Let me not be put to shame, O LORD," the psalmist cries out, "for I have cried out to you; but let the wicked be put to shame and lie silent in the grave" (Ps. 31:17). Though the rich will lose everything in the grave (Ps. 49:12), "God will redeem my life from the grave," says the psalmist, "he will surely take me to himself" (Ps. 49:15). To find one's end in the grave is to suffer the shame of losing the vindication of life (Isa. 38:18). "All who had spread terror in the land of the living went down uncircumcised to the earth below. They bear their shame with those who go down to the pit" (Ezek. 32:24). But God promises to vindicate the righteous: "I will ransom them from the power of the grave; I will redeem them from death" (Hosea 13:14). God will be faithful to mercifully grant this final gift of righteousness: "In my distress I called to the LORD, and he answered me. From the depths of the grave I called for help, and you listened to my cry" (Jonah 2:2).

Final vindication in resurrection is rooted in the gift of the Spirit's embrace of flesh in the Spirit's indwelling of the creature and the foretaste of new life granted in that embrace. Resurrection/exaltation is the hope of those who possess the Spirit and the comfort of those who suffer and seek vindication for their humanity in God. Righteousness in the Old Testament is ultimately an act of mercy as an expression of a covenant faithfulness that exceeds what Israel or the nations can ever claim by their own worthiness. It is an eschatological gift that exceeds the strict standards of legal systems, for it involves the abundant outpouring of the Spirit, the forgiveness of sins, a faithful witness to the merciful justice of God, and redemption from the grave in vindication for an undying hope in God and an enduring witness to God's mercy. There is simply no way of understanding justification from an Old Testament context without drawing attention to God's indwelling presence and all that that implies.

Conclusion

"*This* is to be justified, to receive the Divine Presence within us and be made a Temple of the Holy Ghost."[53] The Old Testament implies that the

---

53. John Henry Newman, *Lectures on Justification* (London: J. G. & F. Rivington, 1838), p. 160.

right relationship that ultimately brings Israel and the nations into the covenant faithfulness of God is not given by the law per se, as important as the law was as the condition of recognizing the Lord and enjoying the Lord's blessing. God will fulfill the divine promise to Israel and, ultimately, to the world and the creation through the gift of the Holy Spirit. Justice is achieved through something unimaginable, namely, the very presence of God through the Spirit, a presence that brings creation into a depth of life and hope ungraspable by current systems of justice or rational frameworks. The gift of righteousness will be abundantly poured out like a rain or a flood. It will be excessively rich in mercy and grace. It will involve the very transformation of creation in the defeat of sin and death for the eternal glory of God. The root of this justice and its very core is the divine habitation or indwelling of creation. Only through this will creation be vindicated as the theater of God's glory that it was created to become.

This indwelling is the dream of sages and the hope of prophets. It is based in the Old Testament on divine faithfulness in covenant relationship with Israel but also, more broadly, with the nations and all of creation. This divine faithfulness places demands on the people of God, especially under the guidance of the law as revealed through Moses and reinterpreted by the prophets. However, righteousness is a gift that exceeds the capacities of legal codes or of strivings among the faithful to bear witness to grace. The law thirsts for the Spirit in search of the ultimate fulfillment of its witness. As Israel is drawn into the despair of exile, the hope increases for a latter-day outpouring of the Spirit to fulfill the witness of the law and the promises of God to bestow righteousness on the world.

We draw closest to the heart of the law when we read that it witnesses to love for God with one's whole being (Deut. 6:4-5). This love is the righteousness of the Spirit, first bestowed on the creature and then returned through the creature's transformed and — ultimately — glorified existence. This righteousness is excessive because it grants a foretaste of the future kingdom of God in which the Spirit will be poured out in abundance upon all flesh, God's very own presence to bring the creation into the intimate union with the Creator. It fulfills the basic calling of all creation to bear the Spirit to the glory of God as the new creation. As such, the promise and foretaste of righteousness in the Old Testament could never be earned or rationally accounted for through any system of exchange or reciprocity. True justice can only find fulfillment in the new world fashioned according to the fundamental relationship with creation willed by the Creator. Its definition cannot be construed according to abstract norms, but rather according to the divine purpose in fulfillment of the divinely willed relationship, namely, an indwelling by the Spirit of God.

The divine indwelling is centered implicitly in the Old Testament on the anointed one. The Messiah is the faithful one, who, in solidarity with God's people, especially the oppressed, ascends to the throne to be vindicated by God as ruler over God's kingdom. He rules in justice as the bearer of the Spirit and the harbinger of hope. Connected to him, the people of God cultivate hope for the coming of the Spirit to indwell all things, fulfill justice with respect to God, and share in the vindication of the Spirit's witness to justice. This justice in the Spirit of life and grace might seem like injustice because it pardons Israel's sin and opens the door of divine favor to the nations. It facilitates an intimate knowledge of God in which one can empathize with God's suffering love for those who are not faithful (as Hosea shows us). Justifying righteousness is thus fulfilled in mercy, grace, and new creation. Even in the face of death, Israel can have hope that their faithful waiting on God will not be shamed but will rather be vindicated in resurrection.

Connected also with the divine presence and favor in the Old Testament is the tabernacle and the Temple. The tension between Messiah and Temple in discerning the central locus of divine righteousness within Israel will only be clarified in the New Testament. Also vital to the future gift of righteousness in the gift of the Spirit is Israel's role as a channel of blessing to the nations. Whether or not the law can provide within its own provisions the needed fulfillment of Abraham's blessing will become a subject that will preoccupy Paul, as we will see shortly.

What is unclear in the Old Testament witness is the precise link between the vindicated Messiah and the outpouring of the Spirit of life on all flesh. The Messiah bears the Spirit in solidarity with the people, but it is God who pours out the Spirit in the latter days (e.g., Joel 2:28-29). The vindicated Messiah rules with God's authority and seems to function as a divine figure in Daniel 7, but nowhere does it say that *he* bestows the divine Spirit. This idea will represent the breakthrough of the New Testament witness, because all four Gospels and the book of Acts, the narrative foundation of the New Testament canon, will introduce Jesus as the Spirit baptizer, or the one who will not only bear the Spirit but also bestow the Spirit. Spirit baptism then becomes the link between the vindicated Messiah as the one who bears the Spirit and the Spirit-indwelt and vindicated creation. Spirit baptism will link the righteous Messiah with the rightwised creation.

Also unclear in the Old Testament is how the excessive gift of righteousness through the coming Spirit will redraw the boundaries of the elect community. There are hints in the Old Testament that the justice of God reaches out to the radically other, to the point of making the divine rightwising seem like an offensive injustice. There are also indications that Israel is destined in its own enjoyment of the blessings of righteousness through the Spirit to be a channel of blessing to the nations. It will take Jesus' table fellowship and Paul's mission to the Gentiles to reveal just how radical the coming reign of righteousness throughout the earth through the coming Spirit will challenge Israel's understanding of the covenant community or the nature of covenant faithfulness with regard to the legal structure of Israelite religion. The baptism in the Spirit through the coming ministry of the Messiah will provide a narrative context for justification that will both challenge and fulfill Israelite tradition.

6 Apart from Us

Justification and the Spirit-Indwelt Christ

The impartation and indwelling of the Spirit is vital as a point of departure for a pneumatological (and hence Trinitarian) doctrine of justification. But justification in the Spirit cannot only be concentrated on the Spirit's indwelling and embrace of *believers,* to their awakened inner life, or to their communal life in witness to justice to an increasingly unjust world. Justification in the Spirit also has an *external* point of reference (which is also deeply internal), namely, Christ — especially in his filial relationship by the Spirit to the heavenly Father as revealed in Christ's redemptive story. This story directs us to the place and time where God has acted to restore justice. But the story also involves Pentecost, where Christ inaugurates justice by becoming the firstborn among many brothers and sisters (Rom. 8:29) and where the Spirit fulfills justice by being the one who anoints the many. This means that the Spirit is at the very substance of justification as a divine act, first in Christ as the Son of the Father and the man of the Spirit, but also in Christ as the Spirit baptizer. I speak here of basing justification on an "objective pneumatology," which is a christological and a Trinitarian pneumatology. I will begin this chapter by giving a preliminary explanation of what I mean by this term.

Objective Pneumatology: Preliminary Thoughts

In part, an objective pneumatology is inspired by Karl Barth, who accused Schleiermacher of making the tragic error of concentrating his pneumatology on religious consciousness rather than on the outpouring of the Spirit at Pentecost.[1] I am also following the insight of Moltmann and others into the significance of the Spirit as the one whose anointing mediates the coming of the divine Son into the flesh (Luke 1:35) and who continues to anoint Christ, sending him forth from the Father into the world. In a sense, the Spirit proceeds from the Father to dwell in the Son! Then, as Moltmann explains, "we would understand that Christ comes from the Father and from the Spirit." The Spirit cooperates with the Word in being, in a real sense, "the subject of Jesus' life until his death."[2] David Coffey even speaks of the "incarnation" of the Holy Spirit in the faithful life of love that characterized the Son in the flesh.[3] He also writes of the Son's making the Spirit his own by returning devotion to the Father through the Spirit and pouring forth the Spirit as the Spirit of Christ, a clear sign of Christ's deity.[4] If the Spirit already rested on the Son in the bond of love enjoyed eternally with the Father, then the incarnation allowed the Spirit, too, to rest on the body of Jesus within the circle of love and justice enjoyed within the triune life. "The Spirit gave the Word a body so that those with bodies might receive the Spirit."[5]

It is important to note, however, that Jesus as the divine Word of the Father also mediated the Spirit into the world (for only God can impart God). He did this in his miracles (Matt. 12:28) and chiefly in his death, resurrection, and exaltation by receiving the Spirit from the Father to pour the Spirit forth onto all flesh (Acts 2:33). Jesus rises "into the full Spirit-life of the resurrection" in order that his ascension and vindication as the Son of man would impart this same Spirit to cre-

---

1. Karl Barth, *Protestant Theology in the Nineteenth Century* (Grand Rapids: Eerdmans, 2002), pp. 457-59. Also helpful here is John Thompson's use of the term "objective pneumatology" to describe Karl Barth's use of the Spirit to counter the liberal attempt to conflate revelation into the subjective consciousness or experience of the divine. Thompson, *The Holy Spirit in the Theology of Karl Barth*, Princeton Theological Monograph Series (Kent, UK: Pickwick, 1991).

2. Jürgen Moltmann, *A Broad Place: An Autobiography* (Minneapolis: Fortress, 2008), p. 329. Moltmann develops this insight in *The Spirit of Life: A Universal Affirmation*, trans. Margaret Kohl (Minneapolis: Fortress, 1992), pp. 58-73.

3. David Coffey, "The 'Incarnation' of the Holy Spirit in Christ," *Theological Studies* 45 (1984): 479.

4. Coffey, "The Holy Spirit as the Mutual Love of the Father and the Son," *Theological Studies* 51 (1990): 219.

5. Eugene Rogers, *After the Spirit: A Constructive Pneumatology from Resources Outside the West* (Grand Rapids: Eerdmans, 2005), p. 126.

ation.[6] As the very impress of the Spirit, Jesus Christ as the divine Son becomes the subject who, on behalf of the Father, sends forth the Spirit into the world to indwell other bodies. This indwelling thus shapes them also into the impress of the Spirit, which is the very image of the Son. It is only after the Son returns to the Father through resurrection and exaltation that the divine Son receives the Spirit from the Father in order to pour the Spirit forth on all flesh (Acts 2:33), thus taking creation up into the Son's journey of love and justice (justice in the service of love, in the service of mutual indwelling or *koinonia*).[7]

An objective pneumatology involves Jesus not only as the vindicated Son of the Father but also as the Spirit baptizer, which is his elect calling by the Father, namely, to be the life-giving spirit (1 Cor. 15:45) or the firstborn among many (Rom. 8:29). It also involves the Spirit's mission to indwell the creation by first indwelling the Son. The embrace of the Spirit thus takes ambiguous creaturely life into the circle of love and justice enjoyed within God as Father, Son, and Spirit. As such, objective pneumatology involves the personal — or, better, the interpersonal. But there is still a distinction to be made between God's act of justice that culminates in the bestowal of the Spirit (God's self-bestowal) and the creature's obedient participation in that justice by the Spirit. Spirit baptism is the place where the "objective" and "subjective" (or interpersonal) meet. In the context of Spirit baptism, justification is based on the former but involves the latter.

In light of my goal to base justification on an objective pneumatology, allow me to start with a few guiding convictions. First, it is vital to overcome the unfortunate fracture between an "objective" doctrine of justification that is solely christological and a "subjective" understanding that is pneumatological. Viewing justification through the lens of Spirit baptism will not allow for such a fracture. The Spirit is enormously significant to the objective basis of justification in Christ and thus provides the essential link to a proper understanding of the role of the creature in justification personally and interpersonally.

Second, it is vital to overcome the gap between justification in the cross and subsequent events involving Christ that are generally more widely recognized as events of the Spirit (resurrection, exaltation, and

---

6. I borrow this helpful phrase from Bernard J. Cooke, *The Distancing of God: The Ambiguity of Symbol in History and Theology* (Minneapolis: Fortress, 1990), p. 366.

7. Moltmann, *A Broad Place*, p. 329; he develops this insight further in *The Spirit of Life*, pp. 58-73.

Spirit impartation). Part of the problem here is the dominance of an Anselmian satisfaction theory of the atonement in the West, in which justification is fulfilled through Christ's restoration of divine honor at the cross. Not only does the Spirit play no necessary role in this understanding of the atonement, justification is typically viewed as objectively accomplished in the cross and not directly in the events spanning the resurrection to Pentecost. As an example of this fracture between the cross and the role of the risen Christ as a "life-giving spirit" (1 Cor. 15:45), note what Everett Harrison says in intentional resistance to the wording of Romans 4:25 (which says that Christ was "raised for our justification"):

> It may be helpful to recognize that justification, considered objectively as an aspect of God's provision, was indeed accomplished in the death of Christ and therefore did not require the resurrection to complete it.[8]

Paul would have strenuously disagreed, writing to the Corinthians that "if Christ has not been raised, your faith is futile; you are still in your sins" (1 Cor. 15:17). The resurrection and Pentecost are vital to justification even as an objectively granted provision. The resurrection of Christ cannot be reduced to a mere "proclamation" or apologetic proof of a justification fulfilled in the cross.

Lastly, the "right relation" that constitutes our justification is not primarily legal or moral but rather communal *in the Spirit.* In the Old Testament the context of covenant faithfulness is defined in other than strictly legal — or even moral — terms. It is viewed, for example, as a marriage relationship that is defined by love and intimate union (as in Hosea), even foretold as coming through a rain or shower of the Spirit (as in Joel). This faithfulness exceeds systems of justice to offer abundant grace and hope where there seems to be no possibility for either in the current situation. This is why doxology and adoration come much closer as the primary context for understanding justification in the Spirit than theories of legal or quasi-legal exchange.

The justice of God will ultimately be fulfilled for creation through a divine self-impartation that will come as a glorious and abundant rain or a flood on the earth. It will be fulfilled when the Spirit does a work on the human heart, making the law's witness to a life directed toward loving God and neighbor ongoing and dynamic. The New Testament teaches that this

---

8. Everett Harrison, *Romans,* Expositor's Bible Commentary, ed. Frank E. Gaebelein (Grand Rapids: Zondervan, 1976), p. 54.

justice is fulfilled in Christ as the man of the Spirit and in us by the indwelling of the Spirit through faith in Christ. Justification is thus "in the name of Jesus Christ and by the Spirit of God" (1 Cor. 6:11). The just relationship is a mutual indwelling between God and the sinful creature involving pardon and new creation in the very image of Christ.

With these thoughts in mind, let us reflect on the Christ event as an event of the Spirit with an eye toward understanding the basis of our justification as a divine decision and an act of self-giving. Romans 8:30 speaks of calling, justification, and glorification. Those three are inseparably linked, because justification is rooted in God's election and finds fulfillment in the glorification of creation as the habitation of God. Moltmann says: "Justification is therefore the beginning of glorification here and now, in the present; glorification is the future completion of justification."[9] Yet we must not forget that the entire purpose of these pneumatological categories is to conform creation to the image of Christ, the very impress of the Spirit (Rom. 8:29). The implication here is that Christ, as the man of the Spirit, is the elect, justified, and glorified Son of the Father in the bond of the Spirit that they share and that is opened to creation through the sojourn of Jesus on earth. We will thus begin this reflection on the objective basis for justification in the Christ event with a pneumatological theology of election and then work our way from there to its christological and pneumatological fulfillment with a special focus on the doctrine of the atonement.

Elect in the Spirit

The connection of justification to election has been a mixed blessing. On the one hand, it has historically caused justification to be wedded to a "timeless metaphysic" that "plants the kiss of death on eschatology, and on the way of salvation, and on the doctrine of justification as well."[10] On the other hand, election more biblically defined has granted justification the possibility of a larger narrative framework than that of the cross, though the latter remains vital to understanding the direction of the story. Such is implied by what I said in the preceding chapter about Israel's elect calling

9. Jürgen Moltmann, *God in Creation: A New Theology of Creation and the Spirit of God* (San Francisco: Harper and Row, 1985), p. 227.

10. G. C. Berkouwer, *Faith and Justification* (Grand Rapids: Eerdmans, 1954), p. 156.

to bear witness to the nations of the life and justice that the law and the prophets foreshadowed. In this witness, they were to channel the blessing of Abraham to the nations, a blessing that the Old Testament implies is connected to the life of the Spirit and the anointed rule of the Son of man. In Romans 9–11, the will of God to vindicate God's covenant faithfulness to both Israel and the nations is revealed in terms of its historical development and eschatological fulfillment. This text functions as the climax of the first eight chapters of Romans, in which justification is arguably the central idea. Romans 8 grounds justification in election and climaxes it in glorification (8:30). So there is no theology of justification in the Spirit apart from election.

As I have noted above, the rightwising of creation is relational and redemptive in thrust and it is also rooted in the judgment and decision of God. This is one point that the Protestants got right. There has thus rightly existed a special relationship between election and justification from the time of Augustine but especially from within the Protestant tradition. Justification in the Spirit by faith in Christ *apart from the works of the law* is really the unexpected twist in the narrative with which Paul wrestles in speaking about justification in the context of election. How can the Gentiles be blessed on the heels of Israel's having to suffer the very curse of the law? Is not the blessing of the Spirit to come to the Gentiles through Israel's faithful witness? In the light of this question, Paul will weave an intricate theological argument that will be based on a few important points. First, Paul argues in Romans 3 that the work of Christ was always the means by which God intended to bestow the Spirit and rightwise the nations. Both the law and the prophets testified implicitly to the cross and to a righteousness that comes as a gift "apart from the law": "But now a righteousness from God, apart from law, has been made known, to which the Law and the Prophets testify" (Rom. 3:21).

Second, in Romans 11, Paul exploits the fact that God has never before allowed the nation's rebellion to get in the way of the fulfillment of the promises. There have been times in which a faithful remnant needed to participate in a blessing intended for the larger nation, which is how Paul interprets the fulfillment of the promises in the context of the young but growing messianic movement. The twist is that God even used Israel's rejection to channel the promised blessing to the nations as well as to Israel.

Third, Paul's deeper argument consists of Christ's role in bearing the curse of the broken law for Israel so that, through his faithful journey in the Spirit and his impartation of the Spirit, the promised blessing could still come to the Gentiles as well as to faltering Israel. Consider Galatians 3:13-14 in this light: "Christ redeemed us from the curse of the law by becoming a curse for us, for it is written: 'Cursed is everyone who is hung on a tree.'" He redeemed us in order that the blessing given to Abraham might come to the Gentiles through Christ Jesus, so that by faith we might receive the promise of the Spirit.

Israel is still in "exile" due to the curse of the law, and Christ as the righteous King is crucified in a state of exile in the midst of Israel's failure. He bears Israel's curse and the deeper curse of Adam in which Israel participated so that, through resurrection and Spirit baptism, the Spirit might come to both Israel and the nations.[11] In his masterful conclusion of Romans 1 to 11, Paul notes that in the depth of the divine wisdom, God saw to it that both Jew and Gentile were relegated to disobedience so that both might receive the mercy of God's righteous favor in the same way, through faith in Jesus Christ as the channel of the blessing to which the law and the prophets looked forward (Rom. 11:32-36). The justification of the creation through Christ as the channel of the Spirit was not an afterthought; rather, it was built into the elect will of God, God's own self-determination and self-vindication as Creator and Lord. Justification is implicitly tied here to divine election.

Karl Barth's understanding of election is valuable to our purposes in proceeding beyond these seminal points because he defines it essentially as God's predetermined act of *self-giving* for the creation. Barth thus defines election according to its actual historical and eschatological development, especially in the story of Jesus, rather than as an abstract or timeless *decretum absolutum* (absolute decree). He begins with the insight that there "can be no Christian truth which does not from the very first contain within itself as its basis the fact that from and to all eternity God is the electing God."[12] The divine steadfastness or righteousness constitutes election for Barth (p. 126). But Barth complains that election has historically not been tied to the divine justice of God's redemptive acts but rather to the whims of a capricious and tyrannical God. "It cannot be denied," he wrote, "that there has taken place such an absolutising of the concept of electing, or of its freedom, with the accompanying influence of a non-

---

11. I am dependent in part here on N. T. Wright, *Jesus and the Victory of God,* vol. 2 of *Christian Origins and the Question of God* (Minneapolis: Fortress, 1996), pp. 576-604.

12. Karl Barth, *Church Dogmatics,* vol. 2, *The Doctrine of God,* pt. 2, ed. G. W. Bromiley and T. F. Torrance (Edinburgh: T. & T. Clark, 1957), p. 77. Hereafter, page references to this work will appear in parentheses in the text.

Christian conception of God in the history of the doctrine" (p. 25). The God of election has been described in a way closer to that of a capricious monarch than of the self-giving God depicted in the story of Jesus.

Against this trend, Barth proposes a point of departure for election in the "decision of the divine will that was fulfilled in Jesus Christ, and which had as its goal the sending of the Son of God" (p. 25). Since the Son of God is the eternal Word that was always with the Father as the Father's self-communication (John 1:1-14), there can be no elect will for creation that is somehow prior theologically to Christ (p. 101). Barth thus criticizes the historic Protestant tendency to posit an eternal "absolute decree" that is theologically prior to Christ, "which is independent of Jesus Christ and is only executed by Him" (p. 65). Under this decree, Christ becomes a subordinate and secondary decision, reduced to an instrumentalist function of bringing about what was theologically prior to him. Barth responds to this absolute decree by remarking, "What an abyss of uncertainty is opened up!" (p. 65) One then cannot know for sure who this God is who elects or what lies at the basis of this will to act. An election that is meant to be a source of security, gratitude, and joy now becomes a source of uncertainty and anxiety. Rather than looking to the depth of Jesus Christ in fathoming God's elect will for creation, we end up looking for something prior to and other than Christ, which for Barth can only be "nothingness, or rather the depth of Satan" (p. 25).

Certainly, Jesus Christ in the New Testament warrants a more central role in election than that of a mere secondary decision to serve as the instrument in the election that remains theologically prior to him. Calvin thus comes close to the truth when he refers to Jesus Christ as the "mirror of free election."[13] Taking this one insight as his point of departure, Barth is adamant that Jesus Christ "is the decree of God behind and above which there can be no earlier or higher decree and beside which there can be no other, since all others serve only the fulfillment of this decree" (p. 94). Indeed, "[b]efore Him and without Him and beside Him God does not, then, elect or will anything" (p. 94). Besides or above or behind Christ "there is no election, no beginning, no decree, no Word of God" (p. 95). Barth asks concerning the eternal Word made flesh, "If this is not election, what else can it be? What choice can precede the choice by which God has of Himself chosen to have with Himself in the beginning of all things the Word which is Jesus?" (pp. 100-101) For this reason, Christ is

---

13. Calvin, *Institutes of the Christian Religion*, 3.22.1.

"God's Word, God's decree, and God's beginning. He is so all inclusively, comprehending absolutely within Himself all things and everything, enclosing within Himself the autonomy of all other words, decrees, and beginnings" (p. 101).

Jesus Christ as the eternal Word thus "crowds out and replaces the *decretum absolutum*" (p. 103). "Jesus Christ is the divine election of grace" (p. 104). Christ is then not merely the means of bestowing favor — he *is* the favor. He is not merely one gift among others, he *is* the gift within which all others are found. He is not merely the revelation of the mystery of God in election, "He is the thing concealed within this mystery, and the revelation of it is the revelation of Himself and not of something else" (p. 104).

The election that is Jesus Christ means first of all an act of divine self-determination in which God wills from all eternity to be the God who bears this name as the covenant partner present to humanity (p. 100). "Primarily, God elected or predestined Himself" (p. 162) to be the self-giving God in Jesus Christ, and Jesus in his self-giving becomes the revelation of this electing God. It is within this elect self-determination to be the God of the Word who will bear the name Jesus that God "decides for the existence and nature of the creature" (p. 101). In the Word that was destined to become flesh in Jesus, God determined before the foundation of the world by grace and in freedom to "put Himself under obligation to man" (p. 101).

The Father chose to be the one who would send and offer up the Son for the creation, but the divine Word also determined to be the elect, "to offer up Himself and to become man in order that this covenant be made a reality" (p. 101). Election means that God does not just will to send help or aid but rather wills to send Godself into flesh to stand in the place of humanity. This self-giving or self-bestowal is essentially what Barth intends when he says that "what God ultimately wills is Himself" (p. 169). In fact, God's very "being" is this elect decision of self-giving: "God Himself is predestination" (p. 175). The salvation that flows out from this understanding of election is not an aid to human progress but rather the gift of God's own indwelling for the liberation or the death and new birth of creation.

The decree of election is thus not abstract or timeless but rather the event of Jesus Christ in which the Word became flesh and went to the cross and rose again. The decree is "not abstract but clear" because it is essentially a historical act, the event of God's becoming human and redeeming humanity in Jesus Christ (p. 158). "This decree is Jesus Christ and for this very reason it cannot be the *decretum absolutum*" (p. 158). As an extension of the election tied to the divine Word that was chosen to become flesh, "this man Jesus Christ was taken up into the will of God and made a new object of the divine decree, distinct from God" (p. 159). The eternal event of self-determination or of self-election by which God wills to be the God who is the covenant partner to humanity is played out and fulfilled in the event of Jesus Christ. In fact, election *is* this event, the entire story of Jesus. The result is that to the election of the event of Jesus "there belongs . . . electing man as well as the electing God" (p. 162).

This is Barth's understanding of double predestination: in Christ, God elects Godself to be the faithful covenant partner to humanity, and humanity is elected to be the faithful covenant partner to God. Both take place in Christ, namely, the electing God and the elected creature. "Both are God's Self-giving to man" (p. 162). Election "stands or falls with the view that in regard to the electing God and the elected man we must look and continue to look neither to the right hand nor to the left but directly at Jesus Christ" (p. 174). In Jesus Christ, humanity is taken up into God's election of the Word. This election that takes place in Jesus Christ involves both grace and judgment, but this double decree is not salvation for some and damnation for others. In Christ, God has willed salvation for humanity and damnation for Godself (p. 163). Lost humanity is elected in Jesus Christ: "It is the lost son of man who is partner of the electing God in this covenant" (p. 164). In the story of Jesus we find the story of election, in which God "took the author of evil to His bosom, and willed that the rejection and condemnation and death should be His own" (p. 167). In the eternal Word, the divine Judge has determined to be the judged for the sake of creation, because "His justice is a merciful and for this reason a perfect justice" (p. 124). Justice is fulfilled in merciful self-giving.

The creature is not excluded from election. Indeed, "God elects man in order that man may be awakened and summoned to elect God" (p. 181). Election thus has a dynamic history and an eschatological horizon. But Christ is the primary arena of decision between the electing God and the elected creature. The eternal will of God is "identical with the election of Jesus Christ," and as such "is a divine activity in the form of the history, encounter, and decision between God and man" (p. 175). We are elect only by sharing in Christ's election, only by sharing in the history of his participation in the divine favor. The fact that we are chosen "in Him" (Eph. 1:4, 11) "means in His Person, in His will, in His own divine choice, in the basic decision of God which He fulfills over against man" (p. 117). Christ's election is unique in that he is also the electing God. As such, it is only in union with this elect man that we attain the electing God: "His election is the original and all-inclusive election; the election which is absolutely unique but which, in this very uniqueness, is universally meaningful and efficacious, because it is the election of Him who Himself elects" (p. 117). Nevertheless, election extends over history to include human decision, for there is no election "except in the movement from electing God to elected man, and back again from the elected man to the electing God" (p. 186). The relationship between the electing God and elected humanity is thus "constantly renewed and refashioned" as a living history. But the two parties are not equal, and God's decision is decisive (see pp. 193-94).

There is no question but that Barth has taken the doctrine of election to another level. He has gone beyond the Calvinist reduction of election to a mysterious and hidden decree concerning those among the human race who will be saved (while leaving the others to be damned). He has also transcended the Arminian reduction of election to a rubber-stamping of human decisions. Barth wisely saw that both of these choices end up removing election from its foundational place in Christian worship and life. By wedding election to the Christ event — indeed, to Christ's very person as the eternal Word made flesh — he restores the doctrine to its role in inspiring assurance and joyful gratitude and praise.

As for the substance of Barth's teaching on election, one could only but affirm its major thrust. How could there be any divine judgment or decree that takes precedence to the divine Word made flesh? Ephesians 1:1-14, the *textus classicus* concerning election, locates election "in Christ" — or some variation of this phrase — no fewer than eleven times! Romans 8:29 makes conformity to Christ's image the very goal and purpose of election. Interestingly, 1 Peter is addressed to the elect (1 Pet. 1:1) but notes in 1 Peter 1:20 that Christ was the one who "was chosen before the creation of the world" and revealed as the chosen one "for your sake." Christ as the Son of God is the elect one, whose election was foreshadowed by Israel's election (and before that, Adam's and Eve's) and in whom we are adopted as sons and daughters of God today. There is no election prior to or beyond Christ. It may be hard for us to swallow given our anthropocentric tendencies, but we are not the central players in the drama of redemption. God is, and that also means that Christ is.

The Spirit is as well. Indeed, by the logic of Barth's own position, the Spirit is essential to election as a divine act of self-determination and self-giving into which we are drawn. Just as there is nothing theologically prior to the Word with respect to the Father, so there is also nothing prior to the

Spirit. There is no will to redeem, no openness to the other, without the Spirit of God, who enriches the bond of love between the Father and the Son and is destined to be the one in the many. Moreover, there is no event of Christ as God's election that is not also an event of the Spirit. Since Christ is called to be the Spirit baptizer, election cannot stop with the incarnation, not even with the cross and the resurrection, for Christ was destined from the beginning to be the firstborn among many brothers and sisters (Rom. 8:29). Spirit baptism links Christ as the elect to the church as those who are elect in him. Spirit baptism shows this election to be potentially without boundaries — *on all flesh.* Seen from a pneumatological lens, election does not merely lead to covenant as a legal relationship, but to mutual indwelling. Barth thus comes close to describing the goal of election when he writes that God "took the author of evil to His bosom, and willed that the rejection and condemnation and death should be His own" (p. 167). God took the sinners into the divine bosom, not only in the incarnation and the cross but also at Pentecost by indwelling them and allowing them to indwell God.

Unfortunately, Barth does not discuss the Spirit at any length in his massive treatment of election, except for an occasional reference to the electing God as triune, or to the role of the Spirit in fellowship with the electing Father and Son (pp. 53, 101, 158). There is one significant passage from Barth's discussion, however, that makes election at its very substance a drama carried out through the Spirit as "itself history, encounter, and decision, since it is an act of God Himself in His triune being as free love" (p. 184). If election involves the triune God being in self-giving love and in a way that has history, encounter, and decision, it must be pneumatological at its core. The fulfillment and vindication of God's covenant faithfulness to Israel and the nations in Jesus the Messiah essentially involves the restorative presence of the very Spirit of God. The problem is that Barth does not develop this pneumatological dimension of election, leaving the doctrine a largely binitarian one that takes place between the Father and the divine Word.

Let us pause for a moment to see how we might expand Barth's understanding of election pneumatologically. If election is eternally an act of free love by the triune God, as Barth states, then the Spirit must play a vital role in it. Concerning the Trinity, Barth notes that the Father and the Son are not in a mere relationship alongside one another; rather, they are in an "active mutual orientation and interpenetration of love" that constitutes their unity as the one God. They "are not just united but are united in the

Spirit of love."[14] Now, if the Spirit is indeed involved in the "active mutual orientation and interpenetration of love" involving the Father and the Son, then the Father eternally elects the Son "in the Spirit," and the Son determines to be the faithful Son in the same loving bond of the Spirit in response to the Father. Spirit baptism would then be the elect means by which God seeks to bring humanity into this "interpenetration" of divine love. There is dynamism to election in the correspondence between the immanent and economic dimensions of the Trinitarian life of God. Election would in effect be an eternal decision mediated by the Spirit.

Election is thus not only a divine decision to be wedded to flesh but more intimately to inhabit flesh through the Spirit-indwelt Christ. God actually created humanity to bear the divine Spirit and thus to conform to the fullness and glory of pneumatic existence in the image of the Son. Note 2 Corinthians 5:4-5:

> For while we are in this tent, we groan and are burdened, because we do not wish to be unclothed but to be clothed with our heavenly dwelling, so that what is mortal may be swallowed up by life. Now it is God who has made us for this very purpose and has given us the Spirit as a deposit, guaranteeing what is to come.

This is why Adam and Eve become living souls by the very breath of God (Gen. 2:7). We were made to eventually rise in resurrection and glorification into the fullness of pneumatic life in intimate communion with the Father through the Son.

Sin is not just breaking a commandment; it is an alienation from life. Spirit baptism through the Spirit-indwelt Christ becomes the goal of creation and the fulfillment of justice for creation. Irenaeus brilliantly points out that the Spirit rested on Jesus in order to "get accustomed to dwell in the human race, to repose on men, to reside within the work God has modeled, working the Father's will in them and renewing them from oldness to newness in Christ."[15] Indeed, Jesus was raised to be a "life-giving

---

14. Barth, *Church Dogmatics,* vol. 1, *The Doctrine of the Word,* pt. 1, trans. G. W. Bromiley, ed. G. W. Bromiley and T. F. Torrance, 2nd ed. (London: T. & T. Clark, 1975), p. 487; I am grateful to David Coffey for drawing my attention to this quote (Coffey, *Did You Receive the Holy Spirit When You Believed? Some Basic Questions for Pneumatology,* Père Marquette Lecture in Theology, 2005 (Milwaukee: Marquette University Press, 2005), pp. 91-92.

15. Irenaeus, *Against Heresies,* in *The Apostolic Fathers: Justin Martyr and Irenaeus,* rev. A. Cleveland Coxe, *Ante-Nicene Fathers,* vol. 1, ed. Alexander Roberts and James Donaldson (Peabody, MA: Hendrickson, 1994), 3.17.1.

Spirit" (1 Cor. 15:45). All flesh is elect in Christ through his role as the Spirit baptizer, for the outpouring of the Spirit upon all flesh occurs only through him. Both Christ and the Spirit are mutually at the very substance of election and of justification.

How else, we could ask, is Christ concretely the electing God and the elect creature? Is he not this as the Spirit baptizer? In other words, does Jesus not reveal the elect creature as the one who receives the Spirit, while also revealing the electing God as the one who lavishly bestows the Spirit on all flesh so that all may be sealed as God's possession or place of habitation? As I noted in the preceding chapter, the Messiah is considered vindicated as chosen of God by bearing the Spirit (cf. Isa. 61:1-3). 1 Timothy 3:16 is key here:

Beyond all question, the mystery of godliness is great:

He appeared in a body,
was *vindicated* by the Spirit,
was seen by angels,
was preached among the nations,
was believed on in the world,
was taken up in glory.

Christ is justified by the Spirit but in a way that involves other witnesses, since he appeared in the flesh, was seen even by angels and was supported by the voices of faithful witnesses to the nations. His justification "by the Spirit" could be seen as key to the entire passage, especially the blessing intended for the Gentiles, since the Holy Spirit is here the supreme witness to Christ as the vindicated Son. The justification by the Spirit may be a reference to his baptism and/or resurrection. Theologically, it could also involve his exaltation because, as Acts 2:33 implies, Christ received the Spirit in exaltation as the crucified and risen Christ in order to bestow this same Spirit on all flesh. How can Jesus represent the elect creature and the electing God aside from this event of Spirit baptism?

Paul's understanding of election is also richly pneumatological. Ephesians 1, the *textus classicus* of election, concludes with the Spirit as the agent of election. Those who have been chosen in Christ "were marked in him with a seal, the promised Holy Spirit, who is a deposit guaranteeing our inheritance until the redemption of those who are God's possession — to the praise of his glory" (Eph. 1:13-14). The elect were thus chosen in the outpouring of the Spirit, "in accordance with the riches of God's grace that he lavished on us with all wisdom and understanding" (Eph. 1:7-8). How else is grace lavished on us except in the outpouring of the Spirit? The goal of this lavish outpouring of grace is to "bring all things in heaven and on earth together under one head, even Christ" (Eph. 1:10). By faith we grasp this participation in Christ as the wellspring of grace through the indwelling of the Spirit. Christ as the elect one is the locus of the Spirit's indwelling so that in him God can take possession of creation by indwelling it.

From the incarnation to Pentecost, the divine election of humanity played out in the Christ event is expansive in nature. Barth's focus on the incarnation implies that election has broad boundaries. The divine Word was made "flesh," implying that all of humanity — indeed, the entire suffering creation — was laid claim to by God in the incarnation, when the Spirit gave the Word the anointed body of Jesus in order to anoint all flesh through him. If the Spirit is the substance of election, Pentecost must also be viewed as equally important for our understanding of the expanse of divine election. The Spirit, who wedded an anointed body to the divine Word, is to be poured out on all flesh to anoint all flesh in Christ as an inclusive and reconciling force (Acts 2). The Spirit incarnates the Word in flesh so that the Spirit-filled Christ might serve as the wellspring of life in bringing creation into the divine indwelling or divine favor. As the divine Word, Christ can pour out the Spirit on behalf of God and as God upon all flesh. As Saint Augustine reminded us, "How much must he who gives God be God! . . . He received it as a man, he poured it out as God."[16]

The creation, in which God creates life from the void by the hovering Spirit, becomes the beginning of an elect story that finds fulfillment in the work of the Spirit and the Word in the restoration and redemption of the creation as the dwelling place of God. Later, God as Word and Spirit will reach into the abyss at Jesus' crucifixion in order to bring creation into the divine embrace. Only in inhabiting the sinful creature does God fulfill humanity's calling to bear the Spirit to God's glory (Gen. 2:7; 2 Cor. 5:4-5). Justification and glorification fulfill creation in the narrative of the God who elects Godself as the self-giving God who indwells creation: "[F]or God made us for this very purpose and has given us the Spirit as a deposit, guaranteeing what is to come" (2 Cor. 5:5).

Therefore, the divine Son is eternally the Word of election deter-

---

16. Augustine, *De Trinitate*, in *On the Holy Trinity*, trans Arthur West Hadden, 1st ser., ed. Philip Schaff, NPNF (reprint; Peabody, MA: Hendrickson, 1994), 15:26.46.

mined to occupy the household created by and for him (John 1:10-12; Col. 1:15-16). Only in the regeneration and resurrection by the Spirit can the household receive the Son as the man of the Spirit and, through the Son, the heavenly Father (John 1:12-13). Election is no hidden or mysterious absolute decree but a decision and an act that is both eternal and historical. As such, it is pneumatological through and through. If God is the Spirit baptizer, or the self-giving, self-transcending God of love, the Spirit must be essential to election. The Spirit is essential to the divine self-determination as Creator and Redeemer, who will create all things to be the habitation of God and then represent the means by which the Word becomes the vehicle of the Spirit to creation (is made flesh, lives, is offered up, and raised to new life). The Spirit is the means by which the divine life is imparted to creation and the creation is taken up into the Son as the Father's will for creation. Election is a historical and an eschatological act of the Spirit, for we are chosen as recipients of lavish grace and sealed as God's possession in Christ (Eph. 1:1-14).

Since election is an eternal judgment that is enacted in history with an eschatological fulfillment, the righteousness by which we are justified in the New Testament is in essence the triumph of the divine presence in creation to bring all things into the justice and vindication of Jesus as the man of the Spirit. Justification brings life (Rom. 5:18), a life that triumphs over sin and death and reigns eternally. The divine life inhabits all things, fulfilling the purpose for which they were created and fulfilling justice for them in the context of God's covenant faithfulness or covenant *presence* as the "God with us" to make all things new. It is to this part of the drama of justification through Christ that we now turn.

Jesus' Life: Justification and the Righteousness of the Kingdom

The insight of our last chapter into justifying righteousness as covenant presence and new creation brings us to Ernst Käsemann's interpretation of divine righteousness and justification within the context of intertestamental Jewish apocalypticism. The righteousness of God is basically "God's sovereignty over the world revealed eschatologically in Jesus."[17] Re-

---

17. Ernst Käsemann, *Perspectives on Paul,* trans. Margaret Kohl (Mifflintown, PA: Sigler Press, 1996), p. 180. Hereafter, page references to this work will appear in parentheses in the text.

ferring to Galatians 5:5, Käsemann notes that justification is also future oriented, "for the ultimate righteousness of God is still to be realized." In the present situation, justification is to be viewed as the power "by which God makes his cause triumph in the world" (p. 180). The "gift itself has thus the character of power" (p. 170). Interestingly, Käsemann notes that righteousness "becomes God's gift when it takes possession of us and, so to speak, enters into us" (p. 173). The point is that "the gift which is being bestowed here is never at any time separable from the Giver. It partakes of the character of power in so far as God himself enters the arena" (p. 174). Käsemann rightly concludes that justification and sanctification "must therefore coincide, provided that by justification we mean that Christ takes power over our life" (p. 175). Justification demonstrates that "God's power reaches out for the world, and the world's salvation lies in its being recaptured for the sovereignty of God" (p. 182). "For you shall receive power when the Holy Spirit comes on you" (Acts 1:8).

Though Käsemann does not explicitly conclude that the gift of righteousness granted in justification is pneumatological in substance, his entire discussion seems to cry out for that conclusion. In speaking about the Spirit in the New Testament, we are certainly referring to the power of God present among us to reestablish us within the lordship or righteousness of Christ (cf. Matt. 12:28; Acts 1:8; 1 Cor. 2:4-5; 12:3; Eph. 3:16-19). There is, in fact, an implied doctrine of justification in Jesus' inauguration of the kingdom of God in his lifetime as the man of the Spirit.

The righteousness of God as a coming power that enters into us in order to reestablish God's lordship on the earth should be seen within the context of the Old Testament prophecies concerning the coming righteousness or the coming of the Spirit as a rain or a flood that will envelop and pervade our beings, create in us a heart dedicated to God's law, and cause us to walk in God's ways. According to N. T. Wright, this understanding of righteousness should also be viewed in the context of the centrality of the Temple to Jewish understandings of God's presence and lordship on the earth.[18] As I have noted above, Jeremiah 7:5-11 points out that the Temple was to be the place where God dwells with his people so long as the people do not forget God's ways of justice (pp. 418-19). The Temple had become the focal point of hope and national liberation as well as security against the pagans (p. 420). The destruction of the Temple led to a theol-

---

18. Wright, *Jesus and the Victory of God*, 2:333-428. Hereafter, page references to this work will appear in parentheses in the text.

ogy of the *Shekinah* as the presence of God to bear Israel's suffering in exile and to lead them back to the land of promise.[19]

The centrality of the Temple to the divine presence and favor within Israel would change with the coming of the Spirit-anointed Messiah. John the Baptist's ministry was already seen as a challenge to the central place of the Temple in the piety of Judaism, or "as an alternative to the temple ritual."[20] His announcement of the coming Messiah as the *Spirit* baptizer sealed Jesus' revolutionary identity as the one who will function to both fulfill and replace the Temple as the center of restoration through the life of God's Spirit. Jesus, in the Gospels and Acts, thus announces a coming judgment on the Temple that implies his own role in taking its place as the locus of the divine presence and favor (Mark 14:58; 15:29-30; Matt. 26:61; 27:39-40; John 2:19; Acts 6:14), as Wright points out (pp. 334-35). It is not the Temple that will guarantee the presence and favor of God, but Jesus as Immanuel, meaning "God with us" (Matt. 1:23). Jesus will be the new temple and his people the New Jerusalem (Acts 7:46f.). Israel's center in the presence and favor of God shifts to Jesus and the vindication of God's people, and their witness shifts to Christ as well (pp. 338-39).

The cleansing of the Temple called into question deeply entrenched segregations between pure and impure, accepted and outcast, and Jew and Gentile; and it shifted the locus of God's presence and favor to Jesus in his table fellowship with sinners. As the Spirit baptizer, Jesus justifies by opening the sacred presence and favor of God to the impure and the outcast. Jesus' act of cleansing the Temple, while quoting Jeremiah 7:11, indicates that God's judgment had decisively come down on the current religious system in favor of Jesus himself as the locus of God's redemptive presence. Most likely, this action in the Temple was prominent in causing Jesus' crucifixion for blasphemy.

Jesus' Last Supper was connected to the Passover meal, but it was probably observed on the day before Passover (according to John's testimony in John 13:1-2) as a distinct act that again signaled a shifting of Israel's journey with God from the Temple and the religious life of Israel to Jesus (pp. 557-58). Such a shift in the center of Israel's life to Jesus must have seemed like a lofty claim to those who caught glimpses of it. But Jesus

19. Moltmann, *The Spirit of Life*, pp. 47-51.

20. James D. G. Dunn, *Christology in the Making*, vol. 1, *Jesus Remembered* (Grand Rapids: Eerdmans, 2003), p. 359, quoted in David A. Brandos, *Paul on the Cross: Reconstructing the Apostle's Story of Redemption* (Minneapolis: Fortress, 2006), p. 34.

would be vindicated in his claim to be the new temple of God's presence. Wright notes that the destruction of the Temple in the Olivet Discourse (e.g., Mark 13) was implicitly tied to Jesus' vindication as the rightful king in the kingdom of God and center of God's presence and favor on the earth (p. 342). His actions in setting people free, healing them, and pardoning sins shifted the locus of the divine presence and favor to him, "implicitly making the Temple redundant" (p. 362). His resurrection from the dead and exaltation to the right hand of the Father was the decisive vindication. It was then that Christ received the Spirit from the Father to bestow it upon all flesh, thus opening God's presence and favor to all people and setting in motion an eschatological turning of God's people into the new temple, the New Jerusalem, and all of creation into the habitation of God. The Temple in Jerusalem will be destroyed, but when Christ's body (temple) is killed, he will raise it up in three days (John 2:19-21). Christ's vindication as the vehicle of the Spirit's presence in Israel becomes part of the "controlling story" of Jesus' life (p. 363). No wonder all four Gospels and Acts announce him chiefly as the Spirit baptizer.

Jesus' life ministry thus appropriately begins with the descending of the Spirit upon him at his baptism, accompanied by the Father's heavenly voice affirming Jesus as indeed the beloved Son (e.g., Matt. 3:16-17). This decisive shift in the location of God's presence and favor occurs at the Jordan at John's baptism or at the margins of Israel's religious life. But this event is central to the dawn of the kingdom of God in the world. This event is prefaced by John the Baptist's preaching both the nearness of the kingdom of God (Matt. 3:2) and the Messiah's coming role as the one who will bestow the Spirit in judgment and restoration (Matt. 3:11-12). The implication is clear: the Messiah as the possessor of the Spirit will inaugurate the kingdom of God by becoming the decisive dwelling place of God and by mediating the Spirit to others. Jesus provides a foreshadowing of his role as Spirit baptizer by setting people free in the realm of the Spirit's presence: "But if I drive out demons by the Spirit of God, then the kingdom of God has come upon you" (Matt. 12:28).

God's rule will be accomplished not by enslaving creation, for this is the practice of the dark powers that he has come to overthrow. Jesus inaugurates God's rule by liberating people to righteousness in the realm of the Spirit. The righteousness of the kingdom reaches out especially to the weak and oppressed, to those who cry out for mercy and justice; it is present at that place of utter helplessness for all, even those who live the deluded existence of power and feed off exploitation but who wish to repent.

Its doors are wide, inviting all who seek freedom through genuine repentance. It is a gift in the realm and in the power of the transforming Spirit before it ever becomes a work. It opens possibilities for life where all religious and political systems fail. Michael Welker insightfully reminds us:

> Liberation from sin is brought by the bearer of the Spirit, Jesus Christ, who intercedes prior to the level of our capacity for betterment, be it moral or whatever. That liberation intercedes *before* the forces of public capacity for renewal can be put to the test — and fail. . . . When Jesus cures the sick or drives out demons, he intercedes in situations in which we see ourselves condemned to helplessness and feel ourselves paralyzed; where patience is of no avail and time does not heal; where the empty phrases by which we seek to assuage and encourage stick in our throat; where one lives between a sense of powerlessness and apathy and outbreaks of anxiety and despair.[21]

As Welker notes, sin is not just a moral wrong but an idolatry that alienates one from the very life force that brings people into relationship with God and others and that causes life to flourish as God intended. Sin ultimately defined is thus a blasphemy against the Spirit, the Spirit of life (Matt. 12:30-32). "Sin issues in the *destruction of the foundations of regeneration.*"[22] Therefore, pardon for sin can never be a mere clean slate or a declared word from a distant court but rather deliverance and new birth through a divine embrace at the very core of our existence. Miroslav Volf says that for*giving* is a form of divine self-*giving*.[23] Justification or rightwising can never be a mere legal declaration or an enabling for the attainment of virtues. It is a reaching into the alienation and hopelessness of the hell into which creation has fallen in order to bring that hell into the divine presence and embrace — so as to restore true life and hope. Only the truly repentant can enter in, only those who ride the stream of the Spirit toward letting go of the idolatry that binds and alienates, so that all that is left is a cry for mercy that can press through to liberty.

Jesus always taught that the Temple functioned as the place where God's favor is concentrated as long as it remained a place of humble repen-

---

21. Michael Welker, "The Holy Spirit," *Theology Today* 46, no. 1 (April 1989): 13-14 (italics in original).

22. Welker, "Holy Spirit," p. 13 (italics in original).

23. Volf, "Being as God Is: Trinity and Generosity," in *God's Life in Trinity*, ed. Miroslav Volf and Michael Welker (Minneapolis: Augsburg Fortress, 2006), p. 7.

tance and just regard for others, which is why his role as the new temple is linked to God's judgment on Israel. We must read Luke's understanding of justification in this context, and I will quote the passage in full:

> To some who were confident of their own righteousness and looked down on everybody else, Jesus told this parable: "Two men went up to the temple to pray, one a Pharisee and the other a tax collector. The Pharisee stood up and prayed about himself: 'God, I thank you that I am not like other men — robbers, evildoers, adulterers — or even like this tax collector. I fast twice a week and give a tenth of all I get.' But the tax collector stood at a distance. He would not even look up to heaven, but beat his breast and said, 'God, have mercy on me, a sinner.' I tell you that this man, rather than the other, went home justified before God. For everyone who exalts himself will be humbled, and he who humbles himself will be exalted." (Luke 18:9-14)

Luke includes this tradition in order to take aim at the Pharisees, "who were confident in their own righteousness." This confidence finds expression in the pharisaical prayer of gratitude for a perceived superiority over the tax collector with regard to faithfulness to the law. On the other hand, the tax collector has no such illusions of superior standing; he only wants God's mercy. Luke has Jesus conclude the story with the notion that the repentant tax collector who confessed his sin went away "justified," and the Pharisee, who relied on his outward observance of the law for his approval from God, did not. The implication is clear: the temple can be a place of both self-righteousness and repentance. But justification will come only to those who cry out for mercy with repentant hearts.

It is clear on the surface of this story that what is at stake hinges on whether or not one is dependent on God's mercy alone for access to the gift of God's righteousness. Of course, this dependence is crucial to the story. Jesus rejects any other dependence, even on God's holy law. In its witness to God's righteousness, the law cannot make one righteous. Rightwising is God's work. To absolutize anything other than God shifts the credit from God to humans and grants people a capacity that they do not possess. Ironically, it even contradicts the very witness of the law to the prior grace and power of God to redeem, as in the exodus from Egypt, which originally provided the framework in which the law was to be interpreted (Exod. 20:1-3), or in the promise of the coming circumcision of the heart by the Spirit (Deut. 30:6).

Jesus thus "taught a doctrine of the justification of sinners by the outgoing righteousness of God."[24] One could refer to the parables of the prodigal son (Luke 15:11-32), the laborers in the vineyard (Matt. 20:1-16), and the Great Supper (Luke 14:16-24). One could also quote Jesus' sayings concerning his mission to save sinners and his relationships with sinful people (e.g., Zacchaeus; see Luke 19:1-10). Jesus' merciful acts of healing also supported a rightwising by grace. Indeed, Jesus identified himself with the suffering servant who will "justify many" (Isa. 53:11).[25] His open table fellowship invited both the outcast and the guardians of the law to sup together in fulfillment of the righteousness of the kingdom (Luke 15). Jesus will arise as the new temple of God's righteous presence and favor.

There is no question but that the above Lukan text about the Pharisee and the publican reveals that justification in Luke implicitly contains a social dimension, since the tax collector, receiving no mercy from others due to his life as an outcast, can only seek mercy from God. The Pharisee, on the other hand, enjoys social recognition due to his standing within the Jewish community, denies mercy to the tax collector, and instead boasts of his superiority.[26] In other words, the one who cries out for mercy in the midst of social rejection is justified rather than the one who denies mercy in an effort to celebrate or to protect his own social standing. In this parable, justification cuts to the root of social privilege and its use to both celebrate one's own attainment of God's bounty and to deny this bounty to others.

In a similar vein, Jesus tells another parable about a man who is journeying from afar to the Temple to leave an offering at the altar. Just before he completes this act, however, he remembers his offense against his brother. He places the offering to the side and journeys back home to reconcile with his brother before traveling back to the Temple to complete the ritual. Clearly, Jesus is foreshadowing a doctrine of justification in the midst of a justly reconciled and reconciling community that is open to all and centered on Jesus as the new temple of God, or the locus for the Spirit's dwelling.

This is how justification functioned in the life of Jesus as the bearer of

24. Alan Richardson, *An Introduction to the Theology of the New Testament* (New York: Harper and Row, 1958), p. 81.

25. Richardson, *Theology of the New Testament*, pp. 81-82.

26. Stephanie Harrison, "The Case of the Pharisee and the Tax Collector: Justification and Social Location in Luke's Gospel," *Currents in Theology and Mission* 32, no. 2 (Apr. 2005): 99-111, esp. 99-100.

the Spirit in the larger context of ancient Jewish society. It is up to theologians today to discuss how it can function in the secular, pluralist, or religious societies of our world. How do we, in celebrating our privilege, deny grace to others who lack the qualities that we attribute to being young, intelligent, wealthy, white, male, or physically "able"?[27] How does justification cut at the root of such privilege, and what kind of community in the Spirit of all grace does justification by grace suggest today? Can we bear witness to the vindicated Messiah, who was unjustly executed, if we do not cultivate among ourselves the justice of God as a community of the Spirit?[28] Can we worship an unjustly condemned but vindicated Jesus while ignoring the unjustly condemned of the earth?

Luke may help us connect Paul's doctrine of justification with Jesus' teaching about the righteousness or justice of the kingdom of God. In 1997, Jürgen Moltmann wrote an essay entitled "Was heist heute 'evangelisch'?" (What does the term "evangelical" mean today?), which aimed to probe that connection.[29] Under the influence of Christoph Blumhardt, a pietist-turned-socialist pastor, Moltmann there describes his own journey as an evangelical theologian from justification to the kingdom of God, "from a theology of faith to a theology of hope."[30] He elaborates on this shift in a subsequent essay, entitled "Die Rechtfertigung Gottes" (The Justification of God).[31] In both these essays Moltmann takes aim at the historical limitations of the justification doctrine, which was shaped more by the medieval preoccupation with penance than by the scriptural teaching about the life-giving reign of God's righteousness in the world. His complaint about traditional Protestant understandings of justification by faith is that they tended to restrict themselves to a theology of the cross and to pardon for

---

27. I am grateful to Amos Yong for introducing me to the issue of the oppression suffered by persons with disabilities by the prevalence of "ableism" in our culture. See Yong, *Theology and Down Syndrome: Reimagining Disability in Late Modernity* (Waco, TX: Baylor University Press, 2007).

28. This is Mark Heim's riveting question with regard to the atonement of Jesus. Using René Girard's understanding of the role of the scapegoat in society, Heim develops an understanding of Jesus' death as an unjust murder due to the effort to scapegoat him. Jesus returns in resurrection — not in vengeance but in grace. The result is a just community that gathers around him and resists the injustices attached to scapegoating. See Heim, *Saved from Sacrifice: A Theology of the Cross* (Grand Rapids: Eerdmans, 2006).

29. Moltmann, "Was heist heute 'evangelisch'? Von der Rechtfertigungslehre zur Reich-Gottes-Theologie," *Evangelische Theologie* 57 (1997): 41-46.

30. Moltmann, "Was heist heute 'evangelisch'?" p. 42.

31. Moltmann, "Die Rechtfertigung Gottes," *Stimmen der Zeit* 7 (July 2001): 435-42.

the sinner, which is then expanded as a universal human category without a proper differentiation between perpetrators and victims of injustice.

The righteousness of the kingdom of God, however, involves hope for those who suffer as victims of evil in the world, as well as those who benefit from injustice in isolation from them. It is not restricted to the cross but also involves the resurrection and Pentecost. It is not restricted to pardon for sin but also promises liberation from sin's oppression, especially for the victims of sin, and for those who are most responsible for perpetrating it as well. In the same year that Moltmann's more elaborate essay appeared, I published an essay that forged a direction similar to his but that was independent of his essay: I used Käsemann's development of the Pauline doctrine of justification as an apocalyptic concept dedicated to the victory of God's righteousness in the world through the Spirit of life.[32]

Though I centered my focus on Paul in that essay, I could very well have focused on Luke and other synoptic Gospels as well. The thrust of Luke's story of the Pharisee and the publican fits well with Luke's emphasis on Jesus as the man of the Spirit who has come to bring divine favor to the poor and the oppressed (Luke 4:18), especially through Spirit baptism. As in the other synoptics, the righteousness of the kingdom of God sets people free and ushers them into the realm of God's favor by ushering them into the realm of God's Spirit. The inauguration of the kingdom of God and its righteousness in the world comes by the Spirit of mercy and justice, to which the law has implicitly borne witness — and not the guardians of the law. Therefore, Luke is hard on the guardians of the law who seek to justify their rejection of the outcasts via their perceived obedience to the law (note the parables of the elder son [Luke 15:1-2, 11-32] and the Good Samaritan [Luke 10:25-37]).

The righteousness of the kingdom not only relativizes the law, it also fulfills the law's true inner witness. In this prioritizing of mercy, the righteousness of the kingdom fulfills the heart of the law, which is love for God and neighbor (Mark 12:33; Deut. 6:4-5). Jesus fulfills righteousness by going into the baptismal waters in search of the lost and the outcast and then announcing the coming reign of God through a justice defined by mercy (Matt. 3:15). Mercy and justice trump religious ceremony as the truly "weighty" matters of the law (Matt. 23:23).

But it is not the law that will bring the promised fulfillment of righ-

---

32. Macchia, "Justification through New Creation: The Holy Spirit and the Doctrine by which the Church Stands or Falls," *Theology Today* 58, no. 2 (July 2001): 202-17.

teousness; rather, it is the liberating power of the Spirit required by the heart of the law itself (Matt. 12:28; cf. Rom. 14:17). The righteousness of the kingdom thus reorients life around a table fellowship that involves both the religious and the outcasts who are judged as unclean (e.g., Luke 14 and 15; cf. Gal. 2). It embraces them both in mercy and with the hope that they will all partake of the justice of the kingdom and share the same with each other. The righteousness of the kingdom is a sphere of life into which one enters and by which one lives by trusting in the mercy of God and forming a willingness to be a channel of mercy to others. One is born into it from above (John 1:12-13; 3:3-15). It is described as a feast and a celebration rather than as a set of routine ceremonial obligations (John 2:1-11): it is the realm of the Spirit into which one is "baptized."

It is important at this point to note the crucial role of the cross in the fulfillment of the kingdom of God on earth. The cross is not incidental to the fulfillment of the kingdom. Mark's Gospel, for example, says that the cross is crucial to Jesus' destiny as the man of sorrows and as a ransom for the rescue of sinners (e.g., Mark 10:45). In looking at the drama of justification as enacted and revealed in the Christ event as an event of the Spirit, we should focus for a moment on the meaning of the cross, especially since the New Testament highlights the cross as of particular importance. In an effort to shift the believer's righteousness before God from the sacrament of penance to a more secure foundation, the Reformers placed the theological focus of justification on the atonement, for which they had biblical precedent (Rom. 3:25).

Pentecostals also focus on the power of the cross for justification, except that they tend to see the cross as that which mediates the Spirit of life to the cursed, the diseased, and the dying. We will proceed inspired by this direction of thought rather than the Anselmian direction that influenced historic Protestant and Catholic atonement theories. I will not attempt to merely dismiss that direction, since it had a marginal biblical connection. Instead, I will attempt to take note of the serious limitations of the theory and its problematic influence on the doctrine of justification, especially in separating justification from the life of the Spirit.

Beyond Anselm: Atonement and the Mediation of the Spirit

Jesus died while we were yet sinners (Rom. 5:8). "And with one stroke, justification as occurring through grace alone is all but exclusively tied to

Christ's death."[33] I would say that justification is not *exclusively* tied to the cross, but it is *focused* there. It is focused there, however, as the place where the Spirit's presence is most profoundly at work as a source of grace in the midst of the worst of blasphemy, sin, and death. As I have noted above, the *Shekinah* presence of God became in Judaism the presence of God in the midst of Israel's suffering and as a presence in the return journey to the land of promise. Foundational to a theology of the cross is Jesus' conviction that he inaugurated the kingdom of God by being the new center of God's indwelling presence and hence of divine favor and vindication among sinners and outcasts.

What is often neglected in theologies of atonement is the importance of the cross as a vital component of the means by which the Spirit is bestowed on all flesh in the midst of alienation and death, in spite of the fact that Jesus says in numerous places that his death would lead to the granting of God's eschatological presence to many. For example, Jesus declares that "unless a kernel of wheat falls to the ground and dies, it remains only a single seed. But if it dies, it produces many seeds" (John 7:24). He follows that with an additional commentary about his death: "But I, when I am lifted up from the earth, will draw all men to myself" (John 7:32). Indeed, Paul affirms that Jesus is delivered over to the cross in order to become the first among many brothers and sisters (Rom. 8:29-32). Despite such hints that the cross mediates the eschatological drawing of creation into Christ's body by the Spirit, the cross has tended to be viewed as an abstract drama of justice played out between the Father and the Son that has its own meaning quite apart from Pentecost. It was Anselm who was mainly responsible for this trend, and before proceeding any further, it behooves us to look closely at his understanding of atonement.

Satisfaction in the Middle Ages consisted of a payment that was offered and was sufficient to make amends for a wrong committed or an honor offended. Anselm's satisfaction theory of the atonement assumed that Christ's death was the adequate payment necessary for atonement to occur between God and humanity. This theory of the atonement dominated Western theology, both Catholic and Protestant, from the Middle Ages to the modern era. More recently it has come under a barrage of criticism. In establishing critical distance from this theory, Gustaf Aulen maintains that the *Christus Victor* understanding of the atonement (Christ as

---

33. Roy A. Harrisville, *Fracture: The Cross as Irreconcilable in the Language and Thought of the Biblical Writers* (Grand Rapids: Eerdmans, 2006), p. 98.

victor over the powers of darkness on the cross) was Luther's atonement theory and that Luther held this theory in common with classic descriptions of Christ's death found in the New Testament and the church fathers. I agree with Aulen that the *Christus Victor* understanding of Christ's death is found in Luther and goes back to the patristics and the New Testament; but the satisfaction theory is in Luther as well. For example, quite in line with the prevailing atonement theory of his day, Luther says:

> In addition, it follows that our sins are so great, so infinite and invincible, that the whole world could not make satisfaction for even one of them. Certainly the greatness of the ransom — namely, the blood of the Son of God — makes it sufficiently clear that we can neither make satisfaction for our sin nor prevail over it.[34]

For Luther, only Christ's satisfaction for our sin is adequate to support our assurance of salvation. Though Luther interfaced it with ransom (as did Anselm himself), satisfaction is still part of Luther's theological imagination.

At the core of Anselm's satisfaction theory of atonement is his understanding of divine justice. Anselm viewed justice fundamentally as God the Creator's right to be Lord over the creation, for in atonement "God recover[s] his right." Not always recognized as Anselm's point of departure, this insight into God's right as Creator and Lord is quite biblical. For Anselm, however, God's very *honor* is at stake in maintaining and respecting this right. Anselm says, therefore, that justice in the final analysis supports God's honor and dignity as Lord: "God maintains nothing with more justice than the honor of his own dignity." By sinning against God and submitting to the alien lordship of the devil, humanity made God the "loser."[35] Human sin is the chief injustice because it directly challenges God's right as Creator over humanity, which is an affront to God's honor. Anselm notes: "So then, everyone who sins ought to pay back the honor of which he has robbed God; and this is the satisfaction which every sinner owes to God" (1:11). In the case of God and humanity, however, the debt of an offering that would restore honor to the Creator is too great to imagine. Humanity stands before an unreachable debt with regard to both the mag-

---

34. Luther, "Lectures on Galatians 1535," in *Luther's Works,* ed. Jaroslav Pelikan (St. Louis: Concordia, 1963), 26:33.

35. Saint Anselm, *Cur Deus Homo,* in *Saint Anselm: Basic Writings,* trans. S. N. Deane (La Salle, IL: Open Court, 1968), 1:13. Hereafter, references to this work will appear in parentheses in the text.

nitude of the sin that offends God's honor and the magnitude of the compensation worthy of restoring that honor adequately.

The emphasis on restoring honor to an offended lord made a great deal of sense in Anselm's feudalistic worldview, in which the entire network of life depended on adherence to a reciprocity involving both the lord's commitment to provide protection and care and the serf's obligation to return honor and loyalty to the lord. Anselm expanded this social network, applied analogously to God, to include all of creation. For Anselm, sin would cause "in the very universe that God ought to control, the violation of the beauty of arrangement, and God would appear to be deficient in his management" (1:15). Further, in the background of Anselm's thinking lay the cosmic harmony and hierarchy and their connection with the divine nature so typical of the Neo-Platonic worldview.[36] If God overlooks this affront to the divine honor as Creator and Lord, "either God will not be just to himself, or he will be weak in respect to both parties; and this is too impious even to think of" (1: 13).

Anselm's emphasis on divine honor and dignity helps to explain why God requires satisfaction from humanity for sin. Anselm admits that God is bound by no law and could forgive freely without payment; but to do so would still not restore the honor that was bruised by the human race. Furthermore, to do so would trivialize sin and remove any real distinction between guilt and innocence. If God overlooks sin, "there is no longer any difference between the guilty and the not guilty, and this is unbecoming to God." Anselm concludes, concerning God, that "it does not belong to his liberty or compassion or will to let the sinner go unpunished who makes no return to God of what the sinner has defrauded him" (1:12). For God to be true to Godself, God must require payment from humanity: "God's compassion cannot contradict God's justice for God to be consistent with himself" (1:24). Rather than view divine justice and compassion as mutually defining categories, Anselm sees them in tension and in need of reconciliation.

For Anselm, only humanity can make satisfaction for sin against God, for only humanity has challenged and bruised the divine right of God as Lord over the creation. If the devil had ensnared humans against their will, God could simply overthrow this alien power without the need for satisfaction. Anselm admits that "in an evil angel, there can be no justice

---

36. S. Rodger, "Anselm: An Orthodox Perspective," *Greek Orthodox Theological Review* 34, no. 1 (Spring 1989): 27.

at all. There was no reason, therefore, as respects the devil, why God should not make use of his own power against him for the liberation of man" (1: 7). The problem is that humanity *freely* conspired with the devil against God and submitted to an alien lordship. In this case, it is only fitting that God respond to the seriousness and magnitude of human sin and in faithfulness to God's own honor as rightful Lord over creation require satisfaction from humanity. The principle is ironclad, and God must require sufficient satisfaction from humanity for atonement to occur: "So that, as by man God suffered loss, by man, also, he might recover his loss" (1:8).

According to Anselm, satisfaction made by humanity must be equal to the magnitude of the eternal right and honor that was damaged by human sin. The price paid for satisfaction, therefore, must be "be greater than all the universe" or eternal in significance (2:7). Anselm rejects the medieval notion that satisfaction must be paid to the devil to release humanity from slavery to an alien lordship. Nothing is owed to the devil. But humanity owes a debt to God for freely submitting to the devil's lordship. Therefore, satisfaction must involve the overthrow of the devil's lordship by humanity, something that is equally out of humanity's reach:

> God was in no need of descending from heaven to conquer the devil, nor of contending against him in holiness to free mankind. But God demanded that man should conquer the devil, so that he who had offended by sin should atone by holiness. As God owed nothing to the devil but punishment, so man must only make amends by conquering the devil as man had already been conquered by him. (2:19)

Here arises the quandary in which humanity is found. Humanity must make eternal payment for the magnitude of sin and overthrow the devil in the process, but humans are unable as finite and fallen beings to do so. God is the only one who can perform such satisfaction, but God has no need to make any such payment, since God is not in the wrong. Humanity must make satisfaction but cannot; God can make satisfaction but is not the one for whom it is appropriate to do so. As Anselm puts it, "For God will not do it, because he has no debt to pay; and man will not do it, because he cannot" (2:7). How, then, can satisfaction for sin be made?

The answer for Anselm is the God-man, Jesus Christ. Only Christ is both perfect God and perfect man. Therefore, only he has both the divine power to make satisfaction as well as the fittingness as a human being to make such satisfaction on behalf of humanity (2:7). The person who makes satisfaction must be fully divine, since only God has the power to overthrow the devil and make adequate satisfaction, but also fully human, since it is only fitting and just that a representative of the human race make the payment for it. Though it is only fitting that a human make satisfaction, Anselm is clear that, only in being divine, can the man Jesus do this. Anselm even develops this admission, strangely enough, in order to maintain that in essence it is God making satisfaction after all: "[S]ince he is very God, the Son of God, he offered himself for his own honor as well as for that of the Father and the Holy Spirit" (2:18). But how is this possible if it is morally inappropriate for God to make satisfaction? Does doing it through the agency of a man make the divine agency in satisfaction somehow appropriate? Why? Anselm is nowhere clear on this.

There are, of course, other points of tension and difficulty in Anselm's arguments. First, Anselm assumes throughout his treatise that satisfaction performed by a human being on behalf of humanity is necessary due to the demands of God's moral character, and not only because of the seriousness of sin and the requirements of the moral order created by God. However, when pressed on the sovereignty of God's will, Anselm concedes that human satisfaction is necessary *only because God wills it.* Concerning the necessity of Christ's incarnation and death, Anselm says that "they were to be because they were; and if you wish to know the real necessity of all things which he did and suffered, know that they were because of necessity, because he wished them to be. But no necessity preceded his will" (2: 18). One could argue that, for Anselm, satisfaction as a human payment is fitting to God as "just" because God determined that God should be just in precisely this way. In other words, God is morally self-determining. But, in that case the entire necessity of satisfaction shifts from what is fitting or necessary to God to what God considers fitting or necessary with regard to the world.

But how does one know how God has determined to be just with respect to the world? There is a long-standing tradition within Christian theology in support of looking to *revelation* for this answer, particularly what is revealed in the cross. The whole thrust of Anselm's recoil at the thought of God's providing atonement without human payment loses its force unless we can successfully make the case that revelation supports precisely this understanding of God's moral self-determination. The argument then shifts from assumptions concerning God's moral character to the locus of revelation by which one principally discerns the direction of God's moral self-determination. The question then becomes where revelation is to be found. Is revelation to be found principally in God's law, in some philosophical, cultural, or legal understanding of the moral order of creation? If one interprets God's moral self-determination principally in the light of the cross, which arguably both "fractures" and fulfills all other religious understandings of God, an argument can be made that God required no human satisfaction in order to establish justice out of the *excess* of grace poured out for humanity in the gift of the Spirit.

The notion of a debt required of humanity by God as a precondition of atonement is difficult to establish from Scripture, especially from the narratives most directly dealing with Christ's passion and death. I agree with Martin Hengel's conclusion that the New Testament broke with the martyr cults of the ancient world by defining atonement as God's act of reconciliation rather than a human effort to assuage the wrath of God: "God, as the subject of the saving event, reconciled to himself his unfaithful creatures, who had become his enemies."[37] Anselm would have disagreed, finding in the cross the necessity of payment to assuage God's wrath and to restore honor. However one decides this issue, does not the entire debate now hinge on how one interprets the cross? In other words, rather than our understanding of the cross arising from some presumption about God's moral character or self-determination, or the moral order of the universe, our discernment of God's moral character or self-determination arises primarily from our understanding of the cross. In the end, Anselm needed to make his case for the necessity of satisfaction on the basis of what the New Testament teaches about the death of Jesus. This obligation is especially true in the light of our previous discussion of justice in the Old Testament as defined by God's own covenant faithfulness to humanity rather than by abstract norms or principles.

Furthermore, the Father and the Holy Spirit are largely absent in Anselm's satisfaction atonement theory, functioning as little more than wounded and dishonored spectators waiting to be healed and reconciled. Where is the role of the Father in delivering up the favored Son on behalf of humanity or of the Spirit in anointing the Son and bearing up under the blasphemy of the cross? Where is the faithful Christ as the man of the Spirit and the channel of the Spirit to sinful humanity? Anselm's belief that honor is restored once humanity overthrows the alien lordship of the

---

37. Hengel, *The Atonement: The Origins of the Doctrine in the New Testament*, trans. John Bowden (Philadelphia: Fortress, 1981), p. 31.

devil and submits to God's lordship holds potential for a pneumatological understanding of the atonement. But this requires development, because it functions in Anselm as subordinate to the restoration of honor assumed to be fulfilled in the cross. So long as the conviction exists that the atoning act of payment and overthrow is fulfilled in the quasi-legal metaphor of the cross, the emphasis remains on human payment to God rather than on the liberation of creation caused by God's self-giving and self-offering to humanity.

For Anselm, justice is, in fact, not so much fulfilled in the faithful self-giving of God to sinful humanity as through a payment made in order to fulfill a quasi-legal transaction. Humanity through Jesus frees itself for God and restores honor to God through the satisfaction of the cross. The requirements of payment are met there. In this view of atonement, the resurrection, the exaltation, and the baptizing of all flesh in the Spirit become addenda to the act of justice in the cross rather than as essential components of it. This is precisely how Pentecost was severed from the cross — and the Spirit from justification — in Christian theology. This is not meant to deny that the cross is an event of reconciliation in its own right in the sense that God descends there into the abyss to take the God-forsaken into the divine bosom. It only means that the goal of the embrace of the cross is the embrace of human hearts and communities through Pentecost, and that the two cannot be separated. If we are ever to recover the ancient integration of justification and the Spirit, we must heal the breach between the cross and Pentecost.

Anselm's satisfaction theory has more recently come under critical scrutiny for a variety of reasons, especially for its advocacy of divine violence. Schleiermacher remarks that the notion of righteousness applied to God in the vicarious satisfaction doctrine is taken from "the crudest human conditions."[38] A heavenly Father whose honor or dignity is restored through the brutal murder of his Son conjures up images of an oppressive and even sadistic patriarch and what would now be judged as child abuse.[39] Moltmann has sought to correct the Anselmian image of a heavenly Father as a patriarch or lord whose honor is restored through the sacrifice of a human life by portraying God the Father as suffering with the Son in the Son's act of self-giving on the cross. The cross then becomes

38. Schleiermacher, *The Christian Faith* (Philadelphia: Fortress, 1976), p. 460.

39. Flora A. Keshgegian, "The Scandal of the Cross: Revisiting Anselm and His Feminist Critics," *Anglican Theological Review* 82, no. 3 (Summer 2000): 475-92.

God's way of incorporating the suffering of humanity into Godself so that the divine life could conquer it along with sin and death.[40]

Having difficulty with any notion of human violence as willed by God, J. Denny Weaver has sought a nonviolent theory of atonement in critical distance from Anselm's satisfaction theory. Jesus' death thus becomes the natural consequence of the inauguration of the kingdom of God within a violent world.[41] But this idea of natural consequence does not adequately take into consideration those texts in which Jesus describes his mission as directed toward giving his life (e.g., John 12:23-27). From the Father, Jesus felt a sense of destiny toward this end (e.g., Mark 8–10).

S. Mark Heim probes deeper to note that God could have willed for Jesus to accept death in some way other than crucifixion. But death through violent crucifixion was the divinely strategic means due to the fact that murderous scapegoating is the place where human evil is played out at its worst. Rather than Jesus' crucifixion being romanticized to cover its fundamental injustice, it becomes the means by which the true nature of human evil is exposed and genuine grace offered to overcome it. Heim has brilliantly shown that Anselm's satisfaction theory has played into the tendency described by the French thinker René Girard for cultures to romanticize the unjust murder of scapegoats by turning their murder into an offering for peace, thus silencing their cries of abandonment or for justice, something that the crucifixion narratives do not do. Heim concludes that the cross thus "undermines redemptive violence not glorifies it."[42] I will return to this issue of the cross as a sacrifice in a moment.

The adequacy of Anselm's satisfaction theory of atonement in terms of its faithfulness to the biblical witness has been called into question as well, including by evangelical sources. Joel B. Green and Mark D. Baker conclude that "Anselm offers a less than biblical view of the cross — not because he uses terms like vassal or satisfaction that are foreign to biblical texts on the cross but because he uses them in a way that gives the cross and the atonement a meaning at odds with what is found in the Bi-

---

40. Moltmann does this throughout his book *Trinity and the Kingdom: The Doctrine of God* (Minneapolis: Augsburg Fortress, 1983). At some consternation to Moltmann, feminist theologians under the influence of Dorothée Sölle have sometimes accused him of advocating a patriarchal view of God despite his clearly expressed theological developments to the contrary. See Moltmann, *A Broad Place*, pp. 198-99.

41. J. Denny Weaver, *The Nonviolent Atonement* (Grand Rapids: Eerdmans, 1991).

42. Heim, *Saved from Sacrifice*, p. 11. See also René Girard, *The Scapegoat*, trans. Yvonne Freccero (Baltimore: Johns Hopkins University Press, 1986).

ble."[43] Besides the problems I have noted above, the emphasis of the New Testament when it comes to atonement is not on the payment of a debt owed to God but rather on the liberation of humanity and creation from slavery among enemies of God.[44] The "ransom" (Mark 10:45) is not meant to be traced to its object (which then becomes the point of emphasis) but rather to convey the depth of sacrifice and redemptive power involved in the liberation of humanity. Besides, the use of the term "ransom" may have been taken from a military metaphor, in which prisoners of war are set free from bondage.

On the other hand, Anselm's sensitivity to issues related to God's vindication as rightful Lord of creation places him closer to the biblical teaching on atonement than many of his contemporary critics may realize. The whole issue of honor, shame, and lordship is close to the cultural world of atonement texts. Yet, unlike Anselm's atonement theory, Scripture relates atonement to these issues in ways that do not conform to cultural expectations. Rather than God's providing an offering on the cross and through Pentecost to restore divine honor out of divine self-regard, God restores divine honor out of regard for the other. Let me explain.

Walter Brueggemann notes that there is a fundamental tension in the Old Testament between Yahweh's honor through self-regard and through regard for Israel (and the world).[45] There are texts in which God's graciousness is limited to the faithful and in which God acts faithfully only out of self-regard. For example, in Ezekiel, God acts faithfully to manifest God's holiness (Ezek. 20:41), to sanctify God's great name (Ezek. 36:23), and to support God's holy name (Ezek. 39:25). It would even seem that "Yahweh in effect has no interest in Israel, but Israel is a convenient ready-at-hand vehicle for the assertion and enactment of Yahweh's self-regard." Also in Exodus 14:4, 7, God declares that God will deliver Israel "to gain glory for myself over Pharaoh" (p. 308).

Yet this divine self-regard is frequently brought into tension in the Old Testament with a divine regard for Israel and creation, even to the point that God suffers indignity and humiliation in faithfulness to Israel in the midst of its unfaithfulness. God's pursuing of Israel in Hosea 1–2 as some-

---

43. Joel B. Green and Mark D. Baker, *Recovering the Scandal of the Cross: Atonement in New Testament and Contemporary Contexts* (Downers Grove, IL: InterVarsity, 2000), p. 132.

44. Green and Baker, *Recovering the Scandal*, pp. 131-36.

45. Brueggemann, *Theology of the Old Testament: Testimony, Dispute, Advocacy* (Minneapolis: Augsburg Fortress, 2005), p. 303. Hereafter, page references to this work will appear in parentheses in the text.

one might pursue an unfaithful spouse is a prominent example (as is God's yearning for Israel as a parent yearns for the return of an unfaithful child in Hosea 11:1-4). "Yahweh moves back and forth between self-regard and regard for Israel, sovereignty and pathos" (p. 309). The tension between God's sovereign self-regard and "pathos" or fidelity is there in the Old Testament text and seems "unimaginable and unbearable" to Israel. That is especially true when God decides God must abandon Israel out of self-regard, for example, in Lamentations 5:20-22 and Isaiah 49:14 (p. 309).

The central thrust of the Old Testament, however, is to ultimately resolve the tension through a convergence of sovereignty and fidelity in God's saving deeds. God's righteous self-regard as sovereign Lord is fulfilled in God's loving compassion and saving deeds (Isa. 45:8, 23-24; 51:6-8; Ps. 71:19; 89:17; 96:13; 98:9; 111:3; Dan. 9:16-18). In fact, such "convergence of sovereignty and compassion is the staple of Israel's faith" (pp. 304-6). Brueggemann suggests that texts that support this convergence "should be regarded as normative for theological interpretation and be allowed to govern other texts" (p. 309). Such a conclusion is particularly relevant for Brueggemann in the light of the cross. He refers especially to Moltmann's "cruciform discernment of the character of God . . . who completely risks sovereignty in solidarity" (p. 311).

Though Brueggemann does not mention Anselm in his discussion of the Old Testament tension between sovereignty and mercy, we may draw from his insights to locate Anselm legitimately within the biblical witness, even if Anselm is located there only with significant criticism and qualification. For Anselm, God's honor has been bruised in humanity's disregard for divine lordship, and God is compelled out of self-regard to withdraw mercy. The separation of divine justice and mercy that occurs in Anselm's *Cur Deus Homo,* which causes the ire of its critics, does occupy an undercurrent in the biblical witness. However, it is problematic that Anselm sought the convergence of sovereign justice and compassionate mercy through an offering paid to God in Christ's death on the cross. The convergence arrived at in the biblical witness, however, is not mediated by an offering to God to restore honor but is rather achieved in a theological overlapping of justice and mercy within the context of God's saving deeds. In the biblical witness, God's justice and glory are ultimately served in acts of mercy and deliverance.

This insight would have caused Anselm, had he attended to it, to emphasize the cross as the place where God's honor is upheld in an act of redemptive self-giving. There is an *offering* for atonement in the sending of

Christ and the Spirit (both Christ and the Spirit are referred to as the first fruits: 1 Cor. 15:20; Rom. 8:23), but one that vindicates God as Creator and Lord and blesses creation with the privilege of participation in the divine vindication and glory. God's glory is served in mercy to the other, and God glorifies Godself in order that creation might be glorified. As with the God of the Old Testament, who overcomes wrath in suffering love (e.g., Hosea 11:7-9), the God of the cross overcomes the dishonor of the human denial of divine lordship through a wounded love and an offer of embrace by the indwelling Spirit.[46] Justice is fulfilled through mercy and redemption by God's taking injustice, shame, and death into Godself in order to bring all things into the intimate communion of the Spirit.

This biblically orthodox resolution to the tension between sovereignty and pathos in God's relationship to sinful humanity has the additional benefit of delivering theologies of the cross from their confinement to a rational *economy of exchange,* in which divine justice is reduced to a quasi-legal tit for tat. In a helpful discussion of this issue, Kevin Vanhoozer contrasts such an economy of exchange with an *economy of excess,* which pictures the cross as the place where divine justice is accomplished through an inexplicably abundant outpouring of grace in the divine self-giving for sinful humanity.[47] Humanity through Christ does not provide God with an offering equivalent to the weight of their offense; rather, God in the cross provides the means by which creation can be brought into the excessive grace of God's faithful self-giving and self-vindication. Christ's faithfulness becomes revelatory of the faithfulness of God, and the exchange of faithful love between the Son and the Father through the Spirit ends up being the very fountain of excessive grace opened to undeserving sinners.

The economies of exchange and of excess may be seen as paralleling the realms of sin and of grace. Hence, Paul Ricoeur wrote that the "logic of punishment was the logic of equivalence (the wages of sin is death); the logic of grace is a logic of surplus and excess."[48] We might add that the logic of surplus is the logic of the abundantly poured out Spirit. Indeed,

---

46. This is the main thesis of Kazoh Kitamori, *Theology of the Pain of God* (Eugene, OR: Wipf and Stock, 2005).

47. Kevin Vanhoozer, "The Atonement in Postmodernity: Guilt, Goats, and Gifts," in *The Glory of the Atonement: Biblical, Historical, and Practical Perspectives,* ed. Charles Hill and Frank A. James III (Downers Grove, IL: InterVarsity, 2004), pp. 367-404, esp. pp. 374-75.

48. Paul Ricoeur, "Interpretation of the Myth of Punishment," in *The Conflict of Interpretations: Essays in Hermeneutics,* ed. John Ihde (Evanston, IL: Northwestern University Press, 1974), p. 375.

"where sin increased, grace increased all the more" (Rom. 5:20). Paul wrote earlier (Rom. 1) about the excessiveness of sin, but in Romans 5 he makes it clear that grace increased all the more. Paul provides a pneumatological setting for this excessiveness of grace in Romans 5:5 by writing about the love poured out into us in the gift of the Spirit. The point is that the divine self-giving in the gift of the Spirit does not fit any rationally justifiable exchange or ideology. As I have argued earlier, the Spirit points to a transcendent reality, namely, the new creation as the habitation of God. Excess through the Spirit has its own "economy" in the gratuitous nature of *gift.*

Jacques Derrida and Jean-Luc Marion explore the possibility of such an economy of excess in a provocative discussion about the nature of the "gift." Derrida notes that the entire notion of "gift" is problematic, because every gift provokes a comparable gesture from the recipient (equivalent exchange), creating an economy of exchange that cancels out the very nature of a gift as gratuitous. Thus, for Derrida, a true gift is "impossible." If a gift did exist, it would appear as impossible, making it something that defies all description or phenomenological identification. As such, it cannot be known, for, "as soon as you know it, you destroy it."[49]

By way of response, Marion notes that the gift is rooted ultimately in God's *self-giving.* The giftedness is preserved, since no comparable or adequate reciprocation or description is possible; yet some kind of phenomenological descriptions of this gift are possible "in such a way that new phenomenological rules appear," which preserve the novelty, mystery, unexpectedness, and uniqueness of the gift.[50] Toward the end of his discussion of this debate, Vanhoozer suggests that the cross can ultimately be seen as the means by which the abundance of the *Spirit* is graciously mediated to sinful humanity.[51] How else can true excess be understood except in the context of the outpouring of the Spirit "without limit" (John 3:34), across boundaries (Acts 2:17-18), in eschatological expanse (Acts 2:19), and in ultimate resurrection and glorification (Rom. 8:11, 30)?[52]

Indeed, all legal and quasi-legal atonement theories are binitarian in nature, played out between the Son and the Father. A pneumatological

---

49. "On the Gift: A Discussion between Jacques Derrida and Jean-Luc Marion (moderated by Richard Kearney)," in *God, the Gift, and Postmodernism,* ed. John D. Caputo and Michael J. Scanlon (Bloomington: Indiana University Press, 1999), p. 60.

50. Derrida and Marion, "On the Gift," pp. 63-64.

51. Vanhoozer, "The Atonement in Postmodernity," pp. 399-400.

52. I follow Eugene F. Rogers here in claiming that the Spirit is the principle of excess in the Godhead. See Rogers, *After the Spirit,* passim.

atonement theology introduces an element of excess that bursts all systems of exchange to pieces and has the sacred inexplicably invading the hell of God-forsakenness in order to transform it into an ocean of hope. Such an atonement theology fits well with the pneumatological understanding of justification that I seek to develop in this book. It also helps us heal the breach between the cross and Pentecost that is characteristic of Western theologies of atonement. Let us explore this possibility a bit more, looking at a few prominent metaphors for atonement in the New Testament in the light of the mediation of the Spirit.

Overlapping Metaphors of Atonement

There are a number of metaphors that are used in the New Testament and beyond to describe the atoning significance of Jesus' death in the New Testament. The New Testament authors were at a loss to describe the excessive abundance of grace released in the cross and beyond. As Frank Ewart says, "Calvary unlocked the flow of God's love, which is God's very nature, into the hearts of his creatures."[53] These biblical metaphors for atonement are distinct and cannot be fully harmonized, but I think they do overlap and can be shown to be complementary to one another. We should first explore the notion of vindication, since it helps us look again at what Anselm got right — but also where he essentially missed the mark. Despite the numerous problems with Anselm's atonement theology, he did intuit the importance of God's rightful claim as Lord of the creation over against the dark powers that unjustly hold it captive. As I have noted above, this insight motivated Anselm's desire to place the blame on humanity for willfully deciding to renounce God's lordship in favor of an alien lordship. For God to renounce this lordship would be unthinkable for Anselm, since it is so contrary to what we know of God from Scripture.

So far, so good. What is problematic is Anselm's assumption that it is only fitting for humanity to restore the honor of lordship to God. Another, more fruitful, theological path in the light of the cross, the resurrection, and Pentecost is to emphasize the Christ event as the place where God vindicates Godself as Lord by entering into the depths of human sin, suffering, and death in order to raise humanity to justice through Christ as the

---

53. Frank Ewart, "The Revelation of Jesus Christ," in *Seven Jesus Only Tracts*, ed. Donald W. Dayton (New York: Garland, 1985), p. 5.

man and bestower of the Spirit. "How are you and I righteous? In that God is God."[54] As Karl Barth suggests, God thus restores proper honor to Godself by fulfilling justice through merciful redemption for humanity's sake. God the judge becomes the judged so that humanity might know the righteousness of God. In the process of this redemptive victory, God did not weakly overlook human wrong but rather overcame it in grace. Barth explains further:

> What we have to see here is that God does not weakly submit. He does not renounce the grace of election and the covenant. He does not yield in His will to save. He does not surrender the right in which He is in this will towards man. This will has to be done and it is done in the justification of man. In this way, God in the first instance justifies Himself.[55]

As I have noted above, the Son of man in Daniel 7 rises on a cloud from earth to the throne of God in solidarity with the oppressed in order to be vindicated by receiving the right to rule God's righteous kingdom. Christ is the king and the Spirit is the kingdom (Gregory Nazianzus). Jesus came not only as the Son of man but implicitly as the one who will replace the temple as the new center of God's presence and favor, to endure the sufferings at the end of the age in order to provide the means by which others may partake of God's justice. In the Gospels, the resurrection and exaltation of Christ as the man of the Spirit — as well as the fall of Jerusalem and the temple — serve to vindicate Christ as the locus of the Spirit, the locus of God's future justice. The cross is central to this divine self-vindication, as Romans 3 makes clear. But so is the resurrection and Pentecost. Let us explore this point further.

To vindicate a person is to justify or to validate that person or that person's claim. No creature can vindicate God, since God as the sovereign Lord does not stand before the judgment seat of any standard external to Godself. But God can and has vindicated Godself as Creator and Redeemer precisely by showing mercy to the sinful creature in Christ. The vindication does not come through punishment or wrath but rather through mercy, since the God of abundant grace is the one being vindicated. In this light, Romans 3:26 notes that God redeems sinners in order to "demonstrate his

54. Jenson, *Systematic Theology*, vol. 2, *The Works of God* (Oxford: Oxford University Press, 1999), p. 299.

55. Barth, *Church Dogmatics*, vol. 4, *The Doctrine of Reconciliation*, pt. 1, trans. G. W. Bromiley (Edinburgh: T. & T. Clark, 1956), pp. 550, 563.

justice at the present time, so as to be just and the one who justifies those who have faith in Jesus." God mercifully accepts sinners in Christ in order to demonstrate *divine justice.* Justification not only creates a just relationship between the Creator and the creature through the Christ event and the indwelling Spirit, but in doing so it also vindicates God as the God of justice. Note the larger passage surrounding Romans 3:26 (vv. 21-26):

> But now a righteousness from God, apart from law, has been made known, to which the Law and the Prophets testify. This righteousness from God comes through faith in Jesus Christ to all who believe. There is no difference, for all have sinned and fall short of the glory of God, and are justified freely by his grace through the redemption that came by Christ Jesus. God presented him as a sacrifice of atonement, through faith in his blood. He did this to demonstrate his justice, because in his forbearance he had left the sins committed beforehand unpunished — he did it to demonstrate his justice at the present time, so as to be just and the one who justifies those who have faith in Jesus.

There are a few points that I wish to emphasize in this text that lead up to the reality of justification as divine self-vindication in the Spirit. First, justification was a scandal in that it brought Gentiles — considered "sinners" as opposed to righteous Jews — into the righteousness of God. However, the judgment called down on Jerusalem and the Temple by Christ implied that all people, Jew and Gentile alike, are "sinners" and are thus brought into the justice of God in the same way, through faith in the redemption wrought through Jesus: "There is no difference, for all have sinned and fall short of the glory of God, and are justified freely by his grace through the redemption that came by Christ Jesus" (v. 23). Jews are "Gentilized" by being called sinners, and Gentiles are made into spiritual Jews in Christ by being called righteous. Apart from Christ, both Jews and Gentiles find themselves outside the glory of the Temple, of the *Shekinah* presence of God, or of salvation. Only through Christ are they restored to such glory.

Second, the cross is not just a scandal, since it fulfills that to which the law and the prophets testified or bore witness, namely, God's justice through a divine act of mercy and redemption toward sinners. The above passage is all about the *witness* to divine justice in the world, and the first witness is the Old Testament law and prophets. "But now a righteousness from God, apart from law, has been made known, to which the Law and the

Prophets testify" (v. 21). The law bore witness to a justice that would be ful-filled apart from the law! In other words, in bearing witness to justice through crucifixion, resurrection, and Spirit baptism, the law bore witness to something it could not impart, something transcendent that only God can inaugurate. In bearing witness to God's strength, the law bore witness to its own weakness, for the letter kills but the Spirit gives life (2 Cor. 3:6). "For if a law had been given that could impart life, then righteousness would certainly have come by the law" (Gal. 3:21). The law and prophets tes-tify to the fact that divine justice is fulfilled directly by God essentially through mercy and redemption and not punishment, though those who re-sist this mercy will be judged as a result (the wrath of God revealed from heaven, Rom. 1:18). The three *dia* clauses in the Romans 3 text serve to focus further on faith in Christ and his atoning self-sacrifice (symbolized in the spilling of blood) as a decisive focal point for the public demonstration of divine justice: "through faith in Jesus Christ," "through the redemption that came by Jesus Christ," and "through faith in his blood" (Rom. 3:22-25).[56]

Third, not only the law and the prophets implicitly vindicate the cross as the place of justice in our text, but *God* also bears direct witness to the justice implied by the cross in the past and the present. Our text declares no fewer than three times that in the atonement the divine justice is "made known" or "demonstrated" among those who have faith in Jesus. Justifica-tion by faith not only brings sinners into God's righteous favor; it also demonstrates or bears witness to divine justice. Notice the combination of past and present tenses: the righteousness of God "has been made known" (v. 21), while Christ died in order that God might "demonstrate his justice at the present time" (v. 26). Implied is the fact that the demonstration of justice through the cross is *ongoing*.

How is the demonstration of justice through the cross ongoing in the present time? In this light, it is noteworthy that, though 3:21-26 centers the demonstration or witness to God's justice in the crucifixion, Romans 4:25 adds that Christ's resurrection is also essential to the demonstration of di-vine justice: "He was delivered over to death for our sins and was raised to life for our justification." This addition of the resurrection fits well with Romans 1:4, which notes that Christ "through the Spirit of holiness was declared with power to be the Son of God by his resurrection from the

---

56. As noted by Leander Keck in his review of Douglas C. Campbell, *The Rhetoric of Righteousness in Romans 3:21-26,* JSNT Sup. 65 (Sheffield, UK: JSOT Press, 1992) in *Journal of Biblical Literature* 112, no. 4 (Winter 1993): 717-18.

dead: Jesus Christ our Lord." It is significant that the declaration of Christ's sonship in the resurrection is "through the Spirit" in Romans 1:4, especially since this verse is arguably programmatic for Romans. Implied in the larger narrative framework of Romans 3:21-26 is that the witness to God's justice in the cross in saving sinners is ongoing (at the present time) due in part to the fulfillment of the cross in the resurrection and glorification of Christ in the power of the Spirit.

Hans Urs von Balthasar has remarked provocatively that the resurrection and enthronement of the Christ were the very first indications that the Father had taken Jesus' part in the crucifixion and that the curse experienced there was not Jesus' decisive end but rather the means by which he entered our poverty so as to offer us the riches of the Spirit. The connection of justification to the cross in the early development of the New Testament *kerygma* was thus secondary and derivative of the seminal context of the resurrection (Rom. 4:25).[57]

Moreover, the Spirit that vindicates the cursed, crucified Son in resurrection and exaltation is now vindicating cursed Gentiles (and Jews!) in him (Gal. 3:13-14). This is how justification by faith is demonstrating God's justice "at the present time" (Rom. 3:26). The demonstration of justice in the cross is ongoing "at the present time," one might say, because of the witness of the Spirit granted at the resurrection and among all peoples through Pentecost, which bears witness to the fact that God has forgiven and liberated sinners by creating a just relationship with them by grace. The formation of the just relationship and the public vindication or witness of God as the God of justice are the same act, because God is revealed as just or righteous precisely in the merciful liberation of the sinful creature as bearer of the Spirit.

Indeed, God bears witness to "his justice at the present time, so as to be just and the one who justifies those who have faith in Jesus" (Rom. 3:26). As Barth notes, "The fact that in the justification of man God in the first instance justifies Himself gives to the justification of man, to the judgment that kills and makes alive in which it is executed, its holiness." This divine justice is God's right as Creator to contradict the contradiction raised against this right. Therefore, love contradicts rejection and life contradicts death.[58] The empty tomb and the outpouring of the Spirit serve to

---

57. Hans Urs von Balthasar, *Mysterium Paschale*, trans. Aidan Nichols (Grand Rapids: Eerdmans, 1990), p. 201.

58. Barth, *Church Dogmatics*, vol. 4, pt. 1, p. 562.

contradict the contradiction. This is justification plain and simple, namely, God remaining true to Godself as the Creator and covenant partner and contradicting the contradiction raised against it by the creature. We are justified as bearers of the Spirit of Christ by sharing in this just relationship and becoming witnesses of it before the world.

Let's restate this in the light of our vocation to bear the divine Spirit. The creation was made to bear the divine Spirit in union with and in witness to God as Creator and Lord (Gen. 2:7; 2 Cor. 5:4-5). Since humanity was created to bear the divine Spirit, how else can they now be justified or vindicated as creatures of God except by once again bearing the Spirit in witness to God's chosen Son for whom all things were made (Col. 1:16)? The merciful transformation of sinful creation into the dwelling place of the Spirit in the very image of Christ then becomes the means by which God restores union and bears witness to divine justice. Barth is correct when he notes that God justifies Godself by crucifying and raising the creature to new life.[59] This is how divine justice is accomplished and demonstrated. It is the work of Father, Son, and Spirit.

What I have said about justification and vindication implies that Christ bore our sin, suffering, and death so that in him we might know life. I am referring here not only to vindication but also to an element of *substitution* as involved in the death of Jesus. Nowhere in the New Testament is the death of Jesus termed explicitly a "substitute" for us, though the closely related notion of "in our place" is strongly implied. That is rooted in Isaiah 53:11, which says that the suffering "righteous servant will justify many, and he will bear their iniquities." In the New Testament, Paul notes that "Christ redeemed us from the curse of the law by becoming a curse for us" (Gal. 3:13). In Romans, Paul characterizes the plight of the sinners as being "delivered over" (παρέδωκεν) to the darkness and sin of their path (Rom. 1:24-28), but he describes the cross with exactly the same term, noting that Christ was delivered over to our plight "for our sins" (Rom. 4:25) or "for us all" (Rom. 8:32). So also a text in 1 Peter says of Christ that "he himself bore our sins in his body on the tree" (1 Pet. 2:24). Paul clearly links his mission to the earliest proclamation of the Jewish church through his atonement message depicting Christ as dying "for" our sins: "For what I received I passed on to you as of first importance: that Christ died for our sins according to the Scriptures" (1 Cor. 15:3). It is *our* sin and *our* curse that he bore in order that we might be free. There is an element of substitution in this idea.

---

59. Barth, *Church Dogmatics*, vol. 4, pt. 1, p. 562.

Martin Hengel points out that the fundamental roots of this notion of atonement through suffering for others in the New Testament is widely assumed to be both Jewish and Greek. From a Jewish and Old Testament context, there is an established tradition of the righteous prophet who is exalted to God through suffering and death.[60] With the exception of Isaiah 53, however, there is not much in the Old Testament linking the death of a righteous sufferer with atonement for others. As I noted in the preceding chapter, Daniel 7 hints of solidarity of the messianic Son of man with oppressed Israel. But even though this vindicated figure rises to the throne from the earth, there is no clear indication that he has suffered or has been sacrificed. Furthermore, the influence of the Old Testament on the New Testament atonement message still leaves unanswered the question as to why the proclamation of Jesus' atoning death for the world found such powerful expression in the missionary literature of the New Testament that was directed to *Gentile* Christians (in the Pauline corpus, the Epistle to the Hebrews, and 1 Peter).[61]

This question has provoked an inquiry into the Greek influence on the New Testament atonement teaching. Though there are traces of heroic martyrdom "for" others in the Jewish Hellenistic period, this concept is prominent in classical Greek literature. Moreover, in the early Greek period, the idea existed that an individual could be sacrificed to assuage the wrath of the gods, but these scapegoats were as a rule from the underside of society, in contrast to the voluntary self-sacrifice of heroes for the common good.[62] However, as I noted above in response to Anselm, there is no clear indication in the New Testament that Jesus' atonement is meant as an offering to assuage God's wrath. Yet there is still some basis in the Greek world for understanding the idea of "substitutionary" atonement.

Interestingly, there was a fairly widespread notion in ancient Judaism of a time of suffering brought upon the world as the birth pangs of the coming kingdom. Jesus assumed that these birth pangs would fall on Jerusalem and the temple as the divine judgment. His cleansing of the temple and the Olivet Discourse concerning the coming destruction of the temple and of Jerusalem (e.g., Mark 11, 13) have been cited as prominent indicators of this assumption. A convincing case can be made for the idea that Jesus

60. Hengel, *The Atonement*, p. 3.

61. Hengel, *The Atonement*, p. 8. Hengel thus quotes K. Koch in calling Isaiah 53 an "erratic block" at the periphery of the Old Testament. See Koch, "Sühne und Sündenvergebung um die Wende von der exilischen zur nachexilischen Zeit," *Evangelische Theologie* 26 (1966): 237.

62. Hengel *The Atonement*, pp. 3, 8, 19-25.

saw himself as bearing this suffering for Israel so that the nation could be reborn through him and function once more as the light to the nations.[63] Though the Greek idea of the suffering martyr was different from the one that emerges from Jewish narrative, it would also have given Gentile readers some point of reference for understanding Jesus' role as the righteous sufferer for others.

It was up to Paul to note that Jesus' acceptance of the judgment placed on the Jewish people brought the nation into solidarity with Gentile sinners, leaving all as having fallen short of the glory of God that accompanies his presence and favor on earth (e.g., Rom. 3:23; Gal. 3:13). Jesus accepted this curse so that, through his role as the locus and mediator of the divine presence and glory, not only Israelites but even Gentiles could become bearers of the Spirit (Gal. 3:13-14). The point here is not that God's wrath is assuaged by the cross, but that Jesus is sent by the Father and empowered by the Spirit to enter into the depths of despair in order to bring those who occupy it into God's glorious presence. He is the faithful Son who is led of the Spirit to the far country to bring the lost sons and daughters into the household of the Father's presence.

Closely connected to this idea of substitution, then, is *ransom.* Jesus is portrayed as functioning as the Son of man not just in riding the clouds toward victory (as in Dan. 7) but also in giving his life as a ransom for many (Mark 10:45). In the ancient Greek world, "ransom" had layers of meaning, usually referring to the deliverance of captives, either slaves or military prisoners, by making an appropriate payment.[64] The attempt to figure out to whom the "payment" of the cross was made is to stretch the application of the metaphor too far and reduce it to a system of exchange. The emphasis of Mark 10:45 was on the limitless self-sacrifice of Jesus as the context for the deliverance of Israel — indeed, of all humanity — from the clutches of slavery to unfaithfulness and death. Gustaf Aulen says this about Jesus' death:

> The New Testament idea of redemption constitutes in fact a veritable revolution; for it declares that sovereign divine love has taken the initiative, broken through the order of justice and merit, triumphed over the powers of evil, and created a new relation between the world and God.[65]

63. Wright, *Jesus and the Victory of God,* 2:576-604.

64. Adela Yarbro Collins, "The Signification of Mark 10:45 among Gentile Christians," *Harvard Theological Review* 90, no. 4 (Oct. 1997): 371-82.

65. Gustaf Aulén, *Christus Victor: An Historical Study of the Three Main Types of the Idea of Atonement* (New York: Macmillan, 1969), p. 79.

The lack of attention to payment in the "ransom" of the cross does not mean that Christ's death is not in some sense an offering or a *sacrifice*. The Father delivered up the Son (Rom. 8:32), and the Son delivered himself up (Heb. 9:14), for our salvation. It is "through the eternal Spirit" that Jesus delivers himself up. Jesus is the Lamb of God who takes away the sins of the world in the Johannine tradition (John 1:29; Rev. 5:6). Jesus is the sacrifice that is perfect in the book of Hebrews as well: it fulfills all other sacrifices once and for all. While the sacrifices in the Old Testament tabernacle were but a fleeting sign of the reality to come (Heb. 10:1-4), Jesus fulfills divine righteousness by entering the most holy place of God and offering himself unblemished "through the eternal Spirit" (Heb. 9:14). What qualifies Jesus as the final high priest is thus not his priestly ancestry but rather his self-giving by the *eternal* Spirit, or, in the words of the author of Hebrews, "the power of an indestructible life" (7:16). The sacrifices under the law cannot make righteous, only the one who does the will of God by offering himself up as the man of the Spirit for the sake of creation. Hebrews 10:8-9 is quite strong: "'Sacrifices and offerings, burnt offerings and sin offerings you did not desire, nor were you pleased with them' (although the law required them to be made). Then he said, 'Here I am, I have come to do your will.'" Jesus' self-giving revealed the self-giving of God, which is the only path to human fulfillment in the image of God.

Jesus' sacrifice is the one ultimately pleasing to God because it is done by the Spirit and the faithfulness of the Son, who has gone to the far country in search of wayward humanity. As D. Lyle Dabney has pointed out, Jesus' final moments in Gethsemane show him admitting in a moment of weakness that the "Spirit is willing, but the body is weak" (Mark 14:38). The Spirit here is the Holy Spirit, for this is the Spirit that moves Jesus to the cross to offer himself up for the redemption of humanity. This very Spirit descended on Jesus as he went into the baptismal waters in identification with the lost, and it is the Spirit who drove Jesus into the desert to face humanity's enemy (Matt. 3–4).[66] Jesus, as the new dwelling place of the Spirit, fulfills not only the temple but the temple cult as well. Jesus fulfills the role of the high priest and the sacrifices in offering proper worship and self-giving to God. In fact, according to Hebrews, the temple cult only

---

66. D. Lyle Dabney, "Naming the Spirit: Towards a Pneumatology of the Cross," in *Starting with the Spirit*, Task of Theology Today II, ed. Stephen Pickard and Gordon Preece (Hindmarsh, Australia: Australian Theological Forum, 2001), pp. 50-52.

existed to bear witness to him. The true temple (Christ) would take the Spirit to the nations, indeed, to all of creation.

The language of offering and sacrifice is not the language of satisfaction but rather the Hebraic language of worship and glory to God. As an offering of worship and glory to God on behalf of humanity, Christ sacrificed himself on the cross as the Father delivered him up for the creation's salvation from bondage to sin and death (Rom. 4:25; 8:32). In sacrificial terms, Christ is thus raised up by the Spirit as the "firstfruits" of the resurrection (1 Cor. 15:23). The Spirit was the agent in that action of sacrificial self-offering of Christ, receiving Christ from the Father to offer him up for the sake of the world (Heb. 9:14). This offering was completed when in Christ's resurrection the Spirit offered the faithful Son to the Father as a fragrant offering (Eph. 5:2). Jesus rises "into the full Spirit-life of the resurrection" in order to impart the Spirit as an offering poured out on the creation.[67] This is the initiation of the baptism in the Holy Spirit.

It is interesting that, in Spirit baptism, not only Christ's but the Spirit's "atoning" work is referred to in sacrificial terms, since we are referred to as having the "firstfruits" of the Spirit (Rom. 8:23). Not only Christ but the Spirit is also offered up as the first fruits of the harvest of new creation for the justification of creation. The Spirit was previously the agent in offering up Christ; now Christ will be the agent in offering up the Spirit. At Pentecost, Christ as the principal offering becomes the high priest in offering the Spirit poured forth on the world for humanity's sake in a way analogous to how the Spirit received the Son from the Father at the cross to offer him up for the world (Acts 2:33).[68] The offering of the Spirit by the Son in Spirit baptism will climax in resurrection as well, but this time it will be the resurrection of his body (the church) surrounded by the renewed creation.

The Spirit who offered Christ to the Father as the faithful Son in the cross and the resurrection is now offered to the Father by the Son at the *eschaton* in the form of the renewed creation indwelt by the very presence of God. In other words, the Spirit offered Christ in resurrection and glorification from the depths of forsakenness to the Father as the gift of the faithful Son in order that the Son might offer the Spirit to the Father from the depths of the enslaved creation but now enshrined in the new creation in the image of the faithful Son. This is when the Son offers the kingdom to

---

67. Cooke, *The Distancing of God*, p. 366.

68. Gunton, *The Actuality of the Atonement: A Study of Metaphor, Rationality, and the Christian Tradition* (Edinburgh: T. & T. Clark, 2003), pp. 127, 135.

the Father, and God is all and in all (1 Cor. 15:20-28). This is atonement through the outpouring of the Spirit on all flesh. This is justification in the Spirit, when God rectifies the alienated creation through the divine indwelling and restores to creation its created purpose of bearing the Spirit in the image of the faithful Son.

Thus there is an exchange that takes place in the cross, but it is an excessive or blessed exchange. As the very locus of God's presence, Jesus descends into God-forsakenness in order to bring the God-forsaken into the embrace of the Spirit. Not only does the cross reveal human election, but also human rejection, so that the depths of rejection might be filled with the justice of the divine embrace.[69] The Spirit descends with Christ into the depths of God-forsakenness in order to take this reality up into God's presence. Indeed, it is "through the eternal Spirit" (Heb. 9:14) or the "power of an indestructible life" (Heb. 7:16) that Jesus — as the new temple of God, the new high priest, the new offering, and all that belongs to the holy temple of God's presence — can function as the new place where the Jews, and also the Gentiles, can once again dwell together in God and God in them. The striking point is that Jesus as the holy dwelling place of the Spirit descends to the place of the God-forsaken in order to open up the sacred to the profane.

As the man of sorrows, the man of the Spirit cries the words of the Psalter, "My God, my God, why have you forsaken me?" (Mark 15:34; cf. Ps. 22:1). Yet the forsaken one is still offering himself "through the eternal Spirit!" The Spirit is not absent at the cross, only profoundly hidden — even to the eyes of God's anointed. Jesus does not cease to be the dwelling place of the Spirit even as he cries out from the depths of God-forsakenness. Because the Spirit "accompanies Christ to the end, he can make this end the new beginning."[70] As Dabney notes, even as the Spirit is blasphemed at the height of human rejection and injustice, the Spirit remains with Christ as the divine possibility of life.[71]

This is without question the deepest mystery of the cross. But it is the mystery that lies at the very substance of how sinners can be simultaneously the bearers of the Spirit by faith in Christ. The hidden Spirit is the key to understanding a pneumatological theology of the justification of sinners by grace through faith. Mark tells us that, after the crucifixion, the temple veil was torn in two, implying that the dwelling place of God is no

---

69. Barth, *Church Dogmatics*, vol. 2, pt. 2, p. 322.
70. Moltmann, *The Spirit of Life*, p. 68.
71. Dabney, "Naming the Spirit," p. 58.

longer to be limited to the sacred confines of the temple. A Gentile is found confessing Jesus as the Son of God at the cross as well (Mark 15:38-39), foreshadowing Christ's future role in channeling God's presence and favor to the nations, thus fulfilling Israel's elect calling. Even today we find the Spirit within the community of faith and in the cries of liberty within the world, often in ways that are profoundly hidden beneath forsakenness and suffering. In the light of the triumph of the cross and the resurrection, however, it is also clear that the Spirit remains the possibility of life.

The cross leads through resurrection and exaltation to Jesus' vindication as the true temple of God, "a fragrant offering and sacrifice to God" (Eph. 5:2), and to the fulfillment of Jesus' mission of opening that divine indwelling to creation. As I will suggest later, the imagery of Acts 2 indicates that the church becomes the temple of the Spirit through participation in Christ as the fullness of the Spirit's presence.[72] Indeed, he is the Spirit baptizer, the one who was raised "a life-giving spirit" (1 Cor. 15:45). In Christ the sacred invades the profane, and hope invades hell. Christ is shown to express hope from the grave that God will indeed not forsake him after all: "You will not abandon me to the grave, nor will you let your Holy One see decay. You have made known to me the paths of life; you will fill me with joy in your presence" (Acts 2:27). The Father will prove through the resurrection an enduring faithfulness that has not failed.

We should also bear in mind that the forsaken creation entered by the forsaken Christ and the blasphemed Spirit at the cross was already a reality sustained by the Spirit in its implicit witness to God (Rom. 1:20) and also precisely in its implicit yearning for the liberty of redemption: "We know that the whole creation has been groaning as in the pains of childbirth right up to the present time" (Rom. 8:22). There is no such thing as a Spiritless creation: "If I make my bed in the depths, you are there" (Ps. 139:8). In the cross, God reaches down into a forsaken creation that is crying out for liberty with the aid of divine pathos, the Spirit of creation. The Spirit who descended with Christ into suffering and alienation at the cross brought to fulfillment the Spirit's longstanding intercession for creation in the midst of its groaning for liberty. In the cross, the Spirit now willfully opens up to be assailed by the dark forces that keep creation in bondage in order to remain

72. See G. K. Beale, "The Descent of the Eschatological Temple in the Form of the Spirit at Pentecost: Part 1: The Clearest Evidence," *Tyndale Bulletin* 56, no. 1 (2005): 73-99; "The Descent of the Eschatological Temple in the Form of the Spirit at Pentecost: Part 2: Corroborating Evidence," *Tyndale Bulletin* 56, no. 2 (2005): 63-90.

true to this intercession. Christ's implicit cry for liberty from forsakenness on the cross is done in harmony with the blasphemed Spirit, to be sure, but also in deep harmony with the Spirit that has long since been groaning with the suffering creation. The cross spans the God above and the God below by connecting the answer of redemption with the groans for liberty. God achieves justice for creation, not only as judge, but also as intercessor and advocate in solidarity with the guilty and shamed defendants.

As implied above, the divine exchange involves incarnation. The incarnation was, from the earliest time of the Christian church, vital to Christ's role as redeemer, vital to the cross. Jesus was not just a virtuous martyr. If so, he would represent only one sacrifice in a long line of sacrifices, still awaiting fulfillment. As a mere martyr, he could ascend to God by God's power, but he could not bestow the Spirit or take anyone with him, for only God could do that. Justice is thus ultimately fulfilled in the Old Testament by the Creator and Lord. The fundamental assumption is that salvation belongs to God alone. Hosea 13:4 is clear: "You shall acknowledge no God but me, no Savior except me." The New Testament affirms this insight in the terse confession of Revelation 7:10: "Salvation belongs to our God." Jesus, as the Lamb of God who redeemed the world, is thus granted the same praise as the God who is seated on the throne (Rev. 5:9-14; cf. Dan. 7:14).

If God alone can save and Jesus is to be regarded also as the Savior, we must then regard Jesus as divine. He is "our great God and Savior" (Titus 2:13), each of the two terms including the other by definition. The same holds true regarding Jesus as the one who imparts the divine Spirit for salvation. As the incarnate Word of the Father, Jesus has life according to John 1:1-14: "In him was life, and that life was the light of men." He is the resurrection and the life (John 11:25). Being identified with the very life of the resurrection, he can impart life to others, "breathing" it upon the disciples in a way analogous to God's breathing the divine breath into Adam (John 20:22; cf. Gen. 2:7), an act soon followed by Thomas's confession to Jesus, "My Lord and my God!" (John 20:28).

The church fathers thus correctly assumed that the one who imparts the divine breath must himself be divine. The one who bears the Spirit must be the incarnate Son if he is to bestow this Spirit and the life that it shapes upon others, so that others might be conformed to his image as the faithful Son. The Spirit gives the Word an anointed and indwelt body as a gift in order that Christ could give all bodies the gift of the same anointing. The Spirit baptizer must be the incarnate Word of the Father.

It is significant that the Old Testament pictures the Messiah as the one who receives and bears the Spirit (e.g., Isa. 61:1-3), but not as the one who grants this same Spirit to others. All four Gospels and Acts highlight this unique idea: that the Christ not only bears but also bestows the Spirit (Matt. 3:16; Mark 1:8; Luke 3:22; John 1:33; Acts 1:5; 2:33). Christ bears the Spirit in order to impart this Spirit of Christ to others, making it possible for Jesus' filial relationship with the Father to become eschatologically an ever-expanding circle. In the light of Spirit baptism, justification is Trinitarian in implication and enriches all aspects of salvation by presenting them in the light of the divine right accomplished by the restoration of creation's vocation of bearing the divine Spirit in the image of the Son and in communion with God as Father, Son, and Spirit.

The idea of the "graced exchange" in which the divine Word, or Son, became flesh so that all flesh could partake of the divine life is very ancient. John's Gospel presents Christ as the Word of the Father that became flesh in order that those who receive him can be born from above and receive the right to become children of God (1:12-14). Similarly, Hebrews says that Christ partook of flesh so that all flesh might be freed from slavery to death and to the devil (Heb. 2:14-15). Paul also notes that Christ partook of our poverty so that we could partake of his riches (2 Cor. 8:9). Paul's use of the classic hymn in Philippians 2, a virtual portal into the earliest hymns of the church, also supports the same notion of Christ as partaking of our humble existence in order that, exalted, he could be Lord of salvation (Phil. 2:6-11). Something similar is at play when Paul declares that Christ was born under the law so that we might be born by the Spirit as children of God (Gal. 4).

Although this notion of exchange was prominent in Eastern soteriology, as I have noted above, it is still widely assumed from early on in the church, both East and West (Catholic and Protestant).[73] For example, Irenaeus writes of Christ, "He who was the Son of God became the Son of man that man, having been taken into the Word, and receiving the adoption, might become the Son of God."[74] Also as I noted earlier, some variation of Athanasius's dictum "God became man so that man might become God" was advocated by the Cappadocians in the East.[75] In the West,

73. See Daniel A. Keating, *Deification and Grace* (Naples, FL: Sapientia Press, 2007), pp. 11-38.

74. *Against Heresies*, 3. 19. 1, quoted in Keating, *Deification and Grace*, p. 11.

75. Athanasius, *De Incarnatione*, quoted in J. A. McGuckin, "The Strategic Adaptation of Deification," in Michael J. Christensen and Jeffrey A. Wittung, eds., *Partakers of the Divine Nature: The History and Development of Deification in the Christian Traditions* (Grand Rapids: Baker Academic, 2006), p. 101.

Hilary of Poitiers and Ambrose of Milan supported similar notions of exchange.[76] Augustine echoes Irenaeus: "The Son of God [became] the Son of man that he might make the sons of men the sons of God."[77] Similarly, Aquinas says that "grace surpasses every capability of created nature, since it is nothing short of partaking of the divine nature."[78] Also well known are Luther's expressions of the "joyful exchange," in which Christ takes on our unrighteousness so that we can take on his righteousness.[79] Concerning Christ, Calvin similarly maintains that, "by taking our mortality, he has conferred immortality upon us."[80]

This blessed exchange idea of salvation has the advantage of viewing the inauguration of justice played out in the story of Jesus as a seamless narrative from the incarnation to the exaltation. Kallistos Ware says that the "mystery of Christ forms an undivided unity. Incarnation, baptism, transfiguration, crucifixion, resurrection, ascension: all the moments in Christ's incarnate dispensation constitute a single whole."[81] All of these events together represent the descent of the Word into flesh from the Father and by the Spirit so that all flesh could be taken up into the divine life by the very same Spirit.[82] Saint Basil writes:

> [Do we speak of] Christ's advent? The Spirit is forerunner. Or of his incarnate presence? The Spirit is inseparable (from him). The working of miracles and the gifts of healing are through the Holy Spirit. Demons were exorcised by the Spirit of God. The devil was deprived of his power by the presence of the Spirit. Remission of sins is accomplished by the grace of the Spirit. . . .[83]

76. See Keating, *Deification and Grace,* p. 13.

77. Augustine, *Tractatus in Iohannis Euangelium,* 21.1, quoted in Keating, *Deification and Grace,* p. 14.

78. Aquinas, *Treatise on Grace,* Q. 112, 1st art., in *Basic Writings of St. Thomas Aquinas,* trans. and ed. Anton C. Pegis (New York: Random House, 1945).

79. See, e.g., *Luther: Letters of Spiritual Counsel,* trans. and ed. Theodore G. Tappert (Vancouver, BC: Regent College Publications, 2003), p. 110.

80. Calvin, *Institutes,* 4.17.2, quoted in Keating, *Deification and Grace,* p. 15.

81. Kallistos Ware, *How Are We Saved? The Understanding of Salvation in the Orthodox Tradition* (Minneapolis: Light and Life, 1996), p. 121.

82. Boris Bobrinskoy, "The Indwelling of the Holy Spirit in Christ," *St. Vladimir's Theological Quarterly* 28 (1984): 56.

83. Basil, *Spiritu Sancto,* in *Basil: Letters and Select Works,* trans. Blomfield Jackson, NPNF, vol. 8, 2nd ser., ed. Philip Schaff and Henry Wallace (reprint; Peabody, MA: Hendrickson, 1994), 19:49.

I would like to add that, within this series of events that feature the accomplishment of justice by the incarnate Christ as the man of the Spirit, each part implies the meaning of the whole as well as its own unique element within it. The incarnation represents the emptying of the Son of God into weak and suffering flesh by means of the Spirit in order that flesh might be joined to God through the Spirit (Luke 1:35) and partake of God. In baptism also, Christ as the man of the Spirit descends down into the water of weak and fallen humanity in order to take upon himself their condition and to provide access to God (Luke 3:22). In his self-sacrificial life, Jesus takes on the role of the servant and eats with sinners in order to inaugurate the kingdom or rule of God by mediating the Spirit upon them for their deliverance (Matt. 12:28). The cross and resurrection especially have Christ descend into the depth of human suffering and sin in order that, by the Spirit, flesh could partake of life (Rom. 1:4; 4:25; Heb. 2:14-15). Christ is exalted in order to definitively receive the Spirit on our behalf so that he can bestow it on all flesh (Acts 2:33). Not only does the entire narrative of Spirit baptism imply a seamless tale of exchange (the incarnate and anointed Christ having flesh in order that flesh might have the Spirit), each element of the narrative implies the same truth in its own right. Yet there is still a development. The Spirit sends Christ from incarnation to crucifixion in order that Christ might send the Spirit through the means of his life, death, and exaltation. The goal of this sending of the Spirit is that all of creation could rise as a holy offering to God as justified through participation in divine communion and in recognition of God as rightful Lord of creation.

Conclusion

God has determined from all eternity to be the God who gives of Godself and takes the other into the embrace of the divine communion. This God is the self-giving Father, Son, and Spirit, a circle of love that seeks to indwell creation. Genesis 1–2 shows that this God creates by reaching into the void in order to bring life into being, life that is graced abundantly by being made to be the dwelling place of the Spirit. Creation finds fulfillment in new creation and the divine indwelling through Christ as the one who imparts the Spirit. In Christ as the man of the Spirit, God reaches down into the abyss of God-forsakenness in order to open creation to the gift of the Spirit, the gift of divine pardon and justice in the very image of the

Son. Creation has always lived from God even in its captivity to sin and death. For God to abandon the creation is to abandon Godself as Creator. God does not relinquish divine lordship and will uphold the honor of that lordship by overcoming evil and death with self-giving love.

In the light of the above summary, there is simply no way of using the cross to exclude the Spirit from the essence of justification. The Spirit that mediates the coming of Christ into the world is mediated by Christ to the world through his life, death, resurrection, and exaltation. The cross is worthy of special focus (1 Cor. 2:2) because it is here that the uniqueness of divine justice in the Spirit comes to sharp focus. I agree with Roy A. Harrisville that the cross "fractures" commonly held ideas about righteousness in the ancient world.[84] Righteousness is fulfilled in mercy, justice is granted in the midst of an unjust act, power is granted in weakness, new life arises from death, victory is accomplished from defeat, and the presence of the Spirit is opened up to the sinful creature through an experience of God-forsakenness. Of course, the cross means all of this only in its continuity with the life that preceded it and the events of resurrection, exaltation, and Spirit impartation that follow it.

Nevertheless, it is quite stunning and overwhelmingly beautiful to view how God has decided to open the Spirit to creation, namely, through the mediation of the crucified Jesus. Count Nicholas Ludwig von Zinzendorf once wrote that Jesus poured forth the Spirit from the wounds of his crucifixion, especially as symbolized in the water that gushed forth from Christ's side.[85] What a wonderful image of the role of the cross in mediating the life of the Spirit. There is no way from this context of understanding the Spirit-indwelt, justified life except as a life fashioned by the self-giving that took Jesus from the incarnation to the cross. Bonhoeffer was right in saying that "the only man who has the right to say that he is justified by grace alone is the man who has left all to follow Christ."[86] Pneumatic existence is cruciform existence. Justification is the justice experienced in this form of existence as well as the vindication of it as glorifying to God.

I proceed now to talk again about the basis of justification in the metaphor of Spirit baptism, but this time with a focus on Spirit outpouring

---

84. Harrisville, *Fracture*, passim.

85. Zinzendorf, *Ein und zwanzig Discurse über die Augsburgische Konfession, 1748, Der achte Discurs, Hauptschriften*, Bd. VI (Hildesheim: Stift Hildesheim, 1963), pp. 159ff.

86. Bonhoeffer, *The Cost of Discipleship*, trans. R. H. Fuller (New York: Macmillan, 1963), p. 55.

rather than the Spirit-indwelt Christ or the events leading up to the resurrection. I have already dropped a number of hints as to how Scripture supports the fulfillment of justification in creation through the gift of the indwelling Spirit, but these hints require elaboration and greater biblical support.

7 Embracing Us

Justification and Spirit Baptism

In contrast to the relative neglect of the Spirit in justification debates of the past, the New Testament highlights the Holy Spirit in most of the contexts in which justification is mentioned. The emphasis on the Spirit throughout nearly all of the New Testament as the very essence of salvation has already been documented by James Dunn. Dunn concluded his important study *Baptism in the Holy Spirit* by recognizing a unified witness among nearly all of the authors of the New Testament that a Christian is essentially one "who has received the gift of the Holy Spirit by committing himself to the risen Jesus as Lord."[1] The indwelling Spirit of God is the "nerve center" of the entire Christian life in the New Testament (p. 102). Indeed, the gift of the Spirit is "the same as justification by faith" (p. 113), for justification "takes place in the Spirit" (p. 122). All soteriological categories must be defined within the realm of the indwelling Spirit, for "the baptism in the Spirit is God's acceptance, forgiveness, cleansing and salvation" (p. 82).

With this pneumatological soteriology in mind, I intend to show that justification in the New Testament is neither primarily the typically Protestant declaration of righteous standing nor the traditionally Catholic fruit of righteousness in us as we cooperate with grace. It is rather in essence God's covenant faithfulness and righteous favor provided for humanity in

---

1. James D. G. Dunn, *Baptism in the Holy Spirit*, Studies in Biblical Theology, 2nd ser., 15 (London: SCM Press, 1970), p. 229. Hereafter, page references to this work will appear in parentheses in the text.

Christ's mediation of the Spirit through his faithful life, death, resurrection, and Spirit impartation as well as the embrace of the indwelling Spirit within. The Spirit bears witness to our Spirit that we are children of God despite our weakness and groaning for the liberty yet to come, even despite the fact that we still await our adoption that will be fulfilled through the fullness of pneumatic existence in the resurrection (Rom. 8:15-23).

Specifically, this favor is bestowed on Jesus as God's Son, both at the very essence of his obedient self-giving for creation, especially during his God forsakenness on the cross, and as vindication of that cruciform life, especially at his resurrection and exaltation. I hope to show that Spirit baptism opened this justification in the Spirit to a creation held captive to sin and death. Through the indwelling of the Spirit and the new birth, sinners are taken up into the righteous favor of God that is inaugurated especially in Christ's death and resurrection. The goal of justification is glorification (Rom. 8:30), at which point God inhabits the creation, and the creation receives the very fulfillment of its calling to become the habitation of God.

What provoked most statements about justification in the New Testament is thus the theologically startling fact of ceremonially unclean Gentile "sinners" becoming bearers of the Spirit by faith in Christ. In the context of the well-known recognition that Israel had indeed not fulfilled its calling to bless the nations, Paul reasoned theologically against the background of Christian tradition — and with respect to the Gentile possession of the Spirit — that Christ had fulfilled the task of channeling the blessing to the nations for Israel. The obvious inability of Israel to fulfill its calling within the provisions of the law pointed additionally to faith in Christ as the means of receiving the Spirit. In fact, the Gentiles were receiving in the Spirit the blessings directed in the prophets to restored Israel, while the Jews were still experiencing the wrath of exile![2] The fact that the blessing was bestowed on the heels of Israel's failure meant that Jews are also sinners and are thus justified by the Spirit through faith in Christ in exactly the same way as the Gentiles are.

It's important to note, however, that justification was not merely the result of Paul's creative theological imagination. At key points Paul quotes what appear to be ancient Christian references to justification (cf. Rom. 4:25; 1 Cor. 6:11).[3] There are indications that the term was known in the

---

2. See Frank Thielman, *Paul and the Law* (Downers Grove, IL: InterVarsity, 1994), p. 79.

3. John Reumann, *Righteousness in the New Testament* (Philadelphia: Fortress, 1982), pp. 31, 38.

earliest Jewish Christian communities, especially within the Hellenistic Jewish Christian community.[4] As I have noted earlier, there is good reason to believe that the notion of the justification of sinners goes back to Jesus himself (e.g., Luke 18:10).[5] Furthermore, it is my conviction that justification through Spirit baptism receives a somewhat neglected development in Luke. Therefore, I will do something relatively unorthodox and begin with Luke in my attempt to develop the usefulness of Spirit baptism as a narrative context for an ecumenical theology of justification that is both theocentric and open to human participation.

A Lukan Framework for Justification?

The Pentecostal movement blessed us all by drawing attention to Spirit baptism as significant for an ecumenical discussion of one's journey into Christ, including justification.[6] The expansively eschatological understanding of Spirit baptism recently favored among a number of Pentecostal and charismatic voices is particularly helpful for providing a perceptive lens through which to view justification as a pneumatological and eschatological gift, especially as developed within the open spaces of the triune God. However, I must pose the question at this point of whether or not we can biblically locate justification within the distinctly Lukan narrative framework of Spirit baptism.

As I have noted earlier, it is interesting that all four Gospels and the book of Acts, which make up the narrative foundation of our New Testament canon, introduce and highlight Christ as the Spirit baptizer (cf. Matt. 3:16-17; Mark 1:11; Luke 3:16; John 1:33; Acts 1:6-8, 2:33). Paul makes Spirit baptism essential to the bringing together of Jew and Gentile into the one

---

4. Hans Dieter Betz, *Galatians*, Hermeneia: A Critical and Historical Commentary on the Bible (Philadelphia: Augsburg Fortress, 1979), pp. 114-15, 119.

5. See Eberhard Jüngel, *Paulus und Jesus: Eine Untersuchung zur Präzisierung der Frage nach dem Ursprung der Christologie*, Hermeneutische Untersuchungen zur Theologie, 2 (Tübingen: Mohr-Siebeck, 1962), p. 275.

6. I do not mean, with this statement, to denigrate the significance of the Holiness movement or other revival groups that have also spoken of Spirit baptism. I only mean to say that it was Pentecostalism that so highlighted the metaphor as to bring it to the attention of ecumenical discussion, provoking key theologians from other traditions to respond from the vantage point of their unique theological heritages, and to help expand the boundaries of the metaphor among Pentecostal theologians who engaged them in conversation.

body united in Christ (1 Cor. 12:13; Eph. 5:18-19), a theme close to the heart-beat of Paul's theology of justification. As Roger Stronstad has noted, however, the Spirit baptismal metaphor is a distinctly Lukan emphasis.[7] Moreover, though the metaphor is fluid in meaning in the New Testament and open to several nuances, it does serve to highlight the work of the Spirit as poured out from the Father through the Son for the purpose of indwelling people (Acts 2:33) and drawing them into the righteous favor, witness, and vindication of the Son, all concepts that are important for a theology of justification.[8]

It is important here to note the fact that Spirit baptism or the gift of the indwelling Spirit in Acts does not occur in a vacuum but rather within a cluster of themes that point to what Paul would term the justification of sinners, indeed, of all flesh through the Spirit. Favor with God through the gift and communion of the indwelling Spirit enters the history of human relationships and affairs for Luke as a redemptive force. This outpouring of the Spirit creates a community of believers richly involved in *koinonia* (Acts 2:42f.). The attention of others to this new reality of communal justice as well as the enthusiastic public witnesses to the redemptive story behind it occasions for Luke a "quasi-legal" conflict between the community of Jesus' Spirit-empowered witnesses and those who opposed them. This conflict also occasions the vindication in the Spirit of the witness to Jesus through signs and wonders, pointing to the ultimate vindication of the end-times fulfillment of salvation. Justification for Luke thus involves righteous favor and communion, witness, and vindication. Let us unpack this cluster of justification themes a bit more.

As Markus Barth has shown, Luke has a justification theology even though the writer does not use the term often (most notably, Luke 18:9-14 and Acts 13:39). Even though the term "justification" is not invoked much in Acts, Barth makes a compelling case that the entire book of Acts implies a justification theology. Acts has the followers of Jesus testifying before the world in concert with the Spirit that Jesus was the "righteous one" (22:14) anointed by God to bring salvation (10:38). The anointed one was condemned and executed unjustly but was vindicated in the Spirit through

---

7. Roger Stronstad, *The Charismatic Theology of St. Luke* (Peabody, MA: Hendrickson, 1988).

8. See Macchia, *Baptized in the Spirit: A Global Pentecostal Theology* (Grand Rapids: Zondervan, 2006). For an indication of the variety of viewpoints on the meaning of the metaphor today, see Henry Lederle, *Treasures Old and New: Interpretations of Spirit Baptism in the Charismatic Renewal Movement* (Peabody, MA: Hendrickson, 1988).

resurrection and exaltation by God (3:19-21; 4:27-31; 5:29-32; 7:51-53; 10:39-43).[9] The church functions in the Spirit of God's righteous favor to witness also to Christ's vindication by God, for Christ "was not abandoned to the grave, nor did his body see decay. God has raised this Jesus to life, and we are all witnesses of the fact" (Acts 2:31-32). As Hans Urs Balthasar notes concerning Christ: "[H]is advocate, the Spirit, will undertake the defense of his innocence . . . on the basis of, precisely, the Cross, and over against the world."[10] Not only against the world but primarily for it. I would add that Spirit baptism in Acts opens up Jesus' righteous favor to history and allows all those indwelt by the Spirit to share in this favor and in the Spirit's witness to the vindicated Christ.

Acts thus begins with the exaltation and vindication of the unjustly crucified Jesus as the one who is anointed and indwelt by the Spirit. Recall that Daniel 7:13 has the Messiah ascend to the throne on clouds from the earth in order to receive final vindication from the Ancient of Days.[11] In Acts 1:9, Luke has Jesus ascend on a cloud to the heavenly Father after being raised from an executioner's death. At the throne, the same Spirit that vindicated Christ in life (Luke 1:35; 3:22) and in resurrection (cf. Rom. 1:4) is now given to him once more to anoint him as the judge over all (Acts 2:33; 10:39-42) but also as the one who justifies in the Spirit all who turn to him by faith (cf. 1 Tim. 3:16, in which Jesus is "vindicated by the Spirit"). We may also note Acts 2:33: "Exalted to the right hand of God, he has received from the Father the promised Holy Spirit and has poured out what you now see and hear." This text summarizes Jesus' entire redemptive journey in which he receives the Spirit from the Father in order to impart it to all flesh. As Irenaeus notes, "The Lord, receiving this as a gift from His Father, does Himself also confer it upon those who are partakers of Himself, sending the Holy Spirit upon all the earth."[12]

This more elaborate explanation of justification in the Spirit is provided by Luke in Peter's pivotal message at the strategic prelude to the Spirit's indwelling of the Gentiles in Acts 10. In obvious reference to the

9. Markus Barth, *Acquittal by Resurrection* (New York: Holt, Rinehart and Winston, 1964), pp. 67-84.

10. Hans Urs von Balthasar, *Mysterium Paschale*, trans. Aidan Nichols (Grand Rapids: Eerdmans, 1990), p. 119.

11. N. T. Wright, *The Resurrection of the Son of God* (Minneapolis: Fortress, 2003), p. 215.

12. Irenaeus, *Adversus Haereses*, in *The Apostolic Fathers: Justin Martyr and Irenaeus*, rev. A. Cleveland Coxe, ANF, vol. 1, ed. Alexander Roberts and James Donaldson (Peabody, MA: Hendrickson, 1994), 3.17.2 (445).

Gentiles who were about to receive the Spirit by faith, Peter starts by proclaiming that God "accepts men from every nation who fear him and do
what is right" (10:35). The message of divine favor with regard to the gift of
the Spirit is then based in Jesus, who was anointed "with the Holy Spirit
and power" to do good for humanity and to deliver those oppressed of the
devil (10:38). This righteous Christ indwelt by the Spirit was executed
("killed"), "but God raised him from the dead" (10:39-40). With the Spirit
baptismal event of Acts 2 in the background, Peter further notes that the
risen Christ "commanded us . . . to testify that he is the one whom God appointed as judge of the living and the dead" (10:42). The implication here
is that the Spirit-anointed Christ was unjustly condemned and executed
but that God vindicated him by exalting him to the position of righteous
judge over history. The condemned one now sits in judgment over the
earthly courts that condemned him unjustly. But the judge is first the Savior who turns to his accusers with the offer of his Spirit and his righteous
favor. Indwelt and anointed by this same Spirit, the followers of Jesus share
in his righteous favor and are taken up into the testimony of the Spirit in
history to the vindicated Christ. This is Luke's understanding of justification in the Spirit: justification is implicitly integral to Spirit baptism for
Luke.

By receiving the Spirit, the Christian community is implicitly the
rightwised community, the justified community, for *"through him everyone is justified"* (Acts 13:39). Indwelt by the Spirit and raised from the dead
(or transformed), we, too, shall ascend to heaven "in the clouds" with Jesus
to be exalted and to have our witness to Jesus vindicated (Acts 1:11; cf.
1 Thess. 4:17). We can add a Pauline phrase here: "those he justified he also
glorified" (Rom. 8:30). In the meantime, the indwelling of the Spirit takes
us up into Christ's divine favor and turns us into living witnesses to the
vindicated Christ.

If Christ was vindicated as the new temple of God's presence, so the people of God become a temple of the Spirit in him at Pentecost. G. K. Beale has
persuasively mounted a case for the fact that the flames accompanying the
speaking in tongues in Acts 2 were part of "a theophany in a newly inaugurated eschatological temple."[13] As the confusion of tongues at the tower of
Babel was a divine judgment of the human effort to build a temple that
could reach God and establish the people's own sense of identity, Pentecost

---

13. G. K. Beale, "The Descent of the Eschatological Temple in the Form of the Spirit at
Pentecost, Part 1: The Clearest Evidence," *Tyndale Bulletin* 56, no. 1 (2005): 74.

establishes the identity of the people of God in Christ through their transformation into a temple of God's holy dwelling.[14] Holy flames do indeed
function in the Qumran literature to signify God's presence in the heavenly
temple.[15] The Lord fills the upper room at Pentecost with God's holy presence just as the glory of the Lord filled God's house in the Old Testament
(1 Kings 8:6-13). The house of God's presence will serve the establishment of
God's reign on the earth and God's vindication as Lord (2 Sam. 7:12-13). The
messianic figure will build the temple from which he will reign (Ps. 132:11;
Zech. 6:13). Christ becomes in his risen body the new temple of the Lord and
will establish God's reign by turning God's people into a temple of God's
presence through Spirit baptism. Both the establishment of a kingdom and
of a temple, therefore, may be in mind in Acts 2:30. The allusion to Psalm
132:11 in Acts 2:30 has to do with an eschatological temple inaugurated
through the baptism in the Spirit at Christ's ascension.[16] Both the temple
and God's kingdom are linked to the vindication of God and of God's
anointed as Lord and King and of the faithful who point to this lordship over
the earth through their Spirit-embodied witness. This is justification in the
Spirit by faith in Christ. Acts also notes that the fellowship of Jesus that
shares in his unjust persecution can be comforted by the hope of sharing in
his vindication as bearers of the Spirit. In fact, the early believers in Acts saw
the opposition and persecution they faced as analogous to the opposition
faced by the unjustly condemned Christ, and they explicitly asked for the
power and miracles in the midst of their suffering to have their own witness
to Jesus vindicated in the Spirit (Acts 4:27-31). The miracles of the Spirit in
Acts offer signs of God's eschatological vindication of Jesus: "It is by the
name of Jesus Christ of Nazareth, whom you crucified but whom God raised
from the dead, that this man stands before you healed" (Acts 4:10).

In the sermons of Acts, God vindicates the unjustly crucified Christ in
resurrection and exaltation and turns the execution into an event of salvation that offers life to all through the Spirit. In Paul's calling in Acts, Jesus
makes the connection between his unjust condemnation and those of his
followers, to the point of saying that Paul is continuing to unjustly persecute him by persecuting them (Acts 26:14). The Paul of Acts then saw his

---

14. Beale, "The Descent, Part 1," p. 75.

15. Beale, "The Descent, Part 1," pp. 84-93; see also Glen Menzies, "Pre-Lucan Occurrences of the Phrase 'Tongue(s) of Fire,'" *Pneuma: The Journal of the Society for Pentecostal
Studies* 22, no. 1 (Spring 2000): 27-60.

16. Beale, "The Descent of the Eschatological Temple in the Form of the Spirit at Pentecost, Part 2: Corroborating Evidence," *Tyndale Bulletin* 56, no. 2 (2005): 64, 67-69.

calling as that of bearing witness to the "Righteous One" before the Gentiles (Acts 22:14-21) in solidarity with the Spirit-anointed Jesus movement that he once persecuted. As N. T. Wright says, the work of the Spirit "causes the Apostle to re-embody the Messiah as the herald of a new age."[17] Implied in Acts is a "forensic" justification wrought in Christ's resurrection/exaltation/Spirit impartation and present in the common life of the Spirit in and among those who bear witness to Christ, especially in the midst of sharing in his suffering.

It is to this divine vindication of the unjustly condemned Christ that the Christians as bearers of the Spirit give forth this witness, thus participating in the divine self-vindication (Acts 3:19-21; 5:30-32; 13:37-39; 17:30-31).[18] For example, in Acts 13, Luke records Paul and Barnabas saying of justification that, through Christ, "everyone who believes is justified from everything you could not be justified from by the law of Moses" (Acts 13:39). Luke then ties this justification text to Jesus' unjust crucifixion (v. 28) and to his vindication by God in resurrection (v. 30). The early witnesses of Jesus' resurrection "are now his witnesses to our people" (v. 31). These Spirit-indwelt and empowered witnesses, including Paul and Barnabas, are meant to be a light to the Gentiles of the risen Christ, to bring salvation to the very ends of the earth (v. 47). Such an outpouring of the Spirit on all flesh is the final vindication of the righteous God against the murderous opponents of the Spirit-anointed Christ. Divine justification triumphs for Luke in Spirit baptism. The Spirit-inspired witness of history ends on the side of the witnesses to the risen Christ rather than on the side of the murderers of Jesus. Justification as both righteous favor and vindicated witness takes place for Luke through the Spirit that gives life from the dead and raises up witnesses who participate in the divine self-vindication in history.

These witnesses for Luke participate in God's righteous self-vindication through the Spirit and not by way of obedience to the law (Acts 13:39). In Acts 10, the Gentiles, considered as sinners under the law, are embraced by the community of the Spirit because they, too, receive the indwelling Holy Spirit from the risen and exalted Christ. They are vindicated and join the witness of the Spirit to the vindicated Christ by faith in him rather than by obedience to the law. This life in the Spirit of the vindicated Christ is in fact the only true fulfillment of the law's inherent witness for Luke (Acts 24:14; 26:22). Peter's lesson at the home of Cornelius is in-

17. N. T. Wright, *Paul in Fresh Perspective* (Minneapolis: Fortress, 2005), p. 146.
18. See Markus Barth, *Resurrection as Acquittal*, p. 70.

deed telling in the context of this Lukan focus on the Spirit and not the law as the entry of Jew and Gentile into one body and one mission of bearing eschatological witness to the justice of God. In a vision, Peter is told by God to kill and eat animals not considered pure by Jewish law. When Peter resists, God declares, "Do not call anything impure that God has made clean" (Acts 10:15). This revelation prepares Peter to accept Cornelius, who would be cleansed by the Spirit received through faith in Christ.

While Peter is yet preaching, Cornelius and his household are filled with the Spirit (Acts 10:44). The emphasis on the reception of the Spirit before Peter is finished preaching may indicate an emphasis on faith and not law as the means of receiving the Spirit. The Spirit came upon them before Cornelius and his household had the opportunity to do anything other than believe and repent. Peter's comrades agree, noting that "God has granted even the Gentiles repentance unto life" (Acts 11:18). That cleansing would come by way of the Spirit and not the law is affirmed by the Jews at the Jerusalem Council, who noted concerning the Gentiles: "God . . . showed that he accepted them by giving the Holy Spirit to them, just as he did to us. He made no distinction between us and them, for he purified their hearts by faith" (Acts 15:8-9). God's acceptance and favor come to the sinners in the gift of the Spirit and not merely in a declaration to be believed. The message of Acts is wholly consistent with Paul's teaching about the justification of Jew and Gentile in the community of the Holy Spirit by faith and not by the law. In the Spirit, justification, sanctification, and empowered witness are overlapping and mutually illuminating concepts for Luke.

If Pentecost at the time of Jesus was a celebration of the giving of the law at Sinai (as some have suggested), then Luke, in his Pentecost narrative of Acts 2, is consciously replacing the law with the Spirit as the source of participation in the life, community, and witness of the vindicated Christ.[19] Luke would then be contrasting participation in the communal life and mission of the Messiah through the gift of the Spirit with participation by way of an attempt at obedience to the law without the gift of the Spirit. Though Luke is uniquely careful to see the fulfillment of salvation through Jesus and the Spirit as consistent with the witness of Moses and the law (Acts 24:14; 26:22), he is also clear that righteousness comes not from the law but from the risen Christ and the Spirit (e.g., Acts 10:28; 13:32-39). Therefore, implied in Acts 2 is Luke's version of "justification" in the

---

19. See, for example, Robert F. O'Toole, "Acts 2:30 and the Davidic Covenant of Pentecost," *Journal of Biblical Literature* 102, no. 2 (1983): 245-58, esp. 245-47.

Spirit by faith "apart from the law," with a special focus on the implications of the term for the living communion and witness of the people of God.

Though the term "justification" is used only once in Acts, its presence may be detected implicitly at key points in the message of the book. It is indeed possible for the content of justification to be featured throughout a biblical passage or book even though the term is not used or highlighted.[20] One could see the entire book of Acts as close to the heartbeat of Paul's concern for the justification of sinners. Moreover, the entire book of Acts shows God as embracing all peoples, Jews and Gentiles, rich and poor, male and female, into one body through the shared gift of the Spirit (Acts 2:17-18, 42-47). If the Gentile reception of the Spirit is part of the impetus behind Paul's doctrine of justification by faith apart from the law (as we will note momentarily), the message of Acts definitely overlaps significantly with Paul's. Indeed, one can use the distinctly Lukan and Pentecostal root metaphor of Spirit baptism to provide a larger narrative framework for understanding justification in the Pauline discussion of that term, one that Paul himself shares and that ties justification richly to the Spirit, the kingdom of God, eschatology, and the Trinitarian self-vindication in history. However, these themes are not far from the mind of Paul, as I will suggest in the next section.

Paul: Galatians and Romans

As with Luke, Paul in Galatians indicates throughout that justification comes or is fulfilled by the gift of the Spirit of new life. The importance of pneumatology to Paul's treatment of justification and the law in Galatians has been neglected in the past.[21] Charles Cosgrove was led by discerning this importance to conclude that the gift of the Spirit is at the heart of Paul's struggle in this book to define the gospel against legalistic opponents.[22] The τοῦτο μόνον of Galatians 3:2 ("I would like to learn *just one*

---

20. I am in agreement with Eberhard Jüngel, *Justification: The Heart of the Christian Faith*, trans. Jeffrey F. Cayzer (Edinburgh: T. & T. Clark, 2001), p. 15.

21. Richard Longenecker, *Galatians*, Word Biblical Commentary, vol. 41, gen. ed. Bruce M. Metzger (Dallas: Word Books, 1990), p. 101.

22. Charles Cosgrove, *The Cross and the Spirit: A Study in the Argument and Theology of Galatians* (Macon, GA: Mercer University Press, 1988), esp. p. 40. However, Crosgrove argues that the Spirit, and *not* justification, is the central issue in Galatians, not recognizing that the two may have been equivalent for Paul.

thing from you") indicates that Paul is arriving at the heart of his concern in the letter. He follows with questions concerning how the Galatians had received the *Spirit:* ". . . because you observed the law or because you believed what you heard?" The Gentile reception of the Spirit by faith apart from the law convinced Paul that justification is by faith and not law (Gal. 3:5). As we will have occasion to note, faith is itself for Paul a vital aspect of pneumatic existence, because the Spirit is an eschatological reality that must be embraced in obedient trust in Christ rather than by sight. The witness of Galatians is clear: "[B]y faith we eagerly await through the Spirit the righteousness for which we hope" (Gal. 5:5).

In fact, justification and the gift of the Spirit serve as functional equivalents throughout Galatians. Paul affirms in Galatians 2:16 that justification is by faith and not law; the gift of the Spirit is by faith and not law in 3:2-5 as well. Justification is the blessing of Abraham in 3:8, while this blessing also involves the Spirit in 3:14. Paul starts chapter 3 (vv. 1-5) with the issue of receiving the *Spirit by faith* and not law, and then he shifts, in 3:6-8, to the example of Abraham and to the issue of *justification by faith* and not law, a shift that is necessary because it cannot be said that Abraham possessed the divine Spirit (though he was reckoned to be righteous by faith).[23] But when the chapter shifts to the contemporary situation involving the Gentiles in 3:14, the subject is once again the blessing of the Spirit by faith and not law. Paul simply assumes, without explaining it in Galatians 3, that the reception of the Spirit by faith and not law automatically implies justification by faith and not law and vice versa. This assumption would be unfounded if the two realities were not identifiable with each other in some way. Ronald Fung rightly observes:

> Paul takes it for granted that Abraham's being justified by faith *proves* that the Galatians must have received the Spirit by faith also; and this argument from scripture falls to the ground *unless* the reception of the Spirit is in some sense equated with justification.[24]

Paul is not merely implying, in Galatians 3, an analogy between justification by faith and the gift of the Spirit by faith.[25] As Dunn says about

23. Sam K. Williams, "Justification of the Spirit in Galatians," *Journal for the Study of the New Testament* 29 (1987): 95.

24. Ronald Y. K. Fung, *The Epistle to the Galatians,* New International Commentary on the New Testament (Grand Rapids: Eerdmans, 1988), p. 136 (italics in original).

25. Here Fung and I are in disagreement with Cosgrove, who makes the relationship be-

Galatians 3: "The gift of the Spirit and justification are two sides of the same coin."[26] Indeed, Galatians 3:2-6 "equates" justification with the reception of the Spirit.[27] There simply is no forensic justification that is in any way "prior" to the gift of the Spirit. E. P. Sanders notes: "In Paul's own letters, righteousness by faith, the Spirit by faith or sonship by faith mix indiscriminately with participationist language in such a way as to exclude the possibility of a systematic working out of righteousness as the forensic preliminary to life in Christ Jesus."[28]

An implication of this Pauline focus on the Spirit as the locus for justification is the equally important point that the law cannot justify because it cannot grant new life in the midst of humanity's bondage to sin and death and Israel's failure to fulfill the law's witness to life from within the provisions of the law. The law bears witness to life, but the law and its obedience cannot by themselves give life. Paul explicitly says as much in Galatians 3:21, where he notes that the law's inability to save is not an indication of its opposition to the promises of God but rather of a basic lack of power to bring these promises to fulfillment: "For if a law had been given that could impart life, then righteousness would certainly have come by the law." Sam K. Williams accurately understands the implication of this verse when he notes that "righteousness *is* by means of *[ek]* that which *can* make alive, namely, the Spirit."[29] As Nils A. Dahl says of Galatians, "Paul makes no distinction between the forensic and the pneumatic."[30] In Galatians 3, receiving the Spirit apart from the law is the same as being justified apart from the law.

The idea that the law could justify and give life if only *we* had the power and freedom to obey it simply begs the question, since there is no such power and freedom apart from the Spirit of life. Even creaturely existence apart from faith is oriented toward God by the Spirit (Acts 17:28). Creaturely freedom and power apart from the Spirit is unthinkable on any

---

tween justification and the Spirit in Galatians merely analogous. Cosgrove, *The Cross and the Spirit,* p. 40; see also Fung, *The Epistle to the Galatians,* p. 136.

26. Dunn, *Baptism in the Holy Spirit,* p. 108.

27. H. W. Heidland, "λογίζομαι," *Theological Dictionary of the New Testament,* ed. Gerhard Kittel, trans. Geoffrey W. Bromiley (Grand Rapids: Eerdmans, 1967), 4:292.

28. E. P. Sanders, *Paul and Palestinian Judaism: A Comparison of Patterns of Religion* (Minneapolis: Fortress, 1977), pp. 506-7.

29. Williams, "Justification of the Spirit in Galatians," p. 97 (italics in original).

30. Nils A. Dahl, "Promise and Fulfillment," in *Studies in Paul: Theology for the Early Christian Mission* (Minneapolis: Augsburg, 1977), p. 133.

level, a nonsensical hypothetical. The law is indeed "powerless" "in that it was weakened by the sinful nature" (Rom. 8:3), but one could add just as easily, as Paul did elsewhere, that the law is powerless also because the Spirit and not the letter is the source of life (cf. 2 Cor. 2:3-6). The law in Galatians is not just weakened by sinful flesh but by the fact that it cannot in itself impart life (Gal. 3:21). Only God can impart life, because only God can impart God. In this light, saying that the flesh without the renewing Spirit strips the law of all power of fulfillment is the same as saying that without the Spirit the letter is powerless. The letter only kills apart from the Spirit (2 Cor. 2:6); indeed, the law "lacks divine power, that power which is the primary characteristic of the Spirit."[31]

As I have noted above, the promise of the law to bring life in the Old Testament was itself qualified in both the law and the prophets by the hope that the law will do this through the coming gift of the Spirit. Life will be received in the excess of the divine outpouring and not through a system of legal exchange. The law has to be taken up in the Spirit to have its witness fulfilled. This is the meaning behind the paradox of a law testifying to a righteousness given *apart from the law* by faith in Christ (Rom. 3:21). The law is fulfilled apart from the law, not in a way that nullifies the law but in a way that fulfills it by exceeding it.

The promised gift of righteousness must then come in the Spirit rather than from within the provisions of the law. Of such the prophets were in agreement (see Ezek. 36:26; 37:13-14). John the Baptist would also note that his ceremonial washing was but the sign that awaited fulfillment in Christ as the one who would impart the promised Spirit (Matt. 3:11-12), for the kingdom of God is not in food laws ("eating and drinking") but in "righteousness, peace, and joy in the Holy Spirit" (Rom. 14:17). The law can be a valuable sign and witness, waiting to come alive via the Spirit in the obedient life, for the law is fulfilled in the life led by the Spirit (Rom. 2:29; 8:4; 13:10). In the final analysis, however, justification and regeneration is the Spirit's work. As with Luke, so also with Paul: it is by the Spirit that the Son of God enjoys the Father's favor and is vindicated (1 Tim. 3:16); so it is by the Spirit of life that we share in that divine love and vindication and are awakened to life in and for God (Rom. 8:10-11). Thus, what really matters for Paul at the heart of justification is not circumcision but rather "new creation" (Gal. 6:15), which is the work of the Spirit of life.

---

31. Williams, "Justification of the Spirit in Galatians," p. 96.

The vindication of the Gentiles apart from the law by the Spirit of God provided the theological context from which Paul would use inherited tradition to reason that Christ has fulfilled the task of Israel to bless the nations. Christ was cursed on the cross under the law but vindicated by the Spirit in resurrection (Rom. 1:4; cf. 1 Tim. 3:16); thus cursed sinners can bear the Spirit of life by faith in Christ. Paul proposed that the Gentiles were receiving the blessing of the Spirit through Christ while Israel was still under judgment. However, Paul then directly linked the risen Christ crucified under the curse of the law with both the redemption of Israel and the reception of the Spirit among the Gentile sinners:

> Christ redeemed us from the curse of the law by becoming a curse for us, for it is written: "Cursed is everyone who is hung on a tree." He redeemed us in order that the blessing given to Abraham might come to the Gentiles through Christ Jesus, so that by faith we might receive the promise of the Spirit. (Gal. 3:13-14)

As Markus Barth says, only those condemned with Christ under the law can rise with him in justification.[32] Paul will reason from there that Jews as well as Gentiles are sinners (cursed under the law) so that they may all be justified in the Spirit by the same faith in Christ crucified and risen.

> We who are Jews by birth and not "Gentile sinners" know that a man is not justified by observing the law, but by faith in Jesus Christ. So we, too, have put our faith in Christ Jesus that we may be justified by faith in Christ and not by observing the law, because by observing the law no one will be justified. (Gal. 2:15-16)

If justification is by the Spirit rather than by the law, it must come to us as a spiritual rebirth, which is precisely what Paul maintained in Galatians. Note that Paul's shift from the law to righteousness by faith in Galatians 2:19 is described as a spiritual rebirth:

> For through the law I died to the law so that I might live for God. I have been crucified with Christ and I no longer live, but Christ lives in me. The life I live in the body, I live by faith in the Son of God, who loved me and gave himself for me. (Gal. 2:19-20)

---

32. Markus Barth, "Jews and Gentiles: The Social Character of Justification in Paul," *Journal of Ecumenical Studies* 5 (1968): 249.

The curse of death vis-à-vis the law leads to identification with the crucified Christ, and in that identification a participation in his risen life and vindication.

Similarly, Paul notes in Romans 6:7 that "he who has died has been justified (δεδικαίωται) from sin," implying that justification involves spiritual rebirth and liberation from the domination of sin. This verse is strong evidence for the view that righteousness is transformative, and it has much to commend it grammatically.[33] Paul also speaks in Romans 8:10 of the shift from righteousness by the law to the righteousness attained by faith as a spiritual rebirth: "But if Christ is in you, your body is dead because of sin, yet your spirit is alive because of righteousness." The new birth by the Spirit provides Paul with the conceptual framework for understanding how justification by faith occurs in the life of the believer.

Paul's argument in Galatians 4 is also that believers are children of Abraham by being justified by faith but also *by being born of the Spirit* (Gal. 4:6, 29). We should not place too much weight on the reversal in the order of justification and new birth in the Spirit between Galatians 4:6 and 4:29.[34] Paul surely does not mean to say in 4:6 that sonship is possible without the Spirit! In the light of 4:29, Paul involves the Spirit in verse 6 at the very essence of justification. Paul's major point in this chapter is that even having the law is not enough to qualify a people as children of Abraham, inheritors of his righteousness by faith. Even the holy covenant of Mount Sinai can be said to bear children who are still enslaved (v. 24). Only those born of the Spirit from above are free as children of Abraham, sharing in the righteousness embraced in faith (v. 29).

As we noted above, the blessing of Abraham involves both justification (Gal. 3:8) and the gift of the Spirit (3:14). Being in the Spirit is being "in Christ," sharing in his sonship and in the inheritance promised to the children of Abraham. Indeed, "all the Gentiles, begotten as children of Abra-

---

33. But then, seemingly out of confessional loyalty (and in tension with the wording of the text), Michael Bird concludes that the link between justification and transformation in this text is "logical" but not "conceptual." Bird, *The Saving Righteousness of God: Studies on Paul, Justification, and the New Perspective*, Paternoster Biblical Monographs (Eugene, OR: Wipf and Stock, 2007), p. 18.

34. This is what Williams does when he highlights this alleged inconsistency to support his conclusion that there is no causal connection between justification and new birth by the Spirit. If there is no such causal connection, then how is one to understand Paul's point in Galatians that he died to the law in order to awaken to righteousness by faith (Gal. 2:19-20; cf. Rom. 8:10)? See Williams, "Justification of the Spirit in Galatians," p. 100n12.

ham by the *Spirit* of God, would be blessed by being reckoned *righteous*."[35] The righteousness reckoned here is not granted from a distant court, but in the context of the Spirit's embrace and in anticipation of the resurrection and the new creation. Justification by grace through faith in Galatians is justification through the life-renewing indwelling of the Spirit of God.

This integral connection between justification and the Spirit is implied in Romans as well. An argument can be made that the entire structure of Romans 1–8 supports the idea that justification involves new life in the place of the condemnation and death brought about by human disobedience.[36] The quotation of Habakkuk 2:4 in Romans 1:17 may well be translated "those just by faith shall *live*," placing the emphasis on life as integral to justification, just as condemnation and death are integral to the reality of sin. Christ was raised for our justification (Rom. 4:25) in fulfillment of the faith of Abraham in "the God who gives life to the dead and calls things that are not as though they were" (Rom. 4:17). Thus, with Adam, "the result of one trespass was condemnation," while, with Christ, "the result of one act of righteousness was justification *that brings life*" (Rom. 5:18). Chapters 6–8 then contrast further condemnation/death and justification/life. Romans 8:4 brings this contrast to a sharp focus by noting that Christ condemned sin in the flesh "in order that the righteous requirements of the law might be fully met in us, who do not live according to the sinful nature but according to the Spirit." Our spirits are said to be alive because of God's gift of righteousness (Rom. 8:10). Dunn rightly concludes the following from these texts:

> [J]ustification or right relationship and the Spirit are so closely connected for Paul — so close that each can be described as the result and outworking of the other (vv. 4, 10) — that we can draw up a similar equation: gift of the Spirit = gift of righteousness.[37]

In Romans, "Christ's 'act of righteousness' issues in 'justifying life.'"[38] As Joseph Fitzmyer notes, the "Spirit of life" in Romans is "nothing other

---

35. Bird, *The Saving Righteousness*, p. 96 (italics in original).

36. Bird, *The Saving Righteousness*, pp. 49-53; see also Mary Sylvia C. Nwachukwu, *Creation-Covenant Scheme and Justification by Faith: A Canonical Study of the God-Human Drama in the Pentateuch and the Letter to the Romans* (Rome: Editrice Pontifica Universita Gregoriana, 2002), p. 326.

37. Dunn, *Baptism in the Holy Spirit*, p. 148.

38. James D. G. Dunn, *Romans 1–8*, Word Biblical Commentary, vol. 38 (Dallas: Word, 1988), p. 432.

than justification."[39] The just relationship for the New Testament is not primarily a legal or a moral relationship but a mutual indwelling by the Spirit of life. God does not just accept sinners; God embraces them, takes them into the divine life and puts the divine life in them. God grants the *koinonia* of divine love.

In the light of the foregoing discussion, we should not be surprised that Paul would root justification in both Christ's death and *resurrection* in the book of Romans. N. T. Wright is correct in noting that "Romans is suffused with resurrection. Squeeze this letter at any point and resurrection spills out; hold it up to the light, and you can see Easter sparkling all the way through."[40] In Romans 4:25, Paul quotes what is most likely an ancient confession concerning Christ: "He was delivered over to death for our sins and was raised to life for our justification."

Seeing that the integral relationship between justification and the gift of new life in the Spirit is already prevalent in Galatians and in Romans 1–8, I find it odd that there are commentators on Romans who find the linkage between Christ's resurrection and justification in Romans 4:25 "puzzling."[41] Efforts to explain the language of 4:25 by ignoring its Semitic parallelism ("for our sins . . . for our justification") — so that the text would read, for example, "he was raised *because* we were justified (by Christ's death)" — cannot stand unchallenged.[42] In point of fact, the thematic focus on the resurrection as the declaration of Christ's sonship in Romans 1:4 leads to the concentration on Abraham in Romans 4 as the one who believed "the God who gives life to the dead and calls things that are not as though they were" (1:17).[43] God's calling into being "things that are not as

---

39. Joseph A. Fitzmyer, *Romans*, Anchor Bible Commentary (New York: Doubleday, 1992), p. 491.

40. Wright, *The Resurrection of the Son of God*, p. 241.

41. "Puzzling" is Douglas Moo's term in *The Epistle to the Romans*, New International Commentary on the New Testament (Grand Rapids: Eerdmans, 1996), p. 289. On a linguistic level, I understand why Moo would say that Rom. 4:25 is at least somewhat surprising. Paul does not often link justification explicitly to Christ's resurrection. But the overall flow of the argument of Romans 1–8 makes the link between justification and Christ's resurrection in Rom. 4:25 not particularly "puzzling" at all. See Dunn, *Romans 1–8*, p. 225.

42. Thus I argue against Adolf Schlatter, *Romans: The Righteousness of God*, trans. Siegfried S. Schatzmann (Peabody, MA: Hendrickson, 1995), p. 118, and H. C. G. Moule, *The Epistle to the Romans* (Fort Washington, PA: Christian Literature Crusade, 1975), p. 126. For the importance of the parallelism, see Peter Stuhlmacher, *Paul's Letter to the Romans: A Commentary*, trans. Scott J. Hafemann (Louisville: Westminster/John Knox, 1994), p. 75.

43. Wright, *The Resurrection of the Son of God*, p. 242.

though they were" in this verse is God's regarding us as raised though we are still in the midst of death.

There is indeed a "reckoning" of righteousness here; however, such is not the reckoning of "merits" (or some such "quantity" of grace or record of righteous accomplishments) but a reckoning of life to be discerned and experienced by faith right in the midst of death! Indeed, as Paul says, "the words 'it was credited to him' were written not for him alone, but also for us, to whom God will credit righteousness — for us who believe in him who raised Jesus our Lord from the dead" (Rom. 4:24). The "justifying grace of God is all of a piece with his life-giving power."[44] Aquinas captured the sense of Romans 4:25 when he referred to the resurrection and ascension of Christ as "the cause of our justification, by which we return to newness of justice."[45]

That Christ was "delivered up" (παρεδόθη) in Romans for our transgressions (Rom. 4:25) recalls God's delivering up or handing over the sinner to the perils of a wayward life in 1:24-26. The excesses of sin described in Romans 1 are outdone by the greater excess of grace poured out abundantly upon sinners in the Spirit of life: "Where sin increased, grace increased all the more" (Rom. 5:12-21). As the Deutero-Pauline text Titus 3:5-7 notes, grace is available in the excessive abundance of the Spirit poured out on undeserving vessels: "the Holy Spirit, whom he poured out on us generously through Jesus Christ our Savior." Indeed, if God delivered up his own Son, none of the Son's benefits will be withheld from those who share in his Spirit by faith (Rom 8:32). This excess of grace in the Spirit of life thus has its roots in the resurrection of the Messiah cursed on the cross. In Romans 4:25, Christ is also delivered up along with the sinners in order that through his resurrection by the Spirit (Rom. 1:4) the undeserving sinners (principally Gentiles, but also Jews) might have the Spirit of new life as well.

Implied in Romans is the connection present in Galatians between the cursed Christ raised from the dead by the Spirit and the cursed Gentiles and Jews justified in the same Spirit. Christ, as the one rejected, is declared by God in resurrection as the favored Son "according to the Spirit of holiness" (Rom. 1:4; cf. 4:25). Indeed, Christ "appeared in a body, was vindicated by the Spirit" (1 Tim. 3:16). So also the Gentile and Jewish sinners reckoned as cursed under the law are embraced in the realm of this very

---

44. Dunn, *Romans 1–8*, p. 241.
45. Aquinas, *Ep. Ad Romanos*, 4:3, quoted in Fitzmyer, *Romans*, p. 390.

same Spirit as sons and daughters of God taken up in the communion of the Spirit, justified in the Spirit of life by faith and not the law. Justification is implicitly about resurrection, substantially about the Spirit. The atonement was viewed from the lens of Pentecost.

Christ's being "delivered up" can also be read in the light of Isaiah 52:13–53:12. Worthy of note is Isaiah 53:11, in which the servant "justifies many," especially in the light of what seems to be his resurrection: "After the suffering of his soul, he will see the light of life."[46] In Romans, God reckons all as sinners in order to have mercy on all (Rom. 11:32). The Gentile category of "sinner" is applied to the Jew in order that the Jew might know the same justification embraced in the resurrection of the cursed and rejected Jesus. The Jewish category of "righteous" is thereby expanded in order to include the Gentile via the gift of the Spirit.[47] All are reckoned as sinners so that all can be justified in the Spirit of the risen Christ.

The conclusion of Romans 4 that Christ was raised for our justification (v. 25) could not be more natural in its scriptural context. Since new life through the Spirit is integral to justification, it is quite natural to see the resurrection and the impartation of the Spirit from the risen and ascended Christ as the root cause of justification. The confusion sometimes expressed in the face of Romans 4:25 is caused in part by an understanding of justification imported from outside of Romans, namely, as a divine declaration based on the cross but essentially distinct from the life of the Spirit. Justification is thus thought to arise from the event of the cross rather than the resurrection, and may be reducible to pardon for sin. As I have noted earlier, Everett Harrison could even write in intentional resistance to the wording of Romans 4:25:

> It may be helpful to recognize that justification, considered objectively as an aspect of God's provision, was indeed accomplished in the death of Christ and therefore did not require the resurrection to complete it.[48]

In a reductionism similar to Harrison's, Charles Hodge takes from Romans 4:25 nothing more than the fact that the resurrection is the mere

---

46. C. E. B. Cranfield, *A Critical and Exegetical Commentary on the Epistle to the Romans* (reprint; Edinburgh: T. & T. Clark, 1985), 2:252.

47. Eugene Rogers, *After the Spirit* (Grand Rapids: Eerdmans, 2005), pp. 87-88, 91.

48. Everett F. Harrison, *Romans*, Expositor's Bible Commentary (Grand Rapids: Zondervan, 1976), p. 54.

"evidence" of a justification fully accomplished in Christ's work of satisfaction in the cross.[49]

Joseph Fitzmyer rightly complains that the resurrection as an event of the Spirit has in the West been treated as "an appendage or even an exemplary confirmation of Jesus' death, which was considered to be the real cause of forgiveness of sins and justification."[50] Markus Barth, too, notes that justification has wrongly been narrowly attributed to the crucifixion and sanctification to the resurrection.[51] The resurrection of Jesus represents both God's solemn acceptance of Christ's sacrifice as well as those who by faith in him have died and risen with him. "There is no righteousness worthy of its name without resurrection."[52]

In the context of incorporation by the Spirit into Christ, the events of resurrection, exaltation, and Spirit impartation become essential aspects of justification. After all, the Christ vindicated in the Spirit shares his righteous favor with us by imparting the Spirit of life. Philip Melanchthon has captured the spirit of Romans 4:25 well in the following summation:

> Not only the death of Christ must be apprehended, but also that our high priest with the Father has been raised again, that he truly hears us, is truly efficacious, truly gives life, gives the Holy Spirit, helps us, frees us from eternal death, will raise the dead, and will give new and everlasting life, wisdom, and righteousness. Paul has included all these things when he says, "he rose again for our justification."[53]

The Spirit is the link for Paul between the justification of the crucified Christ in resurrection and the hope of those who suffer in Christ for final vindication. As in Luke, so also with Paul in Romans, those who suffer with Christ take comfort in their being justified and glorified with him in the fullness of life in the Spirit. The entire logic in Romans 8 leads to this conclusion. Those who suffer are comforted with the hope of glory (8:18); the hope is founded on the presupposition that those justified are also glorified (8:30); then Paul gets right to the point in 8:31-38, showing that there

---

49. Charles Hodge, *Epistle to the Romans,* 9th ed. (Grand Rapids: Eerdmans, 1958), p. 129.

50. Fitzmyer, *Romans,* p. 389.

51. Barth, *Resurrection as Acquittal,* p. 22.

52. Barth, *Acquittal by Resurrection,* pp. 4-5.

53. Philip Melanchthon, *Commentary on the Romans,* trans. Fred Kramer (St. Louis: Concordia, 1992), p. 121.

is no charge against God's elect that can triumph against them, for "it is God who justifies" (8:33). In the end, all of the voices that condemn cannot triumph, for God's verdict over those who suffer will have the final word when they are vindicated in resurrection and glorification, for "those he justified, he also glorified" (Rom. 8:30).

Romans 10 also implies — in concert with Luke — a connection between justification and vindication in the Spirit among those who suffer or are condemned. Verse 10 declares that the heart believes unto justification and the mouth confesses unto salvation. Verse 11 follows that no one who trusts in the Lord *will be put to shame,* pointing to the vindication of the company of the justified. In an allusion to the outpouring of the Spirit in Joel 2, Romans 10:12-13 then notes: "For there is no difference between Jew and Gentile — the same Lord is Lord of all and richly blesses all who call on him, for 'everyone who calls on the name of the Lord will be saved.'" None will be put to shame, for all are vindicated by faith and the "blessing" of the Spirit. As in Galatians 3, both justification and the Spirit are involved in the blessing of Jew and Gentile. Paul's quoting of Joel in Romans 10:13 indicates, through echoes in the text, that a theology of the Spirit is implied here as well.[54] This theology implicitly involves the Spirit in covenant renewal and the vindication of the renewed people of God by faith — both Jew and Gentile.

The gift of righteousness in Romans is thus not a quantifiable record of merits. It is rather an essential feature of life and communion in the Spirit that conquers and reigns in the place of death. I thus agree with D. Lyle Dabney that the Spirit is the very substance of justification for Paul.[55] There is little wonder that Romans 1–8 would lead the Luther expert, Gerhard Ebeling, to speak of "life-giving justice/righteousness" by way of participation through faith in the righteousness of Christ and to conclude that, "understood thus, justice/righteousness by faith cannot be forensic."[56] I would note in passing that it is not forensic in a way that lacks the Spirit of life. I would go so far as to say that justification in the Spirit for Paul has legal or forensic overtones, as we saw with Luke's Acts. But these overtones are dimensions of life in the Spirit rather than an abstract declaration or transfer of merits. As Andreas Osiander says, a fundamen-

54. N. T. Wright, *Paul in Fresh Perspective,* p. 125; see also p. 145.

55. Dabney, "The Justification by the Spirit: Soteriological Reflections on the Resurrection," *International Journal of Systematic Theology* 3, no. 1 (March 2001): 46-68.

56. Ebeling, *The Truth of the Gospel: An Exposition of Galatians,* trans. David Green (Philadelphia: Fortress, 1985), pp. 335-36.

tally forensic view of justification is a "thing colder than ice."[57] Such a view of justification is not Pauline, or even biblical for that matter, for "the decisive fact which Paul cherishes is the presence of the Spirit in the believer: the Spirit is life by virtue of God's righteousness, the Spirit as God's acceptance and sustaining power active in those who trust him."[58]

Paul: Two Baptismal Texts

There are two additional texts (one Pauline and the other Deutero-Pauline), possibly connected to the ancient practice of water baptism, that place justification and the gift of the Spirit within the closest proximity, even to the point of indicating that justification comes to the believer or is fulfilled through the indwelling of the Spirit. The first is 1 Corinthians 6:11, in which Paul writes to Gentile believers, "You were washed, you were sanctified, you were justified in the name of the Lord Jesus Christ and by the Spirit of God." We may not be accustomed to speaking of washing and justification as "by (in) the Spirit of God," but Paul considered such language appropriate. Some hesitate before this verse, noting that "justification" may not have here "its technical Pauline sense."[59] Accustomed to viewing justification in Paul as a legal declaration of pardon in Christ distinct from life in the Spirit, some find it odd that justification in this verse seems "to be located in baptism and new life."[60] A pneumatological reading of Paul on justification, however, will open up the possibility that he was in full agreement with the earlier and broader Christian tradition of making the Spirit the "nerve center" of all soteriological categories, including justification.

Thus do I agree with Gordon Fee that no hesitation or qualification is required in response to 1 Corinthians 6:11. Fee does not locate this text within the rite of water baptism; rather, he regards it as a description of regeneration, sanctification, and justification. Of interest to us, however, is Fee's conclusion that for Paul all of these terms are the result of the work of

57. "Kelter ding dan das eyes"; Osiander, "Eine Disputation von der Rechtfertigung," §73, *Schriften und Briefe 1549 bis August 1551*, hrsg., Gerhard Müller und Gottfried Seebass, *Gesamtausgabe*, Bd. 9 (Gütersloh: Gütersloher Verlagshaus, 1994).

58. Dunn, *Romans 1–8*, pp. 444-45.

59. C. K. Barrett, *A Commentary on the First Epistle to the Corinthians* (New York: Harper and Row, 1968), p. 142.

60. Barrett, *Commentary on the First Epistle to the Corinthians*, p. 142.

the Spirit in the believer's life.[61] James Dunn also wrote of this verse that "the link between the Spirit and justification is very strong," implying that "justification . . . takes place in the Spirit."[62] We may conclude from this verse that regeneration, sanctification, and justification are overlapping metaphors of new life in the Spirit, each with its own unique theological nuance. In the gift of the Spirit we are spiritually reborn, cleansed of our sin, "righteoused," and sanctified (or consecrated) by God. The Spirit is at the base of justification and "it is only pneumatology that fulfills the work of justification."[63]

We may also parenthetically note, before proceeding to our other baptismal text, that a similar connection between justification and the Spirit is implied elsewhere in the Corinthian correspondence. Second Corinthians 3:6-11 tells us that the letter of the law kills but the Spirit gives life. Contrasting the ministries of law and Spirit, Paul writes, "If the ministry that condemns men is glorious, how much more is the ministry that brings righteousness?" The implication here is that the ministry of the Spirit brings with it rightwising, while the ministry of the law brings condemnation.

The other baptismal text relevant to our discussion is Titus 3:5-7, in which the author speaks of Christ:

> He saved us, not because of righteous things we have done, but because of his mercy. He saved us through the washing of rebirth and renewal by the Holy Spirit, whom he poured out on us generously through Jesus Christ our Savior, so that having been justified by grace, we might become heirs, having the hope of eternal life.

As with 1 Corinthians 6:11, this Titus text indicates a role for the Spirit in the reception and fulfillment of justification. The line "he saved us not because of righteous things we have done" parallels the next line: ". . . he saved us through the washing of rebirth and renewal by the Holy Spirit." Salvation by grace equals salvation by the Spirit. The generosity and abundance of grace are defined pneumatologically as God's own abundant self-giving in the Spirit. Then, at the center of the following two references to

---

61. Gordon Fee, *The First Epistle to the Corinthians*, New International Commentary on the New Testament (Grand Rapids: Eerdmans, 1987), p. 247.

62. Dunn, *Baptism in the Holy Spirit*, pp. 122-23.

63. Gottlob Schrenk, "δικαιοσύνη," in *Theological Dictionary of the New Testament*, ed. Gerhard Kittel, trans. Geoffrey W. Bromiley (Grand Rapids: Eerdmans, 1964), 2:209.

salvation ("he saved us . . . having been justified by grace") stands the statement about the renewing and cleansing work of the Spirit.[64] Salvation and justification are thus implicitly linked to regeneration by the Spirit. The *ina* clause in verse 7 confirms this linkage, indicating that justification involves our inheritance of life through the gift of the Spirit and new birth. This line of interpretation leads to Dunn's conclusion that "no Paulinist would think to distinguish the event of being justified from that of becoming an heir 'in hope of eternal life.' The saving purpose of God, which is that we might be justified and become heirs, is effected by the baptism in the Spirit."[65]

These texts imply that justification in the Spirit is a participatory reality in which the Spirit dwells in us and we dwell in God. I wish to briefly explore what the Johannine witness can say to us in this context.

John: Righteousness as Mutual Indwelling

Justification by grace is certainly not a prominent theme in John. But Theo Preiss has shown that John's teaching on the vindication of divine righteousness in the world parallels and overlaps considerably with Paul's own theology of justification, even though the typically Pauline language for justification is lacking in John. Preiss notes that throughout John there is assumed a vast rejection in the world of God's claims to faithfulness and truth, at the end of which God is sure to emerge as victor through the glory of the cross and the resurrection. Christ and the Spirit are present as faithful *witnesses* to the triumph of divine faithfulness, witnesses that are sure to be vindicated.[66] Jesus specifically relates his witness to the faithful Father as together fulfilling the requirements of the law that qualify a witness as faithful.

> The Pharisees challenged him, "Here you are, appearing as your own witness; your testimony is not valid." Jesus answered, "Even if I testify on my own behalf, my testimony is valid, for I know where I came from and where I am going. But you have no idea where I come from or where I am going. You judge by human standards; I pass judgment on no one.

---

64. Philip Towner, *The Letters to Timothy and Titus,* New International Commentary on the New Testament (Grand Rapids: Eerdmans, 2006), p. 787.

65. Dunn, *Baptism in the Holy Spirit,* p. 167.

66. Theo Preiss, *Life in Christ* (Chicago: Alec R. Allenson, 1954), pp. 15-20.

But if I do judge, my decisions are right, because I am not alone. I stand with the Father, who sent me. In your own Law it is written that the testimony of two men is valid. I am one who testifies for myself; my other witness is the Father, who sent me." (John 8:13-18)

Jesus later involves the Spirit as intercessor and witness as well. After the triumph of the cross and the resurrection, the vindication of the Father and Son's witness to divine truth and faithfulness goes on through the ministry of the Spirit. The Spirit's witness will confirm the faithful witness of Jesus and the Father as well as the condemnation of the devil as the cosmic false witness.

> When he [the Spirit] comes, he will convict the world of guilt in regard to sin and righteousness and judgment: in regard to sin, because men do not believe in me; in regard to righteousness, because I am going to the Father, where you can see me no longer; and in regard to judgment, because the prince of this world now stands condemned. (John 16:8-11)

In the Apocalypse, too, there are constant reminders that God's judgments are faithful and true and will be vindicated (Rev. 16:4-5), while the devil, the accuser, will be defeated and shown to be false (12:10-12). In Revelation 11, the two witnesses, arguably a symbol of the people of God, minister under the power of the Spirit. When executed, they rise up and ascend to the throne of God vindicated for their witness to Christ, just as Christ was vindicated in his witness to the heavenly Father. They ascend to heaven on a cloud, as did the vindicated Son of man in Daniel 7 and Acts 1, "while their enemies looked on" (11:12). The Spirit vindicates the witnesses for their testimony to divine righteousness in the world in a way that is analogous to the vindicated Son of man, in his very image, for they conquer by his blood (12:11).

In John's Gospel, the love shared among believers with the heavenly Father in Christ is at the very essence of the fulfillment of divine justice in the world and will represent the chief means by which the witness of the faithful community will convince the world to believe (John 17:20-26). This love is *koinonia,* a mutual sharing of life: "Just as you are in me and I am in you. May they also be in us so that the world may believe that you have sent me" (17:21). The Spirit is implicitly here at the very substance of this love and this witness in the world.

In my examination of righteousness in the Old Testament, I noted that divine righteousness is covenant faithfulness that is concentrated on God's people but extends beyond to reach the entire creation. We also saw that righteousness would be concentrated objectively on God's anointed and would through him involve an outpouring of the Spirit on all flesh. God's justifying righteousness would penetrate to the very core of our being and cause us to dwell in God as the realm of freedom and obedience. The divine rightwising of the sinful creature would come with the gift of the Spirit and be defined substantially as renewed *koinonia* between God and humanity. John marvelously fills out the implications of what the Old Testament looked forward to in terms of the triumph of divine justice or righteousness in the world through the gift of the Spirit and the renewed, just community.

At this juncture it is important to note that, even in those New Testament texts where rightwising is not explicitly tied to the indwelling of the Spirit, it is *implicitly* tied to that indwelling. I will use the Epistle of James as a case in point.

James: Justification as Incarnated "from Above"

I will discuss James again in a later chapter that deals with faith. In this context, however, I am interested in how James's discussion of faith set the context for what he wrote about the term "justification," especially against the background of the Pauline understanding that justification occurs in the Spirit. In dealing with James and justification, I will need to make a few preliminary remarks about James's understanding of faith — only to elaborate on them later. The issue of the relationship between Paul and James is complex. I will only attempt here to cut to the chase by briefly offering my own reading of James in the light of the Pauline tradition. I do believe that James had a certain version of the Pauline legacy in mind when writing; thus it is important to hear his voice as complementary to Paul's legacy before continuing.[67]

There are three aspects of the discussion in James 2 that strike me as important right away in my reading of James on justification. First, I am struck by the fact that justification is not James's major concern. The entire

---

67. I agree here with Wiard Popkes that James's perceived "opposition has some relation to Pauline thought." Popkes, "Two Interpretations of 'Justification' in the New Testament Reflections on Galatians 2:15-21 and James 2:21-25," *Studia Theologica* 59 (2005): 129-46 (quote from p. 133).

discussion in James 2 where justification is mentioned (vv. 14-26) deals mainly with the issue of faith and works. Justification is imported into the discussion as a subsidiary issue. Verse 18 introduces his major concern: "But someone will say, 'You have faith; I have deeds.' Show me your faith without deeds, and I will show you my faith by what I do." He then concludes the passage with the issue of faith as well: "As the body without the spirit is dead, so faith without deeds is dead" (v. 26).

James seems concerned primarily with an erroneous view of faith as a mere confession that is removed from life: "You believe that there is one God. Good! Even the demons believe that — and shudder" (2:19). This biting sarcasm is meant to drive home the point that faith as a mere confession of belief does not even reach the standard of faith met by the demons, for they at least *feel* what they believe, right down to the core of their being! Their feeling is one of terror rather than adoration, but it is a feeling nonetheless, which places it above a formal and abstract confession. Such a confession without life expression is like a disembodied spirit rather than an incarnate reality (2:26). Even the demons have been more deeply affected.

Secondly, I am struck by the spirituality that informs the discussion of faith and works in James, so that justification may find authentic "manifestation" (Calvin) in life. Tellingly, our passage on living faith in James 2 is sandwiched in between a discussion of the need to obey the word of God rather than merely to "listen" (1:19-26) and a passage about unruly speech springing forth from an unruly inner life, like a certain kind of spring that gives forth the same kind of water or a certain kind of tree that bears a corresponding kind of fruit (3:1-12). Obviously, James had in mind a notion of living faith that involves the willful determination of the believer (doing and not only hearing) but that arises even more fundamentally from a change deep within (becoming a certain kind of spring or tree). True faith takes place for James in the context of a relationship with God that changes us into friends of God as a just community, inspiring willful expressions of this loyalty in our treatment of others (3:26).[68] For James, faith does not seem to be very different in substance from what we might term, from a Pauline perspective, the work of the Spirit in new birth. Indeed, for James, God wills to "give us birth through the word of truth, that we might be a kind of firstfruits of all he created" (1:18).

By observing this similarity between James and Paul, I do not mean to deny that, to some extent, James occupied a different thought world from

---

68. Popkes, "Two Interpretations," pp. 135-36.

Paul's. Paul's heavy focus on Christ and the Spirit (implicitly Trinitarian structure) is nowhere to be found in James. James speaks simply of "God" or the "Father of lights." But there is no question that, for James, God alone is the source of the wisdom that leads to good deeds (3:13), for this wisdom "comes from heaven" (3:17) and is received by unwavering faith: "If any of you lacks wisdom, he should ask God, who gives generously to all without finding fault, and it will be given to him. But when he asks, he must believe and not doubt . . ." (1:5-6). This unwavering faith is rooted in God's unchanging faithfulness to give us every good gift, even to grant us spiritual rebirth: "Every good and perfect gift is from above, coming down from the Father of the heavenly lights, who does not change like shifting shadows. He chose to give us birth through the word of truth, that we might be a kind of firstfruits of all he created" (1:17-18). Again, we have a language that is analogous to Paul's emphasis on the reception of the Spirit by faith as the source of every good thing.

We must keep in mind that the teaching about justification as being by works and not by faith alone (2:24) is directed to those who are professing faith in God but contradicting it in life. James's concern is not to describe how one comes to genuine faith but rather what genuine faith in God looks like. The works discussed are the works *of faith,* and the wisdom that produces good works (3:13) is attained *in faith* (1:5-6). Therefore, justification is by faith and works for James, but not in the same sense.[69] Faith has the priority in justification, a justification that faith's works then "complete," or incarnate (1:26). The implication is that justification is by faith, but that this justification is embodied in a changed life that is evidenced in genuine works of faith. James is especially clear that faith is thus also completed by the dedicated life that flows from it, for faith requires embodiment to be genuine, living faith: "As the body without the spirit is dead, so faith without deeds is dead" (2:26). In a sense, "faith" completed by works is functionally the same as living faith as Paul would have understood it. Every other use of the term "faith" in James should be bracketed by quotation marks.

The last striking feature of justification in James is that the righteousness involved in justification, though a gift through and through, is also a harvest to be reaped in life (3:18). Justification is "by works" in the sense

---

69. I find Kenneth Collins's discussion of Wesley's soteriology helpful in arriving at this formulation. See Collins, *The Theology of John Wesley: Holy Love and the Shape of Grace* (Nashville: Abingdon, 2007), p. 163.

that it is continuously sought and grasped in a faith that is embodied in the virtuous life and that bears the fruit of good deeds. James defines good deeds as "deeds done in the humility that comes from wisdom" (3:13). This humility and the wisdom at its base cause one to honor the poor and to resist being seduced by the arrogance of riches or social power (1:9-11; 2:1-4; 3:13; 4:13-16; 5:1-6). The justified life incarnates itself penultimately within the just community that manifests the justice of God and allows that justice to bear genuine fruit in a community formed around humble regard for one another and obedience to God and God's righteous law. The fruit of such good works is but the firstfruits of God's own creation (1:18).

What about justification and the Spirit in the context of James? James did not explicitly write about justification as in the "Spirit," but he came close to doing so when he implied that the life of good works in which justification is embodied is "spiritual" and "from heaven" (3:15) and directed toward the fulfillment of the firstfruits of the new creation (1:18). The fact that the justification that the righteous life embodies is referred to as a harvest to be reaped also implies the presence of God as the nourishment from which this righteousness grows. In addition, this righteousness is a profoundly communal dynamic for James, which locates justification in what might be called the "third article" of the Apostles' Creed, the article of the Spirit.

Conclusion

Justification is more deeply connected to the indwelling and new life of the Spirit in the New Testament witness than is commonly assumed. The strong implication of the New Testament is that justification is a dimension of life in the Spirit, of the baptism in the Holy Spirit. Indeed, the cumulative evidence both implicit and explicit strongly suggests that receiving the Spirit and being justified are equivalent realities in Scripture so that one could rightly regard justified existence as pneumatic existence. The link between justification and the gift of the Spirit is not just "logical" or collateral but rather conceptual and integral. I agree with D. Lyle Dabney that the Spirit is the very *substance* of the justified life.[70] The indwelling of the Spirit through Pentecost fulfills the Old Testament *Shekinah*, the presence of God tabernacling with the faithful from the Exodus to the promised land. In the meantime, N. T. Wright has observed:

---

70. Dabney, "The Justification by the Spirit," pp. 46-68.

[T]he work of the Gospel, by the Spirit, in the individual Christian is the putting to rights in advance of men, women, and children, against the day when God puts the whole world to rights. . . . This is the point at which justification by faith can be firmly located on the map of Paul's reimagining of Jewish eschatology in the light of Jesus and the Spirit.[71]

The Scriptures concentrate all soteriological categories not only on Christ but also on the Spirit, both of whom are sent by the Father to accomplish the Father's will and to fulfill justice by bringing creation into the embrace of their love and communion. Sin is not just a broken commandment but an alienation from the blessings of the divine presence. The grace that justifies is not merely a disposition in God or a favorable turning of God toward the sinful creation from a distance; nor is it a mere enabling for the creature's moral development. Grace is the divine embrace whereby God takes the forsaken creatures into the divine bosom by sending the faithful Son and imparting the divine presence through him within and among them.

Spirit baptism provides the link between the Spirit-indwelt Christ and the Spirit-indwelt church, or between Christ's justification and ours. This link must be viewed as containing both objective and subjective significance. Spirit baptism reveals a justification that is based alone on the faithful and true self-giving of God as Father, Son, and Spirit, but this self-giving does not end with the resurrection and exaltation of Christ. In his death, resurrection, and exaltation, Christ was meant to become the life-giving spirit (1 Cor. 15:45) or the firstborn among many (Rom. 8:29). The objective self-giving of God that forms the basis of justification involves both the economies of the Son and the Spirit. It thus involves Pentecost as well: Pentecost cannot be collapsed entirely into the subjective or interpersonal life of the church; it also belongs to the objective self-giving and outpouring of God into the world, and it belongs to the Christ event as well. As we root justification in what God has done *for us* in Christ, we must not overlook Pentecost.

The strength of Spirit baptism as a lens through which to view justification is that it not only fills out the objective basis of justification so as to unveil its Trinitarian fullness; it also shows how justification objectively viewed is *inseparable* from justification viewed through the lens of its incarnation or embodiment in the life and witness of the people of God.

---

71. Wright, *Paul*, pp. 149, 147.

Pentecost fills out the objective basis of justification but also contains within it the subjective realization of justification as an eschatological and communal reality. We are justified by the Trinitarian self-giving and self-vindication of God, but not to the exclusion of the weak and ambiguous witness of the people of God. Justification in the context of Spirit baptism pardons the sinners by embracing, cleansing, and renewing them with the divine indwelling and then continuing to embrace the ambiguous faith and witness that arise in response, regarding them by grace as corresponding to the faithfulness of Christ. Spiritual presence overcomes ambiguous life. This is not "double justification" — as though there are two causes to justification — since it is but one justification that begins and ends in God. We participate in it by faith, but the source and end is one, namely *God*.[72]

The elements of witness and vindication are a large part of the "legal" overtones of justification, which remains a gift indescribable by any legal system of exchange. In Luke's Acts, the Spirit poured out from the crucified and exalted Messiah brings sinful creation into his righteous rule and his loving embrace, or communion, as the man of the Spirit with the Father (e.g., Acts 10:38-43). Implied here is that one is brought through the Spirit's indwelling into the circle of faithfulness enjoyed by the exalted Christ as the man of the Spirit who sits at the right hand of his heavenly Father, a position of deity, authority, and divine favor. The man unjustly executed rises to the Judge's bench, not with the purpose of exacting revenge but of bestowing the Spirit of righteous favor on all flesh. Judgment only falls on those who spurn that Spirit and the divine self-giving behind the Spirit's presence. Hope continues to be offered, however, that all flesh will receive the Spirit. After all, the Spirit is blasphemed on the cross of the rejected Messiah in order to embrace the blasphemers. This is why those handed over to judgment in Romans 1:24-28 are claimed by God's justification by the handing over of God's own Son (Rom. 4:25; 8:32).

In addition, however, in John, Acts, and the Apocalypse, the Spirit also empowers a strong witness of the crucified Jesus as the exalted ruler of history. This witness will ultimately vindicate God as the faithful Lord of creation. Despite our weakness and the ambiguity of our witness, we are allowed to participate in that witness and vindication, which is our

---

72. I appreciate Brian Lugioyo's insight into the problems involved in the term "double justification." Brian Lugioyo, "Martin Bucer's Doctrine of Justification and the Colloquy of Regensburg 1541" (PhD diss., University of Aberdeen, 2007; forthcoming from Oxford University Press), pp. 38, 89.

vindication, too. Justification is Spirit baptized and empowered witness "by grace." Paul also speaks of justification in the context of the vindication (ultimately through glorification) of creation in the midst of suffering (Rom. 8:28-39). Those suffering the weight of injustice can place their hope in the unjustly condemned but risen and exalted Christ that their hard-fought struggle to bear the image of God with all of the human dignity granted by the Spirit will someday be fully vindicated. Even those who benefit most from injustice, however, can experience the justice of divine mercy and love if they repent and bring forth the fruit of repentance. Justification thus implies — in Luke and Acts — a reconciled and reconciling community.

Our Spirit-baptized existence participates in Christ's, for he takes his anointing from the Father to share with us (Acts 2:33), "so that through him everyone who believes is justified" (Acts 13:39). He shared in our condemnation so that we can share in his Spirit. The indwelling Spirit thus testifies to us that we are indeed children of God even though our Spirit-inspired witness penultimately falls short of the glory of Christ (Rom. 8:15-16). Therefore, pneumatology has the potential to help us see how justification can be both theocentric and open to creaturely participation, a divine judgment and a transformation of life, a witness that is ambiguous but also taken up into the Spirit's own witness of Christ as the locus of the Spirit, or of the divine rightwising of creation. The inner witness comforts especially those who suffer unjustly, so that their witness will never be put to shame or discredited, for those he justified will be glorified (Rom. 8:30). Justification in the Spirit is ultimately the liberty groaned for throughout the suffering creation (Rom. 8:22).

In the light of these insights, I wish to draw several more specific conclusions from the larger discussion of this chapter. First, admittedly there is fluidity in the New Testament descriptions of justification as a theological concept in Luke, Paul, John, and James. But this fluidity represents different nuances of interpretation of God's gracious justification of humanity in Christ and in the Spirit.

Second, the indwelling Spirit is not essentially distinguishable from justification but is at the source, substance, and fulfillment of the gift of justifying righteousness in the world. The major theological context for Paul's doctrine of justification is the Gentile and Jewish reception of the Holy Spirit by faith and not law.

Third, even where the Spirit is not mentioned in relationship to justification (as in James), the implication is pneumatological in the sense that justification is said to come by way of spiritual rebirth, is "incarnated" or embodied within a just community, and is fulfilled in God's act of new creation.

Fourth, the grace at the essence of justification is not primarily a possessed virtue or a set of merits. Neither is it an event detached from us. Rather, this righteousness is a living presence that is abundantly — even excessively — poured out on undeserving vessels and that dethrones sin and death as reigning powers in order to reign in their place. Justification brings life, the very life of the Spirit. Calvin rightly says that God is the "fountain of righteousness" in which we participate by faith, for Christ justifies us "by the power of his death and resurrection."[73] What is this fountain, this power, other than the Holy Spirit of God? Justification is thus not separate from the Spirit at the heart of Jesus' work in inaugurating the kingdom of God in the world, especially in Jesus' death and resurrection, as well as in his act of pouring out the Spirit at Pentecost.

Fifth, justification holds profound implications for the formation of the just community and the social witness of the church. Tied to the resurrection of Jesus and Jesus' impartation of the Spirit of new life, justification will find penultimate fulfillment on the way toward the new creation of the future.

There are still many unanswered questions to be explored from this brief biblical reflection on justification in the Spirit, questions that relate to the role of faith, hope, and love, as well as the significance of the church as the justified community. It is to these issues that we now turn.

---

73. John Calvin, *Institutes of the Christian Religion*, trans. Henry Beveridge (Grand Rapids: Eerdmans, 1979), 3.11.8.

THREE

Justification Among Us

*The Eschatological Fulfillment
of Justification*

8 Participation

By the Spirit through Faith

"All the doctors of the church hold it to be a philosophical truth that man's happiness can be found only in possessing God."[1] Possession of the Spirit is the only means to human fulfillment and justice. But how do we "possess" God? Should we even be speaking of "possession" with regard to God? Did not Christ himself resist "grasping" after deity, choosing instead to give of himself for the other, especially the lowly (Phil. 2)? In fact, our possessing God cannot be a grasping, but a *yielding,* an obedient self-offering in response to the Spirit's embrace. Faith responds to the Spirit by the Spirit and in a way that conforms to Christ. This is the significance of faith as the means by which one possesses the Spirit.

Without this insight into the importance of faith as the means by which the creature receives the Spirit and can thereby participate in the justified life, justification by grace through faith can appear as little more than a vague or empty slogan that one could understand in a variety of ways. Of course, faith involves such characteristics as trust, assurance, loyalty, and faithfulness. But even these terms are vague without the pneumatological and christological substance of faith as a human response to God, which corresponds to God's covenant faithfulness. In the context of Spirit baptism, faith is thus the means by which we possess God as God has possessed us in Christ and in the embrace of the Spirit.

---

1. C. Boyer, *Cursus philosophiae, Ethica generalis,* q. prima, De fine moralitatis, art. 5, 453, quoted in Henri de Lubac, *The Mystery of the Supernatural,* trans. Rosemary Sheed (New York: Herder and Herder, 1965), p. 38 n. 1).

This is why faith is caught up in the confidence that God will reward "those who earnestly seek him" (Heb. 11:6). Faith by the Spirit within seeks to possess God, because God has first possessed us. This is the priceless pearl or the buried treasure, the treasure hidden in jars of clay, the very indwelling of God's Holy Spirit (2 Cor. 4:7). I will attempt to define faith more specifically, realizing all the while that we seek to describe something in which we are involved with the totality of our being, but which transcends human capacities of intellect, will, or emotions.[2] I will begin with the role of faith in the Old Testament as conformity to covenant faithfulness.

Faith as Conformity to God's Covenant Faithfulness

One striking feature about the terms used for "faith" in the Old Testament is that they depend on divine faithfulness for their anchor and meaning. Human faith is drawn from divine faithfulness and lives from it. One might notice in the Old Testament the relative lack of emphasis on believing, an emphasis that is abundantly present in the New Testament. The Old Testament thus has no word corresponding exactly to the New Testament word for "faith," πίστις, which has strong connotations of belief, persuasion, and conviction. The Hebrew root, תמא, was used to refer mainly to such notions as reliance and steadfastness, as well as truth and loyalty.[3] It is used especially of God as the one who is faithful to carry out the divine promises. It consequently could also involve an element of patient waiting and hope.[4]

With regard to the corresponding human response, God is the object of such "steadfastness," even when no preposition is used (e.g., Ps. 78:32), since nothing is as sure, permanent, or reliable as God. One's security is in God alone, and God's steadfast loyalty inspires analogous responses among covenant partners.[5] In a somewhat uneven correlation of meanings, the πίστ word group in the Septuagint consistently represents the Hebrew root תמא.[6] Because of the nuances of difference between πίστις and

---

2. Note Paul Tillich's discussion of this in *Dynamics of Faith*, trans. Marion Pauck, Perennial Classics ed. (New York: Harper Collins, 2001), pp. 35-46.

3. E. C. Blackman, "Faith, Faithfulness," in *Interpreter's Dictionary of the Bible*, ed. Emory Stevens Bucke (Nashville: Abingdon, 1962), 2:222.

4. Avery Dulles, *The Assurance of Things Hoped For: A Theology of Christian Faith* (Oxford: Oxford University Press, 1994), p. 7.

5. Blackman, "Faith, Faithfulness," p. 222.

6. Dennis R. Lindsay, "The Roots and Development of the πίστ- Word Group as Faith Terminology," *Journal for the Study of the New Testament* 49, no. 1 (March 1993): 112.

אמן, πίστις is not prominently used in the Septuagint. Hebrew "faith" terms were sometimes translated by other Greek words, such as ἀλήθεια (truth).

Due in part to the Hebrew emphasis on the communal response to God's faithfulness, the accent of the Old Testament is on God's faithfulness and steadfastness and not on the *individual's* response of faith.[7] Key figures in the Old Testament tended to function as illustrations of faith for the nation. The notion of faith as a steadfastness or security in Yahweh by clinging to divine promises lies behind the stories of Abraham in Genesis. Yahweh reveals something of the divine plan for history, to which Abraham responds by relying on it and "making himself secure in it." Genesis 15:6 designates this faith as a righteous act.[8] That this faith was "counted as righteousness" was a revolutionary formulation for those contemporary with it. But the question of what this phrase meant originally was a living one, since relying on Yahweh's promises as concrete and real was both peculiar to Abraham's circumstance and an ongoing possibility in the life of Israel. Genesis 15:6 is similar to a prophetic formulation supporting personal and national dependence on God's faithfulness in the face of uncertainty and fear. Genesis 15:6 and Deuteronomy 6:25 agree that it is Yahweh who determines who is righteous. Suppliants thus pray to Yahweh for vindication (cf. Ps. 17:2).[9]

Life's challenges call forth other ways of discerning and responding faithfully to the will of Yahweh. There was the Deuteronomist conviction that an appropriate response to divine faithfulness required keeping the commandments (see Deut. 6:25). Such obedience was not antecedent to salvation, as the preface to the law in Deuteronomy 5:6-7 reveals. The commandments had as their preface in this text the divine proclamation: "I am the Lord your God who brought you up out of the land of Egypt, out of the house of slavery" (see also Exod. 20:1-2). The Exodus was thus understood as the historical setting and foundation of the giving of the law, so that the law functioned as "signposts to freedom."[10] In Deuteronomy, Israel speaks of its righteousness "for the first time in connection with its

---

7. Artur Weiser, "πιστεύω (κτλ. B I–II, 1)," in *Theological Dictionary of the New Testament,* ed. Gerhard Kittel and Gerhard Friedrich (Grand Rapids: Eerdmans, 1968), 6:182.

8. Gerhard von Rad, *Old Testament Theology* (New York: Harper and Row, 1962), 1:171.

9. Von Rad, *OT Theology,* 1:379-80.

10. For a richly theological development of this idea, see Jan Milič Lochman, *Signposts to Freedom: The Ten Commandments and Christian Freedom,* trans. David Lewis (Minneapolis: Augsburg, 1982).

creed" (Deut. 6:20-25), which narrates the history of Israel's deliverance as handed down. The demanding will of God, the law, thus implied a "pledge of grace."[11] Although God is sometimes said to reward obedience to law with blessing, the beginning and end of such obedience was always God.

For example, Deuteronomy 6:1-3 promises blessings in life, especially in the land of promise, for those who obey the law. But this promise is quickly followed in verses 10-12 with the important point that the land of promise will involve "houses filled with all kinds of good things you did not provide, wells you did not dig, and vineyards and olive groves you did not plant" (v. 11). In the light of such undeserved favor, the Israelites are not to forget the Lord who delivered them in divine mercy from Egyptian slavery (v. 12). In fact, as noted earlier, the obedience to the law had as its major function the acknowledgment of God as the source and Lord of all blessing:

> Be careful that you do not forget the LORD your God, failing to observe his commands, his laws and his decrees that I am giving you this day. Otherwise, when you eat and are satisfied, when you build fine houses and settle down, and when your herds and flocks grow large and your silver and gold increase and all you have is multiplied, then your heart will become proud and you will forget the LORD your God, who brought you out of Egypt, out of the land of slavery. (Deut. 8:11-14)

Such divine favor at the base and goal of life is the implied setting of texts that speak of the law, even where it is not explicit. For example, Deuteronomy 9:1-8 makes it clear that the land and other blessings are gifts that Israel could not earn. Freedom and justice presuppose the grace and mercy of God, which chiefly serve to order human relationships in the community of faith and the society at large. As I have noted earlier, the prophets would also maintain that the law will only be fulfilled when the Spirit is poured forth and hearts are turned to God in the service of love and justice (e.g., Ezek. 11:19-20; 36:26-27). That is already implied in Deuteronomy by its definition of the law's fulfillment as all-consuming love for God (Deut. 6:4-5) through a circumcision of the heart (Deut. 30:6). How is such a demand within our grasp even in the presence of the law? How can any legal system grant it? The law is certainly witnessing here to a life, a life that it can encourage and guide but cannot grant. It will take faith fashioned by the in-

---

11. Georg Braulik, "Law as Gospel: Justification and Pardon According to the Deuteronomic Torah," *Interpretation* 38, no. 1 (Jan. 1984): 5-7.

dwelling Spirit for the law and its larger witness to find a proper home in human life.

Faith as steadfast fidelity in conformity to divine faithfulness encounters trials that test it. The stories of the great patriarchs and matriarchs in Genesis accent the hiddenness of God's actions, especially with regard to the mystery and difficult postponement of the fulfillment of God's promises.[12] This is the challenge to faith. In faith, God's guiding hand is presumed, even if the narratives rarely mention this. The mounting difficulties for Joseph do not reflect Greek fate but guidance by God. Genesis concludes with Joseph's conviction that God intended the evil actions of Joseph's betrayers for the good of the fulfillment of the divine promises (Gen. 50:20). Assurance of divine guidance in history is also not simply to be taken for granted in Genesis but is tested severely. The story of the divine requirement of offering up Isaac pushes faith to the extreme, where God seems to rise up as the enemy of God's own work. Such divine hiddenness is so deep that the experience of forsakenness seems the only way open to faith. Israel had to experience such forsakenness in its history in which faith is tested in the extreme, since God seemed to contradict God's own promises (von Rad, p. 174).

Though Paul testifies that Abraham did not waver in faith in response to this challenge (Rom 4:19), Genesis shows both Abraham and Sarah laughing at the boldness of God's promises in the light of dismal possibilities (Gen. 17:7; 18:12). Further, in the Exodus story, Moses and the Israelites are asked to believe for a deliverance that seemed impossible in the natural realm (von Rad, p. 176). As Hebrews 11:29 notes, "By faith the people passed through the Red Sea as on dry land." The Israelites were being rescued "by grace through faith" before the law was given to guide such faith. In another Old Testament text, Job struggles to understand the ways of God, but he has his beleaguered faith vindicated and strengthened in the end.

Faith is not held with perfection by any means in the Old Testament witness, so weakness does not disqualify the people of faith. God's grace triumphs in spite of human weakness. This shows both the strength and limits of faith with regard to excessive grace. Faith is a natural and necessary component of life in the circle of divine grace, but not even faith can adequately account for the abundance of that grace. Many of the psalms thus elicit personal confidence in the enduring goodness and mercy of

---

12. Von Rad, *OT Theology,* 1:171.

God despite the trials and failures of life. Later, the embrace of the risen Christ and of the Spirit he breathed on them (John 20:21-22) — despite the weakness of their damaged faith vis-à-vis the cross — will draw deeply from this Old Testament background.

The prophets call Israel back to the original trust in Yahweh. This call to steadfast reliance and faithfulness is especially enriched by Isaiah, the "prophet of faith."[13] Next to Genesis 15:6, the *textus classicus* of faith in the Old Testament is Isaiah 7:9: "If you do not stand firm in faith, you will not understand." The reading of this phrase as "you will not understand" is most likely due to a copyist's error, so that 7:9b should read, ". . . you do not stand at all," referring to faith as steadfast loyalty and dependence on God. Augustine's and Anselm's usages of the former reading influenced centuries of discussion in support of the priority of faith to knowledge.[14] Their theological position was sound, but they had the wrong textual base!

In any event, Ahaz is challenged in Isaiah to rely on God alone for ultimate security. Those who hope in and wait upon God will receive youthful vigor in their courage, steadfastness, and strength (Isa. 40:29-31), because God does not grow faint or weary but is steadfast and reliable (40:28). In Isaiah "the struggle is the universal struggle of faith: in whom will you put your trust?"[15] Those who do trust steadfastly will not be disappointed. The text of Habakkuk 2:4, immortalized among Christians by Paul in Romans 1:17 ("the just by faith will live"), most likely meant in its original context something like this: the just will be vindicated in their steadfast loyalty.[16]

In postexilic Judaism, faith became prominently fidelity to law, though trust in God is still assumed, for "he who trusts in the Lord will not suffer loss" (Sirach 32:24).[17] Faith requires patience, hope, steadfastness, and obedience even in the absence of much evidence that God is near and working out the fulfillment of the divine promises. God is faithful to sustain and to vindicate such steadfast faith. The intertestamental eschatological yearning for final vindication in the resurrection will set the stage for the New Testament notion of faith as trust in God's presence in Christ and the Spirit to fulfill the promises.

---

13. Dulles, *Assurance*, p. 9.

14. Glen Menzies, "To What Does Faith Lead? The Two-Stranded Textual Tradition of Isaiah 7.9b," *Journal for the Study of the Old Testament* 80 (1998): 111-26.

15. Menzies, "To What Does Faith Lead?" p. 118.

16. This is my paraphrase. See Dulles, *Assurance*, p. 9.

17. Dulles, *Assurance*, p. 10.

Faith as Belief

On the surface, it may seem that the New Testament is in some tension with the Old by emphasizing the matter of *belief* as a prominent characteristic of faith. Despite the fact that there is no term for faith in the Old Testament that exactly parallels the usage of πίστις in the Greek context, the use of πίστις in the Septuagint is nevertheless significant. Πίστις sometimes referred in classical Greek to "belief" in the gods. Under the influence of the Greek rhetorical tradition, πίστις also came to refer to persuasion and conviction. This trust was not used merely as a depiction of intellectual assent but also of active commitment to and reliance on the gods.[18] By bringing πίστις into relationship with the Hebrew root אמן, in the context of the Septuagint, πίστις was adjusted to take on something of the Hebraic emphasis on steadfastness and faithfulness. This development set the stage for the rich use of πίστις in the New Testament, which included belief and steadfast trust and loyalty.

Still, the difference between the Old Testament's emphasis on steadfast trust and *loyalty* and the New Testament's emphasis on steadfast trust and *belief* is not as great as some might think. First, Paul is clear that belief is of the heart, as inspired by the Spirit of life and directed to the living trust in Christ as risen from the dead: "'The word is near you; it is in your mouth and in your heart,' that is, the word of faith we are proclaiming: That if you confess with your mouth, 'Jesus is Lord,' and believe in your heart that God raised him from the dead, you will be saved" (Rom. 10:8-9). Romans 1:4 begins with the programmatic theme of Jesus as raised from the dead and declared God's Son "according to the Spirit of holiness," implying that the Spirit who raised Jesus from the dead now inspires the faithful life as vital to our foretaste of the life to come.

Abraham himself "believed the God who gives life to the dead and calls things that are not as though they were" (Rom. 4:17). This witness to life speaks to our hearts that we are children of God as well (Rom. 8:15-16), even though our adoption through the redemption of our bodies as temples of the Spirit is still in the future (Rom. 8:23). This witness to life causes the proclamation of the gospel to be "near to you . . . in your mouth and in

---

18. Lindsay argues that πίστις was increasingly used in the religious sphere in the classical and Hellenistic periods and faults Bultmann for downplaying this fact in the *TDNT*: "The Roots and Development of the πιστ- Word Group." See also, Dulles, *Assurance*, p. 10. Hereafter, references to this work will appear in parentheses in the text.

your heart" (Rom. 10:8). This is what moves us to believe that Jesus has in fact been raised from the dead. We believe in the context of the Spirit's embrace and the word of witness that has dawned in our hearts as a result. Faith as belief is thus something connected in the New Testament to the new birth of the Spirit (Gal. 2:20; cf. John 1:10-13). Faith as belief is not just the intellectual grasping of an external declaration but a step of loyal obedience to a word that grips the heart and urges allegiance because it testifies to life.

Since the age when the Spirit is not yet wholly fulfilled, such faith lacks visible vindication. Paul freely admitted that the gospel of an executed messiah was widely regarded as foolish (1 Cor. 1:18). This made the challenge to believe all the more severe and potentially devastating. Therefore, the classic "faith" texts from the Old Testament that combined both trust and faithfulness — Genesis 15:6, Isaiah 7:9, and Habakkuk 2:4 — were highlighted by Christian theologians under the influence of the New Testament emphasis on believing in the presence of life in the midst of the threats of death. There is thus overlap between the Old Testament faith as "steadfastness" and the emphasis of the New Testament πίστις on believing and trust. They even function as mutually illuminating descriptions of the divine-human relationship as inaugurated and sustained by God's Spirit. Believing was understood as coming by way of the witness of the Spirit and the Word of the gospel (John 20:29-31; Rom. 8:15-16; 10:14-15). The linkage of the Hebrew terms for faith with the Greek πίστις thus represents an interesting example of faith's ability by the enabling of the Spirit to adjust to new contexts. By the time of the writing of the New Testament, the Hebrew and Greek notions of "faith" had converged to provide a rich field of meaning useful for describing steadfast belief and faithfulness in the crucified and risen Christ as the one who ushers sinners into the embrace of the Spirit.

Despite considerable overlap between the Old and New Testament notions of faith, Avery Dulles's remark that one enters into a "different universe of thought" on moving from the Old Testament to the New Testament understandings of faith has a point (p. 10). In the Gospels one is immediately confronted with a notion of faith dominated by belief or trust in Jesus as the one who ushers in the era of the Spirit and of the kingdom of God: "If I cast out demons by the Spirit of God, the kingdom of God has come upon you" (Matt. 12:28). But this belief is not a mere intellectual assent but rather full acceptance that God's very Spirit is behind these liberating events surrounding the message and ministry of Jesus.

The message of both John the Baptist and Jesus is for the people to repent because the reality of the kingdom is near and is, in fact, breaking in already through the powerful presence of the Spirit. It was a time to repent and trust that God is with humanity once more in redemptive power in fulfillment of the promises of old. Jesus thus emphasizes faith as an obedient reception of miraculous healing in the new age (Mark 5:34; 10:52; Luke 7:50; 17:19). Lack of faith can impede the miraculous signs and wonders of the dawning kingdom (Mark 6:5; Matt. 13:58). Faith is inspired by signs and wonders (John 2:11, 23; 4:53; 5:36-38; 10:38), but also by the word of Jesus (John 2:22; 14:10-11). Yet it is not that healing was a reward for faith, for the lame man's walking was faith itself in action (p. 15). Thomas believed upon seeing, but the blessing is held out for those who subsequently believe on the basis of the testimony of the gospel (John 20:31). John concludes that the witness was written down "that you might believe that Jesus is the Christ" or the one anointed by the Spirit (20:31).

In later New Testament books such as Jude, the Apocalypse, and the Pastoral Epistles, faith is commonly used to depict the doctrinal content of the church's proclamation and teaching (Jude 3:20). We keep the faith of Jesus (Rev. 14:12) as well as preserve and defend it (1 Tim. 6:20; 2 Tim. 1:14; 4:7). Paul warns those who would shipwreck the faith, presumably through heresy (1 Tim. 1:19). Faith is the pillar of truth (1 Tim. 3:15) (p. 17). But even here faith as a lived reality is often assumed as foundational. For example, the church at Ephesus is addressed in the Apocalypse as being diligent at testing false apostles and proving their falseness, but is still rebuked for departing from its first love (Rev. 2:2-5). Faith was not here to function merely as a standard for discerning orthodoxy or otherwise judging the message or conduct of others, but more deeply as a source of faithful trust and devotion toward God and others in the service of divine love.

Faith is not conceived in a triumphalist way, for it can and does exist with an element of doubt (Mark 9:24). However, the disciples are still rebuked for their lack of faith (Mark 4:40; Matt. 14:31; 16:8; 17:20). Those who believe are to recognize God in the person and ministry of Jesus.[19] As Peter's confession shows, such recognition at the core of faith has its source in revelation (Matt. 16:17; Mark 8:29), even though the Markan narrative implies, by way of Jesus' subsequent rebuke, that Peter's faith is still in for-

---

19. W. A. Whitehouse, "Faith," in *A Theological Word Book of the Bible*, ed. Alan Richardson (New York: Macmillan, 1950), p. 76.

mation, like the gradually improving sight of the blind man who saw people at first as "trees walking" (Mark 8:24). Jesus thus prays that Peter's faith will not fail (Luke 22:31). Faith receives its severe testing in the experience of the cross in a way analogous to Abraham's challenge to trust God even though God seemed to contradict the divine promises in the command to sacrifice Isaac. After Jesus' resurrection, the disciples' faith rises up from the ashes, especially in the impartation of the Spirit and the subsequent empowerment that it brings for turning their lives into living witnesses of Christ (Acts 1:8).

Faith is a vital component in the baptism in the Spirit and the turning of the disciples into living witnesses of Christ and of divine faithfulness in the world. When threatened, the community of Christians in Acts expresses great faith through a prayer that reiterates God's mighty deeds in history (Acts 4). Their faith is vindicated in part and enhanced through inspired proclamation and signs and wonders of the Spirit's presence (Acts 4 and 8; 9:42; 13:12; 14:9). Indeed, through Christ "everyone who believes is justified" (Acts 13:39). God will not fail to vindicate their witness. Such vindication also comes from the experience of the risen Christ in the Spirit. Divine love, the greatest of gifts, is shed abroad in our hearts by the Spirit of God, guaranteeing that faith will never be ashamed as it clings in devotion to Christ as Savior through the indwelling Spirit (Rom. 5:1-5). Let us explore, therefore, the issue of faith, hope, and love in the presence of the Spirit more closely.

Faith, Hope, and Love

Faith involves loyal trust and belief, but it is not reduced to these. Faith is most deeply *participation* in Christ and his communion of love with the Father through and with the Spirit. As such, faith is a complex and holistic dynamic that involves related elements such as love and hope.[20] In places, Romans and Galatians seem to indicate that one is saved by faith alone, but 1 Corinthians 13 makes faith useless without love. Galatians 5:6 also speaks of faith as expressed or active through love. Faith is thus closely linked in John to the positive response to love others as Jesus loved them in giving his life for them and as God so loved the world (John 15:13-17; 3:16). For John, faith may be said to be integral to love. We love in knowing and be-

20. Whitehouse, "Faith," p. 13.

lieving the love that God has for us (1 John 4:16). By God's love, faith overcomes the world.[21]

Paul also speaks of being saved in hope (Rom. 8:24), implying that hope is also essential to faith. Similarly, Hebrews 11:1 defines faith as the evidence of things *hoped for* and the assurance of things not (yet) seen. Faith is thus essential to the pilgrimage of the people of God toward the heavenly city (Heb. 11:16). This city is not yet seen, though one in faith can gain a foretaste of it in the Holy Spirit or in the "powers of the age to come" (Heb. 6:4-5). The core of faith in Hebrews is a conviction or an assurance of things "grasped" without sight (11:1). The assurance of faith also carries with it certain theological convictions, such as the role of God as creator (11:3) or as rewarder of those who seek divine help (11:6). In addition, faith is closely tied to obedience, since "by faith Abraham obeyed God" (11:8). Faith may be said to be the first step of obedience in Hebrews. People are admonished to find in God nourishment and endurance for their faith, as the water sustains whatever grows from the soil (6:7-8). This direction of life is contrasted with those who begin in the faith but soon part and end up shaming Christ (6:4-8).

Faith thus lives in the tension of the eschatological "now" and the "not yet." Paul can thus speak of seeing through a glass dimly (1 Cor. 13:12) and of being continuously transformed into Christ's image by the Spirit of liberty (2 Cor. 3:18), for we walk by faith and not sight (2 Cor. 5:7), not having seen the Lord "face to face" (1 Cor. 13:12) or directly and fully as "presence to presence." In the meantime, faith involves hope (Rom. 4:18), confidence (2 Cor. 4:14), trust (Rom. 10:11; Gal. 2:16; Phil. 1:29), confession (Rom. 10:9-10; 2 Cor. 4:13), and faithfulness (Rom. 1:5, 8; 16:19).

The vision of faith is weak and somewhat faint, but it is still real and increasingly compelling as we continue to set our hearts and minds on Christ rather than on things of this world (Col. 3:1-3). Bultmann rightly notes that the eschatological nature of faith provides the context for Paul's implication that salvation is by faith.[22] Justification is by faith in that it lays claim to that which is not yet, namely, life eternal in direct communion with God through the indwelling Spirit. The present indwelling Spirit within this reality of flesh is only the down payment of liberty or the foretaste of such communion (cf. Eph. 1:13-14), even in the midst of suffering and yearning (Rom. 8:22-25).

---

21. Whitehouse, "Faith," p. 16.
22. Bultmann, "πιστεύω (κτλ. D II,3–III,1)," *TDNT*, 6:215-19.

There is no question but that for most of the history of theology in the West, faith was viewed as justifying the sinner in inseparable union with hope and love. Fighting against the Gnostic challenge, many of the early church fathers stressed the obedience of faith in the context of allegiance to the law and the necessity of love as the greatest commandment to complete it.[23] Eventually, faith came to be viewed as an infused virtue along with hope and love. Peter Lombard's distinction between unformed and formed faith (faith formed by love, Gal. 6:5) became typical of the Middle Ages.[24] So also Thomas Aquinas: "The movement of faith is not perfect unless it is quickened by charity, and so in the justification of the ungodly, a movement of charity is infused together with the movement of faith."[25]

As I have noted earlier, Aquinas allowed works to be meritorious but added with Augustine that, in regarding human works as meritorious God is merely crowning God's own gifts. I regard the entire system of merits that were characteristic of medieval soteriology theologically misleading and pastorally counterproductive; but I am also pleased that there was a sustained effort among the greatest minds of medieval theology to define grace in ways that cannot be explained ultimately by a strict system of exchange. Indeed, beyond all human achievement, faith yearns for final union with God as a gift of the Spirit. Justification by faith may thus be said to be "stretching forth to justice."[26] Faith yearns for the ultimate justice that will come with the new creation when God tabernacles with creation.

The role of love in justification was called into question by the Reformers. They emphasized faith alone as the thing needed for justification because they believed that this exclusivity would shift the focus from our love or obedience to Christ as the only basis for God's mercy toward sinners. The love of God revealed in Christ cannot be based in any way on our love for God, but only on what Christ has done for us. As a result, justifying faith cannot be completed by the rise of love in us for God. The Lu-

---

23. See Robert B. Eno, "Some Patristic Views on the Relationship between Faith and Works in Justification," in *Justification by Faith: Lutherans and Catholics in Dialogue VII*, ed. H. George Anderson, T. Austin Murphy, and Joseph A. Burgess (Minneapolis: Augsburg, 1985), pp. 113-14; see also Dulles, *Assurance*, pp. 15-20.

24. Karlfried Froehlich, "Justification Language in the Middle Ages," in Anderson et al., *Justification by Faith*, pp. 147-51.

25. Aquinas, *Treatise on Grace*, Q. 113, art. 4, in *Basic Writings of St. Thomas Aquinas*, ed. and trans. Anton C. Pegis (New York: Random House, 1945).

26. Aquinas, *Treatise on Grace*, 113.5.

theran theologian Anders Nygren supported this direction of thought in an essay in which he faulted Augustine for viewing salvation as an *ascent* of the soul to God aided by grace, which Nygren identified with the Greek or Neo-Platonic *eros*. For Nygren, Luther supported the biblical direction of *agape* by viewing salvation as the *descent* of God's love to the sinner so as to awaken the sinner to faith in God.[27]

For Luther, faith is relational and not a metaphysical quality of the soul. It is thus dependent wholly on Christ and not on the content of our character or the level of our spiritual devotion. Luther thus could not see faith as a "dead quality" in the soul that needed to be activated and completed by the virtue of love, since faith for Luther is not a metaphysical quality but a divine gift and a relationship with Christ that involves by nature a laying hold of Christ. Luther says that the "fanatical spirits and sophists. . . imagine that faith is a quality that clings to the heart apart from Christ. This is a dangerous error. Christ should be set forth in such a way that apart from Him you see nothing at all."[28]

For Luther, faith is not the body and love the form; faith is the body, and Christ is the form. Luther says that faith "takes hold of Christ in such a way that Christ is the object of faith, or rather not the object but, so to speak, the one who is present in faith itself." He also notes that faith "is the temple and Christ sits in the midst of it."[29] Thus, for Luther, faith is not adorned by love as a *habitus,* but by Christ. Since faith is by nature a relationship to — and even participation in — the living person of Christ, Christ is seen as that which gives it its dynamism as a living faith. Christ functions for Luther in the place of *caritas,* or the fruit of love in us. This is a position that Luther felt delivers us from self-righteousness or self-preoccupation, turning the believer's attention rather to Christ. Luther explains that faith "does not look at its love and say: 'What have I done? Where have I sinned? What have I deserved?' But it says: 'What has Christ done? What has he deserved?' Faith is adorned by Christ."[30]

Luther's aversion to basing justification on infused virtues shifted the medieval focus on the relationship between grace and nature to the relationship between grace and faith in Christ. Personal and existential categories gained ascendance over metaphysical speculation in the discussion of

27. Nygren, *Agape and Eros* (Chicago: The University of Chicago Press, 1992), passim.

28. Luther, "Lectures on Galatians 1535," *Luther's Works,* ed. Jaroslav Pelikan (St. Louis: Concordia, 1963), 26:356.

29. Luther, "Lectures on Galatians 1535," *Luther's Works,* 26:30.

30. Luther, "Lectures on Galatians 1535," *Luther's Works,* 26:88.

the meaning and role of faith.[31] As I have noted above, more recent ecumenical discussions between Lutherans and Catholics and between Finnish Lutherans and Russian Orthodox have used notions of faith as ongoing participation in Christ to build bridges between these traditions, since, as participation in Christ, faith is both relational and transformational.

In my view, Luther did not intend to make faith "loveless," because, as recent Finnish Lutherans have noted, he did recognize the involvement of *divine* love in the rise of faith in the believer.[32] He even said of his opponents that he would not be offended by their "faith formed by love" gloss if they would distinguish it from false faith rather than unformed faith![33] Such an astonishing admission implies that Luther's "faith alone," which clings in trust and devotion to Christ alone, may not have been very different from the medieval faith as formed by love, depending on how one construes this. Luther also says that it is by faith that Christ dwells in the church and makes the church worthy of the love granted symbolically to it in the Song of Solomon.[34] Such an allusion implies that justifying faith involves a bond of love between the believer and God. But if this is true, then would this bond not imply that faith is nourished by love and will bring forth the fruit of love as well? Hans Küng's notion of faith as sufficient to salvation but as also having the seeds of love within it might be a way of connecting Lutheran with Catholic theology.[35]

Part of the difficulty in forging this connection is Luther's sharp contrast between gospel and law and his related tendency to identify love on the side of law. He notes that the law "can teach me that I should love God and my neighbor, and live in chastity, patience, etc.; but it is in no position to show me how to be delivered from sin, the devil, death, and hell." For this, Luther will listen only to the gospel, the crucified and risen Christ. For Luther, faith formed by love as obedience to law assumes an "I" within the

31. Eric W. Gritsch, "The Origins of the Lutheran Teaching on Justification," in Anderson et al., *Justification by Faith*, pp. 162-71.

32. Simo Peura, "What God Gives Man Receives: Luther on Salvation," in *Union with Christ: The New Finnish Lutheran Interpretation of Luther*, ed. Carl Braaten and Robert Jenson (Grand Rapids: Eerdmans, 1998), pp. 76-95.

33. Luther, "Lectures on Galatians 1535," *Luther's Works*, 26:268-70.

34. Martin Luther, *Lectures on Romans*, trans. Wilhelm Pauck (Philadelphia: Westminster, 1961), p. 134.

35. Hans Küng, *Justification: The Doctrine of Karl Barth and a Catholic Reflection*, trans. Thomas Collins, Edmund E. Tolk, and David Granskou (Philadelphia: Westminster, 1981), p. 256.

law *apart from Christ*. He calls such a notion of faith a "trick of Satan." True faith, Luther writes to believers, is being "so cemented to Christ that He and you are one person."[36] In ourselves we are sinners under the judgment of law; in Christ we are justified by faith alone. Though Luther did in places imply that we are partly just and partly sinner, his overwhelming emphasis, especially after the Romans commentary, is on the believer as simultaneously just and sinner.[37] For Luther, faith does lead to the obedience of love and other works of the law as well, but we never trust in these for our salvation. We trust rather in Christ alone.

So what do we conclude about the integration of faith, hope, and love? Luther was right that justification cannot be based on the quality of human love, but this insight would apply equally to any human responses to God, including faith. Faith, hope, and love are all gifts of grace given in the Spirit. As graced human responses in the Spirit to God, faith, hope, and love are ambiguous forms of obedience. Faith is obedient humility that empties one of all but Christ ("an empty hand, an empty vessel"), as Barth noted — and Luther before him.[38] But is not love fashioned after Christ the same? Did not Christ, out of love for God and humanity, empty himself or "make himself nothing" (Phil. 2:7) by becoming a servant? Both faith and love, loyalty and devotion, are kenotic responses of self-sacrifice to God that deeply involve obedience at its most profound level.

Therefore, justification cannot be based on faith any more than it can be based on the fruit of love. I agree with Barth that in justification "God has to close His eyes to the feebleness of our faith, as indeed he does." One recalls Tillich's reference to justification as Spiritual presence overcoming ambiguous life. Barth notes further that the sinner "is as little justified in faith as in his other good or evil works. He needs justification just as much in faith as anywhere else, as in the totality of his being."[39] In other words, we are justified by faith because faith assumes and arises from the embrace of the Spirit and defers in that embrace to another, namely, to Christ. As Peter bore witness concerning the unclean Gentiles, "God, who knows the heart, showed that he accepted them by giving the Holy Spirit to them, just as he did to us. He made no distinction between us and them, for he puri-

---

36. Luther, "Lectures on Galatians 1535," *Luther's Works*, 26:91, 168.

37. See Gerhard O. Forde, "Forensic Justification and Law in Lutheran Theology," in Anderson et al., *Justification by Faith*, pp. 278-303.

38. Barth, *Church Dogmatics*, vol. 4, *The Doctrine of Reconciliation*, pt. 1, trans. G. W. Bromiley and T. F. Torrance (Edinburgh: T. & T. Clark, 1956), pp. 627, 631.

39. Barth, *Church Dogmatics*, vol. 4, pt. 1, pp. 616-17.

fied their hearts by faith" (Acts 15:8-9). Faith rises from the justice won for us by Christ and the embrace of the Spirit and leads to the incarnation of analogous faithfulness among us in history. Justification is based on the former but involves the latter.

The grace of Christ and of the indwelling Spirit — and not faith as the graced but also human mode of reception — is the foundational element. Faith as a gift from the Spirit is merely the creaturely means of incorporation and participation. Justification cannot be based on any human responses, since this would be to turn grace into a reward within a reciprocal system of exchange, something that Paul clearly forbids (Rom. 4:4-8). Faith lives from the embrace of the Spirit through the proclamation of the word (John 16:7-11; Rom. 10:17). It is not the nobility of our faith that makes us just before God; rather, it is the mercy extended to us in Christ and the gift of the Spirit.

In order to give faith a privileged role in justification, the Reformers emphasized the role of faith as a gift of grace and a clinging to Christ. But is not love also a gift from the Spirit given to us (Rom. 5:5), and is this love not also a clinging to Christ? Is not faith integral to love for Christ and love for Christ implicit in faith, for do we not trust the one we love? How can faith in Christ be even conceptually defined in a way that is abstracted from our love for him? As we saw above, Luther ultimately refused to separate faith from love conceptually. So also Barth: "[F]aith itself would not be faith if it did not work by love."[40] The same can be said of hope. Abraham believed "the God who gives life to the dead and calls things that are not as though they were" (Rom. 4:17). Indeed, "by faith we eagerly await through the Spirit the righteousness for which we hope" (Gal. 5:5), and faith is the assurance of things not yet seen (Heb. 11:1). In seeking to see the one we love face to face (presence to presence), does not faith also involve a vibrant hope? In the face of alienation and death, is it not the love and faith granted to us that inspire fresh hope where there is no hope? If faith is a foundational component in one's relationship with Christ, how is it conceivable apart from love *and* hope?

The integration of faith, hope, and love makes sense in the light of the indwelling Spirit. The right relationship brought about by justification is not merely sustained by *believing* a declaration or a message. Faith is sustained by a *living* presence that brings about participation in Christ and communion with God. Faith cannot be defined in ways detached from

40. Barth, *Church Dogmatics*, vol. 4, pt. 2, p. 627.

love and hope. The greatest mistake of the Protestant Reformation was to define love as a work and to separate it conceptually from faith as that which *alone* receives grace.[41] How can a love granted by the indwelling of the Spirit be seen as anything other than an excessive gift indescribable by any system of exchange?

Faith as Participation in Christ

Faith is thus a vital component of union with, and participation in, Christ. For Paul, faith is a "new mode of existence that involves the gift of the Spirit and a living fellowship and union with Christ (Gal. 2:20; 3:14)."[42] Faith participates in Christ, especially his crucified and risen life, as the locus of the Spirit's presence. Notice Paul's definition of justifying faith as a participation in the crucified and risen Christ:

> For through the law I died to the law so that I might live for God. I have been crucified with Christ and I no longer live, but Christ lives in me. The life I live in the body, I live by faith in the Son of God, who loved me and gave himself for me. I do not set aside the grace of God, for if righteousness could be gained through the law, Christ died for nothing! (Gal. 2:19-21)

In this passage Paul views living faith as a dynamic conformity to the faithfulness of Jesus (and of God) revealed in Christ's death and resurrection. In another passage in which Paul speaks of justification by faith, he also speaks of an intimate knowledge of Christ crucified and risen (Phil. 3:10). Justifying faith is a gift of the Spirit entered into through new birth. In union with Christ through the Spirit, faith gives us a knowledge of God's love that surpasses knowledge (Eph. 3:19). Faith will thus find itself rejecting the wisdom of the world and following instead the wisdom of the cross (1 Cor. 1:30).[43]

41. For example, Melanchthon defended Luther's placing of love on the side of law and works in a lengthy argument with Johann Eck at the Regensburg Colloquy. See Jill Raitt, "From Augsburg to Trent," in Anderson et al., *Justification by Faith*, p. 202. Rahner is correct in seeing love primarily and essentially on the side of grace: "Questions of Controversial Theology on Justification," in *Theological Investigations*, vol. 4, *More Recent Writings*, trans. Kevin Smith (New York: Crossroad, 1982), pp. 202-3.

42. D. M. Hay, "Pistis as Ground for Faith in Hellenized Judaism," *Journal of Biblical Literature* 108, no. 3 (Sept. 1989): 470ff.

43. Dulles, *Assurance*, p. 12.

In one sense, then, baptism is crucial as a dramatization of the birth of faith because it participates in Christ's death and resurrection. The baptismal water is a tomb in which one is buried with Christ. But this tomb is transformed by the Spirit into a womb from which one rises to newness of life (Rom. 6:1-5). Faith comes through the death of the self-centered, self-reliant person and the birth of the true person who is reliant on Christ and devoted faithfully to him in self-sacrificial love. Faith thus lives from the Spirit, which remains that which keeps it ignited and alive as a participation in Christ. The Spirit incorporates one into Christ and the leading of the Spirit to which Christ was dedicated. The Spirit is the power of participation in Christ. Faith is simply a way of describing how we come to be involved as persons in this process. Have no doubts about it, faith glides on the winds of the Spirit.

The importance of faith as a new birth and a participation in Christ helps us to see why it would be potentially legalistic if we were to divorce something like repentance from faith as some kind of separate act required first. How can one step away from sin toward devotion to Christ totally apart from that devotion? Severing repentance from faith as an autonomously prior act throws the door wide open for the legalistic prescription (explicitly stated or not) for what level of godly sorrow, self-denial, or even self-punishment is required before one is "worthy" of biblical faith. We can be reminded here of certain struggles toward adequate penance in medieval piety or the *Busskampf* (repentance struggle) of early modern pietism in Germany. Nietzsche rightly saw a masochistic element in such efforts.[44]

Within these distortions of piety, faith becomes a standard to be reached through self-degradation rather than the inspiration for repentance. The biblical injunction to repent and believe is not meant as a prioritization of separate acts (Mark 1:15). In fact, a case can be made that repentance and faith are two distinct ways of describing the same act of turning to God by the Spirit that are mutually inviting. Notice Acts 3:19: "Repent, then, and turn to God, so that your sins may be wiped out, that times of refreshing may come from the Lord." Repenting and turning can be seen as describing the same act rather than as separate acts. Repentance emphasizes the turning *from* sin and faith the turning *to* God. But they both describe the one act of turning. In reality, however, this act of turning is also a death and a rebirth. The turning by repentance and faith is dependent on the new life of the Spirit.

---

44. Nietzsche, *Genealogy of Morals* (New York: Vintage Books, n.d.), §21.

This is not to say that faith and repentance are not distinct (though inseparable) theological categories that illuminate one another. Faith helps us view repentance as a leaving behind of something destructive for something else that is life-restoring. One is not allowed to wallow in repentance or to think of it as a self-imposed purgation devoid of a positive vision to inspire the journey from leaving behind to pressing forward: "Forgetting what is behind and straining toward what is ahead, I press on toward the goal to win the prize for which God has called me heavenward in Christ Jesus" (Phil. 3:13-14). On the other hand, faith is not simply positive thinking or an optimistic outlook on life (though it often involves such things). Faith is more deeply a leaving behind of the ways of death for the ways of life. Faith and repentance as mutually defining categories are descriptive of one's incorporation into and lifelong participation in Christ as the man of the Spirit and the faithful Son of the heavenly Father. Repentance and faith both glide on the winds of the Spirit.

Living faith embodies the covenant faithfulness of God. It is conformity to God by grace or by the presence of the Spirit of life. James rejects the validity of "faith" as a mere confession and insists that such a thing is dead and not a living, embodied reality. Living, embodied faith will be characterized by obedient works. One must wonder, however, whether or not even James would regard the dead faith of such confessionalism as real faith, especially since he regards even the devils as confessing that there is one God and trembling at the thought (James 2:19). Paul also regards faith as living (Rom. 1:17). In this light one can question whether or not James had in mind Paul's highly theological understanding of faith or even of justification. "One would be hard pressed to show that James is rejecting the true doctrine of Paul."[45]

Paul's contrast of salvation by faith and by works (e.g., Rom. 4:1-4) was never intended to drive a wedge between faith and its obedience, as a number of texts from Paul confirm (e.g., Rom. 6). For Paul, faith is a living reality that corresponds by grace to the faithfulness of Jesus. But Paul cannot view faith as a "work" in the sense that it can be defined within a system of exchange (Rom. 4:4-6). It is, after all, a kenotic reality of faithful self-giving; and it is, for Paul, a relationship of loyalty and conformity to Christ into which we are born of the excessive grace of the Spirit and by the declared word of God (Rom. 10:17). No law can grant us this nor stand in judgment over it (Gal. 5:23). No human effort to obey the law can produce

---

45. Dulles, *Assurance*, p. 10.

the relationship with Christ that faith assumes. To reduce faith to a work worthy of grace as a payment is to reduce it to a reciprocal system of exchange. Faith involves us in an abundant outpouring of grace that comes to us in the gospel and the gift of the Spirit of Christ. That faith involves obedience is to be taken for granted, since faith is a living reality. But faith has an essence and a core in the Spirit that causes it to defy adequate description as a meritorious "work."

As participation in Christ, faith conforms to the very image of Christ. The Spirit mediated the incarnation and anointed the body of Jesus so that Jesus could function as the revelation of the covenant faithfulness of God. Jesus revealed this in many ways, such as bestowing favor on the sinner or the outcast (e.g., Luke 4:18), his faithfulness to his own calling from the Father and to the leading of the Spirit, and his willingness to give of his life toward these ends. A connection between faith and faithfulness is suggested by those who interpret texts such as Galatians 2:20, 3:23, 25 (as well as Rom. 3:25) as references to the faith (faithfulness) "of" or "belonging to" Jesus Christ rather than the faith "in" Jesus.[46] Assumed here is a certain narrative substructure in Galatians, and even Romans, which pictures Jesus as revealing the covenant faithfulness of God in his life and journey to the cross and beyond. Others find this formulation "faith *of* Jesus Christ" uncharacteristic of Paul, so that faith *in* Jesus is saving faith in Galatians.[47] I do regard these texts as referring to the faithful life of Christ, which involved a revelation of God's covenant faithfulness. The revelation of faith as the fulfillment of the law (Gal. 3:23) makes sense if this "faith" means the faithfulness of Jesus. Justification is thus first "by faith" in the sense that it was accomplished through the faithful act of Jesus as the man of the Spirit in giving his life for the sinner and the outcast. Justification is "by faith" among us in the sense that the gift of the Spirit creates a correspondence between Christ's covenant faithfulness and ours.

The revelation of the faithfulness of God that appears in Jesus does not just involve his journey to the cross but also his resurrection, exaltation, and impartation of the Spirit to sinful flesh. The covenant faithfulness of God involves God's self-impartation to sinful flesh in the outpouring of the Spirit. Jesus' revelation of God's covenant faithfulness during his

---

46. See Richard B. Hays, *The Faith of Jesus Christ: The Narrative Substructure of Galatians 3:1–4:11*, 2nd ed. (Grand Rapids: Eerdmans, 2001), esp. pp. 141-62.

47. See, e.g., John J. O'Rourke, "Pistis in Romans," *Catholic Biblical Quarterly* 35, no. 2 (Apr. 1973): 188-94.

lifetime by offering mercy to sinners comes to fulfillment in Jesus' bestowing the Spirit on all flesh in Acts 2. Furthermore, as the Son was offered by the Spirit to the Father through the cross and the resurrection (Heb. 9:14; Rom. 1:4), so Christ now offers the Spirit to the world in Spirit baptism (Acts 2:33) so that the world might be renewed and be raised up in the image of Christ and offered in praise to the Father (1 Cor. 15:20-28). This pneumatological emphasis brings us back full circle to the Old Testament emphasis on faith as conformity to the faithfulness of God, except that we speak now of faith as conformity to Christ.

Of course, our participation through faith in the faithful Christ is imperfect and ambiguous. Rightwising in the Spirit involves a divine embrace that both inspires and exceeds the power and witness of our faith. The mere fact that God accepts our faith and witness as belonging to the Spirit and as participation in Christ is excessive and understandable only in the context of the gift of the indwelling Spirit. Ultimate conformity to Christ and to the Spirit that anointed and led him occurs only at our glorification, at which point our weak and imperfect witness is perfected. At that time we will rejoice that the divine Spirit and pardon have embraced us and our imperfect faith all along. But if justification is by the Spirit through faith, what role does the law play in the era of the Spirit?

By Faith and Not Law

We need to look at the way in which Paul contrasts the righteousness by way of the law and the righteousness through faith in Christ. In the light of the above reflections, note Paul's stunning confession in Philippians 3:7-11:

> But whatever was to my profit I now consider loss for the sake of Christ. What is more, I consider everything a loss compared to the surpassing greatness of knowing Christ Jesus my Lord, for whose sake I have lost all things. I consider them rubbish, that I may gain Christ and be found in him, not having a righteousness of my own that comes from the law, but that which is through faith in Christ — the righteousness that comes from God and is by faith. I want to know Christ and the power of his resurrection and the fellowship of sharing in his sufferings, becoming like him in his death, and so, somehow, to attain to the resurrection from the dead.

Paul starts his contrast between righteousness from the law and righteousness through faith in Christ (Phil. 3:3) by contrasting a glorying in Christ through the Spirit and a confidence in the flesh by way of the law. What Paul means by righteousness "that comes from the law" is not in my view restricted to those obvious boundary markers that distinguished Jews from Gentiles (such as circumcision), as Dunn has maintained, though Paul obviously concentrated his attention there.[48] Paul's reference to being a "Hebrew of the Hebrews" (Phil. 3:5) seems to refer to all of the benefits that the possession of the law brings to the Jewish community.

But this is precisely the issue for Paul, for the benefits of possessing the law as a community, though they have some limited value (cf. Rom. 9:4-5), are not enough to guarantee the new birth or the future resurrection of the dead, not enough to bring about the possession of the Spirit. Recall Paul's reference to children born under the law as still being in bondage, while those born by the Spirit inherit the promise (Gal. 4:21-31). For Paul, the Jewish community's possession of the law and dedication to obey it cannot liberate them from the clutches of sin and death, as Romans 7 makes abundantly clear. The contrast here is between communities, Jewish and Christian, and what can legitimately be claimed by both regarding the means to the promise of life.[49]

The contrast is not between works and a passive trust. After all, Paul admonishes his readers in Philippians 2:12 to "work out your salvation with fear and trembling" and speaks of the strivings of faith to win the prize of conformity to Christ (Phil. 3:12-14). The issue is between the witness of the law (and the community gathered around it) and the fulfillment of that witness in the gift of the Spirit as received by faith in Christ. The community gathered around Moses has not yet inherited the promised gift of the indwelling Spirit belonging to the community gathered around Christ. The difference between the righteousness that comes from the law and the righteousness that wins Christ is the baptism in the Spirit.

The crucial question, then, for Paul was: "Did you receive the Spirit by observing the law, or by believing what you heard?" (Gal. 3:2) The way of Christ brings the Spirit; the way of the law cannot. This is the crucial differ-

---

48. See James D. G. Dunn, *Jesus, Paul, and the Law: Studies in Mark and Galatians* (Louisville: Westminster/John Knox, 1990).

49. I am grateful to Francis Watson for this particular insight into the contrast of communities (in *Paul, Judaism, and the Gentiles: Beyond the New Perspective* [Grand Rapids: Eerdmans, 2007], pp. 148-49), though I expand it to involve the comparison of Spirit and law.

ence between the righteousness of the law and the righteousness that justifies. There are other texts that also contrast righteousness by the law with righteousness by way of the Spirit through faith in Christ (e.g., Rom. 10:1-10). In some places Paul locates the weakness of the law in the law itself, in the fact that it is a set of letters engraved on stone in contrast to the Spirit of the living God, who changes hearts. In other places, the problem lies with Israel (and humanity in general) in that as a nation it did not keep the entire law or in itself fulfill that to which the law bore witness. The two problems are sometimes weaved into the fabric of a single passage. For example, Galatians 3:21 notes that no law has been given that can impart life, while in the very next verse he also notes that not only Israel but the whole world is a prisoner of sin in need of liberation by faith in Christ, implying that we are not able to grasp life within the provisions of the law. Righteousness by way of the law "is not based on faith," but remains locked in a failed effort that has already been judged as falling short by God (Gal. 3:10-12).

It is also important to note that the failure to keep the whole law in its far-reaching demands to love God with the whole heart (Deut. 6:1-6) is not primarily aimed (in Gal. 3) at the individual sins of people but rather at the nation of Israel as a whole. The law's witness to the coming blessing in passages like Deuteronomy 27–30 also contains a curse on the nation for not fulfilling all that the law required: "If you do not obey the LORD your God and do not carefully follow all his commands and decrees I am giving you today, all these curses will come upon you and overtake you" (Deut. 28:15). The curse will involve being besieged and exiled at the hands of pagans (28:49-52): "Then the LORD will scatter you among all nations, from one end of the earth to the other" (28:64). But in the midst of such dire predictions God still offers hope that the curse of the law will eventually be reversed and the blessing realized when God has returned Israel to the land (30:4) and bestowed the gift of the Holy Spirit of God on them: "The LORD your God will circumcise your hearts and the hearts of your descendants, so that you may love him with all your heart and with all your soul, and live" (30:6). Then the law that halted the fulfillment of blessing with a curse can finally find its intended fulfillment. Then Israel can fulfill its ultimate mission of being a channel of Abraham's blessing to all nations.[50]

N. T. Wright uses this narrative framework to make sense of Galatians 3, especially with regard to the curse of the law and how Christ undid the

---

50. See N. T. Wright, *The Climax of the Covenant* (Minneapolis: Fortress, 1993), pp. 144-50.

curse in order to fulfill the law, so that the blessings of Abraham could be channeled to the Gentiles as well as to the Jews through the indwelling Spirit.

> Christ redeemed us from the curse of the law by becoming a curse for us, for it is written: "Cursed is everyone who is hung on a tree." He redeemed us in order that the blessing given to Abraham might come to the Gentiles through Christ Jesus, so that by faith we might receive the promise of the Spirit. (Gal. 3:13-14)

The overcoming of the curse and the release of the flow of blessings cannot come, for Paul, in the context of the law's provisions (repentance and the sacrificial system). Pau naturally denies that the return from exile and the fulfillment of the law's blessings to the Gentiles had already been achieved. Paul's assumption that Israel still falls short of fulfillment and is in a sense under the law's curse would not have sounded strange to a people under occupation by the Romans.

The issue of undoing the curse is implicitly about how Israel can break out of its self-enclosed nationalism to fulfill its God-ordained destiny of becoming a channel of blessing to the Gentiles. N. T. Wright says: "When might it come about that the Gentiles would change from being the agents of Israel's curse, the oppressors through whom the darker side of the covenant was being fulfilled, and become the objects of the blessing of Abraham?"[51] This point is crucial: Paul was convinced through his experience of the Spirit in relation to the risen Christ that the end of Israel's exile and the gift of the transformed heart by the Spirit cannot come from within the law's provisions. Paul saw the redemptive story of Jesus that spanned his birth to his bestowal of the Spirit as the only means by which the curse of the law could be lifted and the blessing come to the Gentiles and to the Jews. Such is only experienced now as the firstfruits of a larger harvest, but the Spirit's indwelling both vindicates and guarantees the way of Christ as the only way to renewal. This means that to continue seeking to find the renewal in devotion to the law alone is to continue to bump up against the curse and an unfulfilled promise.

Similarly, in 2 Corinthians 3, Paul was made a minister of the new covenant "not of the letter but of the Spirit; for the letter kills, but the Spirit gives life" (2 Cor. 3:6). The law that brought death was "engraved in letters

---

51. Wright, *Climax*, p. 148.

of stone" (3:7), while the Spirit of the living God writes the witness to Christ upon the heart (3:1-3). The veil covering the heart and blinding one to the witness to Christ when "the old covenant is read" can only be removed by the Spirit of liberty (3:14-17). Only by the Spirit can we be conformed to the very image of Christ (3:18). The conclusion of the matter, according to Romans 2:29, is that "a man is a Jew if he is one inwardly; and circumcision is circumcision of the heart, by the Spirit, not by the written code."

To say that we could be justified by the law if only we could obey the whole law makes little sense theologically. Romans 2:13 does not offer this as a possibility without the Spirit, as the end of the chapter (2:28-29) shows. First, there is no such capacity to obey the whole law apart from the Spirit of life, whom we were created to bear to the glory of God. Humanity became a living soul responsive to God by the indwelling Spirit (Gen. 2:7). The fulfillment of the Spirit's presence in the creature would come later only through Christ. An autonomous human capacity for the law apart from the Spirit is theological nonsense, regardless of whether it be pre- or post-Fall. How is it conceivable apart from the Spirit of God on any theological terms to imagine a freedom to fulfill the law in loving God with one's whole being? As I have noted earlier, the Old Testament, from Deuteronomy to the prophets, says that the law can only be fulfilled through the gift of the Spirit (e.g., Deut. 30:6; Ezek. 36:26-32).

It is interesting that, in Romans 7:14, Paul locates the role of the law in conveying the holy will of God in the fact that the law's function is "spiritual." Earlier (Rom. 2:29), Paul notes that a true Jew follows the law through a circumcision of the heart "by the Spirit, not by the written code." This is what the prophets foretold. The law's witness to the obedient life would be fulfilled by the Spirit of life. This means that it is theologically impossible for the law apart from the Spirit to deliver on its own promise. As Paul says in Romans 3:21, "But now a righteousness from God, apart from law, has been made known, to which the Law and the Prophets testify." In other words, the law itself testified of a righteousness that would come from a gift that transcends the law! Furthermore, the New Testament makes Christ — and not the law — that which channels the Spirit. To say that we could be justified by the law if only we could keep the whole law is the same as saying that we would not need Christ if only we had an abundance of the Spirit without him. Where would this abundance come from if not from him? Was Christ only a substitute action that entered the world only because we failed to grasp the Spirit without him?

The Christ-Torah contrast in Paul is not due to a one-sided conviction that the law is abrogated because it cursed Christ on the cross or inspired the persecution of Christians.[52] Though the law did result in a curse, Paul allowed the law its dignity in representing a glorious revelation of the holy will of God (Rom. 7:14; 2 Cor. 3:7; Gal. 3:21). Paul is clear: "Is the law, therefore, opposed to the promises of God? Absolutely not!" (Gal. 3:21). The problem Paul notes in Romans 7 is that the law simply cannot deliver on its own promise of life, or, to put it another way, the fulfillment of God's covenant faithfulness to restore God's people and bless the nations with the Spirit were not fulfilled within the provisions of repentance and sacrifice provided by the law. The verdict of history was that the law that intended life ended up confirming the reality of death (Rom. 7:10). Therefore, Paul contrasts the law's spiritual witness with our carnality as flesh, "sold under sin" (7:14).

In God's elect will, Christ was needed to bring about the restoration testified of in advance by both the law and the prophets (Rom. 3:21). Without the reception of the Spirit through faith in Christ, even one's devotion to the law is not enough to grant access to life. One is still in slavery to sin and cries out for liberty from "this body of death" (Rom. 7:24). The implication is that only the Spirit of life received through faith in Christ can bring one the fruits intended by the law's spiritual witness. Thus, in Romans 8, Paul proceeds by noting that "what the law was powerless to do in that it was weakened by the sinful nature, God did by sending his own Son in the likeness of sinful man to be a sin offering. And so he condemned sin in sinful man, in order that the righteous requirements of the law might be fully met in us, who do not live according to the sinful nature but according to the Spirit" (8:3-4). The "law of the Spirit of life" that set us free from the "law of sin and death" is a reference to the Torah under fulfillment by the Spirit of Christ.[53] The rest of the chapter then describes life in the Spirit, which is presented as the only means in the midst of our groans for liberty from sin and death of being released from slavery and of enjoying the promised foretaste of this liberty in the here and now. It is thus the work of Jesus and the presence of the Spirit that fulfills the witness of the law and grants a foretaste of liberty in the midst of the groans of slavery to sin and death typical of creation in general. What the Jewish

---

52. Contra Terrence L. Donaldson, *Paul and the Gentiles: Remapping the Apostle's Convictional World* (Minneapolis: Fortress, 1997), pp. 170-71.

53. See Wright, *Climax*, p. 209.

community yearns for in its devotion to the law is fulfilled through faith in Christ and the life of the Spirit received through him.

In viewing the devotion to the law among his Jewish contemporaries as a dead end, did Paul assume that the Judaism of his opponents was legalistic? E. P. Sanders and others of the "new perspective on Paul" have done much to show that the Judaism of the first century did not fit the stereotype of a legalistic religion.[54] Indeed, Paul's major point in his discussions of Judaism seems to be that they have not proceeded beyond the promise and the law that thrived from it to the fulfillment in Christ as the mediator of the Spirit. Paul admitted that the law's witness was glorious, but that this glory points beyond to an even greater glory in the ministry of the Spirit (2 Cor. 3:7-8).

However, given Sanders's research into the primacy granted grace in ancient Judaism, one can still wonder whether the preoccupation with the external deeds of the law typical of first-century Judaism did not *imply* a kind of legalism, even if it was also assumed that the law was actually a gift of grace within a covenant granted by grace.[55] Furthermore, Paul is clear that denying the Spirit to Gentiles because they transgress Jewish ceremonial laws grants the law absolute significance, contradicting the law's own witness and threatening faith in the all-sufficiency of God's actions in Christ and the Spirit for salvation (see Gal. 2–3). That such a rejection of Gentile believers has legalistic implications is also to be accepted as a legitimate conclusion given the particulars of Paul's theology (e.g., Gal. 2; Rom. 4). The overall recognition of the primacy of grace in ancient Judaism was certainly no guarantee that legalistic implications did not erupt among Christian Jews wrestling with Paul's astounding proclamation that Gentiles have the Spirit apart from their inclusion in the normally accepted rituals of the law. I think Paul was in a better place to judge such matters than are modern scholars who comment on the beliefs of his opponents twenty centuries later, based on incomplete or indirect evidence of what these opponents were actually saying.

Paul's position toward the Jewish communities devoted to the law does raise difficult questions today with regard to theological reflection on Israel. One cannot deny that the Spirit was active among those gathered

---

54. E. P. Sanders, *Paul and Palestinian Judaism: A Comparison of Patterns of Religion* (Philadelphia: Augsburg Fortress, 1977), esp. pp. 84ff., 147ff., 240ff.

55. See Thomas B. Schreiner, *The Law and Its Fulfillment: A Pauline Theology of Law* (Grand Rapids: Baker, 1993), p. 116.

around Moses and the covenant of the law revealed through him (Num. 11), even though the promised indwelling of the Spirit granted by God on all flesh in the latter days was yet to come through faith in Christ. Nor are we compelled by the New Testament to deny that God's covenant with Israel maintains a certain enduring significance even in the light of the fulfillment of that covenant through the gift of the Spirit upon all flesh granted eschatologically in Christ (see Rom. 11). However, Paul's argument was theological. I agree with Sanders that Paul reasoned backwards from the actual fulfillment that came through Christ and the Spirit to the fact that those who lack Christ lack the fulfillment.[56]

Of course, Paul also assumed (as the book of Hebrews does) that the law's entire purpose was to point ahead to something greater, so that to remain confined to the old covenant could be regarded as a path that is now contrary to the full purpose that it once served. Thus, for Paul, Israel cannot remain satisfied with the gifts that devotion to the law granted the nation, since these gifts were ultimately dependent on the fulfillment of a promise. The law itself reaches beyond to the fulfillment of a promise, for the law did not "do away with the promise" but looked ahead to it (Gal. 3:17, 23-24). It is only when one absolutizes or depends exclusively on the law that dependence on the promise is abrogated (Gal. 3:18). Ideally, however, the law is not opposed to the promise but mediates it, so long as one receives it with full recognition of the fact that the commandment itself — without the gift of the Spirit — cannot give life, cannot grant that to which it bears witness (Gal. 3:21), for "a man is a Jew if he is one inwardly; and circumcision is circumcision of the heart, by the Spirit, not by the written code" (Rom. 2:29). Only faith in Christ can bring the Spirit and the justification involved in covenant renewal (Gal. 3:1-5). This is the destiny toward which all of humanity was created, Jewish and Gentile.

All of this is not meant to deny that there are ambiguities and tensions in what Paul wrote about the Jewish law. N. T. Wright observes: "Whatever faults the Rabbis may have had, consistency was not among them."[57] Of course, an inconsistency may represent a seeming contradiction that is actually only a tension placed within a text to "tease a reader into thinking harder about a subject."[58] For example, Paul assumes that his readers will

---

56. See E. P. Sanders, *Paul, the Law, and the Jewish People* (Philadelphia: Fortress, 1983), pp. 47, 140.

57. Wright, *Climax*, p. 4.

58. As Wright notes in *Climax*, p. 7.

follow the essential principles of the moral law, since the love of Christ does not cancel but rather fulfills them (Rom. 13:8-10). Difficult and vague in this light is what Paul then has to say about Christ being the "end of the law" (Rom. 10:4) or as "abolishing in his flesh the law with its commandments and regulations" (Eph. 2:15). Equally difficult is Paul's statement that "through the law I died to the law so that I might live for God" (Gal. 2:19). The law was intended to bear witness to and guide the life of the Spirit according to Hebrew Scripture. What can it now mean that Christ is the *end* of the law or that one must die to the law in order to enjoy the life of the Spirit?

The Ephesians 2 text about Christ's abolishing the law "in his flesh" may grant us a hint as to the world of Paul's thought here. Paul concludes this text with the significance of the gift of the Spirit creating a holy temple of God's indwelling among Jew and Gentile who are now united in the bond of love through faith in Christ: "[T]he whole building is joined together and rises to become a holy temple in the Lord. And in him you too are being built together to become a dwelling in which God lives by his Spirit" (Eph. 2:21-22). I have noted in previous discussions that Christ replaced the Jewish Temple as the chief locus of the Spirit's presence. In doing this, Christ also fulfilled the Temple cult and the regulations of the law in his own flesh as the embodiment of God's presence and favor in the world. The dispensation of the Temple and the law as the center of Israelite piety did marginalize Gentile participation. In fulfilling these, Christ also *replaced* them as the center of the new Israel that shares in the blessing granted to the Gentiles in the gift of the Spirit. The new temple built from both Jew and Gentile is built upon Christ as the new temple of God and as the one who imparts the Spirit as the new source of devotion to God.

For Paul, the shift from one loyalty (the old Temple and law) to the new one (Christ as the source of the Spirit) is nothing short of a bridge-burning experience. Paul thus has to die to the law in order to be born again into Christ. Faith — and not law — grasps the Spirit because faith itself is born from the womb of the Spirit and the seed of the gospel (1 Pet. 1:23). One cannot continue to depend on the law to mediate the blessing of Abraham and believe in Christ to baptize in the Spirit at the same time. For Paul, there is no middle of the road. One cannot say that the center of the new Israel is the Temple *and* Christ, the law *and* the Spirit. Paul tolerated Jewish Christians attending the Temple and following all of the particulars of the law; but he did not tolerate placing these on the same level as Christ as the means of salvation! In terms of ultimate loyalty, there is, for

Paul, no further "plus" when it comes to Christ and the Spirit. There can be no addition to excessive grace. Christ and the Spirit alone are ultimately sufficient for the new Israel as the place for the coming together of Jew and Gentile under the eschatological renewal of life. Even the law and prophets themselves implied as much. The message of Philippians 3 is that one must die to everything else in order to win Christ.

Does this mean that the Jewish law has no meaning to the new Israel? Paul does not go that far, and this is where he is, for me, somewhat vague — or at least less than precise. He does indicate that the law reemerges as fulfilled in the new life of the Spirit (Rom. 2:29; 8:2), but even here it is fulfilled by the love of Christ (Rom. 13:9-10) and the witness of the gospel (Rom. 10:9). I think Albert Schweitzer may have a point when he says that the earthly law is ultimately insufficient for Paul to guide the life of an eschatological reality that points beyond this life. Mystical union with the crucified and risen Christ through the leading of the Spirit becomes the new guide to such an eschatological ethic.[59] Christ is the "end" of the law as its eschatological *telos.*

But the new ethic is not otherworldly in being eschatological, as Schweitzer assumes. Certainly the life example and teaching of Jesus informs the eschatological ethic of the Spirit. Moreover, I think texts such as Romans 13:8-10 suggest that the life of the Spirit or the life in devotion to the love of Christ causes one to fulfill the law's guidance of life in a way that still respects the glory of this older witness. The Word of God that is "God-breathed" and profitable for teaching certainly involved the Torah (2 Tim. 3:15-16). After all, it is still Moses that is read when the veil is removed so that the glory of Christ shines through (2 Cor. 3:15-16). And it is the "perfect law that gives freedom, and continues to do this" that provides James with the mirror into the human soul (James 1:25). The *kerygma* of the apostles did not displace the Hebrew Torah in the church's understanding of the Word of God. That is certainly the case today. Human destiny, however, is fundamentally constituted by the divine calling for the creature to bear the divine *Spirit* (Gen. 2:7), and it is Christ and not the Torah that baptizes in the Spirit. It is this indwelling that will rectify creation and vindicate it as God's possession, our final subject of this chapter.

---

59. See Albert Schweitzer, *The Mysticism of Paul the Apostle* (reprint; New York: Seabury Press, 1968), pp. 189-303.

Faith and Human Destiny

Only when we realize that we were made to bear the divine Spirit (Gen. 2:7) in the image of Christ, to possess God by being possessed by God, do we realize that sin is ultimately alienation from the divine life and from our own calling as a creature made for God. Paul depicts the creature as under the burden of mortal existence, yearning for the glorious immortality of the resurrection body. The firstfruits of the glorious existence of the new creation are centered in the indwelling of the Spirit. Indeed, the new creation is the fulfillment of the God-ordained destiny of the creature to become the dwelling place of God.

In this context, notice what 2 Corinthians 5:4-5 says in reference to the body of the resurrection:

> For while we are in this tent, we groan and are burdened, because we do not wish to be unclothed but to be clothed with our heavenly dwelling, so that what is mortal may be swallowed up by life. Now it is God who has made us for this very purpose and has given us the Spirit as a deposit, guaranteeing what is to come.

I take this text to be a reference to the mortal person yearning for the immortal existence of the resurrected body. The reference to not wanting to be naked is most likely a symbol of not wanting to be shamed or judged as unworthy to be clothed with immortal existence at Christ's return.[60] The point that I wish to emphasize here is that in this text we were made for the very purpose of bearing the immortal Spirit in the image of the exalted and glorified Christ. We can refer to "the evocative, ecstatic soul which is more itself the more God is in it and it is in God."[61] This fact implies that sin is not primarily a moral wrong that can be fixed by obedience to commandments. Sin is primarily a human condition of alienation from the divine presence and from the glorious liberty of becoming the vessel shaped into the very dwelling place of God to God's ultimate glory. The immortal body of the resurrection is the "spiritual body" (1 Cor. 15:44), or the body that has risen into the fullness of pneumatic existence. Restoration is only possible by the gift of the Spirit.

---

60. See G. C. Berkouwer, *The Return of Christ*, trans. James C. Van Oosterom (Grand Rapids: Eerdmans, 1972), pp. 56-59.

61. Michael Hanby, *Augustine and Modernity*, Radical Orthodoxy Series (New York: Routledge, 2003), p. 3.

Indeed, Paul depicts sin and death as alienation from the divine glory of eschatological existence shaped by the habitation of the divine Spirit, "for all have sinned and fall short of the glory of God" (Rom. 3:23). He defines this glory later in the Epistle (Rom. 8) as an eschatological reality connected with liberty from the burden of sin and death through the resurrection. The passage is worth quoting in full:

> Now if we are children, then we are heirs — heirs of God and co-heirs with Christ, if indeed we share in his sufferings in order that we may also share in his glory. I consider that our present sufferings are not worth comparing with the glory that will be revealed in us. The creation waits in eager expectation for the sons of God to be revealed. For the creation was subjected to frustration, not by its own choice, but by the will of the one who subjected it, in hope that the creation itself will be liberated from its bondage to decay and brought into the glorious freedom of the children of God. We know that the whole creation has been groaning as in the pains of childbirth right up to the present time. Not only so, but we ourselves, who have the firstfruits of the Spirit, groan inwardly as we wait eagerly for our adoption as sons, the redemption of our bodies. (Rom. 8:17-23)

There are a few points that I wish to draw from this passage. First, just as with 2 Corinthians 5:4-5, Paul describes sin here not primarily as a moral wrong but rather as a human condition of alienation from the glorious liberty of creation renewed by the Spirit. This glorious liberty is ultimately the liberty of divine love revealed in the incarnation and the cross, but also revealed in victory over sin and death of the resurrection and exaltation. Sin and death are forms of slavery that alienate one from this glorious liberty.

Second, those who are on the way toward the liberty of the new creation are placed on this path through the indwelling of the Spirit. Paul portrays the redeemed as having the firstfruits of the glorious liberty yet to come through the Spirit's presence within. The full harvest is yet to come when the Spirit within so pervades human existence as to shape the person into the very image of the glorified Christ. This is the moment of resurrection, when we possess God as God possesses us. There is thus an integral connection between the current possession of the Spirit and the immortal existence of the resurrection, with the former functioning as the firstfruits of the latter and guaranteeing its outcome. Note Romans 8:11: "And if the Spirit of him who raised Jesus from the dead is living in you, he who raised

Christ from the dead will also give life to your mortal bodies through his Spirit, who lives in you."

Third, the path toward liberty through the Spirit's indwelling does not yet make one immune from the sufferings and yearnings of the creation within this present age. Even we who have the firstfruits of the Spirit groan with the suffering creation for the liberty to come. In fact, the firstfruits of the Spirit grant us the deep hunger for the full harvest yet to come. In the meantime, we have the assurance and the hope that the sufferings of this age will not be worth comparing with the glory to come (Rom. 8:18). The glory to come to us as vessels freed for God and for the mutual indwelling will so far exceed any reality now available to us that there will be no means by which to adequately compare the two modes of existence. The glory to come will vindicate our hope in a way that far outshines any challenge that suffering might level against it. In this way, glorification fulfills justification (8:30).

I have said all of the above in order to locate faith within this yearning for God under the influence of the firstfruits of the Spirit. All of creation is caught up in the groaning for the liberty of the new creation as the habitation of God. As Paul notes, we were made for this (2 Cor. 5:5). What is unique about those who groan in *faith* is that they groan with the first-fruits of the Spirit. Faith thus assumes both the weakness of the flesh and the strength of the Spirit. Faith is weak in that it is essentially characterized as the absence of sight and the full realization of pneumatic existence. We have not yet met the Lord directly face to face (presence to presence), and the divine indwelling has not yet pervaded the life of the body to the point of freeing us from the restraints of mortal existence. On the other hand, faith is also strong in that it draws from the witness of the Spirit to trust and hope for the fullness of the liberty that was "deposited" within us through our possession of the Spirit within. More deeply, faith is the means by which we embrace this treasure within and continue to seek it until the day of final indwelling and liberation. By participating by faith in Christ through the indwelling Spirit, we participate also in the future new creation to be fashioned in his image.

Human destiny is fulfilled in the correspondence of faith between Christ as the man of the Spirit and us as possessors of the Spirit. Faith thus ultimately corresponds to the divine faithfulness originally active in God's reaching to possess us through the divine indwelling. We possess God in a way that is analogous to how God has possessed us. In other words, if God has offered us the gift of the divine presence through the divine *kenosis* of the cross and the victory of the resurrection, then through the gift of the

Spirit, faith follows this same path in possessing God with all that we have. Our destiny is fulfilled in our possession of the Spirit by means of faith in a way that corresponds to Jesus' path as led by the Spirit to the cross through to the empty tomb. "Thanks to his intimate experience of the world, as the incarnate one who knows experientially every dimension of the world's being, down to the Abyss of Hell, God now becomes the measure of man."[62] Faith helps us explain what Dietrich Bonhoeffer means when he says that "the only man who has the right to say that he is justified by grace alone is the man who has left all to follow Christ."[63] It is an extreme statement, to be sure, but one worth contemplating and taking with utmost seriousness, especially in the light of the life witness of the man who wrote it. The only way to the vindication of the Spirit in resurrection is the path of the cross.

In other words, faith means that the creature is not meant to be a passive spectator to the divine embrace, but a willing participant and respondent by the very power of that embrace. This response to God is not a cooperation between two autonomous partners but a participation from, through, and in a divine embrace. The participation of the sinful creature in the mutual embrace or indwelling must be fashioned after the divine faithfulness evident in the divine embrace. Paul writes: "I want to know Christ and the power of his resurrection and the fellowship of sharing in his sufferings, becoming like him in his death, and so, somehow, to attain to the resurrection from the dead" (Phil. 3:10-11). Just as Jesus was handed over to death for our sake, so Paul was handed over to death "for Jesus' sake, so that his life may be revealed in our mortal body" (2 Cor. 4:11). Faith functions to possess and to release that life dwelling within through the way of the cross and toward the day of the resurrection (drawing already from its strength). Faith is Spirit-baptized existence; justification is by, in, and toward Christ. This is what it means to be justified by *faith*.

Conclusion

Justifying faith is a relational reality that takes its very substance from God's covenant faithfulness and self-giving in Christ and in the Spirit. The

---

62. Von Balthasar, *Mysterium Paschale*, trans. Aidan Nichols (Grand Rapids: Eerdmans, 1990), pp. 13-14.

63. Dietrich Bonhoeffer, *The Cost of Discipleship*, trans. R. H. Fuller (New York: Macmillan, 1963), p. 55.

relationship is not essentially legal or moral but redemptive and involving a mutual indwelling through the Spirit of life. According to the Old Testament, those who lean on the enduringly faithful God will be energized by God within and glide on that faithfulness as an eagle on the winds (Isa. 40:31). The prophets awaited the day when the indwelling Spirit would fulfill the law's witness to a life wholly faithful to God (Ezek. 36:36-37). The Old Testament thus emphasizes God's steadfast and enduring faithfulness, especially in the context of promises of deliverance and the advent of the Spirit. God's presence and will are often hidden beneath events that seem contrary to the divine plan and that test Israel's steadfast trust and faithfulness. In the midst of confusion, one leans on the divine promises in order to chart a steady course of obedience in life. The law played a vital role in guiding Israel's faithfulness and in witnessing to the life that will be made possible by the Holy Spirit — in which the liberty of obedience will be made a real possibility. The prophets looked forward to the time when the steadfast faithfulness of Israel would be vindicated in the coming of the Messiah and the Holy Spirit. It is God's vindication that will stand against all charges to the contrary.

The New Testament also includes at its core an understanding of faith via the Old Testament theme of steadfast trust and faithfulness, except with a unique accent on belief in response to the promise of life that the Spirit's own presence confirms within. Belief is not so much in tension with the Old Testament emphasis on covenant faithfulness as a valuable expression of it in the new age of the Spirit's witness to the triumph of grace in Christ. The covenant faithfulness of God is now revealed in the man Jesus Christ as the one who is indwelt and led by the Spirit, especially in his offer of divine favor to outcasts and sinners and, in fulfillment of that offer, his later impartation of the Spirit on all flesh. He does this through a life of self-giving that culminates in the cross, the resurrection, and his role as Spirit baptizer.

As the revelation of God's covenant faithfulness, Christ as the man of the Spirit descended into the realm of God-forsakenness in order to channel the Spirit to sinners in his resurrection, exaltation, and Spirit impartation. The Spirit gave the Word an anointed body so that the Word could impart this anointing to other bodies. The Spirit mediated Christ to the world so that Christ as the Word could mediate the Spirit to the world. This anointing shaped Jesus as the archetypal revelation of covenant faithfulness in history, a witness that is rejected in crucifixion but vindicated in resurrection and exaltation and offered to the sinful creature in Spirit baptism. This anointing passed on to sinful creatures causes them to be born anew in order to participate in the justice of divine communion and in faithful witness to this justice before the world.

Faith involves belief but cannot be reduced to it. Faith more deeply involves mutual indwelling and participation. Human faith is possible by the indwelling Spirit, who indwelt and led Jesus on his path to the cross. We are made by the Spirit to participate in Christ, in his witness to covenant faithfulness in history. By participating in Christ, faith participates in the future new creation to be fashioned in his image. We are baptized in the Spirit so as to become living witnesses of Christ in the world (Acts 1:8) and harbingers of the new creation. In this participation in Christ, we share in his favor with the Father and in his vindication as the faithful Son. Bound by the Spirit to Jesus as crucified and risen, faith is shaped into his image and Spirit-led witness. Faith thus follows the path of the cross or of self-sacrificial service, especially to the weak and the suffering.

Faith mimics God's self-giving in Spirit baptism. Clinging to Christ, we shape this faith by love and we inspire it afresh by an enduring hope. Though flowing from and sustained by the Spirit, this faith is still weak, since it exists in the absence of sight and as part of the yearning of the suffering creation for the liberty of the new creation. One faithfully believes the gospel against all challenges and clings in the hope of its fulfillment in the new creation, the fulfillment of the justice of the kingdom of God on earth. Justification by faith means that justifying righteousness is not fully revealed until the resurrection of the dead and the new creation makes all things the dwelling place of God. Until then, "by faith we eagerly await through the Spirit the righteousness for which we hope" (Gal. 5:5).

As a humanly conditioned participation in Christ that is still limited by the suffering and weakness of this age, faith cannot be that on which justification is based. We cannot grant faith divine attributes even though it is born through the Spirit. The Spirit embraces us in this faith and participation in Christ, assuring us of our acceptance in the beloved (Rom. 8:15-16). It is this indwelling — first in Christ and then, by extension, in us in relationship to Christ — that is at the core or substance of justification. This is the reality on which we lean in justification and not the faith that shapes the nature of that leaning. Living faith provides the means by which the rightwising of creation is "incarnated" in creation and reaches for the fulfillment of justice in the new creation, the very habitation of the indwelling Spirit. But it is the Spirit's presence and witness as originally incarnated in the faithful Jesus that inaugurates and sustains justification throughout history and at the fulfillment of the kingdom of God. We are justified "by grace through faith" — or "by the Spirit in Christ through participation in his faithful witness." Justification is in one sense the vindication of cruciform existence: *pneumatic* existence under the shadow of the cross.

9 The Spirit and the Other

The Justified Community

Our previous emphasis on divine righteousness as the covenant faithfulness of God and faith as conformity in the Spirit to divine faithfulness implies that justification is communal as well as deeply personal. As Simon Chan has shown, the Spirit is the "third person" of the Godhead in the sense that the Spirit in personal relationship with the Father and the Son goes beyond the two to involve the many.[1] To be justified in the Spirit is to be justified with the many. Justification thus involves more than individual pardon; it involves mutual pardon within the Spirit's embrace and the reality of *koinonia*. In that light, we could very well have included a substantial section in our last chapter on faith as a communal reality. Though I did refer to the communal dimension of faith in my last chapter, I have strategically decided to save the fuller discussion of that subject for separate and more intensive treatment here. Justification is embodied in history and achieves ultimate realization not only within an individual's life with respect to others but also, more broadly, within communities of faith dedicated to the justice of the gospel. To this dimension of justification we now turn.

Justification and the Church: A Contemporary Discovery

The discovery of justification as a communal reality began with Krister Stendahl's provocative essay "The Apostle Paul and the Introspective Con-

---

1. Simon Chan, *Liturgical Theology* (Lombard, IL: InterVarsity, 2006), pp. 32-34.

science of the West." There Stendahl criticizes the tendency in the West after Augustine to view justification as the means by which the troubled conscience of the individual is soothed by the assurance of forgiveness, a legacy given prominence by Luther. Stendahl notes that Paul shows none of the signs of such a search for pardon in the face of a law that stands above as an oppressive tyrant. On the contrary, Paul even reveals a robust conscience concerning his success at following the commandments (e.g., Phil. 3:4-6). Stendahl maintains that the prominence of justification in Paul's theology is tied to the goal of reconciling Jews with ceremonially unclean Gentiles together in Christ rather than to the soothing of an individual's troubled conscience in the face of the law's demands. The reason that justification declined in significance in the second century was that Jewish and Gentile reconciliation lost its significance in the churches.[2]

Of course, there are other issues one could discuss that are relevant to the waning of Paul's emphasis on justification in the early centuries of the church, such as the Gnostic threat and the effort of the church fathers to meet it in part with an emphasis on the Old Testament law and the obedience of faith. Though Augustine's conflict with Pelagianism did set the stage for an understanding of justification as a personal experience of grace, Augustine also transcended this emphasis by viewing justification in relation to *theosis* and new creation. It may also be argued that Luther did indeed connect justification with the life of the church.[3]

Yet, beyond the above reservations concerning Stendahl's thesis, there is much to applaud in his insights. The drift of early Christianity from its Jewish roots represented a great loss to the church, including the apocalyptic flavor of Paul's theology, as well as his passion for the restoration of Israel through the rise of integrated communities of Jews and Gentiles blessed by the presence of the Spirit and the powers of the age to come. Moreover, there is no question but that Paul's major concerns about justification had to do mainly with the larger issues of the vindication of divine faithfulness in history and the fulfillment of the divine promise to Abraham that God would bless all nations. At the heart of these concerns was Paul's vision of an integrated community of faith in which both Jew and Gentile discover together in their joint conformity to Christ the triumph

2. Krister Stendahl, "The Apostle Paul and the Introspective Conscience of the West," *Harvard Theological Review* 56, no. 3 (July 1963): 199-215, esp. 200-205.

3. On Luther, see Scott Hendrix, "Offene Gemeinschaft: Die Kirchliche Wirklichkeit der Rechtfertigung," *Kirche und Dogma* 43 (1997): 98-110.

of God's covenant faithfulness in the world and the ultimate vindication of those who are blessed to share in the divine favor. As John Howard Yoder says: "The problem was not that Jewish Christians wanted to keep the law; Paul was tolerant of that. Nor was it the belief that by keeping the law one could be saved — they didn't believe that. The problem was the inclusion of the Gentiles by faith in Jesus. It was the 'social form of the church.'"[4] The preoccupation of justification theology in the West with the individual quest for personal forgiveness strips justification of its original pneumatological and eschatological expansiveness. The rediscovery of the communal nature of justification can help to restore it.

Markus Barth defended the "social" view of justification in an even more important essay that was published not long after Stendahl's. Though this essay received little attention, it represented a breakthrough toward a social doctrine of justification. Barth began by maintaining that justification is essentially God's gift of the "other" to the just community: "For their salvation, God has given men the gift of fellow-men."[5] This social orientation to the doctrine cuts at the core of the individualistic self-preoccupation of justification teaching in the West. For Barth, "No man can find meaning and fulfillment of his own life, as long as he is directed more and more to himself, his own faith, his personal principles, his private relationship to God" (p. 258). Justifying righteousness is by nature righteousness for and with the other. "No man is ever made righteous for himself; justification by faith is a reality only in community with those fellow-men whom God elected for justification" (pp. 244-45). Hence, the justification of others in the church cannot be mere appendages or parallel cases of my own justification but rather essential to my rightwising. Justification for Barth is essentially a relational reality, not only between us and God but also in conformity to God between us and the *other*. For Barth, justification is thus by faith but also by love: "Briefly: where there is no love there is no faith and no justice" (p. 245).

Barth notes that in Paul's context this meant that no Jew could understand the justice of God without the fellowship of the Gentiles.

> Only together with the Gentiles who come to God does a Jew experience how surprising, how righteous, how social and how universal is the

---

4. John Howard Yoder, *The Politics of Jesus*, 2nd ed. (Grand Rapids: Eerdmans, 1994), p. 216.

5. Markus Barth, "Jews and Gentiles: The Social Character of Justification in Paul," *Journal of Ecumenical Studies* 5, no. 2 (Spring 1968): 242. Hereafter, page references to this essay will appear in parentheses in the text.

judgment carried out in Jesus Christ. No Jew will be justified without the justification of Gentiles because there is no justification which does not involve God's impartial judgment of Jews and Gentiles. (p. 250)

We are indeed justified by the miracle of Jesus' death, resurrection, and Spirit impartation, but this miracle produces not only a just individual but a just community. Justification in Christ is, therefore, "not an individual miracle happening to this person or that person, which each may seek or possess for himself. Rather justification by grace is a joining together of this person and that person, of the near and the far, of the good and the bad, of the high and the low. It is a social event" (p. 259).

In this attempt at reconciliation, all of the parties are changed; no one remains the same (p. 264). As Barth recognizes concerning the justified person with respect to me, "he is a neighbor who, bound and free in his own way, has a right to expect of me that I let myself be free where I was bound and let myself be bound where I felt myself to be free from responsibility" (p. 252). Such change through justifying grace must not only occur within the church but within the world at large. For Barth, the reconciliation and freedom of justification cannot remain locked within the just community of faith. "A peace in the soul experienced at the expense of peace in the world is no peace" (p. 265). Barth pushed for experiences of justice in the world with respect to the other in order to show that all humans live from justifying grace and are thus changed by it.

Barth then applies this secular interpretation of justification to white racism in the United States and other contexts. His remarks, limited as they were by the commonly used language of his time, are remarkably insightful and worth quoting in full:

But the same is true of the well-meaning, liberal white people who are ready to accept and treat colored fellow-men as "honorary white men." Even when we white people forgive our colored brothers their allegedly inferior origin, morality, culture, and when we receive them into "our" schools, "our" residential areas, "our" churches, "our" occupations, "our" families — we contradict the Pauline preaching of God's justice and the neighbor's right. For the expected or promised Europeanization and Americanization of men of African or other derivation resembles all too obviously the imposition of the law and customs of a privileged group upon the lawless. The apostle Paul fought and forbade such imposition. The law given to the Jews justifies neither the Jews nor the

Gentiles. It takes Jesus Christ to justify and to unite both of them by grace. (p. 266)

In Paul's context, justification was not the act of Jews making Gentiles into Jewish proselytes. Both Jew and Gentile had to change in mutual conformity to Christ. So also, we do not accept the "other" by "graciously" adopting them as *one of us*. African Americans are not accepted by adopting them as whites! Seeing Christ in the other *as other*, we are willing to change in being reconciled, as they are similarly willing to change in relation to us. Neither group loses its cultural bearings, but neither imposes this on the other, nor is anything too valuable to be sacrificed in the joint quest to win Christ.

Markus Barth has developed Stendahl's thesis in an extremely helpful direction. There is no question but that justification reaches out to the other since it has its source in the covenant faithfulness of God. Did not God as Father, Son, and Spirit reveal divine justice in devotion and self-giving in relation to one another? In opening the divine indwelling and *koinonia* to creation, did not God in this faithfulness embrace the radically other for the other's sake? How can we be rightwised with God "by faith" or in conformity by the Spirit to the faithfulness of Christ in isolation from others? In our identification with Christ as the man of the Spirit, do we not also become a vessel of Christ's presence to the other?

Though Markus Barth does not develop the pneumatological dimension of his social view of justification, his essay cries out for it. After all, the Spirit is the one who brings us into *koinonia* across boundaries, as Acts 2 shows us. If Robert Jenson is correct that justifying righteousness is rooted in God's Trinitarian *koinonia*, then we should not be surprised to learn that justification creates *koinonia* among the people of God and encourages analogous signs of this grace throughout a fractured and alienated world that implicitly yearns for it in the Spirit.[6] Of course, we who have the firstfruits of the Spirit cry out for it, too. In answer, the Spirit facilitates our justification across boundaries and in genuine embrace of one another, as the Spirit embraces us within.

Jan Milič Lochman also wrote of the wider social implications of justification in terms of its critical function within a world of achievers. In dialogue with Marxists, Lochman came to see that the transcendence of the

---

6. Jenson, *Systematic Theology,* vol. 2, *The Works of God* (Oxford and New York: Oxford University Press, 1999), p. 300.

kingdom of God within history serves to prevent humanity from absolutizing any cultural vision or political agenda. Transcendence must be respected. From within a Christian context, we understand this transcendence to exist in God. Only God's eschatological righteousness fulfilled in Christ can claim our unqualified allegiance. Freedom depends on refusing any absolute status to anyone or anything besides the liberating God who opens up a new future for us in Christ.[7]

In this light, Lochman shows sensitivity to the perception that justification by faith has been emptied of all meaning due to increasing confidence that humanity can creatively master its own future.[8] In response, Lochman seeks to overcome dualistic or individualistic doctrines of justification by faith in order to expose the doctrine's communal and larger social significance. Justification orients the community of disciples to the life, death, and resurrection of Jesus as the liberating hope for a new future that cannot be domesticated within any particular personal or social agenda. In the light of this liberating hope, the community's vision seeks to restructure our own history from the small to the great, even social and world history (p. 210).

Lochman takes particular aim at the "culture of performance and profit" prevalent in the world, "which limits the 'polyphony of life'" and urges "a 'one-dimensional man,' manipulated and manipulative in the process of production and profit" (pp. 211-12). Justification offers freedom from the "merciless consequences" of this dominant social vision. Though performance of truth has a place, justification cuts at the roots of ideologies of performance that grant absolute significance to the goal of profit or control (p. 212). In addition, labor may be our right, but it is not our justification, which is a gift from God (p. 213). Moreover, though justification incarnates itself in works, avoiding all forms of "cheap grace," all efforts at granting these works absolute significance conforms to an enslaved gracelessness. Instead, justification urges signs of grace in a graceless world (pp. 212-13).

Allow me to respond here to Markus Barth and Jan Lochman (both of

---

7. Lochman, "The Doctrine of Justification in a Society of Achievers," *Reformed World* 35 (Mar. 1978–Dec. 1979): 212-14. Hereafter, page references to this essay will appear in parentheses in the text.

8. Such was the challenge faced by the Evangelical Lutheran Church of Germany: "Thesen zur Rechtfertigungslehre der Theologischen Kommission der VELKD," in *Rechtfertigung zur neuzeitlichen Lebenszussamenhang* (Gütersloh: Gerd Mohn, 1974), pp. 7-8; see also Lochman, "The Doctrine of Justification in a Society of Achievers," p. 211.

whom were my teachers at the University of Basel). Barth's insights into the critical function of justification with respect to racism are insightful. My only hesitance in accepting Barth's proposals is that he does not nuance specifically enough the relationship between the church as the just community and movements for social justice in the world. Lochman's effort to root justification within the community of disciples as a way of reshaping their vision of society and of history so that they may function in Christ (I would add, in the Spirit!) to offer signs of grace in an increasingly graceless world is helpful as a way of augmenting Barth's social doctrine of justification. In this light, what Barth wrote has tremendous relevance to social relationships within the church and, by way of analogy, in the world. Church and world are indeed interpenetrating and related realities.

But instead of speaking of justification in church and world without adequate distinction, as Barth does, I would rather speak of the church's responsibility to model justice for the world through the formation of a just community in the Spirit as a witness to Christ. The church becomes more properly and truly social the deeper it penetrates through the leading of the Spirit into the core of its own existence, which is Christ. From the vantage point of this discipleship, the church seeks an embodied witness that not only proclaims and models the inauguration of ultimate justice in Christ but also seeks *analogous* experiences of justice in the world. These implicit signs of justice in the world bear powerful witness to the fact that all of creation is laid claim to by God in justification and will be taken up into the new creation by the Spirit. The Spirit's witness to justice is certainly not confined to the community of Christ, but this community is the central *locus* of the Spirit's witness to Christ in the world.

N. T. Wright finds in this communal understanding of justification a way of completing the revolution of the "new perspective on Paul" begun by E. P. Sanders. Sanders did well to show us the problem involved in attributing to first-century Judaism the legalism that Luther fought in relation to medieval Catholic piety. But, for Wright, Sanders did not proceed far enough to actually question the received Protestant tradition concerning the nature of justification itself. Wright refers here to the traditional notion that justification is exclusively the means by which a person enters a relationship with Jesus Christ.[9] In disagreement with this narrow view of

---

9. N. T. Wright, *What Paul Really Said: Was Paul of Tarsus the Real Founder of Christianity?* (Grand Rapids: Eerdmans, 1997), p. 114. Hereafter, page references to this work will appear in parentheses in the text.

justification, Wright highlights membership in the covenant community rather than individual initiation to Christ. Concerning justification he notes: "[I]t has to do quite definitely with how you *define the people of God:* Are they to be defined by the badges of the Jewish race or some other way?" (pp. 120-21; italics in original). Specifically, concerning the church at Antioch, the question had to do with whether formerly pagan and uncircumcised converts are full members of the messianic community. The question is one of membership: "The point is: who will be vindicated, resurrected, shown to be the covenant people, on the last day?" (pp. 126-27).

The answer for Wright is that those who have the Torah written on their hearts by the Spirit through faith in Christ have the right to be members in the covenant community and will be vindicated one day with Christ in the end-time resurrection (pp. 126-27). Wright's discussion is unique in his emphasis on Genesis 15 and Deuteronomy 27–30 as a scriptural context for understanding justification and law in texts such as Galatians 3 (pp. 121, 129). For Paul, these Old Testament texts held out the possibility of blessing if the whole law is fulfilled by the nation of Israel, but also a curse if Israel does not succeed. As Israel failed within the provision of the law to become a channel of blessing to all nations, they fell under the law's curse, especially as a people under pagan occupation. Christ then bore the curse for Israel and in his resurrection became the channel of blessing to the Gentiles as well as the source of renewal for Israel (Gal. 3:13-14). The Gentiles also find in the cross freedom from judgment or God-forsakenness in the embrace of the Spirit. In receiving the blessing of Abraham, which is the indwelling Spirit, Gentiles change from participation in Israel's judgment to participation with Israel in restoration. This framework, then, provides us with a context for viewing justification as the means by which the just community is identified, namely, as consisting of Jews and Gentiles together who believe in Christ and bear the Spirit in anticipation of the final justice of the resurrection.

As is apparent in previous chapters, I regard Wright's narrative framework for justification compelling. Of course, one is not forced to choose between the soteriological (in the context of initiation in Christ) and the ecclesiological when it comes to identifying the meaning of justification in Scripture. The rightwising of the people of God is not *only* to be found in their reconciliation with one another in the church or even in their living witness to the faithfulness of God in the world. It is *also* to be found in the Spirit's indwelling and initiation to Christ, which highlights the mutual indwelling between the creature and God that constitutes the church. Ultimate justice is not *only* the reconciled community or the vindication of the resurrection; it is *also* the turning of creation into the final dwelling place of God so that God could also be the dwelling place of creation. Only then is God's covenant faithfulness toward the creation fulfilled and the cosmos set right in terms of what it was meant to be.

Justification is both soteriological and ecclesiological. In other words, justification is ecclesiological or social because salvation or initiation to Christ involves incorporation and *koinonia*. Moreover, Spirit indwelling is deeply personal and interpersonal, individual and corporate. It is vital not to swing to the other end of the theological spectrum and describe justification in exclusively corporate terms. Justification is also highly personal. In justification, the individual is not dissolved into the corporate *Geist*.

It is clear to me, however, that the recent shift to the ecclesiological or the social dimension of justification has done much to open up the pneumatological, eschatological, and implicitly Trinitarian themes connected to the term in the New Testament. It has also served to open fresh possibilities for understanding Paul's contrast between justification by the works of the law and by Christ or the Spirit. The issue is not only whether an individual can keep every single commandment, and justification is not merely the answer to the cry of desperation coming from someone aware of his or her personal failure. The narrative background to Paul's conviction that justification comes by Christ and not law has to do with the fact commonly accepted among Jews of the first century that the restoration and blessing promised by the law and the prophets have not yet come through the provisions available within the law itself. Paul wished to suggest to his fellow Jews that the Spirit and the blessing have been channeled through Christ instead, for he is the one who has fulfilled the law and has borne its curse. The coming together of Jew and Gentile within the restored Israel blessed by the latter-day Spirit came through Christ. The rightwising of the world promised by the prophets has already begun. Of course, this is highly personal, but it is also profoundly corporate and social in significance. Therefore, let us develop the ecclesiological and social dimensions of justification a bit more.

Justification and the Other

Justification occurs when creation is rightwised by becoming the dwelling place of God and being transformed into the image of God's faithful Son.

Essential to the faithful Son is his incarnation and death in solidarity with the lost or the other. Jesus fulfilled all righteousness by going down into the baptismal water in search of the lost and to announce a future kingdom of justice that will liberate the lost and the forsaken by the Spirit (Matt. 3:15-17). Such becomes his mission (Matt. 12:28), which finds its fulfillment in the decisive self-giving that occurs from the cross to Pentecost. There is thus no rightwising in the image of Christ as the man of the Spirit in isolation from the other. This is why the Lord's Prayer asks for forgiveness of debts "as we also have forgiven our debtors" (Matt. 6:12). This is also why the divine indwelling is both personal and *corporate.* Speaking to the Corinthians about the need to avoid sexual impurity, Paul could write to individuals that their bodies were temples of the Spirit (1 Cor. 6:19), just as he had also said to the entire church that "you yourselves are God's temple" (1 Cor. 3:16).

To lay claim to the privilege of being the one who is taken by the Spirit into the divine life involves taking in the other as well. Jesus opened his blessing to Israel only on the condition that the Pharisees receive it at the banquet table with the outcasts (Luke 15). And the blessing of Abraham is to occur only when the Jews bless the nations and are blessed with their fellowship in return. Rightwising in the Spirit is a relational as well as a personal dynamic. In this rightwising, one forsakes the illusion of an autonomous self who is self-sufficient and self-reliant. Yet the self is not dissolved in the process of rightwising either: the self is "de-centered" and centered on Christ, but not dissolved.[10] "The life I live in the body, I live by faith in the Son of God, who loved me and gave himself for me" (Gal. 2:20). The "I" and the "me" maintain their relevance but are now defined in relation to him, the Son of God who gave himself for the other. Let us unpack this a bit.

"In the beginning is the relation." These words, penned by the great Jewish philosopher Martin Buber in his classic work *I and Thou,* is an obvious play on the words of the Genesis creation account. It resonates with Genesis 1:27, where the image of God is male *and* female in relationship. Buber's meaning is clear: "relation" is not a human luxury or an addendum to human existence; there is something about relationships that is "ontological," or essential to human existence. The longing for relationship is innate, arising out of the interdependence of all of life, which is appar-

---

10. See Miroslav Volf, *Exclusion and Embrace: A Theological Exploration of Identity, Otherness, and Reconciliation* (Nashville: Abingdon, 1996), p. 91.

ent, for example, from the experience of the baby in the womb.[11] Ever since William James's idea of the "social self," the significance of the social environment for the development of self-consciousness has been recognized in the social sciences.[12] Justification in the midst of communion assumes a relational anthropology.

Therefore, it is not difficult to understand that relationship is fundamental to human existence and identity. Child psychologists inform us that a child's life flourishes in bonding with significant others and gains identity in seeing this mirrored in the faces and attitudes of those with whom the child forms relationships. There is even a kind of bonding with another within the womb. That child is then born into a language and a social structure that shapes his or her way of perceiving the self and the world. The self is the self-in-relation, the self-in-community — for good and ill. As a person moves into an ever more complex network of human relationships, his or her sense of identity grows equally complex. A person is a parent, a friend, a sibling, a neighbor, and so on, all labels we place on various kinds of relationships, which are fluid and constantly changing. Humans move in communities other than their own, creating a collision of worlds and a further expansion of one's sense of self.

One is constantly reminded that no person is an island. Relationships are not external to us but represent a complex field of life in which we define our very existence, whether we like it or not. We waffle between alienation and assimilation, both signs of a fallen reality as well as what distorts our souls or inner sense of self. This fallen reality is essentially relational, as are the symptoms of destruction and oppression that we feel in the midst of it. The yearning for the Spirit and foretastes of the liberty to come are also relational. We groan with the entire creation for liberty (Rom 8:26). All of this will help us understand the implicitly relational language of justification in the Bible, as well as the essential role of the communion of saints in occasioning the "incarnation" of justification in history.

By saying that relationships are essential to human existence, I do not mean to imply that there is no sense of self distinct from others. In fact, self-consciousness develops within the social environment: relationship

11. Martin Buber, *I and Thou*, trans. Ronald Gregor Smith (New York: Charles Scribner's Sons, 1970), pp. 76-78.

12. William James, *The Principles of Psychology* (reprint; New York: Dover, 1950), 1:203ff.; see also Wolfhart Pannenberg, *Anthropology in Theological Perspective*, trans. Matthew J. O'Connell (Philadelphia: Westminster, 1985), p. 158.

implies a self that exists distinct (though ultimately inseparable) from others. Bonhoeffer expresses it eloquently in his classic *Sanctorum Communio*: "One could . . . say that by recognizing a You, a being of alien consciousness, as separate and distinct from myself, I recognize myself as an 'I', and so my self-consciousness awakens."[13] In fact, it is quite natural in our development to both take others in and keep others at a distance. The boundaries of our existence have both barriers and bridges.[14]

The upshot of the dialectic of distinction and connection of the self-in-relationship is that unity never necessitates uniformity or the dissolving of the distinct self. If there is no such distinct self, there is no freedom, because the self that is not distinct from others becomes lost or bound within the expectations of others. For example, I live in myriad relationships that mediate my life to me. I am a husband, a father, a friend, a teacher, and so forth. But I engage in all of these relationships from a self-conscious center that I sometimes rediscover and nourish in solitude. Without this sense of self apart from others, I am wholly dependent on the acceptance of others to have any sense of identity. Such dependence can easily turn into an oppressive reality in which the significant others of my life can control me by threatening to withdraw their acceptance if I do not conform to their wishes. An oppressive manipulation of individuals can also be imposed by the state or powerful social or cultural influences. Carl Jung wrote *The Undiscovered Self* as a hard-hitting critique of the "mass mind" that seeks to dissolve the individual psyche into an oppressive corporate identity.[15] The fact that I "have a life" distinct from people and corporate forces grants me the freedom from which I can give of myself unconditionally to others regardless of whether or not they reciprocate in kind.

But how do I gain this "life," or this center within, that grants me the freedom I need to form relationships without being overwhelmed by alienation or assimilation? In the midst of relationships, one seeks to discover an inner core, an "autonomous self" who is free. But such autonomy is a modernist delusion that leads to alienation and oppression. What is really needed is a self in *solitude*. Solitude does not deny the essential nature of relationship but implies a safe space to develop the self without threats of abandonment or oppression. It assumes a supportive context,

13. Dietrich Bonhoeffer, *Sanctorum Communio: A Theological Study of the Sociology of the Church,* trans. Reinhard Krauss and Nancy Lukens (Minneapolis: Fortress, 1998), p. 71.

14. Volf, *Exclusion and Embrace,* p. 47.

15. Carl Gustav Jung, *The Undiscovered Self,* trans. R. F. C. Hull (Boston: Little, Brown, 1958).

ideally one made possible by unconditional love and trust, something that could even be called "sacred." But where is such a context to be found?

Anthony Storr's *Solitude: A Return to the Self* grounds the search for such a trusting context for solitude in the child's early capacity — in the context of trusting relationships — to be alone. During a child's early development, the attachment figure becomes a part of the child's inner world as someone on whom the child can rely in the figure's absence. In other words, the capacity to be alone in the context of trust is an essential aspect of a young child's healthy development. Storr concludes from this childhood experience that the "capacity to be alone thus becomes linked with self-discovery and self-realization; with becoming aware of one's deepest needs, feelings, and impulses." Storr criticizes as one-sided the common assumption that maturity implies only the capacity to form healthy relationships; he also considers the capacity to be alone a sign of emotional maturity.[16] Solitude both assumes and is required for the formation of trusting, graced relationships.

The capacity to resist either alienation from or assimilation into the mass mind is the capacity for solitude, which is the context in which a sense of the self that is distinct from others is cultivated. Solitude as the context for self-realization thus becomes as essential to life as is time invested in cultivating relationships. Without solitude, one can be set adrift in one's identity among myriad relationships with all of their expectations and demands without the capacity to find a center of unconditional trust in which to cultivate a free and creative sense of self-realization. This center for the Christian is essentially the embrace of the Spirit in Christ. The Christian would thus highlight Carl Jung's question: "Have I any religious experience and immediate relation to God, and hence that certainty which will keep me, as an individual, from dissolving in the crowd?"[17]

In this capacity to trust God and to receive from God our calling and gifting for life, we discover who we are in relationship to others. This solitude is the center from which one can give of oneself to others. Our selves are not dissolved in justification; rather, in the Spirit we remain centered in Christ and his will for our lives while we open ourselves to others in genuine self-giving. Miroslav Volf says: "The Spirit enters into the citadel of the self, de-centers the self by fashioning it in the image of the self-giving

---

16. Anthony Storr, *Solitude: A Return to the Self* (New York: The Free Press, 1988), pp. 18-19, 21.

17. Jung, *Undiscovered Self*, p. 33.

Christ, and frees its will so it can resist the power of exclusion in the power of the Spirit of embrace."[18] Rightwising rectifies communities by opening them up to each other in genuine *koinonia*. We avoid both alienation (a quest for autonomy that sacrifices communion) and assimilation (a quest for communion that sacrifices solitude) within the justice of God. Justification is thus a personal — even individual — relationship with God as well as one that is cultivated in relation to others in community.

In his perfect self-giving to God and others, Jesus models the divine justice for us. Though Jesus was conditioned by his setting, he resisted its evil and oppressive impact in order to be a redemptive force within it. He did not let his cultural environment or the expectations of others ultimately define him; only the will of the Father nourished in solitude was his daily sustenance. He fulfilled all righteousness by identifying with the lost in the waters of baptism. Led by the Spirit into the wilderness temptation, Jesus was tested but affirmed again and again his identity as the Son of God over against definitions of him that were fashioned by the interests of the enemy. Had he accepted Satan's offers, the definitions of his being and mission received in the process would have enslaved and destroyed him. In his secure sense of self in communion with the Father, distinct from the exploitative expectations of others, Jesus was able to pour himself out and thus mediate the Spirit of God for the redemption of others.

Jesus descended into the baptismal waters in solidarity with the lost and opened his table of fellowship to outcasts and sinners. In the power of the Spirit he set the captives free, and he went to the cross in solidarity with the God-forsaken. Specifically, he bore the curse of being a Jew as well as the judgment of the pagans who functioned as their occupying force. He rose again to provide justice for both, a justice that is fulfilled in their *reconciliation and communion*. Justification in the Spirit is realized both in the justified individual and in the justified community.

In a Christian context, we thus talk of dying to self, the alienated self in bondage to sin and death, in order to awaken to a new sense of self-in-relation-to-God through Jesus Christ. We also die to the autonomous or assimilated self in order to awaken to the reconciled self in relationship with God and — in faithfulness to God — in relationship with others. This new sense of self in Christ does not abolish our former humanity but rather transforms and fulfills it. The unique self that cries out from infancy for relationship and for freedom is fulfilled in an intimate relationship

18. Volf, *Exclusion and Embrace*, p. 91.

with God through Jesus Christ and the life of his Spirit. Paul summarizes the matter when he declares that he was crucified with Christ: "The life I live in the body, I live by faith in the Son of God, who loved me and gave himself for me" (Gal. 2:20).

It is important to note at this point the implications in the bodily resurrection of Jesus for a holistic understanding that justification involves not just the "inner self" but also the entire realm of our bodily or incarnate life, including the network of relationships in which we live and flourish as individuals.[19] The Gnostic movement in the early centuries of the church's history isolated redemption to the realm of the mind or "spirit," a realm apart from the flesh. The wider Hellenistic detachment of mind from body, as well as the modernist concentration on enlightened consciousness, has plagued Christian theology for centuries. The work of the Holy Spirit was thereby restrictively limited to the realm of spiritual enlightenment. The physical and social realms of existence were neglected in the realm of Christian soteriology, nullifying the significance of Jesus' physical sufferings and death, his bodily resurrection by the Spirit of God unto new life, and the outpouring of the Spirit through his glorified existence upon all *flesh*. Consequently, when it came to our understandings of the Spirit's work and justification, the relational self fell out of view. It was easy to see the reality of the church as a mere addendum to justification.

But the Gnostic gospel is not the gospel of the New Testament. The biblical gospel proclaims a God who enters our sin and death, including the broken and divided relationships that cry out for grace. The Spirit provides the way toward redemption and new life through the bodily resurrection of Jesus from the dead. Within this message of Jesus' resurrection, there is no possibility that the grace of God or justification by faith can be limited to an enlightened mind or to an individual self before God. Such a limitation would effect a realm of existence that is unreal and abstract, removed from life as it is actually incarnated and lived in flesh.

In a sense, Pentecost rightwises the people of God in a way that "reverses" the curse of Babel, where humanity pursued a uniform effort at asserting a corporate identity on God. We must bear in mind that the curse of Babel was not in the scattering and diversification of peoples; that was actually the will of God (Gen. 1:28). The curse was in the confusion and

---

19. See D. Lyle Dabney, "The Justification of the Spirit: Soteriological Reflections on the Resurrection," in *Starting with the Spirit*, Task of Theology Today II, ed. Stephen Pickard and Gordon Preece (Hindmarsh, Australia: Australian Theological Forum, 2001), pp. 77-79.

alienation of a people bent on vindicating their own sense of historical destiny. With regard to Acts, the issue of the scattering of the peoples throughout the world was on Luke's mind when he wrote the Pentecost narrative. Luke depicts the audience at the Pentecost event as consisting of Jews of the Diaspora who knew something about the challenges of being scattered. But Luke knew that the scattering of peoples throughout the globe was not just important to Diaspora Jews. Such a theme allowed Luke to reach back to a divine purpose that predates the Sinai covenant and has implications for all of humanity. It is significant that Luke describes Paul's address in Athens as having this issue of the global dispersion of peoples as its focus, but in a way that held broad implications for the Gentiles as well. In this address (Acts 17:24-27), Paul maintains that God created the peoples of the world so that "they should inhabit the whole earth," precisely as it was stated of the human race in texts such as Genesis 1:28 and 10:18, and was fulfilled with both negative and positive possibilities at Babel in Genesis 11. God also providentially "determined the times set for them and the exact places where they should live" so that they would seek and "perhaps find" God (Acts 17:27).

Most interesting is that Paul's address refers to the scattering of the peoples in the world in God's providence within the context of the futility involved in any effort to capture God through temples made with hands. Implied in Acts 17:24-27 is a positive reading of the Babel narrative — or at least its message. In this Lukan reading, God dispersed the peoples throughout the earth so that they could find God again, but not in a way that sanctions their own self-serving achievements, for God does not ultimately need human-made religious temples or idols (17:24). Rather, God dispersed the peoples of the world in a way that would help them recognize the living God as the gift of life, breath, and being in the midst of their migrations and unique geographical and cultural settings. Pentecost would focus on Christ as the locus of the Spirit's redemptive dwelling and on Spirit baptism as the means by which we participate in Christ's Spirit-baptized existence and become in our ever-increasing diversity a living temple to God's glory.

The outpouring of the Spirit at Pentecost only reverses the *threat* of alienation that arose from the collapse of Babel but not the *promise* of the dispersion at Babel. The peoples that dispersed at Babel faced the threat of an enduring fragmentation; but, as Acts 17 shows, God had other plans. The scattering of Babel held out a promise that humanity might rediscover a unity and a vindication that does not dissolve but rather embraces the diversity of idioms, backgrounds, and stories that God willed to providentially release in history. This is the unity witnessed penultimately in the church. The just community reconciles in mutual devotion to Christ but without dissolving differences. The justice of *koinonia* is not assimilation to a controlling group ego but a communion of diverse voices, all of which are uniquely loyal to God's justice in the world. After all, as John Zizioulas has shown, the communion of Father, Son, and Spirit is a communion that involves unity and otherness in a way that shows *both* to be absolute.[20]

The unity of Pentecost is thus not abstract but rather concrete and pluralistic. As I have noted above, the boundaries crossed are specific: namely, rich and poor, old and young, male and female (Acts 2:17ff.).[21] The "all flesh" targeted eschatologically by Spirit baptism and the justice of God aims specifically at crossing such boundaries socially and culturally. The eschatological freedom of the Spirit bursts open human biases and oppressive structures, and the unity of Pentecost aims to conquer injustice and hate with justice and compassion: it is not arrogant and self-serving but humble and obedient; it is respectful and tolerant of differences; it resists unjust privilege and seeks justice for all; it acknowledges and respects the leading of the Spirit in the unique cultural and religious journeys of different peoples; it glorifies God rather than deifies the creature; it is free and not oppressive or manipulative. In this justification in the Spirit, people will discover their true dignity as bearers of the divine image.

Murray Dempster appropriately notes that there are significant breakthroughs in graced relationships wherever people are filled with the Spirit in Acts, a reality symbolized by the speaking in tongues.[22] Developing Dempster's point further, we may note that the poor are granted access to resources, and reconciliation is accomplished between Jews and Samaritans, between Paul and the Christians he persecuted, between Jews and Gentiles, between followers of John the Baptist and followers of Jesus, and so on — through justified or pneumatic existence. The coming of the Spirit via the laying on of hands is a fitting symbol of the relational dynamic of justification in the Spirit.

Expanding the unity of the church toward that kind of diversity im-

---

20. John Zizioulas, "Communion and Otherness," *St. Vladimir's Theological Quarterly* 38, no. 4 (1994): 353-54.

21. Michael Welker, *God the Spirit*, trans. John Hoffmyer (Minneapolis: Fortress, 1994), p. 148.

22. Murray Dempster, "The Church's Moral Witness: A Study of Glossolalia in Luke's Theology of Acts," *Paraclete* 23 (1989): 1-7.

plies creative conflict, as Acts 11–15 and Galatians 1–2 reveal. It was not easy for the Jewish church to break with tradition in entering the households of Gentiles and accepting them unconditionally as bearers of the eschatological Spirit. The increased diversification of the one church involved conflict and an acceptance of otherness through a painful forsaking of cherished traditions. What will we need to forsake in our search for a diversified justice today, one that respects the otherness of the people who join with us in confessing the one faith and experiencing the one baptism? We must keep in mind that the goal of Spirit baptism is *all flesh,* or all people — and eventually all of creation. Are we, in our claim to justification, bearing witness to the final renewal and reconciliation of all things? If not, we damage our claim to be the justified church.

The Spirit is the "go-between God" and, as such, rightwises people within a realm of relationships shaped by divine love. Since humans are relational beings, Zizioulas notes that "[t]he Church is not simply an institution. She is a 'mode of existence,' *a way of being.*"[23] The life of the church is essential to our new life in Christ, because the new life involves renewed relationships in the context of communion. Our empowerment by the Spirit to bear witness to the divine self-vindication of God as Lord is not some kind of naked energy applied to life from the outside. We are empowered from within by the indwelling Spirit and by being changed and shaped into the image of Christ, able to form and cultivate graced relationships with others in the image of God as a God of self-giving love. The power for justifying witness is the power of love at work among us. There is indeed an integral connection between justification and the church as a communion or fellowship shaped and directed by love, the theme of our next section.

The *Communio Sanctorum* as the Sign and Instrument of Justice

The church does not bear witness to divine justice merely through proclamation or external deeds, but also through the quality of its common life in the Spirit (John 17:20-21; Acts 2:42-47). Yet the church is now justified in the Spirit, but not in the sense that this is fully visible or ultimately realized. In the Spirit, however, the church does offer a penultimate witness to the di-

---

23. John Zizioulas, *Being as Communion* (Crestwood, NY: St. Vladimir's Seminary Press, 1997), p. 15 (italics in original).

vine justice that was inaugurated in the world by Christ as the man of the
Spirit. We can affirm with Simon Chan that the Spirit is "incarnated" in the
church to the point that one can speak of the "ecclesial Spirit."[24] The justice
of the Spirit is thus taking shape in — or being impressed upon — the
church in a way that is analogous to its archetypal revelation in Christ. But
there is no biblical notion of the church as simply the *Christus prolongatus*
(the prolonged Christ). This is because the church is at best a weak and ambiguous manifestation of Christ's justice in the world. The church as indwelt by the Spirit is a broken sign of the righteousness or justice of the
kingdom of God. Justification in part means that Spiritual presence overcomes ambiguous life through the embrace and inner witness of the Spirit.

The justified church is thus not arrogant or dominating but rather
humble and oriented to self-giving servanthood to the least of these. It is
not confident in its own fullness but cognizant of its weakness and utter
dependence on the mercy of God. Its ministers of oversight recognize the
universal priesthood and prophethood of believers and seek to cultivate
breathing room for their diversity and service to the church and the world.
The church's witness is affirmed as approved of God only in the embrace
of the Spirit due to the mercy of God inaugurated in Christ, and its members are always submitting to the judgments of Scripture and sensitive to
the discernment of others. It participates in the justice of the future new
creation by participating in Christ. But in its manifestation before the
world, it is recognized as a real but also as a weak symbol. Therefore, "we,
who with unveiled faces all reflect the Lord's glory, are being transformed
into his likeness with ever-increasing glory, which comes from the Lord,
who is the Spirit" (2 Cor. 3:18).

We are thus to inspire the world to believe by our dynamic unity in the
Spirit, the substance of which is the righteous and dynamic *koinonia*, or
fellowship (John 17:20-21). But *our* witness to justice will not ultimately
convince the world that justice has dawned in Christ and the outpouring
of the Spirit. The Spirit bears witness as well in the context of the church's
witness. The most that we can do is invite the world through our ambiguous witness to share in the richness of our *koinonia* so that in this sharing
they, too, may encounter the living Christ in the presence of the Spirit. It is
indeed the Spirit who will convict the world of "righteousness and judgment" (John 16:8), and the Spirit will do this by granting foretastes of the

---

24. Simon Chan, "Mother Church: Towards a Pentecostal Ecclesiology," *Pneuma: The
Journal of the Society for Pentecostal Studies* 22, no. 2 (Fall 2000): 198.

future liberty for which all of creation implicitly yearns. The church as the sign of justice inspires the others to peer into the center of the church's life so that they too may see the face of Christ and be blessed.

The Spirit and kingdom of God are thus prior to the church and determine its eschatological journey as a pilgrim people. As Lorelei Fuchs notes, "The Spirit forms the church as the continuing presence of Christ in the world, transforming it into the proleptic manifestation of God's eschatological reign."[25] More specifically, Spirit baptism is the chief means of witness to divine justice in the world. The pneumatological constitution of the church through Spirit baptism points to the divine presence in instituting the church and to the divine freedom and expansiveness that cause the church to reach for and signify the eschatological and global transformation of all things into the very dwelling place of God. On the way toward this fulfillment, the church functions as the sign of grace in the midst of an all too graceless world.

I have carefully chosen the word "sign" here because it is analogous to "witness." Both terms imply that the Spirit-baptized church participates in the inauguration and fulfillment of the kingdom of God in the world and can by grace be a living witness to it, embodying it and pointing to it. Spirit baptism essentially binds the church to Jesus and the righteous kingdom he proclaimed. There can be no denial or displacement of the church as that body uniquely called to be the sign and instrument of the justice of the kingdom in the world. On the other hand, the church as sign and instrument of the kingdom of God in the world implies an eschatological reservation with regard to any kind of unqualified identification between the justice of the kingdom proclaimed by Christ and the witness of the church. The church proclaims a true word but not an exhaustive or final word.

There is no critical dialectic between Jesus and the Spirit. He is the king and the Spirit is the kingdom. But, as I have noted above, there is such a dialectic between the Spirit/kingdom and the church: thus the church is not the final word but a penultimate witness to the kingdom, which is the Spirit, and the righteous king, who is Christ. Hence, without denying the integral relationship of the kingdom and the church, we must add that

---

25. Lorelei Fuchs, "The Holy Spirit and the Development of Communio/Koinonia Ecclesiology as a Fundamental Paradigm for Ecumenical Engagement," in *The Holy Spirit, the Church and Christian Unity: Proceedings of the Consultation Held at the Monastery of Bose, Italy, 14-20 October, 2002*, ed. D. Donnelly, A. Denaux, and J. Famerée (Leuven: Leuven University Press, 2005), pp. 164-65.

there can be no unqualified identification of the church with the kingdom or Spirit of Christ. Hans Küng observes: "A church that identifies itself with the Spirit has no need to listen, to believe, to obey." The church would only have to listen to itself; according to Küng, it would view Christ as abdicating in favor of a church that has taken his place. Such a church, "for all its pose of humility, is trying to be self-reliant, for all its modesty is trying to be autonomous. A knowing church has replaced a believing church, a possessing church has replaced a needy church, total authority has replaced obedience."[26]

It is helpful here to note Miroslav Volf's rejection of a transfer of the subjectivity of Christ to the church, forming a collective subject, a "total Christ." Instead, Volf speaks of a "juxtaposition" between Christ and the church that "precisely as such is constitutive of their unity." Volf draws from the ecumenist Lukas Vischer to note that the biblical concept of unity is not an unqualified identity but rather a communion of one with the "other" that does not dissolve the difference between them. Jesus said of our unity with him that we will be in him as he is in us (John 14:20). Our oneness with Christ is through mutual indwelling and not sameness of identity.[27] This is not meant to deny that Christ forms a real solidarity with his people (e.g., he asks Paul, "Why do you persecute me?" [Acts 9:4]). But he also asks the church not to lock him out but to invite him in to the sacred meal (Rev. 3:20). Spirit-baptized justification through the divine infilling implies a solidarity of love and communion, of a mutual indwelling that requires our faithful participation. Such must never be taken for granted but cultivated and lived. Such implies an eschatological reality of a "now" and a "not yet," for now we see through a glass darkly, then "face to face" (1 Cor. 13:12). Our oneness with Christ through Spirit baptism is dynamic and not static. It implies a dialectic of grace and fallenness, which is why we must constantly be renewed in it.

The justified church seeks a love in the service of justice and a justice in the service of love. It realizes that its witness depends on the authentic embodiment of this justice before the world; but it also realizes that it lives from the Spirit's embrace and pardon in the midst of weakness and ambiguity. It cherishes and works for the rise of analogous manifestations of justice in society by first — and always — seeking conformity to the Spirit

---

26. Hans Küng, *The Church* (New York: Sheed and Ward, 1967), pp. 175, 239.

27. Miroslav Volf, *After Our Likeness: The Church as the Image of the Trinity* (Grand Rapids: Eerdmans, 1997), pp. 141-44, 158.

of Christ at the center of its existence as a living body. It sides with the victims of injustice but also seeks grace and *metanoia* for all flesh. Its very first response to the Spirit's witness to justification is trust and submission, worship and praise, for it realizes that it possesses the gift of God's very own presence. This is the justified church.

The Charismatic Structure of Justification

The justified community witnesses to a justice under the direction of divine love and *koinonia*. Grace is thus not a generic power but the life of the Spirit specifically shaping and gifting persons in the direction of unique and diverse forms of bearing witness to Christ. Romans 12:6 notes that we have "different gifts, according to the grace given us," implying that grace is tailored to enable and empower a person as a unique channel of grace to others. The graced church is not a generic whole into which people are assimilated but rather a diversely gifted communion that is empowered by a common source and directed toward a common future. Grace is individuated and diversified by a common experience of the Spirit. Paul writes: "For we were all baptized by one Spirit into one body — whether Jews or Greeks, slave or free — and we were all given the one Spirit to drink" (1 Cor. 12:13). The result is a unity in diversity: "There are different kinds of gifts, but the same Spirit. There are different kinds of service, but the same Lord. There are different kinds of working, but the same God works all of them in all men" (1 Cor. 12:4-6). All bear the Spirit, but all do so in unique ways. All have something to contribute to the common experience of, and witness to, justice because all are bearers of the Spirit. Justification has a charismatic structure.

Hans Küng popularized the notion of the "charismatic structure of the church" in his classic work *The Church,* where he makes it the overall context in which the church's gifts of oversight are to be discussed. He notes that juridical thinking is mistrustful of movements of the free Spirit of God out of fear of unbridled enthusiasm. The tendency has been to "sacramentalize or make uniform the charism, and hence the workings of the Spirit."[28] The result is a clericalism in which the notion of *charism* (gift

---

28. Küng, *The Church,* p. 184. Volf developed this concept in *After Our Likeness,* esp. p. 231. See also Veli-Matti Kärkkäinen, "Pentecostalism and the Claim for Apostolicity: An Essay in Ecumenical Ecclesiology," *Ecumenical Review of Theology* 25 (2001): 323-26.

of service) is overwhelmingly discussed in the context of ordained ministry. Neglected are the richness, variety, and exuberance of spiritual gifts as
pictured in such texts as 1 Corinthians 12–14 and exercised throughout the
lives of "ordinary" Christians.

Küng wished to reverse the historic trend toward clericalism. Rather
than subsume charism under church office, Küng thus wished to do the
opposite, namely, to subsume office beneath charism.[29] Since charisms are
universally exercised by all believers, as everyone in the church is called
and commissioned to serve as bearers of the Spirit, the charisms are not
peripheral but are rather essential and central elements of the church.
Küng does not deny the unique role played by those who exercise the
charism of oversight, but he places both gifts of oversight and other gifts
within an overarching concept of the church as a fellowship in which all
members (including ordained clergy) together submit to the verdict of the
word of God by faith. For Küng, "the church must be seen first as a fellowship of faith and only in this light can ecclesiastical office be properly understood."[30]

Justification in the Spirit promotes a mutually enriching *koinonia* and
not a hierarchical domination. The Pentecostal and charismatic churches
that are becoming so visible globally, and are arguably changing the face of
Christendom in the world, have traditionally emphasized the charismatic
structure of the church as essential to the strength of the church's unity
and witness. The practical result of elevating the church's charismatic
structure to prominence is the strong exhortation for the people of God
not to fall short of any gift while waiting for the Lord's return (1 Cor. 1:9).
Every person has a gift and thus a call to serve others with his or her gift(s).
Everyone is to be involved so that the church can "build itself up in love"
(Eph. 4:16). Tied to this admonition is a vision of the church as an interactive fellowship, filled with the Spirit in order to "speak to one another with
psalms, hymns, and spiritual songs" (Eph. 5:18-19). In the church we thus
"submit to one another out of reverence to Christ" (Eph. 5:21) as we speak
the truth in love to one another (Eph. 4:15).

Miroslav Volf has written an important reflection on the church that
emphasizes the role of every member as a unique bearer of the Spirit and
of the Word of God. Though there is a place for ministries of oversight and

---

29. Küng, *The Church*, p. 187.

30. Küng, *The Church*, p. 363. More recently, Volf has developed this idea in *After Our
Likeness*, esp. p. 231.

contexts in which the pulpit will function as central to the church, there is also a place for seeing the ministry of the Spirit and of the Word in the church as polycentric — in which all members function as Christ to one another. Volf uses the social doctrine of the Trinity as a fitting analogy for this image of the church as a *koinonia,* or communion.[31]

Applied to justification, we can say that justice in the church is mutually experienced and witnessed to in *koinonia* (Acts 2:42). The ministries of oversight are not the only ones who speak the truth in love or bind and loose as agents of justice. We speak the truth in love to one another (Eph. 4:15), and we submit to one another as to Christ (Eph. 5:21). In baptism and the gift of the Spirit we drink from the Spirit so as to form one body in which all become agents of righteousness (1 Cor. 12:13-14). We are clothed with Christ in being clothed with the Spirit (Gal. 3:27) so that we heed the words of admonition to the church that we are "neither Jew nor Greek, slave nor free, male nor female, for [we] are all one in Christ" (Gal. 3:28). The Spirit rests on all flesh so that all may become channels of God's liberating and just words of freedom, each from within his or her own unique context (Acts 2:17). The Spirit does not ignore but rather creates just relationships across boundaries of hurt and discrimination. Men and women prophesy, old and young exercise prophetic gifts, Jew and Gentile share in a joint mission, and Paul is received as a brother though he was previously feared as a murderer. Divine justice in the Spirit reconciles in the power of the cross and the resurrection, which is the very power of the Spirit and of the future new creation.

The covenant community in the Spirit thus fulfills the witness of the law to love supremely God and neighbor. Paul notes that "we, who with unveiled faces all reflect the Lord's glory, are being transformed into his likeness with ever-increasing glory, which comes from the Lord, who is the Spirit" (2 Cor. 3:18). The context of this verse is the witness of the Torah to Jesus, as well as the witness of believers who function as letters from Christ, "written not with ink but with the Spirit of the living God, not on tablets of stone but on tablets of human hearts" (2 Cor. 3:3). It may very well be that Paul intended these witnesses, both as letters written by the Spirit (3:3) and as mirrors that reflect the Lord's glory (3:18), to be understood within the church's *koinonia,* that is, to function in relationship to *each other.* The witness and glory of the Torah is thus fulfilled in the church as the just community precisely as it manifests the Spirit and the

---

31. Volf, *After Our Likeness,* esp. pp. 195-99.

Spirit's work to one another in the image of the crucified and risen Christ. Even — perhaps especially — in suffering does the glory of this covenant righteousness shine through.[32]

In the process, the charismatic structure of the church as a context for covenant righteousness is dynamic, interactive, and developing. John Koenig rightly says that the church is to be a "gift-evoking" fellowship.[33] As such a fellowship, the church encourages relationships that edify and build up, relationships that are grace-filled and directed. Through its charismatic structure, the church expands the capacity of its members to receive grace from God via proclamation and sacrament and enhances the church's ability to show forth relational signs of grace and justice in an increasingly graceless and unjust world.

The Sacramental Occasion for Justification

We turn next to the issue of the sacraments. The justification of creation is announced and prefigured in the life of the Spirit, not only in the context of the church's diverse witness to Christ in the Spirit but also in rituals that have sacramental significance. The justice of the Spirit is *koinonia,* or a sharing of life. The church participates as a body in the justice of the Spirit not only through *charisma* and word but also through rites of the Spirit. These are principally water baptism and the Lord's Supper, but one could add footwashing from the context of certain faith communities. As John Christopher Thomas has shown, there is ample indication in the New Testament and early Christianity that Christ did bequeath footwashing to the church as a rite of the Spirit.[34]

These practices are instituted ultimately by Christ and the Spirit. They are essential to the core practices of the church that we "bear" as vital elements of our legacy from Christ and from the outpoured Spirit.[35] They

32. See N. T. Wright, *The Climax of the Covenant* (Minneapolis: Fortress, 1993), pp. 184-90.

33. John Koenig, *Charismata: God's Gifts for God's People* (Philadelphia: Westminster, 1978), p. 123.

34. John Christopher Thomas, *Footwashing in John 13 and the Johannine Community* (Sheffield, UK: Journal for the Study of the New Testament Supplement, Sheffield Academic Press, 1991).

35. See Reinhard Hütter, *Suffering Divine Things: Theology as Church Practice* (Grand Rapids: Eerdmans, 1999).

fundamentally shape our identification with Christ in the context of worship and devotion to the Word of God. They recall Jesus' own journey in the Spirit toward ultimate vindication as the Son of man, "the entire historical life experience of Jesus as the Word of God and matrix of the divine presence."[36] Jesus initiated his public ministry with the gift of the Spirit at his baptism and began to close it with his footwashing and the Last Supper. These pivotal events were led by the Spirit, for, facing the very reality of the cross, Jesus said that the Spirit is indeed willing though the flesh is weak (Mark 14:38).[37] He washed his disciples' feet and in so doing recalled his servant baptism and thus prepared for his sacred meal.[38]

When believers perform these rites in the power of the Spirit, they recognize that their justification does not come from their own resources or religious devotion. They come again and again by the Spirit through these rites to the story of how God inaugurated justice in the world through Christ, the Son of the living God as the man of the Spirit. They see the disciples in this story confused and afraid and yet embraced by Christ in his resurrection and by the Spirit breathed through Christ upon them. They recall the promise of the Spirit for all flesh. They are reminded time and again that the Spirit within, who embraces *them* with God's favor and grants *them* foretastes of the realization of justice, came to them from the Father, from whom the Spirit proceeds, and through the Son, the righteous judge and king, the savior and the lamb. They are not just reminded, but they participate once more in the very power of these events, for they have the Spirit within. They then seek by such power and through these rites to embody this justice within their fellowship and to be nourished from it in their desire to bless others.

Sacraments provide the publicly recognized means by which divine justice is received and embraced in the presence of the Spirit among the faithful. They provide the principal means by which the justice of the future new creation is performed and grasped in the Spirit. By the Spirit,

36. Bernard J. Cooke, *The Distancing of God: The Ambiguity of Symbol in History and Theology* (Minneapolis: Fortress, 1990), p. 366.

37. I agree with Dabney here that the "Spirit" in this text is the Holy Spirit, the same Spirit that rested on Jesus in his solidarity with the lost at his baptism and who led him into the wilderness to be tried by the devil. The willing Spirit leads Jesus to the cross as well. See Dabney, "Naming the Spirit: Towards a Pneumatology of the Cross," in Pickard and Preece, *Starting with the Spirit*, p. 52.

38. See Frank D. Macchia, "Is Footwashing the Neglected Sacrament? A Response to John Christopher Thomas," *Pneuma: The Journal of the Society for Pentecostal Studies* 19, no. 2 (Fall 1997): 239-49.

they also serve to proclaim the Word of God in order to inspire faith and participation in the justice of Christ. Therefore, Calvin calls the sacraments an aid to faith: "Akin to the preaching of the gospel, we have another help to our faith in the sacraments."[39] The sacrament depends on the reception of the Word by faith for its efficacy. On the other hand, the proclamation of the Word can be seen as akin to the sacramental encounter with the crucified and risen Lord in the power of the Spirit. The Word can be viewed as itself having a "sacramental" function in revealing Christ.

Reformed theologian G. C. Berkouwer finds the proclamation of the Word in preaching to be clearer than what comes through the sacraments.[40] But Calvin would not have agreed: "The sacraments bring with them the clearest promises, and, when compared with the word, have this peculiarity that they represent promises to the life, as if painted in a picture." The Word can be seen as confirming the sacrament rather than simply the other way around. The sacraments are efficacious as the means of embracing justification in the Spirit because they offer the promises of the gospel to the believer who receives them in faith, for, as Calvin notes further, the Spirit performs what is promised. The Spirit's performance involves our performance, which is the meaning of the sacrament. The sacraments thus "do not avail one iota without the energy of the Holy Spirit."[41]

Pentecostals have been ambivalent about ritual as a vehicle of the Spirit's work, even though, as Daniel Albrecht has shown us, their worship is more ritualized than they often recognize.[42] The broader context for the suspicion of ritual is the Enlightenment bias that "rituals are pagan, idolatrous, and popish," says Tom Driver.[43] But there is a deep human longing for ritual that is often frustrated in our culture. This longing is rooted in the fact that ritual is a kind of performance that suggests "alternative worlds" and nourishes "imaginative visions" of God's goals for the world. They are different from the routines of ordinary life even though they are drawn from them. The ritual sacraments thus point to the grace implied in all of life and also to God's desire to renew the creation into the very dwell-

---

39. Calvin, *Institutes of the Christian Religion*, vol. 2, trans. Henry Beveridge (Grand Rapids: Eerdmans, 1979), 4.14.1

40. G. C. Berkouwer, *The Sacraments* (Grand Rapids: Eerdmans, 1969), pp. 45-55.

41. Calvin, *Institutes*, vol. 2, 4.14.5, 7, 9.

42. Daniel Albrecht, *Rites of the Spirit: A Ritual Approach to Pentecostal/Charismatic Spirituality* (Sheffield, UK: Sheffield Academic Press, 1999).

43. Tom F. Driver, *The Magic of Ritual: Our Need for Liberating Rites that Transform Our Lives and Our Communities* (San Francisco: HarperSanFrancisco, 1991), p. 9.

ing place of God. Driver is eloquent when he says that "they move in a kind of liminal space, at the edge of, or in the cracks between, the mapped regions of what we like to call 'the real world.'"[44]

Geoffrey Wainwright also suggests that ritual is the "solemn way by which a community formulates its common mind on the meaning of life and world," except that for Christians this expression is meant to transform the present situation toward the fulfillment of that meaning, which is eschatological. This is because, for Christians, "meaning is in the making: life is oriented toward God's ultimate purpose, and history-making is the way to the attainment of that meaning for both individuals and humanity as a whole."[45] Through the sacraments we "celebrate something that is humanly absurd, something literally unbelievable and beyond all worldly expectation," namely, the new heaven and new earth.[46] Sinners are embraced and indwelt by the Spirit so as to bring witness to the justice of God! As the 1979 "Elucidation" of the Anglican-Catholic dialogue on the Eucharist affirmed, the Lord's Supper is the "food of the new creation," a "sacramental presence in which God uses realities of this world to convey the realities of the new creation."[47] These realities speak of God's justifying sinful flesh through Christ and the Spirit of life.

Justification is tied to the sacraments in the sense that the sacraments both occasion the divine embrace and celebrate and deepen one's reception and participation in the divine presence. Rising with Christ in baptism, the believer washes the feet of the other in preparation for the meal of remembrance. This meal is not only a deepening of one's awareness of the Spirit hidden in God's self-sacrifice in the cross in the midst of forsakenness and death, but also a celebration of the life of the resurrection and the outpouring of the Spirit. The meal is repeated as a feast that celebrates the excess of the Spirit in anticipation of the eschatological banquet. As Jesus showed when he turned the water into wine, God really does invite us to an ongoing banquet in which God saves the best for last.

Sacraments are occasions for participating in the justice of divine *koinonia* with God and one another in the Spirit. The problem with sacra-

44. Driver, *Magic of Ritual*, pp. 80-81.

45. Geoffrey Wainwright, *Doxology: The Praise of God in Worship, Doctrine, and Life* (New York: Oxford University Press, 1980), p. 121.

46. Driver, *Magic of Ritual*, p. 202.

47. "Elucidation" (1979), §6b, of the Anglican-Roman Catholic Dialogue, in *Growth in Agreement: Reports and Agreed Statements of Ecumenical Conversations on a World Level*, ed. Harding Meyer and Lukas Vischer (New York: Paulist Press, 1984), p. 75.

mental theology historically has been the ritual distancing of God from the worshiping community and the effort to overcome the distance through a theology of symbolization. Symbols can both block or occasion an encounter with God's presence, depending on how they are viewed and practiced.[48] The sacraments are meant to be occasions for celebrating and deepening participation in Christ in the presence of the Spirit. The Pauline expression provides powerful poetic support of this fact: "For we were all baptized by one Spirit into one body — whether Jews or Greeks, slave or free — and we were all given the one Spirit to drink" (1 Cor. 12:13). A better translation would be: For we were all baptized *in* one Spirit *for the purpose of* forming one body — whether Jews or Greeks, slave or free — and we were all given the one Spirit to drink. As Robertson and Plummer have observed, "The Spirit is the element in *(en)* which the baptism takes place and the one body is the end to *(eis)* which it is directed."[49]

Sacramental sign is best understood as facilitating a kind of "mediated immediacy" that occasions the experience of the Spirit. Inspired by this pneumatological view of sacramental sign, Driver has studied the wide range of rituals globally and regrets that a wide gulf so often separates Christian liturgists or sacramental theologians from the advocates of Spirit possession. In Christian understandings of the sacraments, he regrets the relative loss of an emphasis on becoming "filled with the immediate presence of the deity" — as essential to the sacramental act. He finds in the Pentecostal emphasis on a fresh Spirit infilling in worship an example of a new definition of sacramental experience. Driver complains that the "experience of possession has been more or less banished, its place taken by an emphasis on symbolism."[50]

Though symbolism or signification is inevitable given the fact that we are physical and linguistic beings, we need to understand that it facilitates the realization of what is symbolized, as a hug brings to realization the love symbolized. A pneumatological theology of justification is most fruitfully developed in the context of viewing baptism, footwashing, and the Lord's

---

48. See Cooke, *Distancing of God,* for an excellent and thorough discussion of this problem.

49. A. T. Robertson and Alfred Plummer, *A Critical and Exegetical Commentary on the First Epistle of St. Paul to the Corinthians,* 2nd ed., The International Critical Commentary, ed. Samuel Rolles Driver, Alfred Plummer, and Charles Augustus Briggs (Edinburgh: T. & T. Clark, 1963), p. 272. For this reference, I am grateful to Howard M. Ervin, *These Are Not Drunken as Ye Suppose* (Plainfield, NJ: Logos, 1968), p. 45.

50. Driver, *Magic of Ritual,* pp. 208, 198.

Supper as occasions in which the divine embrace through Christ and the indwelling of the Spirit is celebrated and deepened. We must view signification in the sacraments as the means by which the reality being signified is realized in the fellowship of the faithful.

Let me address the issue of water baptism more specifically. Water baptism is closely related to the gift of the Spirit, as is shown in Jesus' own baptism (Matt. 3:16-17). A special relationship thus exists between water and Spirit baptism. The water rite of John the Baptist formed the original context for the use of the Spirit baptism metaphor, even if the contrast between them was an aspect of the metaphor's use. Spirit baptism as the eschatological gift of the Spirit transcends the water rite from which the metaphor was birthed by John. The difference between John the Baptist's rite and what endured in Christian contexts is that John's baptism looked forward to Spirit baptism while Christian baptism lives from it and points to its fulfillment. Regeneration through faith in the gospel and the ritual performance of this conversion in baptism depend on the gift of the Spirit for their significance and power as a life-transforming experience.

In the larger context of Spirit baptism, water baptism also has a special relationship to justification. In the early centuries of the church, water baptism was *the* sacrament of justification: "The decisive ritual sign of justification is baptism."[51] Many, including myself, consider the later shift to the sacrament of penance as the context for reflection on justification to have been a problematic detour, entangling the doctrine within a phenomenology of conversion rather than focusing on incorporation into Christ by the Spirit. The neglect of baptism as a context for discussing justification also led in Protestant contexts to the overly forensic doctrine of justification through imputed righteousness — with no proper emphasis on participation in Christ by the Spirit.[52] Recent ecumenical discussion of justification has attempted to bring the doctrine back into a special relationship to baptism. Article 25 of the Joint Declaration on the Doctrine of Justification notes: "We confess together that sinners are justified by faith in the saving action of God in Christ. By the action of the Holy Spirit in baptism, they are granted the gift of salvation, which lays the basis for the whole Christian life."

Because Christ came into solidarity with us as the man of the Spirit in

---

51. Wainwright, *Doxology*, p. 138.

52. So concludes Wolfhart Pannenberg, *Systematic Theology*, trans. Geoffrey Bromiley (Grand Rapids: Eerdmans, 1997), 3:229-30.

the baptismal waters, a solidarity that took him all the way to the cross, we can by the embrace of the same Spirit come into solidarity with Christ in our baptism. Our descent into the water is like descending into a tomb. But unlike Christ's descent into forsakenness, we descend "with him" (Rom. 6:4), meaning in solidarity with him. As such, all that dies in the tank is what is self-bound by flesh or what contradicts his love. In descending, we are already being drawn into the embrace of the Spirit. Dying with Christ leads to our sharing in his rising again. The watery *tomb* then becomes a *womb* from which we rise in newness of life centered on Christ and led of the Spirit. Saint Basil thus wrote of the outpouring of the Spirit occasioned in part by baptism as the possession of the renewal of life: "The water receives our body as a tomb, and so becomes the image of death, while the Spirit pours in the life-giving power, renewing in souls which were dead in sins the life they first possessed."[53] I would not want to make Spirit indwelling absolutely dependent on the rite of water baptism, though I would regard baptism as a ritual means by which faith grasps the new life of the Spirit. In grasping the Spirit, one grasps the gift of God's favor and the privilege of bearing witness to it before the world.

Baptism is the gospel of the divine embrace in action and the participation of the believer in that embrace. Baptism thus occasions justification by grace through faith. In light of the role of baptism in occasioning justification *by faith*, infant baptism has been charged with emphasizing the divine embrace but neglecting the needed accent on human participation by faith. Wainwright notes four ways that supporters of infant baptism have attempted to preserve the needed emphasis on the participation of faith. Faith has been equated with the absence of obstacles put in the way of grace. Implying that this is not adequate faith, some have even assumed some kind of active faith by the infant. That infants can have active "faith" in any meaningful sense, however, is difficult to establish. The faith of others (for example, of family and church) has thus also been proposed as provisionally carrying the justified infant, which is meaningful given the corporate nature of justification. But justification is also personal. Most promising is the idea that the infant is baptized with a view toward the child's future affirmation of faith. The young child's participation in the community of the justified would be "provisional" and based on the hope

53. Quoted in Geoffrey Wainwright, "Veni, Sancti Spiritus: The Invocation of the Holy Spirit in the Liturgies of the Churches," in Donnelly et al., *The Holy Spirit, the Church and Christian Unity*, p. 305.

of future personal involvement.[54] Though believer's baptism is in my judgment the mode most faithful to the biblical text, viewing infant baptism as done in hope of future faith as exercised by the child can approximate the full meaning of justification by faith.

We are baptized into one body and drink the Spirit together. The purpose of our incorporation into the Spirit and through the Spirit into the triune life is so that one body is formed in fellowship (1 Cor. 12:13). Clothed with Christ, we overcome divisions caused by gender, class, or race (Gal. 3:28). *Koinonia* occurs within a dynamic process of transformation in which we reconcile, seek justice, and show forth the glory of the Lord in the Spirit to one another (2 Cor. 3:18). Justification in the Spirit is occasioned in baptism and participation in Christ.

Not only baptism but the Lord's Supper also implies an understanding of justification as received in the context of the divine embrace and participation in Christ through faith and by the Spirit. The Eucharist shows even more clearly the fact that this participation is also a *communion* with the risen Christ. Prior to the Last Supper, Jesus washed the disciples' feet, telling Peter that participation in the ceremony would bring cleansing (John 13:10), and that rejecting it would cause Peter to have no part in Christ (John 13:8). Having part in Christ is elaborated on in John's Gospel as the essence of the church's communion with Christ in which we abide in him as a branch in a vine (15:5). This communion is a mutual indwelling in which we are in Christ and Christ is in us as Christ is in the Father and the Father is in Christ (17:21).

The Lord's Supper occasions our experience of pardon and participation in Christ. We sup with him as he sups with us in a mutual communion of love (Rev. 3:20). The pardon is received from him in the embrace of the Spirit and is shared in *koinonia* with one another. The meal is indeed the meal of reconciliation. In the context of the words of institution (1 Cor. 11:23-25), we recall as a living reality Christ's self-giving in the offering of his body and blood because the indwelling Spirit causes us to dwell in Christ and he in us. The self-giving of Christ on the cross is recalled in power from the experience of God in us and we in God, the ultimate meaning and end of self-giving, of the cross itself. In the light of the way in which the cross mediates the Spirit through Christ's resurrection and Spirit impartation, the words of institution during the Eucharist lead quite naturally into the invocation of the Spirit. Both the words of institution

54. Wainwright, *Doxology,* pp. 139-41.

and the invocation of the Spirit in the church's practice of the Lord's Supper ground justification in the act of the risen Christ in imparting the Spirit from the Father. Justification is "in the name of the Lord Jesus Christ and by the Spirit of our God" (1 Cor. 6:11).

Justification is thus in the Spirit and involves *koinonia,* not only between us and God but also between us and one another. It is important in the context of justification through *koinonia* to note that the sacred meal is the *Lord's* Supper. It is rooted in Christ's open table that included the outcasts and sinners, those whom the "righteous" did not want to accept. Consequently, Jesus' table implied a subversive doctrine of justification with regard to the understanding of righteousness among those who rejected the outcasts as "unclean." Jesus' table implied a notion of righteousness governed rather by mercy and grace, the very gift of God's presence that gives rise to a festive celebration of life. In the parable of the lost son (Luke 15), Jesus appeals to the resistant Pharisees and scribes in the figure of the elder son, who resents the father's shamefully excessive expression of compassion toward his outcast younger brother when he celebrates the latter's return with a banquet fit for a royal guest. In appealing to these Jewish leaders, Jesus reminds them that the heavenly Father's love does not contradict justice but rather fulfills it. Within this justice, the Father's household belongs to them as well, and they will not understand or draw close to the heart of the Father unless they can embrace the outcast sibling at the banquet table. Here grace is inseparably connected to reconciliation and community.

More directly connected to the Eucharist is the Lord's Supper. Unlike Jesus' public meals, the Lord's Supper is reserved for Jesus' followers. But on the horizon of both meals is Jesus' gracious and total self-giving that is implied by the broken body and the spilled blood. As noted earlier, Jesus celebrates the Last Supper as the Passover meal, but on the day before the official celebration, according to John 13:1-2. Jesus' supper, though connected to the Passover, was nevertheless a distinct act that signaled a shifting of Israel's journey with God from the Temple and the religious life of Israel to Jesus.[55] Jesus' entire ministry and table fellowship favored the outcasts and sinners at the margins of Israel's life. Now at the margins again, Jesus shares a meal with his followers in order to prepare them for his chief act of redeeming the outcast and the forsaken. He forms a covenant with them by grace, knowing full well that they will grow weak, even deny him.

---

55. Wainwright, *Doxology,* pp. 557-58.

At the resurrection, he will visit them with God's righteous favor in order to renew and enrich their covenant relationship with him, especially through the excessively gracious gift of the Spirit.

The implication is that the Lord's Supper is to strengthen the church's covenant relationship with Christ in the Spirit so that the church can in his image invite the world to the larger table of God's festive banquet of grace. The private meal is covenant enrichment, and the public one is covenant invitation. Every time the followers of Jesus partake of the meal, they are to realize once more the gift of God's favor, for those baptized in the Spirit also drink of the Spirit (1 Cor. 12:13). They commit themselves once more to the way of the cross and rejoice that Christ remained faithful and true despite their weakness and disloyalty. They know that Christ will seek them out to sup with them again, even if they grow weak (Rev. 3:20).

The church will welcome all who have received Christ through faith and baptism, knowing that those whom the Lord invites to *his* Supper cannot be refused by the church. It is not ultimately the church's supper, for the saints are not the source of this meal. Their body and blood did not account for the table that the Lord wishes to share with us. He is the sacrificial lamb, and he is the one with whom we commune in breaking this bread and drinking this cup. It is his Spirit who calls us to dine and who gives rise to the richness of communion at the table. It is his Spirit who guarantees a future supper in the kingdom of God (Luke 22:18) and who proclaims the Lord's death in the meal until Christ returns (1 Cor. 11:26). It is his Spirit who guides us in our remembrance of Christ, in our self-examination, and in our discernment of the Lord's body during the meal (1 Cor. 11:24-32). Those the Lord has invited cannot be turned away if they come to repent and believe on the Lord of the meal, for the meal is the supper of divine favor or of justification by the Spirit through faith. At the messianic banquet in the new creation we will enjoy the Lord's favor as royal guests at the Lord's table. Our communion will be "face to face," and we will enjoy the fullness of his Spirit within.

Conclusion

Justification in Christ and by the Spirit means justification through communion, which is the fulfillment of covenant faithfulness and of life in the Spirit. As Christ rose from the dead into the fullness of life in the Spirit, so his body, the church, rises with the same fullness. We rise in him because we rise by his Spirit, the Spirit that binds us to him and to one another in him. We thus rise not only as individual humans but as persons in communion, both with God and with one another. We are also made as bearers of the Spirit to correspond in our own lives with the love of the Father, the Son, and the Holy Spirit, who love in self-giving and communion, or mutual indwelling. This is the supreme experience of justice, namely, new creation defined by a justice fulfilled in love.

Humanity is thus rectified in reconciliation and communion with the "other." There can be no justice without the other or without such interpersonal and communal renewal, for we were made to bear the Spirit as persons in relationship. As the charismatic community, we speak and embody the truth of Christ in the love of God with the aid of our unique gifts, enhancing the justice of our life together. Through baptism and communion, we participate in Christ by the Spirit of life through faith. We realize together the basis of our justice in the Christ event and live from its power in the here and now. We seek through our life together to bear witness to the justice of the Spirit and of Christ before the world. We also seek to inspire an analogous witness to the justice of God's kingdom in the world. The goal is the final new creation where righteousness dwells as well as the communion of saints at the messianic banquet where the favor and covenant faithfulness of God find fulfillment. Together as dwelling places of God, we will commune face to face with Christ and receive the vindication of our hope. This hope cannot fail because it is placed in the Father of the heavenly lights, "who does not change like shifting shadows" (James 1:17), and in the faithful Son, and in the Spirit's enduring witness. It is to the Trinitarian structure that we finally turn.

10 The Embrace of the Spirit

Toward a Trinitarian Theology of Justification

In this final major chapter I need to highlight the role of pneumatology in leading us toward a Trinitarian integration of justification. Trinitarian theology is a vast topic, so all I can do here is sketch how a Trinitarian theology of justification can benefit from a concentration on the Spirit, especially in the context of the root metaphor of Spirit baptism. I will begin with the need to move beyond a mere knitting together of Protestant and Catholic understandings of justification. My goal will be to show that the Spirit brings about justification not only through participation in Christ by the divine embrace but also through Christ in the mutual love and *koinonia* of Father, Son, and Spirit. I will use the mutual indwelling of Trinitarian *koinonia* as a context for understanding the overlapping and integrated nature of justification and sanctification and, more broadly, the theological categories of creation, redemption, and the giving of life. Something more, then, is needed than a mere patching together of imputed and imparted righteousness.

Beyond Patchwork Solutions

We need to eliminate from discussions about justification the conflict between the Protestant declared righteousness and the Catholic righteousness through the fruit of justice in us. We should not play the two off against each other, but neither should we merely knit them together without deeper integration. Nothing short of a full-blown Trinitarian integration will be sufficient, and the place to start is with the most neglected participant, namely, the Holy Spirit. The outpouring and indwelling of the Spirit bring declared righteousness to the consciousness and experience of obedient communities of disciples, and they plant the seeds that bear the fruit of justice in us. In the Spirit we are reborn and embraced, made to participate in Christ and his favor with the Father, as well as the witness that corresponds analogously to his own, a witness that will culminate in our conformity to Christ's image in the new creation. The Son's favor with the Father is actually a love and communion shared through mutual self-giving and *koinonia*. In the Spirit we participate in the righteousness yet to come in the new creation and in ultimate communion because of our participation in the crucified and risen Christ. Without the Spirit, the Protestant and the Catholic emphases fly apart or, at best, are awkwardly knitted together. They lose their grounding and link because they lack adequate substance in the indwelling Spirit. This substance is not only declarative or ethical but is more interactive and truly relational, involving indwelling and communion.

As I have explained in earlier chapters, the extreme expressions of both traditions have tended to detach justifying grace from the indwelling Spirit. Only by placing the Spirit at the very substance of justification is it possible to arrive at a Trinitarian integration of imputed and imparted righteousness. Justification as a Trinitarian act must be accessed by the Spirit and in relationship to the Son. It is thus possible to bring a Trinitarian framework to justification by restoring the baptism in the Spirit to its role as the root metaphor of salvation. Spirit baptism makes the outpouring and indwelling of the Spirit essential to the heavenly Father's rightwising of creation and vindication as Creator and Lord. It also makes the Spirit essential to Christ's identity and mission, including Christ's work of atonement. It finally makes the gift of the Spirit essential to justification, as well as all other soteriological categories (1 Cor. 6:11).

In the light of this integrative soteriology, Christ's act of fulfilling all righteousness for the sinful creation did not climax on the cross or at the resurrection, but in his pouring out the Spirit as the Spirit baptizer. Indeed, Jesus' death was meant to draw all people to himself (John 12:32), and his resurrection — "as a life-giving Spirit" (1 Cor. 15:45) — was meant to make him the "firstborn among many brothers" (Rom. 8:29). The atonement is not fulfilled without the gift of the Spirit. And the gift of the Spirit is not meant to be detached from the atonement or from justification in order to serve as a mere collateral addendum, or an added bonus, within a larger doctrine of salvation. The Spirit is essential from the first to the last in all of the categories of salvation that we may wish to discuss, from justification to glorification. The so-called objective and subjective dimensions of justification can fruitfully be linked in the baptism in the Holy Spirit.

Merely saying, as some Protestants do, that God's declared judgment performs what it speaks is not enough. The Word of justification in Christ glides on the winds of the Spirit and only performs in the Spirit's embrace. This is true in part because the Father who justifies imparts the Spirit, and the Son who justifies is the Spirit baptizer. Declarative judgments from God do carry out what they proclaim. When God said, "Let there be light," there was light! When creatures receive by faith God's declaration of justice announced in the gospel, that declaration changes the person involved. But the Spirit not only brings this declaration to the heart of the believer as a life-changing presence; the Spirit is also essential to the very act of justice through Christ of which the declaration speaks. In other words, the gospel not only announces that Jesus died and rose again for our sins, but also that the promise of life has been poured out upon flesh through this Jesus, who was crucified. Therefore, Jesus announced, "I have come that they may have life, and have it to the full" (John 10:10). The gospel cannot be dissected into christological and pneumatological "branches." The Spirit is not just the instrument of faith or a collateral gift alongside the right-wising of creation. The Spirit is at the very substance of justification and all soteriological categories (1 Cor. 6:11).

The Spirit's embrace also deepens the historic Catholic emphasis on justification through the infusion of virtues in us. The rise of moral virtues in us shows us that justification imparts a virtuous life and involves life-transforming effects in anticipation of the new creation in which righteousness will dwell. But this concentration on moral formation can also serve to eclipse the basis for justification in the indwelling Spirit and in Christ as the man of the Spirit. A theological concentration can end up being displaced by its properly subordinate anthropological correlate. Justification is primarily through the embrace of the indwelling Spirit and not through charity as a supernatural enabling distinct from the Spirit of life. Of course, the creature comes to cooperate with the Spirit as the creature participates in the Spirit and in Christ. But the gift of the indwelling Spirit is both the beginning and the end of this cooperation. Moreover, Christ's redemptive work does not just impart virtues or fund one's moral conversion. Rather, justification is the Spirit's embrace of the creature and the creature's *liberating participation* by the indwelling Spirit in Christ as crucified and risen and in the *koinonia* that will pervade the new creation and the final communion of saints. New birth, resurrection, and glorification go way beyond and burst asunder any vision of moral formation.

As we have seen, recent ecumenical discussion on both sides of the justification debate has reached at least implicitly for the Spirit as the link between extrinsic and imparted righteousness, a link that shows how justification can be based alone on the former but also involve the latter. This implicitly pneumatological and Trinitarian approach to justification can deepen past efforts to bring the Catholic and Protestant worlds closer together as two different but inseparably related affirmations of the fundamental insight into salvation by the grace of God. George Lindbeck, in his classic *The Nature of Doctrine,* proposes that the two sides of the debate represent a difference between ecclesiastical cultures within the larger church. Doctrine is viewed as functioning to regulate church life and witness rather than as immutable, timeless principles. In this light, it is possible to appreciate both Catholic and Protestant understandings of justification, given the very different situations within both churches that seemed to require the guidance provided by both doctrines. It is then possible to see the two positions as variations within a larger affirmation of salvation as fundamentally via the grace of God alone.

Similarly, the Joint Declaration on the Doctrine of Justification, which was signed in 1999 by the Vatican and the Lutheran World Federation, concluded that the differences between Catholic and Protestant understandings are not worth dividing the church over, but are instead a family difference. Without discussing the thorny issue of how the two views of justification might find deeper integration, both sides affirmed that justification is based on Christ alone and leads to renewal in the Spirit. There is no question but that the impasse between Catholic and Protestant views of justification has seemed like a collision of two very different worlds theologically. That these worlds represent a family difference is an important and helpful assumption, but it does not in itself help us link them theologically.

A Trinitarian framework for justification would seem to represent the way forward, since recent ecumenical efforts are attempting to steer clear of playing a Protestant christological view of justification off against a Catholic concern with inner renewal. The Joint Declaration does in fact suggest a Trinitarian linkage. Note section 15: "In faith we together hold the conviction that justification is the work of the triune God. . . . Justification thus means that Christ himself is our righteousness, in which we share through the Holy Spirit in accord with the will of the Father." However, the Trinitarian proposal in the Joint Declaration is not further explained, nor does it play a programmatic role in the remainder of the document.[1] But this section does imply that a Trinitarian framework involves a participatory doctrine of justifying faith. We share in Christ through the Holy Spirit.

As helpful as this seminal reference to the Trinitarian framework of justification is, the statement still merely assumes a linear view of the involvement of the Trinity in justification, in which Christ's accomplishment of righteousness is accessed subjectively by the Spirit. The Spirit here is limited to an instrumental role in giving rise to faith as participation in Christ; but it does not, from the start, substantially define the justice inaugurated in Christ or the full extent to which Christ fulfills justice as the Spirit baptizer. More recent Trinitarian theology has moved significantly beyond the limitations of this linear approach to the involvement of the Trinity in salvation — in the direction of a more *interactive* (perichoretic and *koinoniac)* model.[2] Within this model, the Spirit's role in the giving and sharing of life would be involved in both Christ's accomplishment of righteousness and our participation in it, with no possibility of confining the Spirit to the subjective appropriation of an atonement that can be described quite well without the Spirit's help.

At this point, Robert Jenson helps us describe more fully the challenge that we face in defining a Trinitarian theology of justification. At first glance, it seems that he shares the linear approach of the Joint Declaration and other ecumenical breakthroughs, such as the Finnish interpretation of Luther. The accent here is on the Spirit as the agent by which one participates in Christ by faith. This participatory soteriology represents a valuable corrective to the older Catholic emphasis on cooperative grace. Participation points to a properly theocentric emphasis and opens the door to a Trinitarian theology of justification. A participatory understanding of grace in the presence of the Spirit also helps us bring deeper integration to the Regensburg Agreement, which, under the influence of Martin Bucer, advocated a twofold doctrine of justification as outwardly based on Christ

---

1. See my essay "Justification and the Spirit of Life: A Pentecostal Response to the Joint Declaration," in *Justification and the Future of the Ecumenical Movement,* ed. William C. Rusch (Collegeville, MN: Liturgical Press, 2003), pp. 133-58.

2. See, e.g., Anne Hunt, *The Trinity and the Paschal Mystery: A Development in Recent Catholic Theology,* New Theology Series 5 (Collegeville, MN: Liturgical Press, 1997).

alone but inwardly involving renewal toward justice. Participation by the Spirit in Christ helps us begin to understand how the two sides are linked.

It is interesting that Jenson, remaining true to his linear understanding of the Trinitarian framework for justification, connects the emphases of Paul, the Protestant Reformation, and Catholicism to the three persons of Father, Son, and Spirit. He locates the emphasis on the Father in Paul, the emphasis on Christ in Protestantism, and the focus on the Spirit in Catholicism (it is noteworthy that he limits his remarks here to the Augustinian heritage). First, Jenson maintains that Paul's emphasis in justification is on God's self-vindication as the God of justice. God the Father is the God who is just in justifying the sinner (Rom. 3:26). The Protestant emphasis is then on Christ as the righteousness of God: justification comes through the fulfillment of righteousness in Christ for us, especially in his atoning death on the cross. Here the accent is on justification as *extra nos* (apart from us), that is, distinct from our morality or the quality of our moral development. Finally, Jenson notes that the Catholic (Augustinian) emphasis, when talking about justification, is on the Spirit as the subjective source of righteousness produced *in nobis* (in us). In justification, we are made righteous or just by being morally transformed in ways that bring forth the fruit of justice or charity in our lives.[3]

Jenson's proposal is helpful as a point of departure for a deeper discussion of the challenges we face in developing a Trinitarian theology of justification. There is no question but that recent biblical scholarship on justification has tended to favor the view that justification in Paul is primarily concerned with the triumph and vindication of God's righteousness in the world.[4] God's own self-vindication as the God of justice is increasingly seen as vital to the biblical understanding of justification. Furthermore, who can question that the *solus Christus* (Christ alone) emphasis is indicative of the historic Protestant doctrine of justification? As Luther wrote, "There is nothing under the sun that counts for righteousness except Christ alone."[5]

---

3. Robert Jenson, "Justification as a Triune Event," *Modern Theology* 11, no. 4 (1995): 421-27. See also his more elaborate discussion in *Systematic Theology*, vol. 2: *The Works of God* (Oxford: Oxford University Press, 1999), pp. 292-303.

4. See, e.g., Ernst Käsemann, "'The Righteousness of God' in Paul," in *New Testament Questions of Today*, trans. W. J. Montague (Minneapolis: Fortress, 1969), pp. 168-82; see also Manfred T. Brauch, "Perspectives on God's Righteousness in Recent German Discussion," in *Paul and Palestinian Judaism*, ed. E. P. Sanders (Minneapolis: Fortress, 1977), pp. 523-42.

5. Luther, "Lectures on Galatians 1535," *Luther's Works*, ed. Jaroslav Pelikan (St. Louis: Concordia, 1963), 27:138.

Though, as I have noted earlier, Luther does in places involve the Spirit in justification, his overwhelming emphasis is on Christ as the one who fulfills all righteousness, so that it is only by faith in Christ that we are justified or made right with God. And the Catholic emphasis on justification that comes out of Augustine has tended to focus on the life-transforming power of grace that comes from the Spirit. Augustine says about justification that "it is not by that law that the ungodly are made righteous, but by grace; and this change is effected by the life-giving Spirit, without whom the letter kills."[6] Justification here is wrought in large measure by the function of grace transforming or perfecting nature. Jenson brings Paul together with historic Catholic and Protestant emphases on justification by appropriating these aspects of justification to the persons of the Trinity. In this effort, he does not criticize or question those emphases; rather, he assigns them a place within the unique actions appropriate to the Father, the Son, and the Spirit.

As helpful as Jenson's discussion is, one still looks for more. We can ask how Jenson moves beyond merely knitting together these dimensions of justification without integration. A "patchwork" construction can end up sidestepping those problems theologically that have prevented the formation of a more integrated Trinitarian theology of justification. As we have seen, Luther called the Regensburg Agreement a patchwork solution for much the same reason.[7] Also, Jenson's linear move from God's self-vindication (the Father) to the accomplishment of righteousness in history (Christ), and, finally, to the perfection of justification eschatologically (the Spirit) has significant but limited value. Unanswered within this framework is the substance of justifying righteousness, particularly with respect to Trinitarian *perichoresis* and *koinonia*.

One could legitimately answer that Christ provides this substance, but a close examination of the story of Jesus will also take note that it is willed

---

6. Augustine, *De Spiritu et Littera*, 34, in *St. Augustine's Anti-Pelagian Works*, trans. Peter Holmes and Robert Ernest Wallace, NPNF, 1st ser., vol. 5, ed. Philip Schaff (reprint; Peabody, MA: Hendrickson, 1994).

7. Brian Lugioyo argues that the Regensburg Agreement finds integration within the singular formal cause in the *will of God*. See Lugioyo, "Martin Bucer's Doctrine of Justification and the Colloquy of Regensburg, 1541" (PhD diss., University of Aberdeen, 2007 [forthcoming from Oxford University Press]), pp. 38-39, 89. This is a helpful insight. Yet, is this enough to adequately integrate the "objective" christological view of justification with the "subjective" (implicitly pneumatological) view? Arguably, we cannot entirely overcome the charge of a patchwork solution if we cannot show how the persons of the triune God work *cooperatively* in both the objective and the subjective dimensions of justification.

by the Father and led of the Spirit and that Trinitarian self-giving in the context of communion occupies its core. Jesus' baptism powerfully symbolizes this fact. The Father pours out the Spirit on the Son while declaring his love for the Son, precisely at the moment that the Son has gone into the waters in search of the lost (Luke 3:16). Notice also the offering of the obedient Son to the Father as empowered by the Spirit (Heb. 9:14) precisely at the moment of his descent into the realm of the God-forsaken. Justification occurs in the opening of the divine circle of self-giving love to alienated flesh. Those who are afar off are brought into the triune communion through the embrace of the Spirit, which is also the embrace of the Father and the Son. Jesus prayed to the Father: "Just as you are in me and I am in you, may they also be one in us . . ." (John 17:21). Since, as the "third Person," the Spirit is the one for and in the many, Christ's own identity as the firstborn among many (Rom. 8:29) is unfulfilled without the Spirit. Both Christ and the Spirit are at the substance of the justification of the sinner.

Jenson does in fact indicate that he wishes to suggest something more than a patchwork solution. He notes elsewhere that the fulfillment of justifying righteousness as a Trinitarian act involves "a mode of the divine persons' mutual life" and that every work of God is "begun by the Father, accomplished in the Son, and perfected in the Spirit and has its unity in their *perichoresis*."[8] This statement implies a move beyond a mere patching together of classic Protestant and Catholic emphases toward a focus on a mutual working of the triune God at every dimension of the justification of creation. I refer here to a pneumatological Christology and a christological pneumatology in support of the recent emphases of Trinitarian theology on *perichoresis* (interpenetration and cooperation) and *koinonia* (the sharing of life) among the divine persons in the fulfillment of divine justice in the world. Such a Trinitarian perspective will grant the Spirit a far more expansive role in justification than that of a mere instrument in the subjective moral formation or faith formation of believers. Even the helpful conclusions that the Spirit facilitates participation in Christ or perfects redemption eschatologically will be qualified by the knowledge that the Spirit is perfecting that in which the Spirit has substantially participated all along, especially in the context of the Christ event, but also eternally in the triune life. We thus need to unpack what we mean by discussing the Spirit as the bond of love within the triune life and between God and creation.

8. Jenson, *Systematic Theology,* 2:300.

The Spirit in Mutual Dependence and Self-Giving

The accomplishment of justice through incarnation and indwelling is rooted theologically in the nature of God as the Spirit baptizer or as the God who indwells the other and takes the other into God's very self. Such is true of God's life of communion as Father, Son, and Spirit. Trinitarian *perichoresis* involves the three persons of the Godhead emptying themselves into each other and receiving from each other's fullness.[9] The three persons exist totally in one another, "realizing themselves in one another by virtue of self-surrendering love."[10] Jesus said that the Father was in him and he in the Father (John 17:21). The Spirit contributes to the essence of the love involved in this mutual indwelling, actively participating in it to inspire and bear witness, creating a circle of divine *perichoresis* that is dynamic and celebrative, a holy dance of love.

God's embrace of the other through self-giving and indwelling thus has its roots within the triune life. John Zizioulas points out that otherness is built into the very being of God as triune: within the Trinity, unity and otherness are not opposed; rather, otherness is constitutive of unity. The three in relationship are not the same person, and yet there is but one God. Within the triune life, therefore, unity and otherness are both absolute.[11] God thus exists as a communion of persons that embraces otherness and does not dissolve it. As Moltmann has noted, homogeneity cannot be open to anything else, "because then it would no longer be homogeneous." In the Spirit, God's unity is inviting and open to integration. As a result of this insight, we should define personhood as "otherness in communion and communion in otherness."[12] Personhood is to be defined as the self-giving to the other and the reception of the other in the freedom and justice of divine love, a mutual sharing of life. Jesus as the man of the Spirit in communion with the Father thus reveals both God and ideal humanity at the same time.

Here is where we need to speak cautiously about the Augustinian concept of the Spirit as the bond of love *(viniculum amoris)* between the Fa-

---

9. Geoffrey Wainwright, *Doxology: The Praise of God in Worship, Doctrine and Life* (Oxford: Oxford University Press, 1980), p. 23.

10. Moltmann, *The Trinity and the Kingdom of God* (New York: Harper and Row, 1981), pp. 173-74.

11. John Zizioulas, "Communion and Otherness," *St. Vladimir's Theological Quarterly* 38, no. 4 (1994): 353-54.

12. Moltmann, *The Trinity,* pp. 149-50, 358.

ther and the Son. Augustine says that "those who have understanding begin also, however feebly, to discern the Trinity, to wit, one that loves, and that which is loved, and love."[13] The Father is the one who loves, the Son is the beloved, and the Spirit is love itself. Does Augustine imply that the Spirit is merely the impersonal force of love in the "I-Thou" relationship between the Father and the Son? We need to exercise caution here so that we do not de-personalize the Spirit by eliminating the Spirit's participation as person in the *koinonia* of Father and Son, relating to them in ways appropriate to the Spirit.

Eugene Rogers argues that the Spirit is not the bond of love or deity between the Father and the Son in some *unqualified* sense. Instead, the Spirit adds excess and superfluity to the love and deity of the Father and the Son in their bond of love, thus opening this love to the radically other (even the bodies of cursed Gentiles) as well as to the eschatological (even infinite) expanse of love's reach.[14] In this qualified sense, the Spirit is at the essence of the bond of love and even deity between the Father and the Son. As the "third" person of the Godhead, the Spirit is the one who opens God's communion and mutual indwelling beyond the "I-Thou" relationship between the Father and the Son in order to include the many.[15] The "third" includes the many. Through the Spirit, God becomes the Spirit baptizer, the one who opens the mutual love and indwelling of the Godhead to all flesh. Within a proper Trinitarian soteriology, there is no election, incarnation, atonement, or resurrection without Pentecost. All flesh is to be justified by the Spirit and in the Son through Spirit baptism and participation in the just *koinonia* of God.

The Spirit as contributing significantly to the bond of love does not de-personalize the Spirit but rather hyper-personalizes the Spirit as essential to the revelation of self-giving love in communion, the ideal revelation of personhood. The late Pope John Paul II, in Article 10 of his *Dominum et vivificantem,* notes that the Spirit is the bond of love, but in a way that includes a deep searching of the depths of God and an equally deep gracing of this love as pure gift.

---

13. Augustine, *De Trinitate,* in *On the Holy Trinity,* trans. Arthur West Hadden, 1st ser., ed. Philip Schaff, NPNF (reprint; Peabody, MA: Hendrickson, 1994), 15:7.13.

14. Eugene Rogers, *After the Spirit: A Constructive Pneumatology from Resources Outside the Modern West* (Grand Rapids: Eerdmans, 2005), e.g., p. 47.

15. Simon Chan reaches for this insight in *Liturgical Theology* (Downers Grove, IL: InterVarsity Press, 2006), pp. 32-33.

In his intimate life, God "is love," the essential love shared by the three divine Persons: personal love is the Holy Spirit as the Spirit of the Father and the Son. Therefore he "searches even the depths of God," as uncreated Love-Gift. It can be said that in the Holy Spirit the intimate life of the Triune God becomes totally gift, an exchange of mutual love between the divine Persons and that through the Holy Spirit God exists in the mode of gift. It is the Holy Spirit who is the personal expression of this self-giving, of this being-love. He is Person-Love. He is Person-Gift.[16]

Saint Augustine's psychological model of the triune life of God lacked an adequate acknowledgment of the interrelationality of the divine persons, but his insight into the role of the Spirit as the bond of love between the Father and the Son warrants greater attention (though it also warrants qualification). Through the Spirit, God becomes an abundant gift poured out from the rich relationship and communion enjoyed between Father, Son, and Spirit.

I find the Athanasian principle of "mutual dependence" of the persons particularly helpful here. The Father is the Father because of the Son (one cannot be a father without a son or daughter); the Son is the Son because of the Father. Athanasius also notes that the Father without the Word is "wordless and wisdomless . . . whence it will follow that there is no longer a Fountain, but a sort of pool."[17] In other words, the Father needs the Son to be the self-giving Word that flows outward toward the other. The Word is spoken and is meant to be incarnated and received.

This insight certainly carries over into the relationship between the Spirit and the Father and Son. There is no incarnation or reception of the Word among the others without the Spirit. In fact, we can qualify Athanasius's statement to say that, without the Spirit, the Father would still not be a fountain but a kind of pool, a deep and circulating pool of love enjoyed with the Son, to be sure, but a pool nonetheless. But the Spirit makes the Father a fountain and the Son a river, both leading to the eternal ocean of the many in God. Incarnation is possible and is not static. Father and Son both become Spirit baptizers. The third mandates the many. The Father becomes the one who elects the Son to become the firstborn among

16. John Paul II, *On the Holy Spirit in the Life of the Church and the World,* http://www.vatican.va/holy_father/john_paul_ii/encyclicals/documents/hf_jp-ii_enc_18051986_dominum-et-vivificantem_en.html, Article 10.

17. Athanasius, *Defence of the Nicene Definition,* trans. Archibald Robertson, 2nd ser., ed. Philip Schaff, NPNF (reprint; Peabody, MA: Hendrickson, 1994), IV.15.

many, and the Son becomes the one who obediently fulfills that calling by being wedded to flesh, setting the captives free, dying and rising again, and pouring forth the Spirit.

The Father is the Creator who makes the creation as the household of the firstborn Son and the place of the divine indwelling. The Son is the one who takes on flesh in order to be the preeminent Son of the household, but he does this by pouring forth the Spirit. The Spirit fashions the creation from the void in order to anoint this creation as a gift to the Son and the Father. The Spirit gives anointed flesh to the Son in order that all flesh could under this anointing receive the Son and the Father, indeed, the divine *koinonia* as well. The Son receives the anointed body so that he might, as divine, pour forth the Spirit on all flesh. The Spirit offers the incarnate Son to the Father in the Son's death and resurrection in order that the Son may offer the Spirit to the Father along with the redeemed creation in the *eschaton* (1 Cor. 15:27-28).

Wolfhart Pannenberg is known for reviving attention to the Athanasian interdependence of the three persons of the Godhead. He notes that an understanding of Trinitarian relationships in terms of origin is problematic. The Father is understood as the only person of the Godhead that is "Unoriginate," while the Son and the Spirit originate from the Father. The characterization of the Son and the Spirit as originate implies a certain ontological inferiority of the Son and the Spirit to the Father.[18] It was precisely this inferiority that was rejected by Arius as pagan, similar to the Greek deities, who were emanated or derivative. Since deity is by nature unoriginate, Arius opted instead for a restriction of deity to the Father alone, with the Logos as a created essence connected only to the Father through the Father's will to create.

In the light of Arius's challenge, Pannenberg has raised an interesting issue: Do the generation of the Son and the procession of the Holy Spirit from the Father imply their ontological inferiority? This is a difficult question to answer. On the one hand, the nature of God as a fountain and river of love implies an *eternal* springing forth of life that calls to mind some notion of eternal *origin*. Scripture does seem to grant the Father a certain primacy in the springing forth of divine love and its return (e.g., 1 Cor. 15:24-28). On the other hand, Scripture is silent about the question of the eternal origin of the Son and the Spirit. The begetting of the Son (John 3:16) and

---

18. Pannenberg, *Systematic Theology*, trans. Geoffrey W. Bromiley (Grand Rapids: Eerdmans, 1988), 1:325.

the procession of the Spirit (John 15:26) have salvation history and not the immanent life of the triune God as a context. The question of the eternal origin of the Son and the Spirit is speculative, based at most on an assumption of correspondence between the economic and immanent Trinity. In fact, as Simon Chan reminds us, the eschatological purpose of the Father's sending of the Son and pouring forth of the Spirit is a much more fruitful and biblical focus of attention than the issue of ultimate origins.[19]

In my view, the issue here is not so much a question of origin or of the *Filioque.* If pressed, I would accept the ancient ecumenical formula of the Spirit as proceeding from the Father *through* the Son, and back to the Father (1 Cor. 15:20-28). Rather, the issue is the interdependence of the persons of the Trinity in the fulfillment of divine love and of redemptive history. The immanent Trinity is the economic Trinity (to use Rahner's axiom) but mainly because of the metaphor of Spirit baptism as descriptive of both the interdependent dynamism of divine love within God and from God in redemptive history. The person of the Spirit reveals the Creator to be the Spirit baptizer, who makes creation to enjoy immortal existence by bearing the Spirit. Note again 2 Corinthians 5:4-5:

> For while we are in this tent, we groan and are burdened, because we do not wish to be unclothed but to be clothed with our heavenly dwelling, so that what is mortal may be swallowed up by life. Now it is God who has made us for this very purpose and has given us the Spirit as a deposit, guaranteeing what is to come.

God creates so that the creation may rise to the fullness of pneumatic existence! The Spirit is not an addendum to any divine work, from creation to glorification. It is not that God enjoys communion within Godself by necessity but gives to creation freely. Through the Spirit, it is all abundantly and excessively free, both in the context of God's self-determination within the immanent Trinity and God's self-disclosure and vindication in the economic Trinity.

The Spirit in the context of Spirit baptism thus empowers the outward flow and the eschatological reach of the divine embrace of the radically other. The Spirit thus mediates the journey of the Son into the far country on behalf of the Father, because the far country is uniquely the Spirit's home. The Spirit mediates the journey because the Spirit is already with sinful flesh and its cry for God. But the Spirit is there already as the power

---

19. Chan, *Liturgical Theology,* pp. 32-33.

of the yearning of the radically other for freedom, willing to mediate the incorporation of the radically other into God (Rom. 8:22). God takes the radically other in through the Christ event, including his pouring out of the Spirit, meaning that we also participate in this communion with both God and others through the self-giving defined by the incarnation, the cross, and Pentecost.

Personal freedom causes one to embrace one's own otherness in God but is directed toward the other as well. It is the freedom of love.[20] Justification thus involves an overflow of God's presence to indwell flesh and to bring flesh into the divine *koinonia*. The creature is rightwised in this divine embrace of the Spirit. As Moltmann has noted, love cannot be satisfied with mere pardon for sin. Sin is not simply a wrong done but a divine life spurned and rejected, an alienation and a source of bondage. In overcoming sin, the God of love fulfills justice and vindicates Godself as Creator and Lord by making creation the divine dwelling place.[21] Pardon for sin thus does not occur from a distant judge but rather from within the indwelling embrace of the Creator, whose justice involves mercy and love.

Koinonia and Trinitarian Justice

Is there justice in divine love or *koinonia?* In asking this question, Nicholas Wolterstorff admits that common understandings of justice would cause one to answer this question in the negative. Indeed, justice is commonly understood as blind and neutral, resolving conflicts by meting out appropriate punishments or rewards that come to people because of their actions. Under this definition, love seems biased and entirely separate from justice, even in tension with it, for "love casts out justice" by replacing it with something else. There seems no place for love in justice, for love is passionately bent toward the benefit of the other and, in the context of divine love, for *all* others. "Where love rules, justice has no room. Justice has room only when love breaks down."[22] If love casts out justice, then love can only occur once justice is fulfilled and then as a postscript.

Penal theories of atonement often separate justification from the gift

---

20. Chan, *Liturgical Theology,* pp. 354-58.

21. Moltmann, *The Trinity,* pp. 116, 125.

22. Wolterstorff, "Is There Justice in the Trinity?" in *God's Life in Trinity,* ed. Miroslav Volf and Michael Welker (Minneapolis: Fortress, 2006), pp. 177-78.

of the Spirit on the basis of a deeper separation of divine justice from divine love. Justice is fulfilled (one is justified) in the assuagement of divine wrath and the pardon of sins, so that love can finally be bestowed through the gift of the Spirit. Justice is assumed here to be an appropriate response to an offense or a payment made that satisfies the demands of law or some external system of exchange. Even in those atonement theories that assume a turning of God toward the sinners in the making of payment, justice itself is still assumed to be located theologically in the payment. Within this vision, basing justification in the gift of the Spirit implies a neglect of the external or legal demands of justice, with the result that we presume to be able by the Spirit to warrant God's favor ourselves.

What is often missed in this protest is that there is no divine favor apart from the Spirit. The triune God experiences and shares favor and justice in communion. Even with regard to Christ, the heavenly Father declares love for him in relation to the Spirit, who rests upon him in witness to — and celebration of — this love (Luke 3:16). Jesus offers himself as a sacrifice by the Spirit who participates in offering Jesus up in devotion to God even as he descends into God-forsakenness (Heb. 9:14). Jesus is declared God's Son in the resurrection from the dead by the Spirit (Rom. 1:4) and is vindicated at the Father's throne upon his ascension by receiving the Spirit from the Father in order to pour it forth onto all flesh (Acts 2:33). He is vindicated precisely as the Spirit baptizer, the firstborn among many brothers and sisters (Rom. 8:29). Hence it is the Spirit who brings us into the Spirit's witness to the sonship of Jesus (Rom. 8:15-16). There is no justice for creation apart from the participation of the Spirit as "third person" in the love, communion, witness, and vindication.

Furthermore, there is no justice without the embrace of the Spirit, for divine justice is not blind or neutral, but is caught up in the divine self-giving and witness. By the Spirit, the sinner is taken up into the divine favor enjoyed by Christ and in eschatological fulfillment. Ambiguous life is embraced and overcome by the divine life, for justification "brings life" (Rom. 5:18) and "reigns in life" (5:17). As I have shown earlier, divine justice is thus redemptive and driven by love. Miroslav Volf's statement is to the point: "Justice is impossible in the order of calculating, equalizing, legalizing and universalizing actions. If you want justice and nothing but justice, you will inevitably get injustice. If you want justice without injustice, you must want love." Embrace can take place beyond the fulfillment of justice only if justice is restricted to some kind of system of exchange. The alternative is to redefine justice as a redemptive concept fulfilled in love. The result is that "the grace of embrace has become part and parcel of the idea of justice."[23]

Is there justice in the Trinity? There can be no justice within the Trinity if justice is understood as the meting out of recompense for a wrong done or a discernment between right and wrong according to a system of exchange. Surely God is not eternally beholden to any external standard, and there is no evil or injustice in God that requires justice as a resolution. Justice would strictly be regarded only secondarily as a soteriological concept — with no direct reference to divine attributes. It would tell us nothing about the relationships of the persons in the Godhead. It would only function to tell us how God would act once God confronts evil. It would function directly only as a soteriological concept to describe how God works to bring about adequate payment for wrongs committed by humanity. It would have no direct analogue within the triune life. In fact, justice would be severely limited in its application, since it would not have been needed if sin had not entered creation and it would have had no presence in the *eschaton* or new creation once sin is eliminated.[24]

Yet, primary justice is deeper than recompense or discernment between right and wrong, having to do with a relationship that is governed by the fundamental right involved in freedom, the enjoyment of the good, and, ultimately, love. This positive and substantial notion of justice can indeed function as relevant to the new creation as well as analogous to the relationships among the persons of the Godhead. In disagreement with Anders Nygren, Wolterstorff refuses to contrast *agape* (love for the sake of the other) and *eros* (love for one's own sake). In God, the two are mutually defining: something is done for God's own sake when it is done for the sake of the other. Wolterstorff would rather contrast love as "attachment," which is limited to one's own benefit, and love that also enjoys the other for the sake of the other and in respect for the other's intrinsic worth. He concludes: "Justice within the Trinity is a constituent of love within the Trinity."[25]

Wolterstorff raises these issues with respect to the ethical life as analogous to the immanent triune life. Also enlightening, I believe, would be an application of his insights to the issue of justification. What deeper and

---

23. Volf, *Exclusion and Embrace: A Theological Exploration of Identity, Otherness, and Reconciliation* (Nashville: Abingdon, 1996), pp. 223-24.

24. See Wolterstorff, "Is There Justice in the Trinity?" p. 177.

25. Wolterstorff, "Is There Justice in the Trinity?" pp. 186-87.

higher understanding of justice can there be than divine *koinonia?* *Koinonia* refers to a sharing of life, an intimate communion, a mutual indwelling. Implied is a relationship that is right and good because it belongs to God, to the abundance of the divine goodness, to the self-giving and indwelling of the other for the other's enjoyment and in infinite regard for the other. This is a love that is just in the ultimate sense of the term; it is a just love that is celebrated through communion and mutual indwelling. This is a just relationship par excellence. It is one that triumphs over the dark powers and is shown in the end to be just.

The upshot of this insight into primary justice as Trinitarian love and *koinonia* is the impossibility of restricting justification to faith alone or to an individual quest for a gracious God. Justification is not simply a divine judgment or declaration received through individual belief or assent. Neither is it primarily a moral renewal through infused virtues. It is a divine infilling and new birth that causes one to participate in the embrace of the divine *koinonia*. It is not individualistic, though it is deeply personal. It creates the communion of saints, vibrant witness to divine justice, and ultimate vindication of this witness in resurrection, glorification, and direct communion with God. If faith conforms the believer to the faithfulness or righteousness of God as the Spirit baptizer, faith must be seen as a form of self-giving in response to the divine indwelling, as working through love and hope within the context of justification itself. Justification transforms believers by conforming them to the image of Christ and to the impress of the Spirit in the justice of divine *koinonia*. The just relationship with God is a mutual indwelling and participation in life. Faith is not simply a believing of a message or a moral response to the enabling of grace. Faith is an embrace and participation in the life that has possessed us deep within. It must be a faith working in love and nourished by hope.

Final Vindication as a Trinitarian Act

If the substance of justification is *koinonia* in Christ and in the Spirit, the goal is the vindication of the sinner by the Spirit in Christ. This is true due to the fact that God's embrace of the sinner through Christ and the gift of the Spirit faces opposition, which calls forth among the faithful vibrant witness and hope for final vindication. Our vindication is first based on God's self-vindication as the faithful Creator and Lord. Since God's self-vindication is ultimately fulfilled in both Christ and the Spirit (or in God as the one who baptizes in the Spirit), divine vindication involves the vindication of the creature. These are the reasons for the legal overtones typical of justification in Scripture and so emphasized among traditional Protestant polemics. Witness and vindication have legal overtones, though they have as their substance an excess of grace in the life of the Spirit that defies any legal system of exchange. As a "legal" metaphor, however, justification involves the embrace, empowered witness, and final vindication of all flesh in Christ and in the Spirit.

This vindication is granted presently in signs and wonders of the Spirit's presence, "powers of the age to come" that may be experienced in the here and now (Heb. 6:5). We especially show forth the love of God, even the glory of the Lord, to one another in communion (2 Cor. 3:18) and in service to others. Final vindication, however, is our resurrection and glorification, which is also the fullness of pneumatic life in the sphere of ultimate love and communion. What are vindicated are not just the divine will and judgment (the Protestant preoccupation) but rather the divine embrace and redemptive presence in the world.

Concerning God's self-vindication, what I have said about the mutual dependence of the persons of the Godhead applies to the witness and vindication of God as loving Creator and Lord. The Father bore witness to Jesus through the Spirit as the favored Son who descends into God-forsakenness in order to rise for them into the fullness of pneumatic existence (Luke 3:16; Rom. 1:4). By the very same Spirit, the Son bore witness to the Father as the Righteous One (John 17:24-25), for Jesus is "the faithful witness, the firstborn from the dead" (Rev. 1:5). There is also an implicit witness by Jesus to the Spirit as the bearer of truth and justice (John 16:7-10), even deferring to the Spirit as the ultimately decisive agent of divine favor (Matt. 12:28-32). Moreover, once poured out upon flesh, the Spirit will bear witness to Christ and to all that Christ has from the Father (John 16:12-15) and will empower those who are incorporated into Christ to share in this witness (Acts 1:8). The Father sends the Son and pours out the Spirit to bear witness to a justice that is fulfilled in mercy and love, a love that embraces all flesh from the cross to Pentecost, so that all flesh can participate in Christ and, through Christ, in divine *koinonia*.

As the Spirit baptizer, God vindicates the sinner by embracing and filling flesh with the divine Spirit, ultimately in the resurrection and glorification of flesh, which is the new creation in which righteousness dwells. This is the final vindication of the *Father*, who sent the Son and poured out the Spirit; it is the vindication of the *Son*, who came from the Father and gave himself to flesh as the man of the Spirit so that he could pour out the Spirit on behalf of the Father on all flesh; and it is the vindication of the *Spirit,* who was sent from the Father through the Son to indwell all flesh so that the many could share in the justice of Father, Son, and Spirit. When flesh is raised and glorified in the image of the Son, the Spirit will achieve final vindication as the Spirit of justice who convicts the world of truth and righteousness and proves to be the one for the many in the self-giving flow of divine love.

Implied here is a mutual dependence in the vindication of Father, Son, and Spirit. When the Father is vindicated as the one who sends the Son and pours out the Spirit, the Son is also vindicated as the one sent from the Father and the Spirit as the one poured out from the Father upon the many. When the Son is vindicated as the Son of the heavenly Father, the Father is vindicated as the Father of the Son, and the Spirit is vindicated as the true source of truth and justice in anointing the Son and bearing witness to him. When the Spirit is vindicated in the divine indwelling and glorification of the many, the Father is vindicated as the faithful Creator who made humanity to bear the Spirit and who stays true to the creation, and the Son is vindicated as the firstborn among many brothers and sisters. The vindication of each is dependent on the vindication of the others. In general, God is vindicated through the indwelling and glorification of creation as the loving God, who fulfills justice for creation by embracing it with the divine *koinonia.*

Conclusion

A Trinitarian theology of justification in the light of Spirit baptism implies the following points. First, justification through *koinonia* has its basis in the Trinitarian life of God as Father, Son, and Spirit. Justification does not merely have its basis in the will of the Father or in the fulfillment of the law by Jesus. Nor does justification have its basis in the moral virtues exemplified by Christ and infused in us by grace. It has its basis in the righteousness of divine love and *koinonia* enjoyed in the triune life and opened to creation through Christ and the Spirit.

Second, justification cannot be restricted to the elect will of the Father and the justice of the cross. As a Trinitarian reality with love at its substance, justification culminates in resurrection, exaltation, Spirit baptism, and the indwelling of the Spirit. Justification occurs "in the name of the

Lord Jesus Christ and by the Spirit of our God" (1 Cor. 6:11). Justification is an eschatological reality that reaches all the way to the resurrection of the saints and the glorification of creation, which is the ultimate in pneumatic existence in the image of Jesus. It vindicates the witness of the saints and fulfills that witness by glorifying God as Creator and Spirit baptizer.

Third, the substance of justification is not "legal" according to anything that we might have experienced in the context of everyday life. The substance of the divine justification of the sinner is precisely a mutual embrace between God and the sinner that comes through Christ as crucified and risen and as the Spirit baptizer. Justification is a just relationship that has self-giving and indwelling as its substance. There is a divine excess and abundance of life at the essence of the just relationship that exceeds even the commonly used metaphor of covenant.

Fourth, justification is not only by faith without further qualification, but rather by faith as fulfilled in love and nourished by hope. It is not confined to the individual struggle with legalism; but it is communal in that it also involves a social witness. *Koinonia* bears witness to a just sharing of life that has love and hope as its horizon. The community of faith bears witness to the gospel fundamentally in its communal life, and it seeks analogues of justice in the world at large, including structural changes that improve the capacity of social contexts to occasion the flourishing and sharing of life. Life flourishes when it is reconciled and healed across boundaries in such a way that the other is respected as other. Life is shared and enjoyed in an expanding and increasingly diverse circle of love. In a way analogous to the divine life, both unity and otherness are absolute in a vibrant sharing of life.

11 Justified in the Spirit

A Concluding Reflection

Turn to Ezekiel 37 and see the prophet standing at the edge of a vast valley of dry bones. He has just been given a tour of the extent of the damage. The Lord has set him in the midst of the valley and led him back and forth, from one end to the other so that he could view how thoroughly lifeless Israel had become. It was at the point at which the full extent of Israel's despair and hopelessness had settled into Ezekiel's heart and mind that the startling question came to him, "Son of man, can these bones live?" Moved deeply by the depth of Israel's hopelessness, Ezekiel answers in the only way that seems to make any sense at the moment: "O sovereign LORD, you alone know."

Even in the midst of Ezekiel's element of uncertainty, the command immediately confronts him: "Prophesy to these bones and say to them, 'Dry bones, hear the word of the LORD!'" The message of hope strikes at the heart of Israel's problem:

> I will make breath enter you, and you will come to life. I will attach tendons to you and make flesh come upon you and cover you with skin; I will put breath in you, and you will come to life. Then you will know that I am the LORD.

How will Israel come once more to know that God is Lord? When the divine breath that originally breathed life into Adam and Eve comes into them to raise them up from total devastation in the field of battle, then they will know that the God is Lord.

The good news that came to Israel at that moment was the possibility of life in the midst of failure, death, and despair. The good news was that the Creator who had called the Israelites and delivered them from Egypt would not abandon them to the field of battle, where they had lost and given up all hope. New life was still a possibility, though their defeat seemed in the distant past and their dead bodies had long since decayed and turned to dust. Though there was no potential for life left, life was still possible through the breath of Yahweh. Though there remained no basis for partnership or negotiation, for self-redemption of any kind, God would graciously breathe into them the new life possible to raise them up from the dust in a way analogous to how Adam was taken from the dust and made a living soul. Though they stood at fault and guilty before the Lord of hosts, the Lord was ready to embrace them with life and turn them into witnesses of abundant grace.

The way forward seemed clear. The Spirit of Yahweh had to be invoked before the new beginning was possible. Ezekiel is told to prophesy to the breath, a symbol of God's Spirit. Ezekiel bore witness to what happened: "So I prophesied as he commanded me, and breath entered them; they came to life and stood up on their feet — a vast army." He then identifies the Lord as the one who raises life from the grave:

> I am going to open your graves and bring you up from them; I will bring you back to the land of Israel. Then you, my people, will know that I am the LORD, when I open your graves and bring you up from them. I will put my Spirit in you and you will live.

Again, the Lord reiterates the fact that Israel will know that God is the Lord when the divine breath takes them up into the new life that conquers all failure and despair. Where there is no hope left, where all seems lost, where there is nothing but failure and death all around, God's breath offers the hope of redemption. The God of Israel, of the entire world, is known and vindicated as Lord precisely in this act of mercy and embrace through the Spirit of God.

This story from Ezekiel 37 is not just a figurative account of how Israel was renewed and encouraged in the midst of its hopelessness. This story would gain another horizon that would enhance its meaning in the death and resurrection of Jesus. Killed in the midst of Israel's failure and exile as a people, the Son of man cries out in despair and forsakenness. Descending into the pit of despair, where no hope is left, Jesus took upon his shoulders the sins and despair of the world. He lay in the tomb, his body dead and cold. All that he was and stood for had been decisively mocked and rejected. Was this the end?

If that had been the end, divine justice through this act of mercy would have been discredited. Humanity would remain guilty and condemned, not just for breaking commandments, but more deeply for alienation from the divine life and love to which the law bore witness. Rather than a life nourished by love and communion with God and others, sinful flesh had become entangled in self-preservation and exaltation. The life from which flesh was to be nourished grew dim in the captivity of flesh to forces of sin and death. The judgment of condemnation was thus strangely the same as the effects of the crime itself. The Creator had made the creature to bear the Spirit and eventually to be caught up into the fullness of pneumatic existence in direct communion with God and in sharing the divine glory. But God also respected human freedom. In the midst of the human rebellion in choosing death over life, God handed all flesh over to an atrophy of life and to the alienation of the far country.

The injustice into which humanity had fallen was not simply moral but also deeply existential and ontological. God the Creator would not submit to this state of affairs. God would not resign the divine right with regard to creation, nor the covenant, the exchange of life, and the ultimate glory of immortal existence in the fullness of the Spirit, in the fullness of love planned by the Creator for the creation. The justice planned for creation was dependent on the *koinonia* of the divine life as well as on reversing the alienation of flesh from life. The alienation would be reversed, to be sure, but only by the gift of the divine presence that gives life and that takes the creature up into the mutual exchange of life characteristic of the life of God as Father, Son, and Spirit.

If the crucifixion of Jesus had been the final act, God's decisive act of self-giving would have been spurned before it could reach the creature, and the rejection of the sinful creature would have had the final word. The forces of darkness would have tightened their grip on the cosmos, and utter darkness and despair would have proved to be insurmountable. The hope of the prophets would have dimmed and burned out. All would have been lost. As unimaginable as it is, the self-vindication of God as Lord would have been thwarted, and the opposition would have gained the upper hand. God's very deity would have been radically called into question.

With this utter hopelessness on the imaginative horizon, the burning question that one confronts at the thought of that dead body of Jesus lying in the tomb is Ezekiel's: "Can this corpse live again?" Christ was now in the grip of the forces of injustice that sought to mock the justice of God and assert themselves as the determining elements of the cosmos. The scene had thus shifted somewhat from Ezekiel 37. The context was still Israel's failure, of course, but the apostolic witness would make it abundantly clear that all sinful flesh was at stake as well, an expansive thought that was not unknown to the prophets but now brought to the forefront and presented with bright colors. At issue was not the promised land but, more prominently, the resurrection from the grave. Everything was held captive to dark forces and thus subject to the curses of sin and death. Christ as the man of the Spirit had come from the heavenly Father to penetrate this vast imprisoned reality, which yearned for freedom. As the man of the Spirit, he descended to the realm of alienation from God in order to take the sinners into the divine embrace of the Spirit.

The embrace would come from the gift of the Spirit of life, just as Ezekiel had foreseen. This is why the divine Son came from the Father in order to be wedded to flesh. The Spirit gave the Son a Spirit-indwelt body so that all flesh could, in him, be taken up into the Spirit's embrace. The only justice possible for the sinners would take place not only through liberation *from* sin and death but also liberation *to* a different redemptive relationship with the Lord of life. This relationship would exist as an exchange of life, or as a mutual indwelling. The formation of the right relationship would require the life and embrace of the Spirit. It would ultimately need the fullness of pneumatic existence, the immortality of the risen and glorified Christ.

Everything depended on this man who cried out in despair from the clutches of death on the cross and who now lay in the cold dark tomb. Those who descend into the pit cannot find hope. This hopelessness and loss of life in the deepest sense could not continue unanswered. More was happening, however, than one could ever have imagined. The Spirit of life had not left the crucified Christ; instead, the Spirit remained hidden beneath the blasphemy of the rejection of life that characterized the crucifixion. The rejection of life was taken up into the divine life, striking at the very heart of God as Father, Son, and Spirit. But that striking would not ultimately prove fatal. Incarnation and indwelling had facilitated an exchange of life between God and the creature in which the rejection of life could meet the divine self-giving and excessive outpouring of life. This exchange would be called "blessed," for God's exchange of life was infinitely greater than the excessive rejection of life confronted at the foot of the cross and in the tomb.

As Jesus lay there in the tomb, the question about whether this body could live again was answered in ways that transcend the human imagination. In conquering sin and death in the resurrection, Jesus had taken flesh up into the fullness of pneumatic existence in ultimate glory and depth of communion. What happened in the story of Jesus, however, must also happen in creation. Therefore, the story of Jesus is not decisively fulfilled until Pentecost. The Son dies as a seed so that he will bear much fruit. The Son bestows the Spirit on flesh so that the Spirit can one day raise all flesh in Christ as the Spirit has raised Jesus, raised to the fullness of life in the Spirit. The atonement through the resurrection of the Son as the firstfruits must also involve the resurrection of others through the firstfruits of the Spirit. Justification would occur only through the fulfillment of the purpose for which humanity was created, namely, to bear the Spirit in fullness or in the image of the risen and glorified Son.

When the day of Pentecost had come, the Spirit was poured out with the theophanic signs of speaking in tongues, the sound of a mighty wind, and flames of fire — signs of God's holy presence (Acts 2:1-4). These signs implied the breaking down of barriers to the realization of justice through the fellowship of the Spirit. Signs of the sharing of life, or *koinonia,* also emerged in the church due to God's indwelling of flesh (Acts 2:42-47). Both are fulfilled in the final appearing of God, surrounded by "wonders in the heaven above and signs on the earth below" (Acts 2:19), but mainly in the new creation and the fullness of life in the Spirit. As Pentecostals have noted, the event of Pentecost is at the core of the apostolic faith. The baptism in the Holy Spirit is the context for understanding justification, and that points to the fact that God's purpose for creation is fulfilled in the embrace of the Spirit. This implies that the work of the Creator and Redeemer is fulfilled in the giver of life. The Pentecostal pioneer Frank Ewart says: "Calvary unlocked the flow of God's love, which is God's very nature, into the hearts of his creatures."[1] This also implies the idea that justification and sanctification cannot be rigidly separated along christological and pneumatological lines, but instead are overlapping and mutually defining categories of the rightwising of creation. In the Spirit, justification is both

---

1. Frank Ewart, "The Revelation of Jesus Christ," in *Seven Jesus Only Tracts,* ed. Donald W. Dayton (New York: Garland, 1985), p. 5.

personal and communal; it is also both a present experience and an eschatological reality.

The embrace of the Spirit among the justified corresponds ultimately to the mutual indwelling and sharing of life enjoyed in the context of the Trinitarian *koinonia*. Through Spirit baptism, this *koinonia* was opened to creation in the process of fulfilling justice. The Father had proved faithful to the Son and, in the process, to creation as well. The Son had proved faithful by descending into the abyss wedded to human flesh in order to rise again as the one who imparts the Spirit to all flesh. The victory of the cross and the resurrection would find fulfillment in the role of Jesus as the Spirit baptizer. The Spirit would prove faithful as the one for the many who would bind the creature to Christ and anoint all flesh in him. This faithfulness, however, would ultimately find fulfillment in the creature's participation in the divine *koinoina,* especially in the fullness of pneumatic existence.

This is the just relationship willed by the Father, won by the Spirit-indwelt Son, and perfected in the Spirit's witness to Jesus. This is the just relationship enjoyed in God as Father, Son, and Spirit and accessible in the life-transforming embrace of the Spirit. The declaration of extrinsic righteousness from Protestant pulpits and the infusion of virtues in the creature's cooperation with grace assumed in traditional Catholic settings has required a developed appreciation of the baptism in the Spirit to link and anchor them both. Though relatively undeveloped, this metaphor came to prominence through the Pentecostal movement in the twentieth century. Ecumenical responses and a deeper analysis of the richness of the metaphor in the history of the Pentecostal movement has provided the possibility for constructive theological reflection. It has become clear to me, through dialogue with colleagues and through my own reflection, that this metaphor can fruitfully be applied to the subject of justification. In fact, recent ecumenical discussions about justification reach for precisely this pneumatological and broadly Trinitarian link between opposing viewpoints. I have become convinced that, in the Spirit, justification can fruitfully be developed in the wide open spaces of the reach of the Spirit, both within the life of the triune God and in the global and eschatological expanse of communion in the love of God.

Bibliography

Achtemeier, E. R. "Righteousness in the Old Testament." In *Interpreter's Dictionary of the Bible.* Edited by George Arthur Buttrick. Nashville: Abingdon, 1962.

Achtemeier, P. J. "Righteousness in the New Testament." In *Interpreter's Dictionary of the Bible.* Edited by George Arthur Buttrick. Nashville: Abingdon, 1962.

Albrecht, Daniel. *Rites of the Spirit: A Ritual Approach to Pentecostal/Charismatic Spirituality.* Sheffield, UK: Sheffield Academic Press, 1999.

Anselm. *Cur Deus Homo.* In *Saint Anselm: Basic Writings.* Translated by S. N. Deane. La Salle, IL: Open Court, 1968.

Aquinas, Thomas. *Treatise on Grace.* In *Basic Writings of St. Thomas Aquinas.* Edited and translated by Anton C. Pegis. New York: Random House, 1945.

Auer, Johann. "Grace (II. Theological, A. History of the Doctrine)." In *Sacramentum Mundi: An Encyclopedia of Theology.* Vol. 2. Edited by Karl Rahner et al. New York: Herder and Herder, 1968.

Augustine. *Confessions.* In *The Confessions and Letters of Augustine with a Sketch of His Life and Work.* Nicene and Post-Nicene Fathers, 1st series. Translated by J. G. Pilkington. Edited by Philip Schaff. Reprint; Peabody, MA: Hendrickson, 1994.

———. *De Natura et Gratia.* In *St. Augustine's Anti-Pelagian Works.* Nicene and Post-Nicene Fathers, 1st series. Translated by Peter Holmes and Robert Ernest Wallace. Edited by Philip Schaff. Reprint; Peabody, MA: Hendrickson, 1994.

———. *De Perfectione Justicia Hominis.* In *St. Augustine's Anti-Pelagian Works.* Nicene and Post-Nicene Fathers, 1st series. Translated by Peter Holmes and Robert Ernest Wallace. Edited by Philip Schaff. Reprint; Peabody, MA: Hendrickson, 1994.

———. *De Spiritu et Littera.* In *St. Augustine's Anti-Pelagian Works.* Nicene and Post-Nicene Fathers, 1st series. Translated by Peter Holmes and Robert Ernest Wallace. Edited by Philip Schaff. Reprint; Peabody, MA: Hendrickson, 1994.

———. *Enarratio in Psalmos.* In *St. Augustine's Exposition on the Psalms.* Nicene and

Post-Nicene Fathers, 1st series. Translated by A. Cleveland Coxe. Edited by Philip Schaff. Reprint; Peabody, MA: Hendrickson, 1994.

Aulén, Gustaf. *Christus Victor: An Historical Study of the Three Main Types of the Idea of the Atonement*. Eugene, OR: Wipf and Stock, 2003.

Barrett, C. K. *A Commentary on the First Epistle to the Corinthians*. New York: Harper and Row, 1968.

Barth, Karl. *Church Dogmatics*. Vol. 1, pt. 1. *The Doctrine of the Word of God*. Translated by G. W. Bromiley. Edited by G. W. Bromiley and T. F. Torrance. 2nd ed. London: T. & T. Clark, 1975.

————. *Church Dogmatics*. Vol. 2, pt. 2. *The Doctrine of God*. Translated by G. W. Bromiley et al. Edinburgh: T. & T. Clark, 1957.

————. *Church Dogmatics*. Vol. 3, pt. 2. *The Doctrine of Creation*. Translated by Harold Knight et al. Edinburgh: T. & T. Clark, 1960.

————. *Church Dogmatics*. Vol. 4, pt. 1. *The Doctrine of Reconciliation*. Translated by G. W. Bromiley. Edinburgh: T. & T. Clark, 1956.

————. *Protestant Theology in the Nineteenth Century*. Translated by Brian Cozens and John Bowden. Grand Rapids: Eerdmans, 2002.

Barth, Markus. *Acquittal by Resurrection*. New York: Holt, Reinhart and Winston, 1964.

————. "Jews and Gentiles: The Social Character of Justification in Paul." *Journal of Ecumenical Studies* 5 (1968): 241-67.

Beale, G. K. "The Descent of the Eschatological Temple in the Form of the Spirit at Pentecost: Part 1: The Clearest Evidence." *Tyndale Bulletin* 56, no. 1 (2005): 73-99.

————. "The Descent of the Eschatological Temple in the Form of the Spirit at Pentecost: Part 2: Corroborating Evidence." *Tyndale Bulletin* 56, no. 2 (2005): 63-90.

Basil, Saint. *Spiritu Sancto*. In *Basil: Letters and Select Works*. Translated by Blomfield Jackson. Nicene and Post-Nicene Fathers, 2nd series. Edited by Philip Schaff and Henry Wallace. Reprint; Peabody, MA: Hendrickson, 1994.

Beasley-Murray, George Raymond. "Interpretation of Daniel 7." *Catholic Biblical Quarterly* 45, no. 1 (January 1983): 44-58.

Beck, Johann Tobias. *Erklärung des Briefes Pauli an die Römer*. Bd. 1. Gütersloh: Bertelsmann, 1884.

Bell, E. N. "Believers in Sanctification." *Christian Evangel* (September 19, 1914): 3-4.

Berg, George E. "Pentecostal Testimonies." *The Apostolic Faith* 1, no. 6 (February-March 1907): 8.

Berkouwer, G. C. *Faith and Justification*. Translated by Lewis B. Smedes. Grand Rapids: Eerdmans, 1954.

————. *The Return of Christ*. Translated by James C. Van Oosterom. Grand Rapids: Eerdmans, 1972.

————. *The Sacraments*. Grand Rapids: Eerdmans, 1969.

Bernard, David K. *Justification and the Holy Spirit: A Scholarly Investigation of a Classical Christian Doctrine from a Pentecostal Perspective*. Hazelwood, MO: WAP Academic, 2007.

Betz, Hans Dieter. *Galatians*. Hermeneia: A Critical and Historical Commentary on the Bible. Philadelphia: Augsburg Fortress, 1979.

Bird, Michael F. "Incorporated Righteousness: A Response to Recent Evangelical Discussion Concerning the Imputation of Christ's Righteousness in Justification." *Journal of the Evangelical Theological Society* 47 (2004): 253-75.

———. *The Saving Righteousness of God: Studies on Paul, Justification, and the New Perspective*. Paternoster Biblical Monographs. Eugene, OR: Wipf and Stock, 2007.

Blackman, E. C. "Faith, Faithfulness." *Interpreter's Dictionary of the Bible*. Vol. 2. Edited by Emory Stevens Bucke. Nashville: Abingdon, 1962.

Blake, H. L. "A Minnesota Preacher's Testimony." *The Apostolic Faith* 1, no. 6 (February-March 1907): 5.

Blumhardt, Christoph. *Ansprachen, Predigten, Reden, Briefe: 1865-1917*. Bd. 2. Neukirchen-Nuyn: Neukirchener Verlag, 1978.

Bobrinskoy, Boris. "The Indwelling of the Holy Spirit in Christ: 'Pneumatic Christology' in the Cappodocian Fathers." *St. Vladimir's Theological Quarterly* 28, no. 1: 49-65.

Body, A. A. "Testimony of a Vicar's Wife." *The Apostolic Faith* 1, no. 11 (January 1908): 1.

Bonhoeffer, Dietrich. *The Cost of Discipleship*. Translated by R. H. Fuller. New York: Macmillan, 1963.

———. *Sanctorum Communio: A Theological Study of the Sociology of the Church*. Translated by Reinhard Krauss and Nancy Lukens. Minneapolis: Fortress, 1998.

Bouyer, L. *The Spirit and Forms of Protestantism*. Translated by A. V. Littledale. Westminster, MD: Harvill Press, 1956.

Brandos, David A. *Paul on the Cross: Reconstructing the Apostle's Story of Redemption*. Minneapolis: Fortress, 2006.

Brauch, Manfred T. "Perspectives on God's Righteousness in Recent German Discussion." In *Paul and Palestinian Judaism*. Edited by E. P. Sanders. Minneapolis: Fortress, 1977.

Braulik, Georg. "Law as Gospel: Justification and Pardon According to the Deuteronomic Torah." *Interpretation* 38, no. 1 (January 1984): 5-7.

Brown, Dale. *Understanding Pietism*. Grand Rapids: Eerdmans, 1978.

Brueggemann, Walter. *Theology of the Old Testament*. Minneapolis: Fortress, 2005.

Brunner, Emil. *Dogmatics*. Vol. 3. *The Christian Doctrine of the Church, Faith, and the Consummation*. Translated by David Cairns. Philadelphia: Westminster, 1962.

Buber, Martin. *I and Thou*. Translated by Ronald Gregory Smith. New York: Charles Scribner's Sons, 1970.

Calvin, John. *The Epistle of Paul the Apostle to the Romans*. Translated by John Owen. Grand Rapids: Baker, 1999.

———. *Institutes of the Christian Religion*. 2 vols. Translated by Henry Beveridge. Grand Rapids: Eerdmans, 1979.

Canlis, Julie. "Calvin, Osiander and Participation in God." *International Journal of Systematic Theology* 6, no. 2 (April 2004): 169-84.

Carlson, Charles P. *Justification in Earlier Medieval Theology*. The Hague: Martinus Nijhoff, 1975.

Chan, Simon. *Liturgical Theology*. Lombard, IL: InterVarsity, 2006.

———. "Mother Church: Towards a Pentecostal Ecclesiology." *Pneuma: The Journal of the Society for Pentecostal Studies* 22, no. 2 (Fall 2000): 177-208.

Childs, Brevard. *Biblical Theology of the Old and New Testaments: Theological Reflection on the Christian Bible.* Minneapolis: Fortress, 1992.

Chung, Tak-Ming. "Understandings of Spirit Baptism." *Journal of Pentecostal Theology* 8 (1996): 115-28.

Coffey, David. *Did You Receive the Holy Spirit When You Believed? Some Basic Questions for Pneumatology.* Père Marquette Lecture in Theology. Milwaukee: Marquette University Press, 2005.

———. "The Holy Spirit as the Mutual Love of the Father and the Son." *Theological Studies* 51 (1990): 193-229.

———. "The 'Incarnation' of the Holy Spirit in Christ." *Theological Studies* 45 (1984): 466-80.

Collins, Adela Yarbro. "The Signification of Mark 10:45 among Gentile Christians." *Harvard Theological Review* 90, no. 4 (October 1997): 371-82.

Collins, Kenneth. *The Theology of John Wesley: Holy Love and the Shape of Grace.* Nashville: Abingdon, 2007.

Cooke, David. *The Distancing of God: The Ambiguity of Symbol in History and Theology.* Minneapolis: Fortress Press, 1990.

Cosgrove, Charles. *The Cross and the Spirit: A Study in the Argument and Theology of Galatians.* Macon, GA: Mercer University Press, 1988.

Coulter, Dale. "'Delivered by the Power of God': Toward a Pentecostal Understanding of Salvation." *International Journal of Systematic Theology* 10, no. 4 (October 2008): 447-67.

Cranfield, C. E. B. *A Critical and Exegetical Commentary on the Epistle to the Romans.* Reprint; Edinburgh: T. & T. Clark, 1985.

Cremer, Hermann. *Die Paulinische Rechtfertigungslehre in Zusammenhange Ihrer geschichtlichen Voraussetzungen.* Gütersloh: Bertelsmann, 1900.

Cross, Terry. "Finitum Capax Infiniti." Address to the Society for Pentecostal Studies, Duke University Divinity School, March 15, 2008.

Dabney, D. Lyle. "'He Will Baptize You in the Holy Spirit': Recovering a Metaphor for a Pneumatological Soteriology." Paper delivered at the Society for Pentecostal Studies. Tulsa, OK: March 8-10, 2001.

———. "The Justification by the Spirit: Soteriological Reflections on the Resurrection." *International Journal of Systematic Theology* 3, no. 1 (March 2001): 46-68.

———. "Naming the Spirit: Towards a Pneumatology of the Cross." In *Starting with the Spirit.* Task of Theology Today II. Edited by Stephen Pickard and Gordon Preece. Hindmarsh, Australia: Australian Theological Forum, 2001.

———. "Starting with the Spirit: Why the Last Should Now Be First." In *Starting with the Spirit.* Edited by Stephen Pickard and Gordon Preece. Hindmarsh, Australia: Australian Theological Forum, 2001.

Dahl, Nils Alstrup. "Promise and Fulfillment." in *Studies in Paul: Theology for the Early Christian Mission.* Minneapolis: Augsburg, 1977.

Dayton, Donald. *Theological Roots of Pentecostalism.* Grand Rapids: Zondervan, 1988.

Del Colle, Ralph. *Christ and the Spirit: Spirit Christology in Trinitarian Perspective.* Oxford, New York: Oxford University Press, 1994.

De Lubac, Henri. *The Mystery of the Supernatural.* Translated by Rosemary Sheed. New York: Herder and Herder, 1965.

Dempster, Murray. "The Church's Moral Witness: A Study of Glossolalia in Luke's Theology of Acts." *Paraclete* 23 (1989): 1-7.

Donaldson, Terrence L. *Paul and the Gentiles: Remapping the Apostle's Convictional World.* Minneapolis: Fortress, 1997.

Donnelly, Malachi J. "The Indwelling of the Holy Spirit according to M. J. Scheeben." *Theological Studies* 7, no. 2 (June 1946): 244-80.

Driver, Tom F. *The Magic of Ritual: Our Need for Liberating Rites That Transform Our Lives and Our Communities.* San Francisco: HarperSanFrancisco, 1991.

Dulles, Avery. *The Assurance of Things Hoped For: A Theology of Christian Faith.* Oxford: Oxford University Press, 1994.

———. "Justification in Contemporary Catholic Theology." In *Justification by Faith: Lutherans and Catholics in Dialogue.* No. 7. Edited by H. George Anderson, T. Austin Murphy, and Joseph A. Burgess. Minneapolis: Augsburg, 1985.

Dunn, James D. G. *Baptism in the Holy Spirit.* Studies in Biblical Theology. London: SCM Press, 1970.

———. *Christology in the Making.* Vol. 1. *Jesus Remembered.* Grand Rapids: Eerdmans, 2003.

———. *Jesus, Paul, and the Law: Studies in Mark and Galatians.* Louisville: Westminster/John Knox, 1990.

———. *Romans 1–8.* Word Biblical Commentary. Vol. 38. Edited by David Hubbard and Glenn Barker. Dallas: Word, 1988.

Ebeling, Gerhard. *The Truth of the Gospel: An Exposition of Galatians.* Translated by David Green. Philadelphia: Fortress, 1985.

Eno, Robert B. "Some Patristic Views on the Relationship between Faith and Works in Justification." In *Justification by Faith: Lutherans and Catholics in Dialogue.* VII. Edited by H. George Anderson, T. Austin Murphy, and Joseph A. Burgess. Minneapolis: Augsburg, 1985.

Ervin, Howard M. *These Are Not Drunken as Ye Suppose.* Plainfield, NJ: Logos, 1968.

Ewart, Frank. "The Revelation of Jesus Christ." In *Seven Jesus Only Tracts.* Edited by Donald W. Dayton. New York: Garland, 1985.

Fairbairn, Donald. *Grace and Christology in the Early Church.* Oxford Early Christian Studies. Oxford: Oxford University Press, 2003.

Farkas, Thomas. "William H. Durham and the Sanctification Controversy in Early American Pentecostalism, 1906-1916." PhD diss., Southern Baptist Theological Seminary, Louisville, KY, 1993.

Faupel, David William. *The Everlasting Gospel: The Significance of Eschatology in the Development of Pentecostal Thought.* Journal of Pentecostal Theology. Reprint; Dorset, UK: Deo Publishing, 2008.

Fee, Gordon. *The First Epistle to the Corinthians.* New International Commentary on the New Testament. Edited by Gordon Fee. Grand Rapids: Eerdmans, 1987.

Finger, Thomas. "An Anabaptist Perspective on Justification." In *Justification and Sanctification in the Traditions of the Reformation*. Studies from the World Alliance of Reformed Churches, 42. Edited by Milan Opočenský and Páraic Réamonn. Geneva: World Alliance of Reformed Churches, 1999.

————. *A Contemporary Anabaptist Theology: Biblical, Historical, Constructive*. Downers Grove, IL: InterVarsity, 2004.

Fitzmyer, Joseph A. *Romans*. Anchor Bible Commentary. Edited by William F. Albright and David N. Freedman. New York: Doubleday, 1992.

Flower, Joseph Roswell. "How I Received the Baptism in the Holy Spirit." *Pentecostal Evangel* 14 (Jan. 21, 1933): 1-12.

Forde, Gerhard O. "Forensic Justification and Law in Lutheran Theology." In *Justification by Faith: Lutherans and Catholics in Dialogue*. VII. Edited by H. George Anderson, T. Austin Murphy, and Joseph A. Burgess. Minneapolis: Augsburg, 1985.

Fox, Richard Whiteman. *Jesus in America: A History*. San Francisco: HarperSanFrancisco, 2004.

Franzen, Piet F. *The New Life of Grace*. New York: Herder and Herder, 1972.

Fuchs, Lorelei. "The Holy Spirit and the Development of Communio/Koinonia Ecclesiology as a Fundamental Paradigm for Ecumenical Engagement." In *The Holy Spirit, the Church and Christian Unity: Proceedings of the Consultation Held at the Monastery of Bose, Italy, 14-20 October, 2002*. Edited by D. Donnelly, A. Denaux, and J. Famerée. Leuven: Leuven University Press, 2005.

Fung, Ronald Y. K. *The Epistle to the Galatians*. New International Commentary on the New Testament. Edited by Gordon Fee. Grand Rapids: Eerdmans, 1988.

Gelpi, Donald. "Breath Baptism in the Synoptics." Paper delivered at the Society for Pentecostal Studies. Pasadena, CA, November 20, 1982.

Girard, René. *The Scapegoat*. Translated by Yvonne Freccero. Baltimore: Johns Hopkins University Press, 1986.

Green, Joel B., and Mark D. Baker. *Recovering the Scandal of the Cross: Atonement in New Testament and Contemporary Contexts*. Downers Grove, IL: InterVarsity, 2000.

Grundmann, Walter. "The Teacher of Righteousness of Qumran and the Question of Justification by Faith in the Theology of the Apostle Paul." In *Paul and Qumran: Studies in New Testament Exegesis*. Edited by Jerome Murphy-O'Connor. Chicago: The Priory Press, 1968.

Hagner, Donald A. *Matthew 1–13*. Word Biblical Commentary. 35A. Edited by David Hubbard and Glenn Barker. Dallas: Word, 1993.

Hanby, Michael. *Augustine and Modernity*. Radical Orthodoxy Series. New York: Routledge, 2003.

Hardon, John. *History and Theology of Grace*. Ypsilanti, MI: Veritas Press, 2002.

Harrison, Everett. *Romans*. Expositor's Bible Commentary. Edited by Frank E. Gaebelein. Grand Rapids: Zondervan, 1976.

Harrison, Stephanie. "The Case of the Pharisee and the Tax Collector: Justification and Social Location in Luke's Gospel." *Currents in Theology and Mission* 32, no. 2 (April 2005): 99-111.

Harrisville, Roy A. *Fracture: The Cross as Irreconcilable in the Language and Thought of the Biblical Writers.* Grand Rapids: Eerdmans, 2006.

Hart, Larry. "Spirit Baptism: A Dimensional Charismatic Perspective." In *Spirit Baptism: Five Views.* Edited by Chad Brand. Nashville: Broadman and Holman, 2004.

Hausmann, S. "Leben aus Glauben in Reformation, Reformorthodoxie und Pietismus." *Theologische Zeitschrift* 27 (1971): 273-74.

Hay, D. M. "Pistis as Ground for Faith in Hellenized Judaism." *Journal of Biblical Literature* 108, no. 3 (September 1989): 461-76.

Hays, Richard B. *The Faith of Jesus Christ: The Narrative Substructure of Galatians 3:1–4:11.* 2nd ed. Grand Rapids: Eerdmans, 2001.

Hayford, Jack. *The Beauty of Spiritual Language: My Journey Toward the Heart of God.* Dallas: Word, 1992.

Heim, Mark. *Saved from Sacrifice: A Theology of the Cross.* Grand Rapids: Eerdmans, 2006.

Hendrix, Scott. "Offene Gemeinschaft: Die Kirchliche Wirklichkeit der Rechtfertigung." *Kirche und Dogma* 43 (1997): 98-110.

Hengel, Martin. *The Atonement: The Origins of the Doctrine in the New Testament.* Translated by John Bowden. Philadelphia: Fortress, 1981.

Hezmalhalch, T. "Among the Indians at Needles, California." *The Apostolic Faith* 1, no. 5 (January 1907): 3.

Hocken, Peter. "Baptism in the Spirit as a Prophetic Statement: A Reflection on the New Testament and on Pentecostal Origins." Paper delivered at the Society for Pentecostal Studies. Springfield, MO, Nov. 12-14.

Hollenweger, Walter. *The Pentecostals.* Peabody, MA: Hendrickson, 1991.

Hunt, Anne. *The Trinity and the Paschal Mystery: A Development of Recent Roman Catholic Theology.* New Theology Series 5. Collegeville, MN: Liturgical Press, 1997.

Hütter, Reinhart. *Suffering Divine Things: Theology as Church Practice.* Grand Rapids: Eerdmans, 1999.

Irenaeus. *Against Heresies.* In *The Apostolic Fathers: Justin Martyr and Irenaeus. Ante Nicene Fathers.* Vol. 1. Edited by Alexander Roberts and James Donaldson. Translated by A. Cleveland Coxe. Reprint; Peabody, MA: Hendrickson, 1994.

James, William. *The Principles of Psychology.* Reprint; New York: Dover, 1950.

Jenson, Robert. "Justification as a Triune Event." *Modern Theology* 11, no. 4 (1995): 421-27.

———. *Systematic Theology.* Vol. 2. *The Works of God.* Oxford: Oxford University Press, 1999.

Jung, Carl Gustav. *The Undiscovered Self.* Translated by R. F. C. Hull. Boston: Little, Brown, 1958.

Jüngel, Eberhard. *Justification: The Heart of the Christian Faith.* Translated by Jeffrey F. Cayzer. Edinburgh: T. & T. Clark, 2001.

———. *Paulus und Jesus: Eine Untersuchung zur Präzisierung der Frage nach dem Ursprung der Christologie.* Hermeneutische Untersuchungen zur Theologie, 2. Tübingen: Mohr-Siebeck, 1962.

Kapic, Kelly M. "The Trajectory of Trinitarian Eschatologies." In *Trinitarian Soundings in Systematic Theology.* Edited by Paul Lewis Metzger. Edinburgh: T. & T. Clark, 2006.

Kärkkäinen, Veli-Matti. *One with God: Salvation as Justification and Deification.* Collegeville, MN: Liturgical Press, 2005.

————. "Pentecostalism and the Claim for Apostolicity: An Essay in Ecumenical Ecclesiology." *Ecumenical Review of Theology* 25 (2001): 323-26.

Käsemann, Ernst. *Perspectives on Paul.* Translated by Margaret Kohl. Mifflintown, PA: Sigler Press, 1996.

————. "'The Righteousness of God' in Paul." In *New Testament Questions of Today.* Translated by W. J. Montague. Minneapolis: Fortress, 1969.

Kasper, Walter. *Jesus the Christ.* Mahwah, NJ: Paulist, 1976.

Keating, Daniel A. *Deification and Grace.* Naples, FL: Sapientia Press, 2007.

Keshgegian, Flora A. "The Scandal of the Cross: Revisiting Anselm and His Feminist Critics." *Anglican Theological Review* 82, no. 3 (Summer 2000): 475-92.

Kitamori, Kazoh. *Theology of the Pain of God.* Translated by W. H. H. Norman. Eugene, OR: Wipf and Stock, 2005.

Koch, K. "Sühne und Sündenvergebung um die Wende von der exilischen zur nachexilischen Zeit." *Evangelische Theologie* 26 (1966): 217-39.

Koenig, John. *Charismata: God's Gifts for God's People.* Philadelphia: Westminster, 1978.

Küng, Hans. *The Church.* Translated by John Bowden. New York: Sheed and Ward, 1967.

————. *Justification: The Doctrine of Karl Barth and a Catholic Reflection.* Translated by Edward Quinn. Philadelphia: Westminster, 1981.

Ladd, George Eldon. *Theology of the New Testament.* Grand Rapids: Eerdmans, 1993.

Land, Steven J. *Pentecostal Spirituality: A Passion for the Kingdom.* Sheffield, UK: Sheffield University Press, 1988.

Lane, Anthony. *Justification by Faith in Catholic-Protestant Dialogue: An Evangelical Assessment.* New York: Continuum Imprint, T. & T. Clark, 2002.

Larbi, E. Kingsley. *Pentecostalism: The Eddies of Ghanaian Christianity.* Dansoman, Accra, Ghana: Centre for Pentecostal and Charismatic Studies, 2001.

Lederle, Henry. "Initial Evidence and the Charismatic Movement." In *Initial Evidence: Historical and Biblical Perspectives on the Pentecostal Doctrine of Spirit Baptism.* Edited by Gary B. McGee. Peabody, MA: Hendrickson, 1991.

————. *Treasures Old and New: Interpretations of Spirit Baptism in the Charismatic Renewal Movement.* Peabody, MA: Hendrickson, 1988.

Lehmann, Karl. "Heiliger Geist, Befreiung zum Menschsein — Teilhabe am göttlichen Leben." In *Gegenwart des Geistes: Aspekte der Pneumatologie.* Herausgegeben von Walter Kasper. Basel: Herder, 1979.

Lella, Di, Alexander. "One in Human Likeness and the Holy Ones of the Most High in Daniel 7." *Catholic Biblical Quarterly* 39, no. 1 (January 1977): 1-10.

Lindberg, Carl. "Do Lutherans Shout Justification but Whisper Sanctification? Justification and Sanctification in the Lutheran Tradition." Studies from the World Alliance of Reformed Churches, 42. In *Justification and Sanctification in the Traditions of the Reformation.* Edited by Milan Opočenský and Páraic Réamonn. Geneva: World Alliance of Reformed Churches, 1999.

Lindsay, Dennis R. "The Roots and Development of the πίστ- Word Group as Faith Terminology," *Journal for the Study of the New Testament* 49, no. 1 (March 1993): 103-18.

Lochman, Jan Milič. "The Doctrine of Justification in a Society of Achievers." *Reformed World* 35 (Mar. 1978–Dec. 1979): 212-14.

———. *Dogmatik im Dialog.* Bd. 1. *Die Kirche und die Letzen Dinge.* Gütersloh, Germany: Gütersloher Verlagshaus, 1973.

———. *Signposts to Freedom: The Ten Commandments and Christian Freedom.* Translated by David Lewis. Minneapolis: Augsburg, 1982.

Lombard, Peter. *The First Book of the Sentences.* In *The Four Books of Sentences.* http://www.franciscan-archive.org/lombardus/I-Sent.html.

Lonergan, Bernard. "St. Thomas' Thought on Gratia Operans." *Theological Studies* 2, no. 3 (September 1941): 289-324.

Longenecker, Richard. *Galatians.* Word Biblical Commentary. Vol. 41. Edited by Bruce M. Metzger. Dallas: Word Books, 1990.

Lossky, Vladimir. *The Mystical Theology of the Eastern Church.* Crestwood, NY: St. Vladimir's Seminary Press, 1997.

Lugioyo, Brian. "Martin Bucer's Doctrine of Justification and the Colloquy of Regensburg, 1541." PhD diss., University of Aberdeen, 2007.

Luther, Martin. "Disputation of Doctor Martin Luther on the Power and Efficacy of Indulgences (95 Theses) (1517)." *Works of Martin Luther.* No. 30. Translated and edited by Adolph Spaeth, L. D. Reed, and Henry Eyster Jacobs. Philadelphia: A. J. Holman Company, 1915.

———. "Lectures on Galatians 1519." *Luther's Works.* Vol. 27. Edited by Jaroslav Pelikan. St. Louis: Concordia, 1963.

———. "Lectures on Galatians 1535." *Luther's Works.* Vol. 27. Edited by Jaroslav Pelikan. St. Louis: Concordia, 1963.

———. *Lectures on Romans,* in *Luther's Works.* Vol. 25. Edited by Helmut T. Lehman. St. Louis: Concordia, 1972.

———. *Letters of Spiritual Counsel.* Translated and edited by Theodore G. Tappert. Vancouver, BC: Regent College Publications, 2003.

———. "Preface to the Latin Writings." *Luther's Works.* Vol. 34. Edited by Lewis Spitz. Philadelphia: Muhlenburg Press, 1955.

Macchia, Frank D. *Baptized in the Spirit: A Global Pentecostal Theology.* Grand Rapids: Zondervan, 2006.

———. "Finitum Capax Infiniti: A Pentecostal Distinctive?" *Pneuma: The Journal of the Society for Pentecostal Studies* 29, no. 2 (2007): 185-87.

———. "Is Footwashing the Neglected Sacrament? A Response to John Christopher Thomas." *Pneuma: The Journal of the Society for Pentecostal Studies* 19, no. 2 (Fall 1997): 239-49.

———. "Justification and the Spirit of Life: A Pentecostal Response to the Joint Declaration." In *Justification and the Future of the Ecumenical Movement.* Edited by William C. Rusch. Collegeville, MN: Liturgical Press, 2003.

———. "Justification through New Creation: The Holy Spirit and the Doctrine by Which the Church Stands or Falls." *Theology Today* 58, no. 2 (July 2001): 202-17.

McDonnell, Kilian. *The Baptism of Jesus in the Jordan: The Trinitarian and Cosmic Order of Salvation.* Collegeville, MN: Liturgical Press, 1996.

MacCormack, Bruce. "What's at Stake in Current Debates over Justification? The Crisis of Protestantism in the West." In *Justification: What's at Stake in the Current Debates?* Edited by Mark Husbands and Daniel J. Treier. Downers Grove, IL: InterVarsity, 2004.

Mannermaa, Tuomo. *Christ Present in Faith: Luther's View of Justification.* Translated by Kirsi Irmeli Stjerna. Minneapolis: Augsburg Fortress, 2005.

———. "Justification and Theosis in Lutheran-Orthodox Perspective." In *Union with Christ: The New Finnish Interpretation of Luther.* Edited by Carl E. Braaten and Robert W. Jenson. Grand Rapids: Eerdmans, 1998.

———. "Why Is Luther So Fascinating? Modern Finnish Luther Research." In *Union with Christ: The New Finnish Interpretation of Luther.* Edited by Carl E. Braaten and Robert W. Jenson. Grand Rapids: Eerdmans, 1998.

Marshall, Bruce D. "Ex Occidente Lux? Aquinas and Eastern Orthodox Theology." *Modern Theology* 20, no. 1 (January 2004): 23-50.

McDonnell, Kilian, and George Montague. *Christian Initiation and Baptism in the Holy Spirit: Evidence from the First Eight Centuries.* Collegeville, MN: Liturgical Press, 1991.

McGrath, Allister. *Iustitia Dei: A History of the Christian Doctrine of Justification.* Vol. 1. *The Beginnings to the Reformation.* Cambridge: Cambridge University Press, 1982.

McGuckin, J. A. "The Strategic Adaptation of Deification." In *Partakers of the Divine Nature: The History and Development of Deification in the Christian Traditions.* Edited by Michael J. Christensen and Jeffrey A. Wittung. Grand Rapids: Baker Academic, 2006.

Melanchthon, Philip. *The Apology of the Augsburg Confession.* In *The Book of Concord: The Confessions of the Evangelical Lutheran Church.* Translated by Charles Arand et al. Edited by Robert Kolb and Timothy J. Wengert. Minneapolis: Fortress, 2000.

———. *Commentary on Romans.* Translated by Fred Kramer. St. Louis: Concordia, 1992.

———. *Formula of Concord. Solid Declaration III.* In *The Book of Concord: The Confessions of the Evangelical Lutheran Church.* Translated by Charles Arand et al. Edited by Robert Kolb and Timothy J. Wengert. Minneapolis: Fortress, 2000.

Menzies, Glen. "Tongues as the Initial Physical Sign of Spirit Baptism in the Thought of D. W. Kerr." *Pneuma: The Journal of the Society for Pentecostal Studies* 20 (Fall 1998): 175-89.

———. "To What Does Faith Lead? The Two-Stranded Textual Tradition of Isaiah 7.9b." *Journal for the Study of the Old Testament* 80 (1998): 111-26.

Meyers, Carol. "Temple, Jerusalem." *Anchor Bible Dictionary.* Vol. 6. Edited by David Noel Freedman. New York: Doubleday, 1992.

Moeller, Charles, and Gerard Philips. *The Theology of Grace and the Ecumenical Movement.* London: Mowbray, 1961.

Moltmann, Jürgen. *A Broad Place: An Autobiography.* Translated by Margaret Kohl. Minneapolis: Fortress, 2008.

———. "Die Rechtfertigung Gottes." *Stimmen der Zeit* 7 (July 2001): 435-42.

———. *God in Creation: A New Theology of Creation and the Spirit of God.* Translated by Margaret Kohl. New York: Harper and Row, 1985.

———. *The Spirit of Life: A Universal Affirmation.* Translated by Margaret Kohl. Minneapolis: Fortress, 1992.

———. *Trinity and the Kingdom: The Doctrine of God.* Minneapolis: Augsburg Fortress, 1983.

———. "Was heist heute 'evangelisch'? Von der Rechtfertigungslehre zur Reich Gottes-Theologie." *Evangelische Theologie* 57 (1997): 41-46.

Moo, Douglas. *The Epistle to the Romans.* New International Commentary on the New Testament. Edited by Gordon Fee. Grand Rapids: Eerdmans, 1996.

Moomau, Antoinette. "China Missionary Receives Pentecost." *The Apostolic Faith* 1, no. 11 (January 1908): 3.

Morgenstern, Julian. "'Son of Man' of Daniel 7:13f: A New Interpretation." *Journal of Biblical Literature* 80, no. 1 (Mar. 1, 1961): 65-77.

Moule, H. C. G. *The Epistle to the Romans.* Fort Washington, PA: Christian Literature Crusade, 1975.

Newman, John Henry. *Lectures on Justification.* London: J. G. and F. Rivington, 1838.

Niebuhr, Reinhold. "Christian Faith and Natural Law." In *Love and Justice: Selections from the Shorter Writings of Reinhold Niebuhr.* Edited by D. B. Robertson. Cleveland: World Publishing Co., 1957.

Nietzsche, Friedrich. *Genealogy of Morals.* New York: Vintage Books, n.d.

Nolland, John. *Luke 1–9:20.* Word Biblical Commentary 33A. Dallas: Word, 1989.

Nwachukwu, Mary Sylvia C. *Creation-Covenant Scheme and Justification by Faith: A Canonical Study of the God-Human Drama in the Pentateuch and the Letter to the Romans.* Rome: Editrice Pontifica Universita Gregoriana, 2002.

Nygren, Anders. *Agape and Eros.* Translated by Philip S. Watson. Chicago: University of Chicago Press, 1992.

Oberman, Heiko A. *The Harvest of Medieval Theology: Gabriel Biel and Later Medieval Nominalism.* Grand Rapids: Baker Academic, 1963.

Ohlemacher, J. *Das Reich Gottes in Deutschland Bauen.* Göttingen: Vandenhoeck & Ruprecht, 1986.

"On the Gift: A Discussion between Jacques Derrida and Jean-LucMarion (moderated by Richard Kearney)." In *God, the Gift, and Postmodernism.* Edited by John D. Caputo and Michael J. Scanlon. Bloomington: Indiana University Press, 1999.

Osbourne, Kenan B. *Reconciliation and Justification: The Sacrament and Its Theology.* Eugene, OR: Wipf and Stock, 1990.

Osiander, Andreas. "Eine Disputation von der Rechtfertigung." In *Schriften und Briefe 1549 bis August 1551.* Gesamtausgabe, Bd. 9. Herausgegeben von Gerhard Müller und Gottfried Seebass. Gütersloh: Gütersloher Verlagshaus, 1994.

O'Toole, Robert F. "Acts 2:30 and the Davidic Covenant of Pentecost." *Journal of Biblical Literature* 102, no. 2 (1983): 245-58.

Pannenberg, Wolfhart. *Anthropology in Theological Perspective.* Translated by Matthew J. O'Connell. Philadelphia: Westminster, 1985.

―――. *Systematic Theology.* Vol. 3. Translated by Geoffrey Bromiley. Grand Rapids: Eerdmans, 1998.

Pelikan, Jaroslav. *Reformation of Church and Dogma. The Christian Tradition: A History of the Development of Dogma.* Vol. 4. Chicago: University of Chicago Press, 1982.

Pesch, Otto Hermann. *Die Theologie der Rechtfertigung bei Martin Luther und Thomas von Aquin.* Mainz: Grünwald, 1967.

Peura, Simo. "What God Gives Man Receives: Luther on Salvation." In *Union with Christ: The New Finnish Lutheran Interpretation of Luther.* Edited by Carl Braaten and Robert Jenson. Grand Rapids: Eerdmans, 1998.

Popkes, Wiard. "Two Interpretations of 'Justification' in the New Testament Reflections on Galatians 2:15-21 and James 2:21-25." *Studia Theologica* 59 (2005): 129-46.

Preiss, Theo. *Life in Christ.* Chicago: Alec R. Allenson, 1954.

Rahner, Karl. "Questions of Controversial Theology on Justification." In *Theological Investigations.* Vol. 4. *More Recent Writings.* Translated by Kevin Smith. New York: Crossroad, 1982.

Reumann, John. *Righteousness in the New Testament: Justification in Lutheran-Catholic Dialogue.* Philadelphia: Fortress, 1982.

Rhodes, Arnold B. "Kingdoms of Men and the Kingdom of God: A Study of Daniel 7:1-14." *Interpretation* 15, no. 4 (October 1961): 423-24.

Richardson, Alan. *An Introduction to the Theology of the New Testament.* New York: Harper and Row, 1958.

Ricoeur, Paul. "Interpretation of the Myth of Punishment." In *The Conflict of Interpretations: Essays in Hermeneutics.* Edited by John Ihde. Evanston, IL: Northwestern University Press, 1974.

Ritschl, Albrecht. *The Christian Doctrine of Justification and Reconciliation.* Edinburgh, 1872.

Robeck, Cecil M., Jr. "William J. Seymour and the 'Bible Evidence.'" In *Initial Evidence: Historical and Biblical Perspectives on the Pentecostal Doctrine of Spirit Baptism.* Edited by Gary B. McGee. Peabody, MA: Hendrickson, 1991.

Rogers, Eugene. *After the Spirit: A Constructive Pneumatology from Resources Outside the West.* Grand Rapids: Eerdmans, 2005.

Ruokanen, Miikka. *Spiritus vel gratia est ipsa fide: A Pneumatological Concept of Grace in Luther's De servo arbitrio.* Helsinki: University of Helsinki Press, 1991.

Sanders, E. P. *Paul and Palestinian Judaism: A Comparison of Patterns of Religion.* Minneapolis: Fortress Press, 1977.

―――. *Paul, the Law, and the Jewish People.* Philadelphia: Fortress Press, 1983.

Sauter, Gerhard. "God Creating Faith: The Doctrine of Justification from the Reformation to the Present." *Lutheran Quarterly* 11, no. 1 (Spring 1997): 17-102.

Scheck, Thomas P. *Origen and the History of Justification: The Legacy of Origen's Commentary on Romans.* Notre Dame, IN: University of Notre Dame Press, 2008.

Schlatter, Adolf. *Romans: The Righteousness of God.* Translated by Siegfried S. Schatzmann. Peabody, MA: Hendrickson, 1995.

Schleiermacher, Friedrich. *The Christian Faith.* Philadelphia: Fortress, 1976.

Schmidt, Hans Heinrich. "Gerechtigkeit und Glaube: Genesis 15,1-6 und sein biblisch-theologischer Kontext." *Evangelische Theologie* 40 (January-February 1980): 417-19.

Schmidt, M. "Spener's Wiedergeburtslehre." In *Zur neueren Pietismusforschung.* Herausgegeben von M. Greschat. Darmstadt: Wissenschaftliche Buchgesellschaft, 1977.

Schreiner, Thomas B. *The Law and Its Fulfillment: A Pauline Theology of Law.* Grand Rapids: Baker, 1993.

Schweitzer, Albert, *The Mysticism of Paul the Apostle.* Reprint; New York: Seabury, 1968.

Seymour, William J. "The Holy Ghost Is Power." *The Apostolic Faith* 2, no. 13 (May 1908): 3.

———. "River of Living Water." *The Apostolic Faith* 1, no. 3 (November 1906): 2.

———. "The Way into the Holiest." *The Apostolic Faith* 1, no. 2 (October 1906): 4.

Shepherd, Michael B. "Daniel 7:13 and the New Testament Son of Man." *Westminster Theological Journal* 68, no. 1 (Spring 2006): 99-111.

Steinmetz, David C. *Reformers in the Wings.* Grand Rapids: Baker, 1981.

Stendahl, Krister. "The Apostle Paul and the Introspective Conscience of the West." *Harvard Theological Review* 56, no. 3 (July 1963): 199-215.

Storr, Anthony. *Solitude: A Return to the Self.* New York: The Free Press, 1988.

Stronstad, Roger. *The Charismatic Theology of St. Luke.* Peabody, MA: Hendrickson, 1988.

Studebaker, Steven. "Pentecostal Soteriology and Pneumatology." *Journal of Pentecostal Theology* 11, no. 2 (2003): 248-70.

Stuhlmacher, Peter. *A Challenge to the New Perspective: Revisiting Paul's Doctrine of Justification.* Downers Grove, IL: InterVarsity, 2000.

———. *Paul's Letter to the Romans: A Commentary.* Translated by Scott J. Hafemann. Louisville: Westminster John Knox, 1994.

Thielman, Frank. *Paul and the Law.* Downers Grove, IL: InterVarsity, 1994.

Thomas, John Christopher. *Footwashing in John 13 and the Johannine Community.* Sheffield, UK: Journal for the Study of the New Testament Supplement. Sheffield Academic Press, 1991.

Thompson, John. *The Holy Spirit in the Theology of Karl Barth.* Princeton Theological Monograph Series. Kent, UK: Pickwick, 1991.

Tillich, Paul. *Dynamics of Faith.* Translated by Marion Pauck. Perennial Classics edition. New York: Harper Collins, 2001.

———. *Systematic Theology.* 3 Vols. Chicago: University of Chicago Press, 1973-76.

Torrance, Thomas F. *The Doctrine of Grace in the Apostolic Fathers.* Grand Rapids: Eerdmans, 1959.

Towner, Philip. *The Letters to Timothy and Titus.* New International Commentary on the New Testament. Edited by Gordon Fee. Grand Rapids: Eerdmans, 2006.

Volf, Miroslav. *After Our Likeness: The Church as the Image of the Trinity*. Grand Rapids: Eerdmans, 1997.

————. "Being as God Is: Trinity and Generosity." In *God's Life in Trinity*. Edited by Miroslav Volf and Michael Welker. Minneapolis: Augsburg Fortress, 2006.

————. *Exclusion and Embrace: A Theological Exploration of Identity, Otherness, and Reconciliation*. Nashville: Abingdon, 1996.

————. "Materiality of Salvation: An Investigation in the Soteriologies of Liberation and Pentecostal Theologies." *Journal of Ecumenical Studies* 26, no. 3 (Summer 1989): 446-67.

Vanhoozer, Kevin. "The Atonement in Postmodernity: Guilt, Goats, and Gifts." In *The Glory of the Atonement: Biblical, Historical, and Practical Perspectives*. Edited by Charles Hill and Frank A. James III. Downers Grove, IL: InterVarsity, 2004.

Von Balthasar, Hans Urs. *Mysterium Paschale: The Mystery of Easter*. Translated by Aidan Nichols. Grand Rapids: Eerdmans, 1990.

Von Rad, Gerhard. *Old Testament Theology*. Vol. 1. Translated by D. M. G. Stalker. New York: Harper and Row, 1962.

Wainwright, Geoffrey. *Doxology: The Praise of God in Worship, Doctrine, and Life*. New York: Oxford University Press, 1980.

Ware, Kallistos. *How Are We Saved? The Understanding of Salvation in the Orthodox Tradition*. Minneapolis: Light and Life, 1996.

Watson, Francis. *Paul, Judaism, and the Gentiles: Beyond the New Perspective*. Grand Rapids: Eerdmans, 2007.

Weaver, J. Denny. *The Nonviolent Atonement*. Grand Rapids: Eerdmans, 1991.

Welch, Claude. *Protestant Thought in the Nineteenth Century, 1799-1870*. Vol. 1. New Haven: Yale University Press, 1972.

Welker, Michael. *God the Spirit*. Translated by John Hoffmyer. Minneapolis: Fortress, 1994.

————. "The Holy Spirit." *Theology Today* 46, no. 1 (April 1989): 5-20.

Wesley, John. "The Principles of a Methodist." In *The Works of John Wesley*. Vol. 8. 3rd edition. Grand Rapids: Baker Book House, 1979.

————. "Sermon 5: Justification by Faith." In *The Works of John Wesley*. Vol. 5. 3rd edition. Grand Rapids: Baker Book House, 1979.

————. "Sermon 107: On God's Vineyard." In *The Works of John Wesley*. Vol. 7. 3rd edition. Grand Rapids: Baker Book House, 1979.

Whitehouse, W. A. "Faith." *A Theological Word Book of the Bible*. Edited by Alan Richardson. New York: Macmillan, 1950.

Williams, E. S. *Systematic Theology*. Vol. 3. Springfield, MO: Gospel Publishing House, 1953.

Williams, Sam K. "Justification of the Spirit in Galatians." *Journal for the Study of the New Testament* 29 (1987): 91-100.

Willig, I. *Geschaffene und Ungeschaffene Gnade: Bibeltheologische Fundierung und systematische Erörterung*. Münster: Aschendorff Verlag, 1964.

Wolterstorff, Nicholas. "Is There Justice in the Trinity?" In *God's Life in Trinity*. Edited by Miroslav Volf and Michael Welker. Minneapolis: Fortress, 2006.

Wright, N. T. *The Climax of the Covenant.* Minneapolis: Fortress, 1993.

———. *Jesus and the Victory of God.* Minneapolis: Fortress, 1996.

———. *Paul in Fresh Perspective.* Minneapolis: Fortress, 2005.

———. *The Resurrection of the Son of God.* Minneapolis: Fortress, 2003.

———. *What Paul Really Said: Was Paul of Tarsus the Real Founder of Christianity?* Grand Rapids: Eerdmans, 1997.

Yoder, John Howard. *The Politics of Jesus.* 2nd edition. Grand Rapids: Eerdmans, 1994.

Yong, Amos. *The Spirit Poured Out on All Flesh: Pentecostalism and the Possibility of Global Theology.* Grand Rapids: Baker Academic, 2005.

———. *Spirit-Word-Community: Theological Hermeneutics in Trinitarian Perspective.* Ashgate New Critical Thinking in Religion, Theology, and Biblical Studies. Hampshire, UK: Ashgate, 2002.

———. *Theology and Down Syndrome: Reimagining Disability in Late Modernity.* Waco, TX: Baylor University Press, 2007.

Ziesler, J. A. *The Meaning of Righteousness in Paul: A Linguistic and Theological Inquiry.* Cambridge: Cambridge University Press, 1972.

Zinzendorf, Ludwig Count von. *Ein und zwanzig Discurse über die Augsburgische Konfession. 1748, Der achte Discurs.* In *Hauptschriften.* Bd. VI. Edited by Erich Beyreuther. Hildesheim: Stift Hildesheim, 1963.

Zizioulas, John. *Being as Communion.* Crestwood, NY: St. Vladimir's Seminary Press, 1997.

———. "Communion and Otherness." *St. Vladimir's Theological Quarterly* 38, no. 4 (1994): 353-54.

Author Index

Albrecht, Daniel, 284
Anselm, 156-65, 226
Aquinas, Thomas, 18, 20, 21, 42, 51, 65, 182, 203, 232
Aristotle, 18
Arius, 304
Athanasius, 26, 181, 303
Aulén, Gustaf, 156, 175

Baker, Mark D., 163
Balthasar, Hans Urs von, 29, 172, 190
Barth, Karl: creation pneumatology, 34; divine self-vindication, 169, 172; election, 137, 138, 141, 142; faith, 235; objective pneumatology, 131; righteousness and mercy, 107, 109; subjective pneumatology, 6
Barth, Markus, 189, 199, 205, 260, 261, 264
Beale, G. K., 191
Beck, Johann Tobias, 67
Berg, George E., 79
Berkouwer, G. C., 47, 135, 283
Biel, Gabriel, 41
Blumhardt, Christoph, 67, 153
Bonhoeffer, Dietrich, 72, 254, 269
Bouyer, L., 31
Brueggemann, Walter, 108, 164, 165

Brunner, Emil, 70
Buber, Martin, 267
Bucer, Martin, 65, 66, 297
Bultmann, Rudolf, 231

Calvin, John: blessed exchange, 182; election, 138; pneumatology and justification, 218; regeneration, 46; union with Christ, 55, 58-60; sacrament, 284
Chan, Simon, 258, 276, 305
Childs, Brevard, 108
Coffey, David, 132
Cosgrove, Charles, 195
Cremer, Hermann, 106
Cross, Terry, 77
Cyril, 28, 29

Dabney, D. Lyle, 176, 178, 206, 214
Dahl, Nils, 113, 197
Del Colle, Ralph, 23
Dempster, Murray, 274
Derrida, Jacques, 167
Dodd, C. H., 120
Driver, Tom F., 284-86
Dulles, Avery, 24, 228
Dunn, James, 186, 201, 208, 209, 242
Durham, William H., 86, 91

Subject Index

Atonement: blessed exchange, 178-83; economy of exchange and excess, 166-68; ransom, 175-76; sacrifice, 176-78; satisfaction, 156-66; substitution, 173-75; vindication, 169-73

Cappadocians, 26-27
Church: and justification, 258-74; and social justice, 275-79; charismatic structure, 279-82; sacraments, 282-96
Council of Chalcedon, 27-29

Deification. *See Theosis*

Election, 135-45

Faith: and hope and love, 230-37; and human destiny, 251-54; and law, 241-50; and repentance, 238-39; and works, 239-40; Old Testament view of, 222-29; participation in Christ, 237-41; weakness of, 50-55
Finnish Lutheran, 51-55
Forensic Justification, 39, 40-50, 60-61, 81, 110-11

Grace: cooperation, 25-29, 72; habitual, 18-24, 31; participation, 25-29, 51-54,

61, 63; recent Catholic theology of, 30-36; supernatural, 31-36

Imputation, 59

Law, 113-18, 241-50

Merit, 21

Oneness Pentecostalism, 87, 92

Pelagianism, 18-19
Penance, 41-43
Pietism, 67-68

Regeneration, 62-65, 67, 70, 82-83, 88-89
Regensburg Agreement, 65-66
Righteousness (New Testament), 146-55
Righteousness (Old Testament): covenant faithfulness, 105-14; law, 113-18; messianic reign, 118-21; pneumatological fulfillment, 122-28

Sacraments: baptism, 282-88; Lord's Supper, 289-96; sign, 57
Sanctification, 69, 87
Spirit baptism: and justification, 188-

Scripture Index